MW01156160

NON-PHOTOREALISTIC COMPUTER GRAPHICS
MODELING, RENDERING, AND ANIMATION

The Morgan Kaufmann Series in Computer Graphics and Geometric Modeling

Series Editor: Brian A. Barsky, University of California, Berkeley

NON-PHOTOREALISTIC COMPUTER GRAPHICS
MODELING, RENDERING, AND ANIMATION

Thomas Strothotte
Stefan Schlechtweg

*Otto-von-Guericke University of Magdeburg
Magdeburg, Germany*

MORGAN KAUFMANN PUBLISHERS

AN IMPRINT OF ELSEVIER SCIENCE

AMSTERDAM   BOSTON   LONDON   NEW YORK
OXFORD   PARIS   SAN DIEGO   SAN FRANCISCO
SINGAPORE   SYDNEY   TOKYO

Executive Director   Diane Cerra
Assistant Publishing Services Manager   Edward Wade
Editorial Assistant   Mona Buehler
Cover and Interior Design   Frances Baca Design
Cover Image   Erich Lessing/Art Resource, NY
Composition   Windfall Software, using ZzTEX
Copyeditor   Robert Fiske
Proofreader   Jennifer McClain
Indexer   Ty Koontz
Printer   Courier Corporation

Morgan Kaufmann Publishers
An Imprint of Elsevier Science (USA)
340 Pine Street, Sixth Floor
San Francisco, CA 94104-3205, USA
www.mkp.com

06   05   04   03   02   5   4   3   2   1

Library of Congress Control Number: 2001099792
ISBN: 1-55860-787-0

This book is printed on acid-free paper.

For my daughter Josephine (born 8 November 1995),
already a frequent computer graphics conference attendee,
and my son George (born 17 November 2000).

— **THOMAS**

Meiner Familie – meinen Eltern
und meiner Großmutter – gewidmet.
Im Andenken an meinen Großvater.

— **STEFAN**

FOREWORD

David Salesin
Senior Researcher, Microsoft Research
Professor, Department of Computer Science & Engineering,
University of Washington

The Quest for Realism has motivated much of the history of rendering, the process of creating synthetic imagery with computer graphics. The earliest work in this area concerned the development of plausible *local illumination* models, the study of how light reflects off a surface. Later work concerned the problem of solving for the equilibrium solution of light reaching all surfaces as the light reflects about an environment, a problem known as *global illumination*. The careful characterization of these problems as physical processes that can be simulated with ever-increasing speed and accuracy ranks among the great successes of the computer graphics field.

However, with this ability to simulate scenes of ever-increasing realism comes a new problem: depicting and visualizing these complex scenes in a way that communicates as effectively as possible. Thus, over the past decade, a new type of quest has emerged—a quest more subtle and actually more interesting, in my opinion, than the quest for realism. This new (and in some sense larger) quest has more to do with creating imagery that is useful, first and foremost, and also beautiful—rather than just physically realistic. To this end, we can no longer turn to the physical sciences. Instead, we must look to the cognitive sciences, as well as to the fields of art, graphic design, and traditional illustration, where the challenges of structuring and abstracting information so that it can be communicated most effectively—and attractively—have been most carefully studied.

This new area of endeavor, which by way of contrast with the earlier quest for realism has become known as *non-photorealism,* or NPR for short, has provoked a tremendous level of interest in recent years. Indeed, there has been an absolute blossoming of fascinating papers and techniques in the research literature: from *artistic screening* methods for printing images using microdots with meaningful shapes that might deliver their own message; to techniques for rendering images in pen-and-ink, watercolor, or engraved etchings styles; to procedures for lighting and even distorting three-dimensional models in order to clarify shapes or direct a viewer's attention. The variety and cleverness and even audacity of these manifold techniques never cease to amaze me as I see each new one presented for the first time at SIGGRAPH (the premier computer graphics conference), or at some other research forum.

Now, a great number of these remarkable techniques have been comprehensively assembled, organized, and presented for a larger audience—in the form of this book that you have in your hands. *Non-Photorealistic Computer Graphics: Modeling, Rendering, and Animation* provides the most systematic and in-depth study of the field of NPR that has been published to date, and I believe it will go a long way toward making the field accessible to practitioners and researchers alike. By disseminating the many early research results in NPR to a much larger audience, my sincere hope is that this book will also play a pivotal role both in enticing practitioners to refine these approaches—making them really practical for computer graphics production—and in inspiring researchers to develop ever more creative and audacious techniques.

CONTENTS

PREFACE

The term *non-photorealistic computer graphics* has come to denote the area of scientific and technological endeavor dealing with the computer generation of images and animations that, generally speaking, appear to be made in part "by hand." Such images often resemble those that, for example, architects, industrial artists, or scientific illustrators produce to communicate more or less specific information, often accompanied by text. They are characterized by their use of randomness, ambiguity, or arbitrariness rather than completeness and adherence to the portrayed objects' properties.

Non-photorealistic computer graphics involves all phases of processing that computer graphics in general uses. By far the most work has been has been done in what is denoted in this book by non-photorealistic rendering (NPR). It has its roots in early papers that appeared in the 1980s (in particular Strassmann, 1986a or Sasada, 1987). Two very influential papers were published at SIGGRAPH 1990 (Saito and Takahashi, 1990, and Haeberli, 1990), but the techniques they presented were still treated in isolation. In 1994, the contours of this new area began to emerge with the papers published at SIGGRAPH (Winkenbach and Salesin, 1994, and Salisbury et al., 1994) and Eurographics (Strothotte et al., 1994). These papers effectively broke open the dam by demonstrating the generality of the underlying principles.

After these publications in 1994, international conferences began having sessions devoted to non-photorealistic computer graphics. The first international symposium devoted solely to this topic was organized in Annecy, France, in June 2000. By the time of this writing, it is estimated that the literature on this topic encompasses some 300 papers.

The time has become ripe for a systematic assessment of the literature. Having grown "organically," the methods and techniques that have been developed have lacked a uniform terminology and notation. The area has thus far been unstructured, making it increasingly difficult to identify and assess new open problems. Indeed, sometimes papers have even "reinvented the wheel," albeit in a different context and application concern. Indeed, this lack of a systematic study has led to the fact that at the time of this writing there is no single, all-encompassing tool for non-photorealistic computer graphics, neither in the market nor in research labs.

Structure of the Book

This book provides a systematic, in-depth insight into non-photorealistic computer graphics as an emerging area within computer science. The text emphasizes the structure of the area and unifies the major results reported on in the literature.

- Chapter 1 provides the background for the area by reviewing its historical roots, why it is of such particular interest today, what fundamental algorithmic approaches are taken, and what the long-range visions are.
- Chapters 2 through 5 structure and treat methods that are based on two-dimensional data structures. This includes pixel manipulation, drawing lines, curves, and other graphical primitives, and simulating natural media.
- Chapter 6 takes a first step in adding some information about the depth of objects portrayed within an image. However, this information is again stored in two-dimesional data structures.
- Chapters 7 and 8 move into the realm of exploiting the three-dimensional information encoded within geometric models for non-photorealistic computer graphics.
- Chapter 9 deals with distorting images and models.
- Chapter 10 discusses a variety of applications of non-photorealistic computer graphics.
- Chapter 11 concludes the book by presenting a conceptual framework for binding everything together.

Target Audience

The book's use is threefold. First, it is intended to accompany a course within a computer science curriculum for *students* at the senior undergraduate or beginning graduate level. Preliminary drafts of the book were used by the authors for teaching such a course at the University of Magdeburg on four occasions (fall 1999, summer 2000, fall 2000, and fall 2001). The course encompassed four hours of lectures per week for a semester of 14 weeks. The students had all had at least one undergraduate computer graphics course covering the basics of 2D and 3D computer graphics. The students were expected to be proficient in a programming language.

The same course was taught by the authors at Simon Fraser University (Vancouver, Canada) as a two-week crash course with four hours of lectures per evening in weeks two and three of the semester (fall 2000). The students were given a take-home midterm in week 7 of the semester, and asked to submit a final project in week 13. This format worked well and enabled the students to take several other regular courses at the same time.

Students should be presented the material of the book in the order in which it is written. A sprinkling of the exercises at the end of the chapters should be given as homework. If there is not enough time to cover the whole book, some of the chapters can be thinned out. For example, Sections 2.3, 2.4, 3.3, 4.2, 4.3, 5.3, 7.3, 8.4, and 9.4 can be left out of the classroom but assigned as further reading without harming the students' basic understanding of the topic.

Second, the book will be useful to *practitioners in the field*. It contains a wealth of examples, particularly in the form of images, which the authors hope will excite the reader and motivate the use of non-photorealistic computer graphics. The methods introduced are explained in enough detail that programs can be written directly without major conceptual effort.

Computer graphics professionals wishing to get into the topic of non-photorealistic computer graphics either can read the chapters in order or, to save time in a first pass at the topic, can read more selectively. They should read Chapter 1, one of Chapters 2 through 5, Chapter 6, Chapter 9, and Chapter 10, if necessary skipping the sections mentioned above, which can also be skipped by students.

The third use of the book is for reference by *researchers in the field*. It unifies the literature and introduces terminology. Wherever possible, the terminology introduced in the original papers is used within the book. However, in some cases, particularly where different articles use varying terminology, the book decides on one wording. The bibliographic references at the end of the chapters give the necessary pointers to the important publications.

In the case of researchers in the field of non-photorealistic computer graphics, the chapters can be read in just about any order because methods that are built upon are referenced appropriately. A comprehensive index aids in selective reading.

Why Study Non-Photorealistic Computer Graphics as a Computer Scientist?

Should a course on a leading-edge topic such as NPR be part of a graduate degree program in computer science?

This question is really asking what is expected of computer science graduates. Presumably, students can no longer be endowed with an equally high level of specific engineering knowledge in all subdisciplines of computer science. Instead, there is an increasing demand for distilling what is being taught to core skills. These lie at the heart of the approach a computer scientist is to take when solving a problem. Such skills should be studied in the context of one another using any one of a number of example areas. The idea is that if these skills are mastered within one area, the graduate will be equipped with the ability to transfer the approach to other areas that may arise at their future workplace.

The area of NPR is one that exemplifies this approach. It takes an area of scientific endeavor that is treated with the methods and tools of theoretical, practical, and applied computing. The treatment of the subject matter as it appears in this book is to be exemplary for how computer scientists decompose problems into parts, bring individual solutions together again, and embed them in systems that actually help users carry out their tasks at hand.

Furthermore, you can observe that there has been a shift in the emphasis during the late 1990s toward providing graduates with a more user-centered view of their work. Whereas many areas within computer science, even within computer graphics, can be studied without ever carrying out empirical work with users, this book treats NPR as a subject area that begins with questions pertaining to what users really want to get out of using its methods and tools.

In keeping with the trend to more user-centered computing, there has been a tendency in recent years for Departments of Computer Science to devise new degree programs to meet the demands of the media industry. One example among many is the undergraduate and graduate program in computational visualistics offered at the University of Magdeburg. Here the emphasis is on methods and tools for visual communication, both from an algorithmic (computer science) and a user-centered (humanities) point of view. A course in NPR is of particular importance in this context because it demonstrates one aspect of the flexibility of graphical communication that will lie at the heart of Web-based systems in the first decade of the new millennium.

Acknowledgments

The material presented in this book draws on research results and the thoughts of many scientists. Our thanks go to Kees van Overveld for contributing his many deep insights into the topic in the final chapter of the book. A number of other colleagues spent time with us in Magdeburg and provided their insights into the topic, among them Lyn Bartram, John Buchanan, Sheelagh Carpendale, Dave Forsey, and Simon Schofield. Many of the first author's Ph.D. students produced results that turned out to be instrumental in the development of this book. Thanks in this regard to Oliver Deussen, Bert Freudenberg, Frank Godenschweger, Nick Halper, Jörg Hamel, Knut Hartmann, Stefan Hiller, Axel Hoppe, Tobias Isenberg, Maic Masuch, Bernhard Preim, Andreas Raab, and Michael Rüger.

We wish to thank those persons who provided the support to make this book happen, including the administrative, technical, and secretarial staff at our institute who keep things up and running, even under adverse workloads (Heiko Dorwarth, Volkmar Hinz, Petra Janka, Thomas Rosenburg, Petra Specht, and Sylvia Zabel); the students at the University of Magdeburg and Simon Fraser University who studied the topic with previous versions of the manuscript; and all of our colleagues around the world who did great research and who gave us the copyrights to their images.

Finally, our particular thanks goes to the superbly professional staff at Morgan Kaufmann who turned our loose-leaf pages into a book we are proud of: Mona Buehler, Diane Cerra, and Edward Wade.

1 | INTRODUCTION

Since its inception in the 1960s, computer graphics has been dominated by the goal of generating images that mimic the effect of a traditional photographic camera. At the time, the term *photorealism* was taken from a style of painting popular in North America. Artists had developed techniques to simulate by hand the workings of a camera. The techniques were perfected to the point where the resultant handmade images could hardly be distinguished from real photographs (see Figure 1.1). Thus, the term *photorealistic computer graphics* was chosen to denote algorithmic techniques that resemble the output of a photographic camera and that even make use of the physical laws being involved in the process of photography.

After over 30 years of research and development on the problem of generating photorealistic images by computer, many problems pertaining to the modeling and rendering of objects with smooth and regular shapes have been solved. Even very complex scenes with many objects found in nature can be generated: Figure 1.2 shows an example of a rendition of a countryside based on 100,000 individual plants that were modeled by about 50 million polygons. More recent research work in this area concentrates now on special effects that increase even more the realism of the computed images, such as modeling and rendering the influence of weather phenomena on surfaces consisting of a specific material.

To formulate the goal to be able to generate *photorealistic* images by computer was a stroke of genius by the founding fathers of the area. Although it is difficult to pinpoint who actually set the goal and recognized its potential, perhaps the most prominent pioneer was Ivan Sutherland working in the early 1960s. As a research

FIGURE 1.1 Example of a handmade photorealistic image.

goal, photorealism has a number of appealing attributes. First, it is "technology driven" in that computers are to be used to model the workings of another kind of machine, a camera; this was certainly *en vogue* at the time and still has its fascination today. More important, however, is that it is relatively clear how to measure scientific progress in the area: by direct comparison with photographs taken by a camera. Practically all members of our Western society, particularly non-computer scientists, can appreciate the goal and can assess its progress by simple inspection. These are the essential ingredients that have contributed to the success of this area of scientific endeavor.

Since the computer graphics community has made such enormous progress within the area of photorealistic rendering, the question where new frontiers may lie was left hanging in the air for most of the 1990s. Indeed, a look at the spectrum of topics of papers presented at leading scientific meetings on computer graphics reveals that few papers still address techniques that have a direct bearing on photorealistic rendering or modeling for it. One major direction in which attention has shifted is to view photorealism as just one of many rendition styles.

FIGURE 1.2 A computer-generated rendition of a countryside.

1.1 **Before and After Photorealism**

Before the age of photography, humankind was already doing well making images to convey information. Deviance from such features as a uniform scale, the lifelike use of color, and the precise reproduction of all details of images as seen by the human eye were the method of choice. This will be illustrated with two examples.

Consider first an image taken from literature on the ancient Egyptians, as illustrated in Figure 1.3. Note how the artist has taken the liberty to draw the subjects in a way in which they cannot possibly have really looked. Moreover, the drawing emphasizes shape at the expense of surface texture and other aspects of realism.

Next, consider the reproduction of a painting of a European town made in the 16th century, as shown in Figure 1.4. This was a typical style of drawing

FIGURE 1.3 Examples of images produced in the times of the ancient Egyptians. Note the posture of the figures; no human can, in fact, hold his body in this position. However, this "inaccuracy" probably did not disturb anyone at the time.

views of towns in the period; many paintings such as these exist. Here the artist has chosen a particular perspective that emphasizes certain aspects of the scene. Notice how the church in the lower left blends into the background while the one in the city is dominant. The latter is drawn much larger, even though it is probably of similar size and is farther away from the viewer.

These examples show how artists, either consciously or unconsciously, have taken advantage of being able to define a "point of view." Drawing by hand, it is possible to free oneself from physical constraints of reality and to convey an impression rather than just to convey details of a scene's appearance. Indeed, there

FIGURE 1.4 View of Nîmes (France), as drawn by Sebastian Manster in 1569.

are artists who contend that *to draw* by hand means *to observe*; some artists carry out their work with the primary goal of studying the details of the scene. Such artists often look down upon photography, which in their opinion circumvents the process of observation. Indeed, it is possible to take a photograph of a scene without really looking carefully at it, whereas the same is not true for a painting!

How did photography change the activity of making images by hand? Aside from the direction of art called photorealism mentioned at the outset of this chapter, people have continued to draw and paint, although the styles have evolved over time. Indeed, even in the 20th century when photography already had a firm footing in print media, many of those wishing to communicate through pictures have preferred to work with traditional methods. As a case in point, we will look at two examples in Figures 1.5 and 1.6, which parallel those of Figures 1.3 and 1.4.

FIGURE 1.5 *Portrait de Dora Maar*, painted in 1937 by Picasso. Note how selected features of the face—visible only from different points of view—are merged into one painting.

An example of the work of Picasso is shown in Figure 1.5. Like the ancient Egyptians, he, too, freed himself from reproducing a scene the way it would look from a single point of view. Instead, the juxtaposition of the individual elements provides for multiple views in one painting. It is left up to the viewer to merge these mentally.

Furthermore, Figure 1.6 shows a map of the city of Plzeň taken from a present-day brochure for visitors to the city. It has been thoroughly distorted so as to provide the viewer with a great deal of information all at once. Indeed, almost every map that meets the eye of cartographic laypersons has been distorted in some way so as to improve the view on the information.

Where do these examples leave us? Both before photography and after its advent, artists have made effective use of deviating from "realistic" renditions of scenes. This freedom to encode an impression rather than being forced to follow physical constraints is considered the key to conveying information.

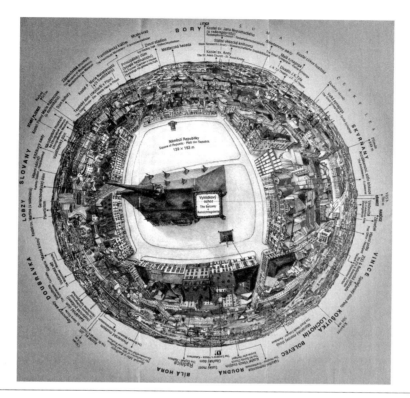

FIGURE 1.6 A map of the city of Plzeň (Czech Republic), as it appears in a brochure for present-day tourists.

1.2 Non-Photorealistic Rendering

The goal of NPR is to be able to specify formally the way in which a rendition is to appear and subsequently to write computer programs that produce non-photorealistic renditions. The first step in our study, however, is to examine in more detail why this is a useful task. We will show how each goal to be achieved by NPR suggests criteria that can be used to measure its success. This will then lead to a discussion of the term *non-photorealistic rendering* itself.

1.2.1 Goals and Criteria for Success

At a superficial level, NPR can be pursued in its own right, void of any deeper reason. This can be justified by treating NPR as a scientific challenge, irrespective of the application of the research results. From this point of view, NPR certainly is an interesting and potentially rewarding area of endeavor. It is unclear, however, how to measure the success of the work under these circumstances. In photo-realistic rendering, the measure of success is the closeness of the resulting images to photographs; although this is a useful measure equally void of an application, there is no analogous measure for NPR.

The following is a possible list of reasons why it is a good idea to try to produce non-photorealistic images. Each of the reasons implies a goal to be achieved with the resultant renditions. These goals enable us to derive criteria to assess the quality of the images.

1. *Simulating intelligence* The area of NPR can be pursued on a basis similar to that of much of the early work in the area of artificial intelligence (AI). The goal of this work was, and sometimes still is, to be able to model human intelligence. Analogously, the goal of NPR could be defined as an attempt to emulate human facilities for producing graphics by hand. Interestingly enough, rendition styles often result from limitations of the tools available for making images by hand. For example, using a sharp pencil to draw makes it hard to shade a surface accurately; cross-hatching based on crisp lines has developed as a good method of approximation. Interest has been expressed recently from the AI community to produce what is sometimes provocatively called smart graphics. However, the goals of the AI community go well beyond NPR and emphasize more adaptivity in user interfaces. Nonetheless, this approach has a built-in measure of success: how close computer-generated images can emulate images rendered by hand. You can imagine a "Turing test for NPR": can images be generated by a computer that are mistaken for renditions that were handmade by people? Still, the fundamental tenet remains at the level of a purely scientific challenge.

2. *Conveying meaning* There are other fundamental reasons beyond scientific curiosity for pursuing NPR. The first is that there is ample evidence that non-photorealistic renditions are in fact more effective for communicating specific information than photographs or photorealistic renditions in many situations. This point was already alluded to in the previous section by showing examples of handmade graphics that bear practically no resemblance to photographs being used to convey information. These are used despite the existence of photography and photorealistic rendering by computer. Over and above this empirical evidence, many studies have been carried out by cognitive and

educational psychologists that attest to the superiority of such handmade graphics over photolike images. The criterion for assessing NPR under these circumstances is whether viewers ascertain the intended meaning of a graphical message. Parameters that can be used in an assessment include the time to understand a message, the error rate, and intercultural aspects.

3. *Clarifying relationship between language and pictures*   Another fundamental reason for pursuing NPR deals with the study of the relationship between pictures and language. Using natural languages undisputedly is the dominant method of communication in the world. This is based on hypotheses about the relationship between language and thinking and the assumption that language has in fact shaped our mental capabilities. Learning to read and write is one of the fundamental facilities that schools teach, and the ability to use these facilities is generally considered to be the ticket to economic prosperity. By contrast, pictures are most often used merely as an add-on to show the major results described in a text that the pictures accompany. Schooling generally contains little or no education on using pictures for communicating ideas or for picture interpretation.

An interesting question that arises is whether language is really inherently so much better for communication or whether its superior development and its widespread use is just more a matter of habit. Hypothesizing the latter case, it will be highly useful to master the computer generation of graphical expressions, since most members of our society are not trained to produce such materials by hand. NPR will play an important role here because of its flexibility and large repertoire of possible nuances that can be associated with an expression. A criterion for measuring the success of NPR under these circumstances is the uniformity with which a complex message can be conveyed to users: a test might be to show subjects an extensive graphical presentation and ask them to write down in a natural language what they ascertain. Variables pertaining to the similarity of the accounts of several subjects and how well these match the intended meaning represent possible variables of assessment.

4. *Offering new products and services*   There are also very good practical goals to achieve when pursuing NPR. It can be hypothesized that one prerequisite for online reference materials and so-called e-books to become a serious alternative to printed books is that systems will be developed that can generate effectively non-photorealistic renditions that approach the quality of handmade graphics. Take for instance medical students' books on a subject like

Goals	Criteria of assessment
Scientific curiosity	None
Similarity to handmade graphics	Turing test for NPR
Communication of specific information	Comparison with words
Hypothesis of a language of pictures	Analysis of natural language intepretation of graphical expressions
A better understanding of the mechanisms of meaning transfer	An operational model of meaning transfer

TABLE 1.1 Goals when pursuing NPR and criteria of assessment of the resulting images.

anatomy: such books contain almost exclusively handmade graphics; they are made by highly skilled illustrators who have undergone specialized training. If such materials are to be made available online, given the lack of methods and tools for NPR, such online materials will be able to contain only scanned versions of these handmade graphics. This will, for example, severely limit interaction with such images, and it will also be difficult to make changes in a handmade image. Moreover, it will also restrict which text manipulations are possible, because image-text coherence cannot be maintained algorithmically. All this means that if NPR is not mastered, online materials will not be able to meet the expectations of an added value associated with interactive graphics.

To summarize, Table 1.1 gives an overview of the goals to be achieved by NPR and the success criteria that result.

1.2.2 A Point of View

As with many new and young areas of scientific endeavor, there is no uniform term by which what we have called NPR is known. Indeed, various researchers have sought to find a name that best describes what is happening. Nonetheless, the name is more than just an eye-catcher; it reflects much about the point of view taken by those developing the area.

When examining the primary literature on the topic, a number of different points of view are taken. These focus on the following:

1. the process of image production that is being mimicked (or, to be more precise, processes that are definitely not being mimicked): *non-photorealistic rendering*,

2. the freedom not to have to reproduce the appearance of objects precisely as they are: *non-realistic rendering,*

3. the process of adapting a presentation to a dialog context and the dynamic information wishes of users: *abstraction,* although this term covers much more ground than that just stated,

4. a specific drawing style: the terms *sketch rendering, pen-and-ink illustration,* and *stipple rendering* are examples,

5. the effect a rendition has (or is hopefully to have) on its viewers: *comprehensible rendering,*

6. the use of renditions for conveying information, perhaps in the context of other media of expression: *illustrative rendering,* or simply *illustration,* and

7. the possible deformations of images: *elastic presentations.*

Another term, *smart rendering,* has recently been introduced to denote image generation with the goal of emulating what can be imagined as being intelligent behavior on the part of the computer. Systems incorporating such rendering are associated with symbolic knowledge representation in applications that themselves are associated with intelligence, irrespective of the graphical rendition. Hence this term has a much wider scope than any of the preceding ones.

For the purposes of this book, we chose the term *non-photorealistic rendering* (NPR for short). The reason for this choice is twofold. First, the term is the one most widely used internationally for this area. Second, the term perhaps most clearly covers all the facets that we cover in our book. Nonetheless, included in our use of the term NPR are aspects of all the aforementioned terms. We include all rendition styles that are covered by the term *non-photorealistic rendering,* including those of the specific drawing techniques previously mentioned (sketch rendering, pen-and-ink illustration, stipple rendering), which can be considered subsets of NPR. The topic covered by this book also encompasses model or image deformations (pliable, elastic, deformable surfaces); hence the book deals not only with "non-photos" but also with "non-realism." The book also deals with aspects of how users perceive graphics; hence it is important that the renditions being studied are comprehensible. Usually the renditions are to be used in the context of linguistic utterances; hence NPR must also be considered to be illustrative in nature.

Notoriously missing from our list of terms is one that indicates that the renditions are to be works of art (*artistic rendering* might be an appropriate term).

Indeed, various authors using one of the other terms have stated that their renditions are to be more or less artistic by nature, but to date no one has seriously argued for the term *artistic rendering* for the entire area. Indeed, the position taken in this book on the place of NPR is that it is not intended to, nor will it in any way, replace the work of humans involved in making works of art by hand. Instead, NPR is intended for generating images in such situations as users would otherwise simply not have any, or at least not as adequate, graphical material at their disposal.

Despite the goals of NPR and the steps toward realizing them documented in this book, it is the firm position of the authors that artists and illustrators will continue to use their creativity for hand-producing graphics. The place of humans will continue to be one of trendsetters in graphics; they will generate styles that will be used as role models for rendering software, they will continue to use drawing or painting as a medium of observing scenes, and they will produce results worthy of putting a signature on. There is ample evidence from other areas of computer science where fears came up among other professional groups that turned out to be unfounded. For example, despite progress in text generation systems, practically all texts that computer users read have still been formulated by other humans; no systems exist, nor will exist in the foreseeable future, for writing computer-formulated novels or poetry or for automatically formulating complex business letters. Indeed, it is the goal that artists and illustrators will continue to carry out such creative processes; this will continue to feed the area of NPR with new challenges and topics of research.

1.3 Approaches to Algorithms for NPR

One of the key distinctions to be made between NPR and photorealistic rendering pertains to artifacts of the renditions produced. In photorealistic rendering, the goal is that all artifacts of the image correspond to features of the underlying model. Another way of formulating this is to say that all *object artifacts* are to be encoded in an image, and nothing else. Just as a good photograph taken with a camera should not contain blurry regions or lines stemming from a dirty or scratched-up lens, photorealistic images generated by computer should not contain artifacts stemming solely from the rendering process. For example, aliasing artifacts do not reflect features of a geometric model but are a side effect of the process of approximating a continuous function by a set of discrete values. Such image artifacts are painstakingly removed in photorealistic rendering by the process of anti-aliasing. This way, each detail of the rendition (ideally) corresponds directly to a detail in the geometric model.

In NPR, by contrast, artifacts encoded within an image may stem from one of several sources. We must differentiate between the image, the geometric model from which it was generated, and the object itself that is modeled and portrayed in the rendition. Indeed, artifacts in an image may result from the manner or style in which the geometric model is rendered; we will refer to these as *image artifacts*. Moreover, artifacts in an image may result from the way in which the geometric model represents the original object; we wll call these *model artifacts*. We will discuss these in turn.

1.3.1 Image Artifacts

Photorealistic images that are well done do not leave behind image artifacts that are visible to the naked eye. The reason is that the "primitives" such images are composed of are very small. Traditional film has a resolution of about 4,000 dpi (dots per inch). By contrast, the naked eye can distinguish between markings on paper that are at least two minutes of arc apart. When printing a photograph in a standard photo album size (say, $6'' \times 4''$), the individual marks are closer together than can be distinguished. Thus there is the possibility to provide a seemingly seamless transition between markings, which in turn makes it possible to record on a photograph the light effects captured by a lens. The same effect can be achieved for photorealistic rendering.

Since NPR generally tries to mimic images made by hand, the individual markings are of a larger size. This means that the markings can be distinguished as image artifacts by the naked eye. For example, in a stipple drawing (see Figure 1.7), a surface is represented by a collection of stipples (dots). This does not mean, however, that the surface itself is polka-dotted; instead, the density of the stipples is typically related to the brightness of the regions they represent. The task of the

FIGURE 1.7 Example of a handmade stipple drawing of an ancient saw. The example illustrates that NPR makes extensive use of image artifacts that do not correspond directly to the objects being portrayed. For example, a trained viewer will never think that the saw shown is polka-dotted.

FIGURE 1.8 Dots of dubious quality. The white dots represent snowflakes in the scene. Their regularity makes them appear as though they were applied to the image.

rendering software is to produce images as a collection of such markings such that information about the underlying model is adequately represented. It is a task of the viewer to interpret such artifacts of the image and deduce what they say about the models or objects that they represent.

By contrast, Figure 1.8 shows an example of image artifacts of questionable quality. Taken from a children's storybook, the large white dots are to represent snowflakes; however, their regularity makes them look as though they are polka dots applied to the image rather than appearing as part of the scene.

1.3.2 Model Artifacts

The other fundamental distinction between photorealistic rendering and NPR is that the geometric models need not correspond exactly to the object being

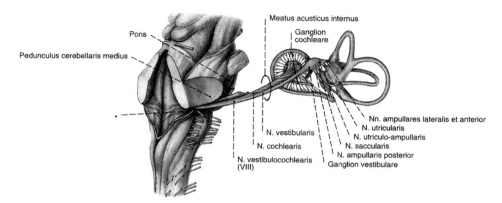

Abb. 456 N. vestibulocochlearis (VIII); häutiges Labyrinth stark vergrößert; von lateral hinten (re).

FIGURE 1.9 Example of a handmade medical illustration and its figure caption taken from a textbook on anatomy. An object of interest has been enlarged, and this has been mentioned in the caption. A translation of the figure caption is "Vestibulocochlear Nerve (VIII), labyrinth strongly enlarged, lateral view."

modeled. Through a process called *graphical abstraction*, certain features of the model are enhanced so as to convey better information.

One reason for carrying out such graphical abstraction is that this enables selected features of the geometric model to be exaggerated in the rendition in order to emphasize them. For example, in medical illustrations an organ of interest in the given context is often enlarged somewhat compared to the other parts of the illustration to provide a better view of it (see Figure 1.9). Sometimes an organ may be rotated somewhat relative to the other parts simultaneously to provide a better view on all objects in a single image and to be able to study several objects in the context of one another. This makes it possible to show more of the relevant parts of an object than would otherwise be possible, while less relevant parts may no longer be visible; this is a second reason for carrying out graphical abstraction. Such changes in the model are often mentioned either in the figure caption or in a disclaimer at the start of the book.

The process of graphical abstraction in NPR can also lead to features of a geometric model being made smaller or otherwise less dominant so as to de-emphasize them relative to other more important ones. Indeed, it is very

FIGURE 1.10 Examples of handmade sketches. In some areas of the portrayed objects, the surface is indicated by cross-hatching, whereas in other parts the surface is not indicated explicitly. Nonetheless, viewers generally will not suspect that the surface has disappeared just because it has not been drawn.

common even to remove small, unimportant details entirely. Nonetheless, trained viewers tend to interpret images correctly in the sense that a detail missing in the rendition is not necessarily assumed to be missing in the object being portrayed. For example, the lack of hatching lines in part of the image of Figure 1.10 will hardly be interpreted as there being a hole in the object; instead, the viewer will conclude that the surface continues in some smooth manner without interruption.

A third reason for changing a model is to enable better recognition of certain features of the object being modeled. For example, in drawings of Disney's Mickey Mouse, the ears are drawn basically in a front view, even if Mickey himself is drawn from the side (Figure 1.11). The ears are one of the fundamental trademarks of Mickey; a mouse without such ears would not be Mickey. Nonetheless, viewers would hardly reason that Mickey's ears were mounted the wrong way.

We contend that it is this reasoning process to interpret non-photorealistic images that gives them their greatest communicative power. The assumption is that viewers will be able to build up a mental model of the object being portrayed. Evidence from psychological research indicates that such mental models may indeed have "holes" where no data is available. Thus NPR enables appropriate graphics to build up incomplete or even vague mental models.

On the other hand, it is not only *possible* to select artifacts to represent certain features of the objects being portrayed, indeed this selection *must* take place

FIGURE 1.11 Mickey Mouse seen from different views. Note how the ears are almost always seen from a front view.

(otherwise, we would be back in the photorealistic mode). This makes NPR in fact more demanding than working with a photorealistic renderer where the question of which object features are represented by which graphical primitive is, by definition, never raised. Thus algorithms must be developed to prepare for this.

1.3.3 A Framework for Computing Image and Model Artifacts

From a computational point of view, the fundamental question in NPR is how to compute the image and model artifacts. Indeed, information sources are needed to derive what a rendition is to look like. These information sources are varied and can be classified by their dimensionality. Generally, the data sources themselves are not rich enough to determine all parameters needed for a rendition; other methods are then needed to narrow down further the possible choices. We shall study these in turn.

Dimensionality of Data Sources for Computing Artifacts

The first aspect that has a marked influence on the kinds of algorithms to be devised for computing artifacts is its dimensionality. In principle, the algorithms fall into the following categories, which we will illustrate with examples of image artifacts.

1. *Linear representations* We will refer to representations of data based on symbols (language or knowledge representation) as linear representations. In situations in which such representations are available for the domain of the

desired image, they may be processed to obtain information on how to choose the artifacts. As a simple example, an algorithm for NPR might determine the subject of a sentence accompanying the rendition and highlight the corresponding object in the image using certain graphical methods.

In essence, the area of *information visualization* deals with some aspects of this topic. The focus of information visualization is to convert inherently non–geometric data into geometric data, which can in turn be rendered using standard graphics tools. This topic is outside the scope of this book, although we will touch on it as an application of NPR (see Section 10.4).

2. *Two-dimensional data* Non-photorealistic images can be generated by analyzing other two-dimensional images, extracting certain information, and assembling the desired non-photorealistic image. For example, to affect image artifacts, a photorealistic rendition can be analyzed with image processing software to compute the positions of edges; these edges can then be enhanced by drawing lines into the original photorealistic image. The result is an NPR. This procedure is common in medical imagery, where a device produces a two-dimensional image that is augmented to draw the doctor's attention to certain features (see Figure 1.12).

3. *Encoding selected three-dimensional information in two-dimensional data structures* In some cases, it is possible to devise special data structures that can be processed to yield directives for non–photorealistic components of an image. For example, Figure 1.13(a) shows a photorealistic rendition of a nut; since parts of it are in a shadow, edges cannot be detected using the method just described. Instead, an additional two-dimensional data structure called a G–buffer (we will come to this in Chapter 6) is computed that contains the normal vector for each pixel in the image. Now discontinuities in the normal vector can be found and lines defining these discontinuities added to the original image. The result is shown in Figure 1.13(b). We shall refer to these two-dimensional data structures containing some three-dimensional data as being $2\frac{1}{2}$D.

4. *Three-dimensional data* If a three-dimensional geometric model of an object to be rendered is available, this can be exploited in the rendering process. For example, Figure 1.14(a) shows a line-drawing rendition of an architectural structure; Figure 1.14(b) shows a rendition of the same building using depth cuing by making thinner parts of lines that are farther away.

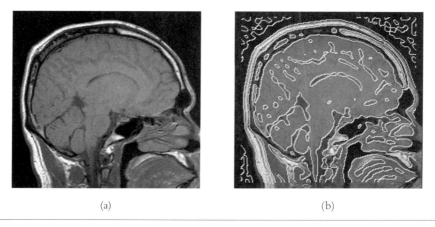

(a)   (b)

FIGURE 1.12 Enhancement of a medical image through edge detection and visualization. An original medical image shows a cross section of a brain (a); edge enhancement software has determined where discontinuities in the surface exist, and these are shown in the NPR (b).

(a)   (b)

FIGURE 1.13 Enhancement of an image using selected three-dimensional information in a two-dimensional data structure. Edge detection on the image of a nut (a) may be inadequate for finding all edges. Instead, an additional two-dimensional data structure, called a G-buffer, is computed that contains the object's normal vector for each pixel in the image. Now discontinuities in the normal vector can be found and lines defining these added to the original image. The result is shown in (b).

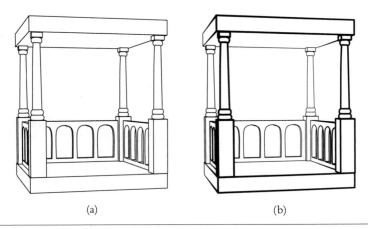

(a)   (b)

FIGURE 1.14 Adding depth cuing using three-dimensional information: a building is shown as a line drawing (a) and the lines not lying in the image plane are tapered to indicate depth (b).

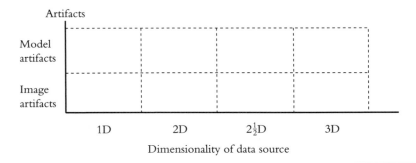

FIGURE 1.15 Artifacts can be classified and related to the dimensionality of their data source.

Model artifacts can also be classified in the same manner. We will see a variety of examples later in this book.

In summary, data is necessary to determine which artifacts are to be combined to yield a non-photorealistic rendition. This data can be classified according to its dimensionality, as illustrated in Figure 1.15.

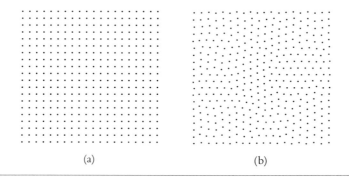

FIGURE 1.16 Placement of stipples. A surface of constant light intensity can be stippled by a regular grid of dots (a). This causes problems when viewers associate the regularity of the grid with non-existent features of the surface. By contrast, a statistical variation in the distribution, as shown in (b), yields more pleasing results.

Computing Artifacts from Data Sources

Once data sources for potential artifacts have been analyzed, it quickly becomes evident that there are many different possible artifacts that can be included in a rendition to convey information. Hence methods must be developed to choose among these.

We will first classify these methods according to the properties that the collection of artifacts is to have:

1. *Random statistical variations* In some situations, statistical variations dictate the possible choices for artifacts (see Figure 1.16). Indeed, statistical variation may be necessary so that a viewer is led to believe that the artifacts are in fact image artifacts and not model or object artifacts.

2. *Arbitrariness* Some object or model features can be visualized with any one of a variety of very different possible choices of artifacts. For example, Figure 1.17 shows a line drawing in which the important parameters for the rendition can be set arbitrarily within certain bounds.

3. *Determinism* Given certain constraints on the properties of a rendition, parameters can, in some cases, be computed deterministically. For example, given a size of a grid to cover a model and the constraint that the object's

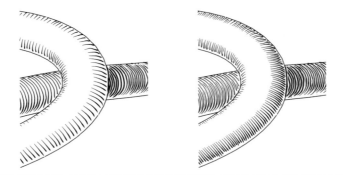

FIGURE 1.17 Arbitrary placement of cross-hatching lines. Note that the hatching is less dense in the left image than in the right one. In any case, the hatching in these images is used to indicate curvature. The precise length and thickness of each line as well as the density of the lines are parameters that can be chosen arbitrarily within certain bounds.

shape is to be recognizable from any orientation, a better parameterization of the grid can be computed (see Figure 1.18).

From where is the data to make these decisions to come? We will see throughout this book that three different sources of data can be exploited when deciding on these properties and their parameterization:

1. *Geometric model* A considerable amount of information can be extracted from the geometric model. Note that the information may stem from the original 3D model, or even some other geometric data structure derived from it (like $2\frac{1}{2}$D or 2D structures). This information goes beyond that necessary to determine the details of what the object being modeled looks like and extends, for example, to a classification of the object's global shape or the complexity of its shape. This information can then be used to decide on the parameterization of the rendition.

2. *User input* User input is an important aspect of systems for NPR. This input is generally contributed by the last user who changes the image. Various methods for enabling user input have been developed specifically for NPR.

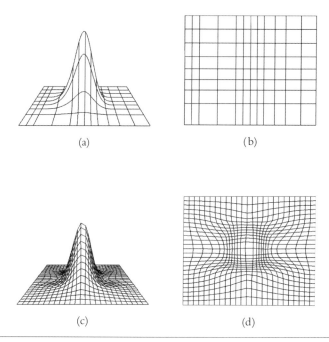

(a)   (b)

(c)   (d)

FIGURE 1.18 Unique positioning of lines. An initial parameterization of a surface is shown in (a). When viewed from the top, the surface's curvature is not evident (b). If the object's curvature is to be recognizable from any viewing direction, a new parameterization can be computed (c). The curvature is now more readily evident from the top view (d). This example is studied in detail in Chapter 7.

3. *Additional symbolic representations*   Experience has shown that to be able to generate high-quality non-photorealistic renditions, geometric models need to be enriched over and above being simply a collection of polygons. On the most fundamental level, this enrichment starts with a hierarchical organization of the polygons into smaller objects; more complex, the enrichment may extend to providing pointers to objects in a knowledge-based system. The latter enables inference mechanisms to be used to compute parameters of the rendition.

These concepts are summarized in Figure 1.19.

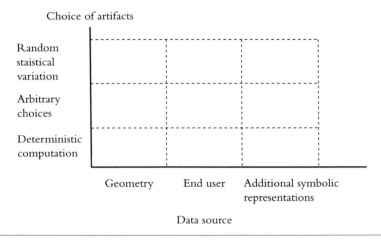

FIGURE 1.19 Methods for computing artifacts can be classified according to the kinds of algorithms used and the data source.

1.4 Visions for NPR

The goal of NPR is to enable users to lead human-computer dialogs with information exchange in a graphical form. The style of the images generated should be flexible so as to be most appropriate for the dialog at hand. To this end, a model of information transfer must be assumed or developed, and methods and tools need to be developed to enable designers and programmers of interactive systems to have appropriate images rendered for their end users.

In this section, we will present several examples of handmade non-realistic images that are to serve as role models. The goal of NPR is ultimately to be able to generate by computer and upon user demand images that are at least as good and appropriate to the dialog context as the exemplars. For the time being, however, these images will remain visions; they are indications of "open problems" to be solved. We will explore images from different areas since each area has its own requirements and conventions. To be successful in creating non-realistic renditions in each of the areas, these conventions have to be followed in order to meet the users' (or viewers') expectations.

1.4.1 Scientific and Medical Illustration

Scientific and medical illustration is perhaps the area of illustration that has achieved the highest level of sophistication. Medical books are full of beautiful samples of unique illustrations. Some of these are so good that they are reused in medical books over many decades; the texts change, but some illustrations are passed on from generation to generation of medical students.

Furthermore, scientific and medical illustration emerged from a field of art into an area of scientific research. The first medical illustrations were published in 1543 in Versalius's book *De Humani Corpus Fabrica*, the first anatomy textbook as we know it. Images in this book were accurately and painstakingly drawn and reproduced as woodcuts by one of Tizian's apprentices. During that time, medical illustration was still a form of art. Today, many universities offer degree programs in scientific illustration or medical illustration.

As a consequence of this development, there exist a number of conventions and standards of how to communicate scientific and medical facts visually. Many of these conventions are so "normal" today that readers of anatomy textbooks do not even notice them as being something special. So, for instance, arteries and veins are almost always depicted using blue and red, whereas muscle tissue is drawn in brown and ligaments in white or gray. Further, lighting conditions are depicted in a way that the light source seems to be placed in the upper right-hand corner of the subject being portrayed. Although these conventions are used consistently throughout the literature today, they are explained in most cases in a special disclaimer to each book. This gives the reader a "translation table" to enable him or her to effectively decode the illustrations.

Figure 1.20 shows an example of such a medical illustration. Note how different lighting conditions are encoded by using different wide lines and different dense hatchings. Also note the use of color to encode additional information (in this case, emphasis).

1.4.2 Technical Illustration

Technical illustrations made by hand tend to be simpler and less varied than scientific or medical illustrations. No doubt this is because they tend to portray industrial products with a more uniform surface structure than, for example, the human body. Indeed, technical illustrations tend to be characterized by larger white surfaces since either the details are not known or unavailable, or they are

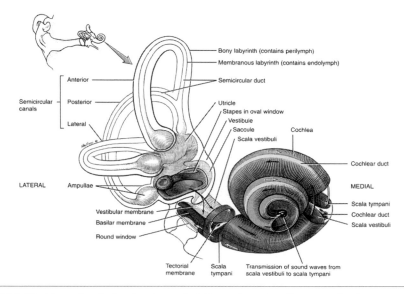

FIGURE 1.20 Example of a handmade medical illustration taken from a textbook on anatomy.

not important for the communicative goal at hand. A second fact is that within the domain of technical illustration, many efforts have been made to develop standards in order to make technical illustrations an effective medium for communication between engineers. This goal has been reached by technical drawings that are standardized even by ISO norms and that are produced nowadays not only by trained draftspeople but also with the help of special software (CAD and CAAD programs).

Nevertheless, technical illustration as an area includes more than just these technical drawings. More illustrative images, as we see every day in user manuals (see Figure 1.21), are part of this area, as well as illustrations in other kinds of technical documentation. Note in these images that they omit many of the details of the portrayed objects and show only these parts that are of interest in the context at hand. What's more, technical illustrations in general tend to include abstract-graphical symbols to show additional information (for example, handling instructions or measurements). It is an interesting question whether these additional symbols can also be generated and placed in the process of non-photorealistic rendering based on the given data.

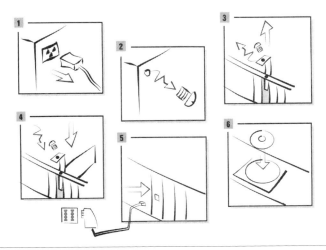

FIGURE 1.21 Example of a technical illustration taken from a user's manual of a PCI device.

1.4.3 Archaeological Illustration

In some branches of science, specific styles of graphics have become the methods of choice for capturing visible phenomena. One such area is archaeology, where scientists draw as a vehicle for observing both minute details and larger patterns in their findings. A great many illustrations in archaeology are drawn primarily using stippling, where the drawing consists of small dots to cover surfaces.

Figure 1.22 shows an example of a handmade archaeological illustration. Note how the various different materials are represented by different kinds of graphical representations. Lines are also added to denote sharp contours like around the edges of individual objects. Note also how the details of the stippling reflect the nature of the material that it represents. Indeed, similar principles also apply in other areas apart from archaeology.

1.4.4 Storytelling

The art of using comics and animation to support telling stories was brought to perfection by the Walt Disney Company. Visualizations convey information to augment what is spoken by the characters. Indeed, though up to now such presentations have been designed manually by human experts, it is an exciting challange to design and implement methods and tools for automatically generating the visualizations for such stories. No doubt NPR methods will lie at the heart

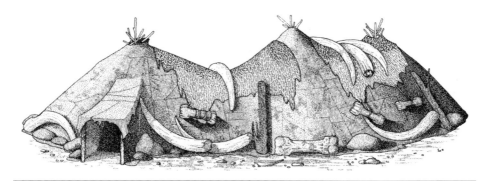

FIGURE 1.22 Example of a handmade archaeological illustration.

FIGURE 1.23 Excerpt of a handmade pictorial presentation for storytelling.

of such systems because this enables abstraction, focus, and subtleties needed for effective communication.

Figure 1.23 shows an excerpt of a handmade graphical presentation reproduced on paper. The long-range vision is to be able to produce such images from verbal descriptions and geometric models.

Exercises

1.1   Find three different handmade images of the same object or the same kind of object as they are used in any area of science or engineering (for example, find three drawings of the heart as they are used in anatomy). Study each image and compare the images.

a. What do you think the illustrators' goal was when they drew the images? How might you assess whether the goals that the illustrators had have been met?

b. For each image, list some features that you would consider to be (i) image artifacts, (ii) model artifacts, and (iii) object artifacts.

c. What conventions do the images make use of? Are they used consistently?

d. What different drawing styles do the images use? Hypothesize why these styles are used.

e. Compare the scale of the drawings. Is each of them to scale?

f. Study the level of detail the illustrators used. Are they the same across the images? Why or why not?

g. What differences would there be between a photorealistic image of your object and the images that you chose? Surmise what dimensionality (linear, 2D, $2\frac{1}{2}$D, or 3D) of a data structure would be needed to affect the changes if the illustrator started with a photorealistic image.

h. Which of the terms that have previously been used for NPR apply to your images?

i. Talk to an expert in the area of application about your answers to these questions. Find out how he or she uses these images, what information he or she expects to take away from them, and in what context this takes place.

1.2 Use a pencil and a piece of paper to draw a sketch illustrating a night out you had recently. Include all details that you consider important for the experience of that evening.

a. Label the objects in the image with respect to the dimensionality of the data source; that is, how do you know that this object should be included in the rendition.

b. For each object, assess how close to the appearance of the real object your drawing is. Is it to scale? Does it have the right orientation? Classify your observations with respect to the terms *statistical variation, arbitrariness, determinism*.

Bibliographic Notes

The need for non-photorealistic image generation methods was already stated quite clearly in the late 1980s. In Foley et al. (1990), one of the standard texts for photorealistic computer graphics, it is said that "If the ultimate goal of a picture is to convey information, then a picture that is free of the complications of shadows and reflections may well be more successful than a *tour de force* of photographic realism." The area of NPR then was of interest at major computer graphics conferences throughout the 1990s. For example, Eurographics'99 and SIGGRAPH'98 both already had sessions dedicated to this topic. Some classical computer graphics textbooks that deal primarily with photorealistic rendering have sections on specific aspects of NPR, for example, Watt and Policarpo (1998). Strothotte and Strothotte (1997) analyzes the role of NPR in human–computer interaction.

In a sense, early papers in rendering can be regarded as having dealt essentially with NPR because the methods were too crude to be classified as photorealistic, even though this was their goal. Among the very first to set what we today call NPR as his goal was Steve Strassman in his paper on hairy brushes (Strassmann, 1986a).

Lansdown and Schofield (1995) were the first to structure in a general way the problems in NPR. In particular, they were the first to observe that such renditions have artifacts that can be attributed to the image rather than only to the objects being modeled.

Various terms have been used in the literature for the general area that we call NPR: non-realistic rendering was first used by the organizers of the Eurographics'99 conference, non-photorealistic rendering by Lansdown and Schofield (1995), sketch rendering by Strothotte et al. (1994), pen-and-ink illustration by Winkenbach and Salesin (1994), stipple rendering by Deussen et al. (1999b), comprehensible rendering by Saito and Takahashi (1990), artistic rendering by Lansdown and Schofield (1995), illustrative rendering by Dooley and Cohen (1990a, 1990b), and finally elastic presentation by Carpendale (1999).

2 | PIXEL MANIPULATION OF IMAGES

The first approach to non-photorealistic rendering that we will pursue is to work on the level of the image's pixels or of small marks. The input to such algorithms is generally simply a pixel matrix, where each entry is either a gray level or a color value (RGB). Indeed, we will concentrate on the former and show how to transform the gray levels to achieve various visual effects. In the terminology of Chapter 1, we will induce *image artifacts* for any one of a number of reasons. Although in the past many authors working on such topics considered these artifacts to be a distraction that had to be minimized, we will show how in many cases this apparent "bug" of having induced image artifacts can be made into an elegant rendering feature in NPR.

The methods we introduce in this chapter can be applied in one of two ways. First, they can be used in a post-processing step to a photorealistic renderer. The renderer initially produces a pixel-based image and then applies algorithms to this image; the pixels are manipulated to produce various different effects. The second way in which most of the methods discussed in this chapter can be used is to apply them to scanned images. Indeed, most of the methods we discuss need no more information than that directly discernible from a gray-level image.

All methods of this and the next chapter operate on the level of pixel manipulation and can be illustrated using what is called an *intensity ramp*. An intensity ramp based on gray levels is shown in Figure 2.1: the intensity varies monotonously from 1.0 on the left to 0.0 on the right; that is, black is represented as intensity value 1.0 and white as 0.0. Hence, the term *intensity* is connected to the "blackness" of the image. If for any reason the opposite notation is needed,

FIGURE 2.1   The intensity ramp based on gray levels.

we will use the term *brightness,* which is represented by a value of 1.0 for white and 0.0 for black. Each method we introduce in this chapter will yield a different way of representing the intensity ramp.

In the following, we will first concentrate on the process of *halftoning,* which carries out a reproduction of a continuous tone image on a bi-level device, that is, each pixel is either set (black) or not set (white). A special kind of halftoning called *screening* can be employed to control the patterns (*dither screens*) used to produce blocks of pixels with given intensity values. In connection with this, the properties of the dither screens have to be observed. We will show how to tune these screens in order to achieve the desired results. We will then show how dither screens can be produced both procedurally and manually, such that they represent certain shapes and how images can be built by combining these shapes. We will then move on to the process of *stippling* in which pencil-point-sized dots are combined to render images. We first introduce automatic methods before we show how user interaction can be used to create expressive images. Finally, image mosaics will be explored, in which the final image is assembled by combining many small discernible images.

2.1   Halftoning Methods

When producing a newspaper or a book in black and white, a considerable amount of work has to be done to prepare images for the printing process. Since only two colors, namely, black and white, are available, all continuous tone images—be they color or grayscale—have to be represented in a manner that the overall intensity distribution stays approximately the same. Here, a process called *halftoning* is the key for producing images in a quality we are used to seeing in daily newspapers.

Originally, halftoning was a process by which each small resolution unit (we are not speaking about pixels yet) is imprinted with a circle of black ink whose area is proportional to the intensity of the corresponding area in the original. Thus the output image is composed of a set of variably sized circles that can be

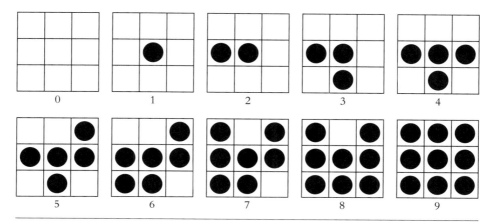

FIGURE 2.2 Example of patterns for representing ten intensity levels of a 3 × 3 pixel area.

seen when looking at a newspaper photograph using a magnifying glass. Usually, newspapers use 60 to 80 variably sized and variably shaped areas per inch, whereas in magazines and books this number is slightly higher, about 110 to 200 per inch.

2.1.1 Ordered Dithering

Modern graphical output devices work with small, indivisible units of uniform size and shape called *pixels* that can be addressed separately and given a unique color (out of a range of colors being determined by the technical specification of the device in question). Thus it is impossible to perform the halftoning process as described earlier since it is impossible to draw areas of different sizes. However, if we consider a group of $n \times n$ pixels, we can switch on and off a different number of them to achieve several intensity levels. Figure 2.2 shows the ten possible patterns for ten intensity levels when using a 3 × 3 matrix. This process of halftoning—often also known as *ordered dithering*—works rather simply by computing the medium intensity of an $n \times n$ pixel area in the original image and replacing this area with the appropriate $n \times n$ pattern for the desired intensity.

The patterns in Figure 2.2 are just one example for setting pixels in a 3 × 3 array. To describe those patterns, so-called dither matrices are used. A dither matrix contains an intensity level in each cell. To get a specific pattern for a region, all pixels represented by cells with an intensity level less than the desired intensity are switched on. For the preceding example, the dither matrix $D^{(3)}$ is

```
1   for x := 0 to width(S)//n do
2     for y := 0 to height(S)//n do
3       R := get n × n region of the image S starting at position (nx, ny)
4       i := mediumIntensity(R)
5       P := pattern[i]
6       place P in the output image O starting at position (nx, ny)
7     od
8   od
```

ALGORITHM 2.1   Ordered dithering based on dither matrices of size n. The output image O is composed of dithering patterns that are stored in the array *pattern* and accessed by the medium intensity of the respective $n \times n$ region of the source image S.

$$D^{(3)} = \begin{pmatrix} 6 & 8 & 4 \\ 1 & 0 & 3 \\ 5 & 2 & 7 \end{pmatrix}$$

For an intensity value of 50% (or $\frac{5}{10}$) of the maximum intensity, the pixels 0 to 4 are thus switched on. Compare this matrix with the patterns in Figure 2.2 to see how the desired intensity levels are reached by switching on a specific set of pixels. To give some more examples, Equation (2.1) shows respective dither matrices for halftoning using 2×2 and 4×4 pixel regions. Note that with an $n \times n$ dither matrix, it is possible to display $n^2 + 1$ intensity levels.

$$D^{(2)} = \begin{pmatrix} 0 & 2 \\ 3 & 1 \end{pmatrix} \qquad D^{(4)} = \begin{pmatrix} 0 & 8 & 2 & 10 \\ 12 & 4 & 14 & 6 \\ 3 & 11 & 1 & 9 \\ 15 & 7 & 13 & 5 \end{pmatrix} \tag{2.1}$$

Putting it all together, Algorithm 2.1 describes the halftoning process using such dither matrices. The dithered intensity ramp in Figure 2.3 reveals one of the characteristics of this algorithm. The intensity range is "discretized" into $n^2 + 1$ regions (given an $n \times n$ dither matrix), each of which is then filled with the appropriate pattern. This yields strong blocking artifacts as would any discretization method.

Such dither patterns must obey certain properties, the most important of which is that they do not form regular patterns or visual artifacts. The visual quality of the dithered image should come close to that of the original image. However, leaving such artifacts in the image or even deliberately producing such

FIGURE 2.3 Intensity ramp dithered using the dither patterns from Figure 2.2.

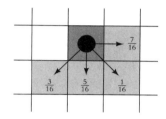

FIGURE 2.4 Distribution of the error within the Floyd-Steinberg algorithm. Note that all portions sum up to one.

artifacts may be used to create renditions with a certain style. We will have a closer look at this in Section 2.1.3.

2.1.2 Error Diffusion

The technique described so far is also known as ordered dithering since clusters of dots are used where the order of the dots is given by the dither matrix and is not changed during execution of the dithering algorithm. Even when the dither matrices are designed very carefully, it is sometimes the case that there are visible artifacts in the resulting image. To circumvent this problem, so-called error diffusion techniques can be used. As the name implies, the error (difference between the exact pixel value from the original image and the approximated value being displayed in the result) is distributed to the neighboring pixels, thus introducing a kind of "smoothing" into the dithered image.

The best-known error diffusion technique was developed by Robert W. Floyd and Louis Steinberg in 1975 and can be considered one of the classical algorithms in computer graphics. The difference between the exact pixel value and the binary representation is distributed among the neighboring pixels with a certain ratio for each direction, as can be seen in Figure 2.4. There exist a wide range of other approaches to error diffusion dithering, which mainly differ in the fractions of the error term being distributed on the neighboring pixels and in the set of pixels being involved.

```
1   for y := height(S) − 1 to 1 step -1 do
2     for x := 1 to width(S) − 1 do
3       K := approximate(S[x, y]);
4       O[x, y] := K;
5       error := S[x, y] − K;
```
6        $S[x + 1, y] := S[x + 1, y] + \frac{7}{16}\text{error};$

7        $S[x − 1, y − 1] := S[x − 1, y − 1] + \frac{3}{16}\text{error};$

8        $S[x, y − 1] := S[x, y − 1] + \frac{5}{16}\text{error};$

9        $S[x + 1, y − 1] := S[x + 1, y − 1] + \frac{1}{16}\text{error};$

```
10    od
11  od
```

ALGORITHM 2.2   Given an input image S, the Floyd-Steinberg algorithm computes an output image O by distributing the approximation error to neighboring pixels. The function *approximate()* returns the closest intensity value possible to display in the output image of the current pixel.

FIGURE 2.5   Intensity ramp dithered using Floyd-Steinberg error diffusion.

To present the procedure more formally, consider the pseudocode in Algorithm 2.2. Note that the algorithm processes the image from left to right and from the topmost pixel downwards so that the error terms are always added to pixels that have not been already involved in the dithering process. Also note that all fractions of the error term that are distributed sum up to one. (That is, exactly the error is distributed; any inaccuracy here results in unwanted visual artifacts.) To show the result, the intensity ramp dithered according to this algorithm can be found in Figure 2.5.

At the end of this theoretical section on the basics of halftoning, an example will show the results that are produced by the different methods when applied to one image. In Figure 2.6(a), an original grayscale image is given. Next, in Figure 2.6(b), a simple threshold quantization has been performed by setting all

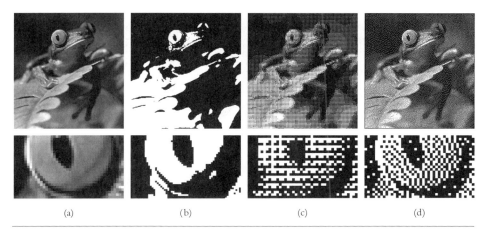

FIGURE 2.6 Different halftoning techniques for the same original image (a): threshold quantization (b), ordered dithering (c), and Floyd-Steinberg error diffusion (d). The lower images show an enlarged part to visualize the pixel distribution.

pixels having an intensity of less than 0.5 to white and all others to black.[1] Figures 2.6(c) and (d) show an example of ordered dithering using the dither patterns from Figure 2.2 and finally the result of the Floyd–Steinberg algorithm.

2.1.3 Applications to NPR

So far we have described the algorithms as they would be described with the original goal of reducing the artifacts being induced in the images. If we turn the page, however, and look at what kinds of possibilities arise when using the same algorithms to introduce artifacts into images, we will find a simple method for creating non–photorealistic renditions.

Non-Photorealistic Dither Matrices

The goal when designing dither matrices used for ordered dithering is usually to distribute the pixels as evenly as possible and to prevent patterns from being introduced in the image. If pixels in the dither matrix are grouped in a way that they form visual patterns, interesting effects are achievable. We will demonstrate

---

1. This is actually how the function *approximate()* in Algorithm 2.2 works.

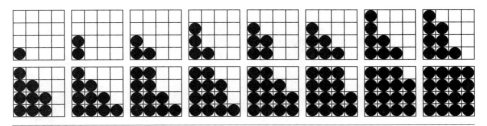

FIGURE 2.7 Dither patterns produced by the matrix in Equation (2.2). Note that the empty pattern (for zero intensity) is not displayed.

this with two examples. The first matrix forms triangular patterns and is built from the bottom left element diagonally up to the top right element. This matrix is given in Equation (2.2); the respective dither patterns can be found in Figure 2.7.

$$D^{(4)} = \begin{pmatrix} 6 & 10 & 13 & 15 \\ 3 & 7 & 11 & 14 \\ 1 & 4 & 8 & 12 \\ 0 & 2 & 5 & 9 \end{pmatrix} \tag{2.2}$$

As can be seen from this example (a dithered image using this matrix can be found in Figure 2.8(a)), the patterns are not clearly visible if the matrix is relatively small. Thus, a larger dither matrix of size, say, 6×6 will yield better results. The strength of the introduced artifacts is increased with the matrix size. As a second example, a matrix that results in linear artifacts is given in Equation (2.3).

$$D^{(4)} = \begin{pmatrix} 6 & 12 & 10 & 1 \\ 2 & 9 & 14 & 5 \\ 4 & 13 & 8 & 3 \\ 0 & 11 & 15 & 7 \end{pmatrix} \tag{2.3}$$

Since in the process of building the dither matrix all pixels have to be used, for some intensity values the patterns are not clearly recognizable. Hence, the matrices introduced here are well designed for an image with medium intensity (many groups of pixels that are replaced by the pattern where the intended shape is most visible). This means also that when designing such matrices or patterns, the target images have to be considered. The images in Figure 2.8 are produced with a 6×6 version of the matrices given earlier.

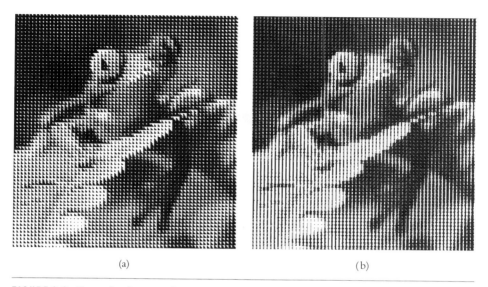

(a)   (b)

FIGURE 2.8 Examples for non-photorealistic dither matrices using bigger versions of the patterns described in the text: derived from Equation (2.2) (a) and derived from Equation (2.3) (b).

Halftoning Using Lines

The following techniques make use of error diffusion to get an initial pixel distribution that is then changed to introduce image artifacts explicitly. The Floyd–Steinberg algorithm offers a good starting point for halftoning using lines instead of dots.

For halftoning with lines, the Floyd–Steinberg algorithm is changed such that

1. short lines are produced as output instead of dots and
2. the error distribution is adjusted so that the image does not get too dark (since short lines blacken more pixels than just a single dot).

Instead of setting a black pixel in the output image, we draw a short line (that is, setting more than one pixel) in a given direction. Doing so, the image gets much darker than we want it to be, so we have to change the *error* term in order to compensate. The only thing we need to change are lines 3 through 5 in Algorithm 2.2. The first approach is Algorithm 2.3, where a line is drawn that covers m pixels. These m black pixels then have to be compensated for by m white

```
1   K := approximate(S[x, y]);
2   if (K = 1) then
3           drawLine(O, x, y, m);
4           error := S[x, y] − K − (m − 1);
5       else error := S[x, y];
6   fi
```

ALGORITHM 2.3 Replacement for lines 3–5 of the Floyd-Steinberg algorithm (see Algorithm 2.2) for hatching lines. The function drawLine(O, x, y, m) draws a line using m pixels, the center of the line being placed at (x, y) in the output image O.

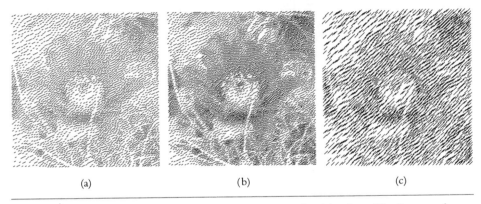

(a)   (b)   (c)

FIGURE 2.9 Using the Floyd-Steinberg algorithm to create hatching lines. The lines are drawn with different slopes, lengths, and densities: slope 30°, lines approximately 3 pixels long (a), more dense hatching as in (a) by changing the error compensation (b), slope 45°, lines 5 pixels long (c).

pixels so the error term is reduced by $m − 1$.[2] This causes the surrounding pixel values to become much brighter and thus not to contribute to the set of black pixels or lines. An example output of Algorithm 2.3 can be seen in the images of Figure 2.9 and the intensity ramp shown in Figure 2.10.

Even though error diffusion approaches generally reduce the number of artifacts left in the image, there are still a few portions that show some kind

---

2. The pixel itself already influences the computation of *error* by the value of K. Thus we only need to subtract $m − 1$.

FIGURE 2.10   Intensity ramp dithered using short hatching lines.

of pattern. This is already the case in the dithered image (see Figure 2.6(d)) and also shows up in the hatched renditions. Here, parallel lines as well as lines being connected to one another introduce even more artifacts than we might wish. To remove these, several possibilities can be considered. First, we can introduce some random changes in the lines' placement, that is, slightly change the position of the endpoints by adding a random offset. This procedure will make the image more vivid but is not a function of the image nor the portrayed geometry itself. A second way is to incorporate geometric properties of the portrayed model into the creation process of the rendition. This can be done either by adjusting the parameters of the halftoning algorithm or—when doing halftoning with lines— by aligning the lines along a specific attribute of the underlying geometry, like the surface normal vector. We will study G-buffers, which are the basis for this kind of application, in more detail in Chapter 6.

2.2 Screening

Using the halftoning techniques introduced so far, the user has no control over the pattern that is used in a block for representing an intensity value. Indeed, the patterns used (recall Figure 2.2) are rather unimaginative and decidedly un-informative. The technique called *screening*, which we shall now study, takes steps toward giving the user control over the pattern that is used to convey intensity. The goal in using such patterns is to employ this level of information display to convey additional information over and above the information contained in the original image. For example, when viewed from a distance, this information may convey texture, or when examined up close, may convey an entirely different mes-sage. Note that the methods that we introduce in this section can be referred to as *image-independent dithering* because the patterns used are chosen independently of the input image.

2.2.1 Basic Method

Ordered dithering approaches use a group of pixels and represent their medium intensity value by a specific pattern (see Section 2.1.1). Error diffusion techniques utilize the result of a simple threshold quantization and redistribute the resulting error to the surrounding region of a pixel. There is a third halftoning technique that is often referred to as *screening*. Here, two images are combined using Algorithm 2.4: the input gray-level image S and an $n \times m$ (gray-level) threshold matrix M that contains intensity values. Given an intensity value $S[x, y]$ at the position (x, y) in the input image, we compute its corresponding binary value in the output image by comparing the value $S[x, y]$ of the pixel with the value $M[x \bmod n, y \bmod m]$ of the threshold matrix. If the pixel intensity is greater than the threshold value, then $O[x, y]$ is set; otherwise, it is not set.

To make life easier and eliminate the modulo operations in Algorithm 2.4, the threshold matrix can be replaced by a second gray-level image—which we call a *dither screen D*—of the same size as the input image. D contains the threshold matrix repeated again and again in the horizontal and the vertical direction. Algorithm 2.4 is then modified as shown in Algorithm 2.5.

---

1   **for** $x := 0$ **to** width(S) **do**
2   **for** $y := 0$ **to** height(S) **do**
3   **if** $S[x, y] < M[x \bmod n, y \bmod m]$ **then** $O[x, y] := 1$ **else** $O[x, y] := 0$
4   **od**
5   **od**

ALGORITHM 2.4   Basic screening as a method of halftoning.

---

1   construct D by repeating M over the image area
2   **for** $x := 0$ **to** width(S) **do**
3   **for** $y := 0$ **to** height(S) **do**
4   **if** $S[x, y] < D[x, y]$ **then** $O[x, y] := 1$ **else** $O[x, y] := 0$
5   **od**
6   **od**

ALGORITHM 2.5   Given a dither screen D of the same size as the input image S simplifies Algorithm 2.4.

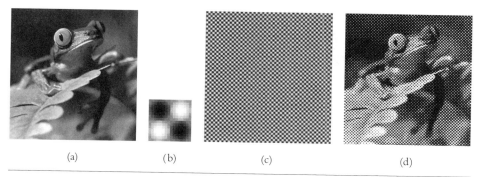

(a)　　　　　　(b)　　　　　　(c)　　　　　　(d)

FIGURE 2.11 Example for image-independent dithering: (a) the original image, (b) the threshold matrix used (enlarged), (c) the dither screen that was formed by repeating the threshold matrix over the image area, and (d) the resulting image after application of Algorithm 2.5.

Figure 2.11 shows an example of this basic method of screening—(a) shows a sample input image S, (b) the dither matrix, (c) the dither screen D, and finally (d) the output image O. As we can see, this technique creates a kind of "texture" in the output image that is determined by the threshold matrix used. This might also be the origin of the name *screening* since it gives the image a look as if a transparent screen containing a pattern is lowered in front of the image.

Although arbitrary images can be used as threshold matrices, to gain better results, they have to possess certain qualities that are needed to approximate the continuous tone image. Those qualities are

1. *Uniform distribution of threshold values* The dither screen should contain an equal number p of pixels of each possible intensity value i ($0 \leq i \leq i_{max}$). This enables the uniform reproduction of the maximum range of gray tones.

2. *Homogeneous spatial distribution of threshold values* Pixels of like threshold value should be spread uniformly throughout the dither screen to approximate the gray tone of the input image in the same fashion in different regions of the image.

Note that the dither screen used in Figure 2.11(b) in fact has the first of these qualities, a uniform distribution of threshold values. It was chosen so that an equally distributed subset of the intensity values between 0 and 255 is present exactly twice. The intensity ramp created based on this basic screening method is shown in Figure 2.12. When dither matrices that do have a uniform distribution

FIGURE 2.12 The intensity ramp using the basic method of screening based on the threshold matrix of Figure 2.11(b).

of threshold values are replicated in tiles over a dither screen covering the input image, as was illustrated in Figure 2.11(c), the second quality, a homogeneous spatial distribution of threshold values, is met automatically.

2.2.2 Tuning Image and Screen Intensities

In cases where the two qualities indicated earlier are not met, the dither screens have to be specially prepared in order to be used properly. To adopt the intensity distribution, we first have to determine which intensities are in the given dither screen and how they are distributed. This is a typical procedure in signal and image processing where *histograms* are employed.

Histograms and Histogram Equalization

A histogram of an image is actually a statistical measure that is also known as the *probability mass function* (PMF) (when normalized to fall in a range between zero and one). It describes the probability with which a pixel in the image has a certain intensity value. To compute the histogram, we simply count up how many pixels there are of each possible intensity and divide these values by the total number of available pixels. Basically, a histogram is then a list describing the distribution of the different gray levels in an image. One attribute of such a histogram or PMF is that its values (probabilities) will always sum up to one. Algorithm 2.6 is used to compute the histogram of an input image; an example—visualized as a bar chart—can be seen in Figure 2.13.

To achieve a uniform distribution of the gray values, we need to perform a *histogram equalization* on the input image. We first compute the cumulative sums of the histogram values as follows:

$$C[i] = \sum_{k=0}^{i} H[k] \quad i = 0 \ldots 255$$

```
1   for i := 0 to 255 do H[i] := 0 od
2   for y := 0 to height(S) − 1 do
3      for x := 0 to width(S) − 1 do H[S[x, y]] := H[S[x, y]] + 1 od
4   od
5   for i := 0 to 255 do H[i] := H[i]/(height(S) · width(S)) od
```

ALGORITHM 2.6   Computing the histogram H of an input image S in which each pixel has one of 256 intensity values.

(a)   (b)

FIGURE 2.13   Gray-level image (a) and the histogram computed for it (b).

As a result, we get the so-called *cumulative mass function* (CMF), which is a statistical measure of the probability that a pixel is of a given intensity or less. Both functions, PMF and CMF, are used in many pixel-level transformation techniques that basically alter the PMF by using the CMF as a look-up table. One of these techniques, histogram equalization, computes for each pixel in the image S a new gray value g' by $255 \cdot C[g]$. As a result, we get an image with a uniform intensity distribution that can be seen easily by computing the histogram of the resulting image again and comparing it with the one from the original image.

Putting it all together, Algorithm 2.7 formalizes the process of histogram equalization, whereas Figure 2.14 shows the resulting image and histogram, again from the input image in Figure 2.11(a). The term *histogram equalization* actually describes a whole class of algorithms, which we shall see shortly. The

```
1   H := histogram(S)
2   C[0] := H[0]
3   for i := 1 to 255 do C[i] := C[i − 1] + H[i] od
4   for x := 0 to width(S) − 1 do
5     for y := 0 to height(S) − 1 do O[x, y] := 255 * C[S[x, y]] od
6   od
```

ALGORITHM 2.7   Histogram equalization for a given input image S.

(a) (b)

FIGURE 2.14   Example of an output image O after histogram equalization (a) together with the resulting histogram (b).

algorithm described here is the most common technique and is also called *non-adaptive uniform histogram equalization* since it works uniformly on the whole image and the transformation of one pixel is independent from the transformation of neighboring pixels.

This process yields an image where the histogram is spread more uniformly, which was our goal for preparing the dither screen. The non-adaptive uniform histogram equalization also enhances low-contrast detail; however, it also increases the contrast of any noise in the input image.

Block-by-Block Histogram Equalization of Dither Screens

In order to achieve the spatial homogeneity of threshold values, you can split the dither screen into small blocks and apply the histogram equalization independently

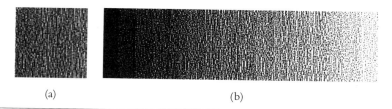

(a)   (b)

FIGURE 2.15 Block–by–block histogram qualization. The dither screen (a) has been blocked into regions of 4 × 4 pixels and histogram equalization applied to each block (b).

---

1   split the input image into small blocks
2   **foreach** block b **do**
3   h_b = cumulative intensity distribution for block b
4   h_b^* = linear approximation of the h_b of all neighboring blocks
5   transform the intensity values of b based on h_b^*
6   **od**

ALGORITHM 2.8 Adaptive histogram equalization.

---

to each block. Thus, the pixels of each block b are transformed using the cumulative distribution of values h_b within this block. Each block is thus equivalent to a small dither screen within the large one. This yields a good approximation of the input grayscale values. Unfortunately, this method yields strong blocking artifacts in the image and destroys some features of the input texture. For example, Figure 2.15(a) shows the dither screen that is processed with this block–by–block histogram equalization, whereas Figure 2.15(b) shows it applied to the intensity ramp. Note that strong blocking artifacts can be seen, and the texture has been changed significantly with respect to the original dither screen.

Adaptive Histogram Equalization of Dither Screens

To avoid the problems with the last method where each block is processed independently, we have to take the neighboring blocks into consideration. This leads to the so–called adaptive histogram equalization (AHE), which also can be used for local contrast enhancement. Though many variations have been developed for a wide range of applications, the version shown in Algorithm 2.8 has been found to work in the context of NPR.

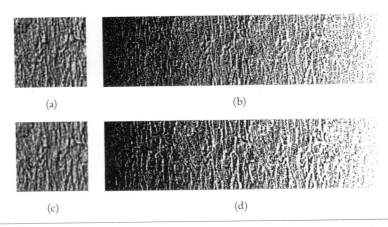

(a)   (b)

(c)   (d)

FIGURE 2.16 Adaptive histogram equalization. The manipulated dither screens are shown on the left, (a) and (c), whereas their effect when halftoning the intensity ramp is illustrated on the right, (b) and (d), respectively. In (a), 4 × 4 blocks were used; in (c), 6 × 6 blocks.

Experience has shown that the algorithm works well with blocks of size between 3 × 3 and 8 × 8 pixels, where the size of the blocks controls the size of the visible features of the original dither screen. Examples are shown in Figure 2.16.

2.2.3 Procedural Screening

The algorithms outlined earlier can be applied to any gray-level image that is to be used as a dither screen. In photorealistic rendering, for simply introducing a certain kind of texture in the image, procedural methods of generating the texture have proved useful. In the same manner, dither screens can be created for use in NPR. Procedural dither screens have a number of advantages, as for instance:

- they are created directly without using a second input image and image processing techniques,
- they can be produced in any scale, and
- non-repeated textures of any size can be produced.

However, there is the disadvantage that such screens can only be created that can be described in mathematical terms. More figurative dither screens, for example, a bark texture, can only be used by image processing techniques.

To satisfy the properties required for dither screens, we have to concentrate on the uniform distribution of values. The spatial homogeneity can then be achieved similarly to conventional dither matrices by periodically repeating one matrix over the whole image region.

For a procedural definition of a dither screen, we thus need a function with a uniform distribution of values. Let $\tau(s, t)$ be such a function defined over the intervals $s \in [0, 1]$, $t \in [0, 1]$. Furthermore, let all values of τ be between zero and one, that is, $\tau : [0, 1] \times [0, 1] \to [0, 1]$. Given such a function, we can now define $\tau_{a,b}$ to be a set of points such that $a \le \tau(s, t) \le b$, where $a, b \in [0, 1]$ and $a < b$. This set contains all possible points for a certain pair of parameter values s and t. The value $|\tau_{a,b}|$ thus counts the number of all elements in such a set. If we want to achieve a uniform distribution of the values of the function $\tau(s, t)$, then we need a function where for any given value of n ($n > 1$) the value of $|\tau_{\frac{i}{n}, \frac{i+1}{n}}|$ is a constant for any value of i with $0 \le i < n$.

We will refer to these functions τ as *dither kernels*. They compute an intensity level for each pair of input values s and t. To use them for dithering, we have to map this dither kernel to pixel positions in the input image. We will then compare the input intensity value with the computed intensity value from τ and thus determine if a pixel in the output image has to be set or not. This mapping is described by a second function $\mathcal{M}$ that transforms input pixel positions (x, y) into pairs of parameters (s, t) lying between zero and one. Thus, a procedural dither screen is composed of a dither kernel $\tau(s, t)$ and a mapping function $\mathcal{M}(x, y)$.

To give an example, we will use the (one-dimensional) function

$$\tau(s, t) = \begin{cases} 2s & \text{if } s \le 0.5 \\ 2 - 2s & \text{otherwise} \end{cases} \tag{2.4}$$

as the dither kernel that constructs a double-sided ramp with which we can approximate tone variations by parallel lines of variable width. Figure 2.17 shows a plot of this function. The most simple mapping of this kernel to an image is to apply the kernel to a small image block and repeat this over the image. Thus the mapping function $\mathcal{M}$ would use the modulo operation to access blocks of size $n \times m$ in the image. To make sure that the input values for τ fall in the interval $[0, 1]$, they have to be manipulated appropriately. For the example here, the mapping would be

$$\mathcal{M}(x, y) = \left(\frac{x \bmod n}{n}, \frac{y \bmod m}{m} \right)$$

This mapping is also illustrated in Figure 2.17 along with the final resulting image of a gray ramp dithered with this approach.

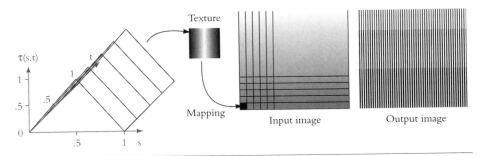

FIGURE 2.17 Procedural screening combines a dither kernel with a mapping function to produce a dithered image.

We can now choose different mapping functions and different dither kernels to adjust the image. In general, texture shape is controlled by the dither kernel $\tau(s, t)$, whereas texture scale and orientation are controlled by the mapping function $\mathcal{M}(x, y)$. We will show a few examples in Figure 2.18 to illustrate the influence of these two functions on the final image. To summarize, Algorithm 2.9 gives a formal outline of the techniques presented.

As we have seen in the preceding examples, texture features depend only on the dither kernel. If this kernel is one dimensional, only one-dimensional effects are achievable; if it is two dimensional, 2D effects—for instance, cross-hatching—can be modeled. For cross-hatching, the following two-dimensional function is used:

$$\tau(s, t) = \begin{cases} It & \text{if } s \leq I \\ (1 - I)s + I & \text{otherwise} \end{cases} \tag{2.5}$$

Here, I determines the lightest intensity that is represented by cross-hatching. Any areas with an intensity below I are hatched using a linear ramp. Moreover, all textures created from one dither kernel are the same all over the image region. To add texture variation, we can work with *displacement maps* as we know it from photorealistic image generation. The resulting texture (dither screen) is then a combination of the dither kernel $\tau(s, t)$ and two displacement functions for s and t, respectively:

$$\mathcal{T}(s, t) = \tau(s + D_s(s, t), t + D_t(s, t)) \tag{2.6}$$

Note that the displacement functions for each variable take both variables, s and t, as input; hence dependencies between s and t can be modeled. Note also

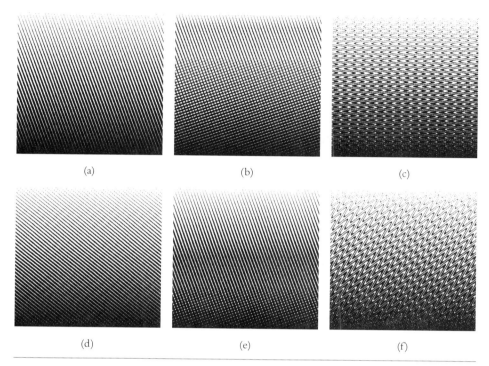

FIGURE 2.18 Different parameters for procedural screening. All images were created using modulo mapping: with an additional 20° rotation (a), using a different dither kernel (Equation (2.5) with $I = 0.7$) (b), using a sine wave as displacement function (c), with an additional 50° rotation (d), again, using Equation (2.5) as dither kernel with $I = 0.3$ (e), and 50° rotation and sine wave displacement (f).

that even when using displacement maps, the resulting function has to satisfy the requirement for uniform distribution of intensity (threshold) values; thus not all functions may be used as displacement maps. No problem arises when using smooth piecewise linear continuous functions (for instance, sine or cosine) as well as procedural noise functions.

Another way to control the features of a procedural texture is to make them depending on local features of the image to be dithered. This *image-based control* of texture features uses so-called auxiliary images, which contain a map of a specific feature in the image. These features can be of a wide variety; some examples include regions that are specified in the image by a user or by

```
1   define a dither kernel function τ
2   define a mapping function M
3   for x := 0 to width(S) − 1 do
4     for y := 0 to height(S) − 1 do
5       (x_m, y_m) := M(x, y)
6       i_s := τ(x_m, y_m)
7       if S[x, y] < i_s then O[x, y] := 1 else O[x, y] := 0
8     od
9   od
```

ALGORITHM 2.9   Procedural screening.

examining the amount of detail (that is, regions with high detail are rendered differently from regions with low detail). If we consider these auxiliary images as being two-dimensional functions $C(s, t)$, we can incorporate them in the general Equation (2.6)

$$\mathcal{T}(s, t) = \tau(s + C(s, t)D_s(s, t), t + C(s, t)D_t(s, t))$$

If the original image is rendered from a 3D model and we have three-dimensional information available, this technique can also be used to map 3D properties onto the texture and thus the rendering style. We will explain this in more detail in Chapter 6. To finish the section on procedural dither screens, Figure 2.19 shows two examples of an image dithered using this method.

2.2.4   Embedding Shapes in Dither Screens

Screening as a method of halftoning has several advantages compared to ordered dithering or error diffusion. The most important is that the shape of the artifacts being introduced in the image can be controlled by the design of the dither screen. Manually designing a correct dither screen that meets all requirements stated earlier, however, is a tedious task. Thus we will first explore a special screening method where letter shapes or texts are used as dither screens. The resultant images look like dithered black–and–white images from a distance and reveal the textual information being brought into the rendition by the dither screen only when viewed from close up. An extension to this method leads to an algorithm to construct dither screens from arbitrary contours that are interpolated so that a smooth transition between different contours is possible.

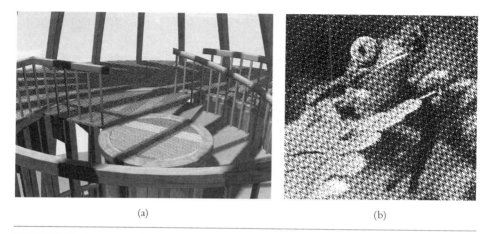

(a)   (b)

FIGURE 2.19 Two examples for the application of procedural screening. Note that this technique is usable to differentiate between objects in a rendition (as in (a)), whereas for a coverage of the whole image area (as can be seen in (b)) different techniques should be the method of choice.

Screening with Texts

In the early days of computer graphics when line printers were the output medium of choice, large graphics were made by combinations of letters to express intensity levels. Dark regions were made by overprinting several characters, effectively covering the entire rectangular area of the character, whereas light regions were denoted by a small character, like a period or an equals sign as can be seen in Figure 2.20. This was an early form of dithering.

Extensions of this method are still of interest today. For example, very small characters, called *microletters*, can be used as the contents of dither screens. This gives the person determining what the rendition is to look like the opportunity to choose a text that can be read when looking at the image up close. From a distance, the image looks like normal digital halftoning. This method has been suggested for printing counterfeit-safe money (bills).

Figure 2.21 shows an example of what can be considered to be "dither rows." The text used is the same for each row, while the intensity varies monotonically from line to line. The characters vary in width, both within a line and between lines, but the height of the lines themselves remains constant.

To render an image S using a text T, the system processes S line by line. The average intensity of the next block is determined and used to select the appropriate

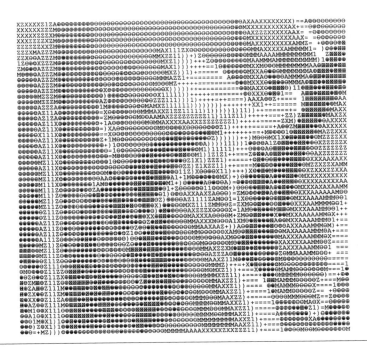

FIGURE 2.20 "Dithering" by combining letters to express different intensity levels.

row of the dither screen. The entry corresponding to the next character in the text T is selected and transferred to the corresponding spot in the output image. Care must be taken that if the character is narrower than the original block, its intensity actually matches that of the smaller block it covers. Around the edges, the last character placed on each line must be clipped appropriately. This procedure is formalized in Algorithm 2.10. An example is shown in Figure 2.22. Note that when the image is printed in a small size or a large rendition is regarded from a distance, the individual letters cannot be discerned. An additional feature is shown in this image. The text lines do not necessarily have to be horizontal and parallel to the image's edges; they can also be bent or applied to any path.

Note that the method of using symbols as the entries in a dither screen is relatively straightforward because the text can be read even if adjacent blocks do not have the same intensity. There are no problems even at the edges of the blocks because the character set is designed so as to leave a blank edge around each character.

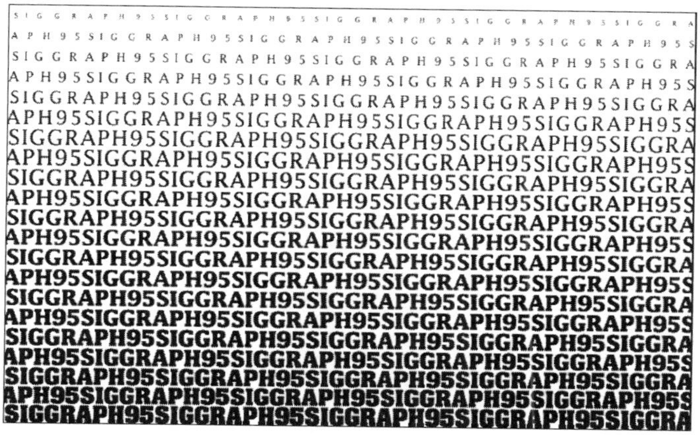

FIGURE 2.21 Dither rows of varying intensity based on symbol-based screening.

```
1   foreach row of blocks r in S do
2       foreach block b in row r of S do
3           i := average intensity of block b
4           place letter T[i, r mod t] at the next available position in O
5       od
6   od
```

ALGORITHM 2.10 Algorithm for screening with texts. Input: matrix S to be screened, one-dimensional array of characters T of length t with the message to be used for the microletters; letter matrix L as shown in Figure 2.21.

Note also that using such very small characters as dither elements makes it very difficult to photocopy the resultant images. Generally, photocopiers cannot capture very small contours as they are used in such microletters. Thus using such microletters is a way of denoting an "original" output, that is, one that originated from a printing process directly from a computer rather than a photocopier.

Embedding Morphed Contours

In some situations, it is desirable to have the dither screens denote graphics rather than just textual symbols. In this case, the graphics will generally spread over more than one block, meaning that we must address potential discontinuities at

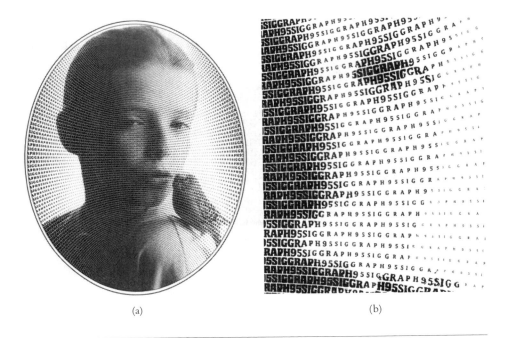

(a)   (b)

FIGURE 2.22 Example of symbol-based screening: full image (a) and enlarged region (b). Note that in the image, not all letters can be discerned by the naked eye.

FIGURE 2.23 The intensity ramp based on contour-based screening. Image based on drawings by Escher.

the edges of the blocks. In particular, *contour-based screening* enables interpolating over block edges so as to enable smooth transitions, even between intensity levels.

This concept was first developed and made popular by M. C. Escher in his famous drawings in which, for example, geese are transformed smoothly into fish. Figure 2.23 shows a computer-generated intensity ramp based on this idea. We will show in the following how the corresponding dither screens can be computed.

FIGURE 2.24 Varying geometric shape across the intensity ramp.

Before showing how to render using a ramp based on Escher's drawings, we will discuss the more simple case of varying the pattern across the ramp. Consider the enlarged dither matrix shown in Figure 2.24: at high-intensity values, it will produce small white circles on a black background, whereas at low-intensity values, it will produce small black circles on a white background. In the middle, it produces a checkerboard-like matrix of squares. This is because the outermost and innermost layers of the dither matrix form circles, whereas the intermediate ones form squares; the matrix represents an interpolation between these two geometric elements.

These notions can now be extended to enable a user to specify any number of geometric objects between which an interpolation is to take place. Different shapes can be defined for different intensity regions so that finally different dither screens are used. The shape of each geometric object is described by a fixed number p of points along its contour. We choose $p = 4k$ points to define the contour of each shape, that is, p is an integer multiple of four so that for each geometric object, k points can be matched with k points on its neighboring shapes when carrying out an interpolation. The algorithm then interpolates between these geometric objects by applying shape-blending techniques. Linear interpolation between two shapes is certainly the simplest technique and works well for many shapes. This may also result in unwanted artifacts when applied to non-regular, more complicated shapes. In these cases algorithms as, for instance, described by Sederberg and Greenwood (1992) can be employed. The whole process for contour-based screening is outlined in Algorithm 2.11, and we will now follow it step by step.

The procedure starts by working in the so-called screen element definition space, which is completely independent of the final image. A screen element is simply a planar region that defines the boundary of what is comparable to the threshold matrix from the basic screening method. The first step in the algorithm

1   define $C = \{c_1, c_2, \ldots c_s\}$ a small set of contours
2   scale each c_i such that it covers a fraction i of the surface of the screen element
3   create intermediate contours by interpolation between the c_i
4   break up the target image into blocks of $n \times m$ pixels
5   **foreach** block b in the target image **do**
6   choose the screen element corresponding to the average intensity of b
7   transform and raster the respective screen element
8   **od**

ALGORITHM 2.11   Contour-based screening overview.

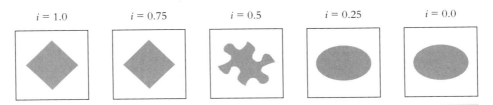

$i = 1.0$ $i = 0.75$ $i = 0.5$ $i = 0.25$ $i = 0.0$

FIGURE 2.25   Step 1: Designing shape contours for a fixed number of intensity levels.

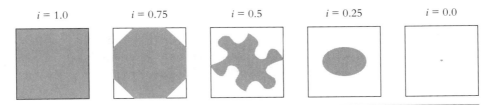

$i = 1.0$ $i = 0.75$ $i = 0.5$ $i = 0.25$ $i = 0.0$

FIGURE 2.26   Step 2: Scaling the contours so that the shapes cover the correct amount of space in the screen element.

is illustrated in Figure 2.25. For a fixed number of intensity levels, contours are defined. In the second step, these contours have to be scaled so that they cover exactly the fraction of the screen element that is determined by the intensity level, at which the shapes are defined. This means that the scaled version of a contour being defined for an intensity $i = 1.0$ will cover the whole area, whereas the scaled shape for $i = 0.5$ covers exactly 50% of the area. For zero intensity (white), we regard the shape as being an infinitesimally small dot (which is still defined via its contour). The result of this scaling process is illustrated in Figure 2.26.

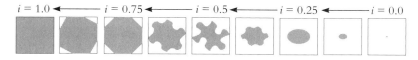

FIGURE 2.27   Step 3: Interpolation between the defined contours for all required intensity levels.

Now that we have defined the shapes and their size for the specified intensity levels, interpolation between these contours is performed to obtain the shapes for all needed intensity values. Basically, if considering gray value target images, 256 different shapes are needed. Interpolation or shape blending (if needed) always takes into consideration two of the predefined contours. Thus, the overall intensity range [0, 1] is subdivided into several intensity regions $[i_k, i_{k+1}]$, where the i_k are given by the definition of the contours. In the first interval $[0, i_1]$, the first shape "grows" from an invisible point to the size required at i_1. If no contour is defined for $i = 1.0$, the last contour also grows until the whole screen element is covered (see Figure 2.27).

As a result so far, a shape is defined for each possible intensity value i, and these shapes are scaled to cover exactly a fraction i of the screen element. We are, however, still working in the screen element definition space. To apply the shapes to the target image, a rasterization of the screen elements has to be performed. This includes possible transformations of the screen element such that it will fit the blocks in the target image that are to be represented by that element. The target image is divided into a set of blocks, each of which will be covered later by one screen element. These blocks do not have to be axis aligned or rectangular. For each block, the medium gray value is calculated, the respective screen element is transformed to match the form and orientation of the target image block, and then the block is rasterized. This is done using well-known shape rasterization techniques as they are, for instance, described in Foley et al. (1990). For obtaining high-quality results, the target image should have a rather high resolution so that for each screen element a rather high number of pixels is available. This helps to reduce aliasing artifacts that cannot be reduced otherwise since standard anti-aliasing techniques are not applicable (there are only black and white pixels and no intermediate values). This final step is illustrated in Figure 2.28.

Compared to the basic screening method, this technique differs in how the target image block is treated and finally replaced by the "halftoned" block. The

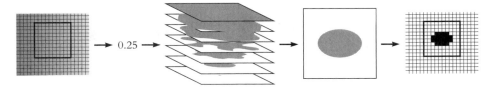

FIGURE 2.28 Step 4: Choosing the correct shape for each target image block depending on the average intensity for that block, transforming and rastering the screen elements, and replacing the target image block.

FIGURE 2.29 Final rendition using the jigsaw puzzle tile shapes.

basic method compares the dither screen pixel by pixel with the target block and uses the dither screen as a threshold matrix. For contour-based screening as well as for text-based screening, the screen elements associated with every intensity level are precomputed and simply replace the target image block. This may lead to unacceptable distortions, especially if rapid transitions (edges) in the target image appear. To circumvent these, the corresponding gray value at the target image's pixel position can be taken into account. The actual pixel being set in the dithered image is then computed as the interpolation between the two dither screens, which could be chosen for the intensities given on both sides of the edges. Nevertheless, the screen shapes have to be designed carefully so that neighboring shapes fit nicely—as it would be required for the jigsaw puzzle tile shape in the preceding example (see also Figure 2.29 and Exercise 2.9).

As an application, Figure 2.30 now shows a mosque rendered by screen dots made of calligraphic Arabic letter shapes and oriental polygonal patterns. Indeed, such buildings are often enriched by patterns in reality. In the lack of geometric models to describe the real patterns, this technique of contour-based screening adds a touch of Islamic culture to the reproduced image.

2.3 Stippling

Another way of reducing the artifacts, which are introduced when using halftoning methods, is by changing the point distribution given by the initial dithering

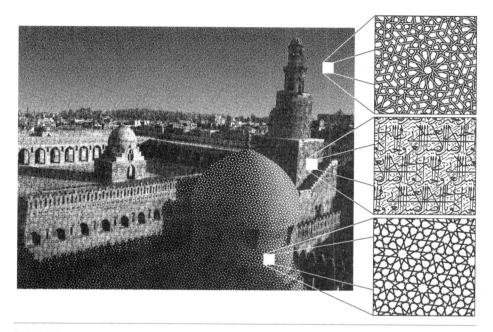

FIGURE 2.30 View of the Ibn Tulun Mosque rendered with artistic screening.

algorithm. This brings us to a technique that is quite common in traditional, handmade illustrations, namely, *stippling*. With stippling, tone as well as texture are created by the placement of small dots (stipples) where the dots are equally, but randomly, distributed. Done properly by hand, stippling is very time consuming and hard for a beginner to learn. Using the computer may at first help to create such images—even for people who do not attempt to be an artist. Even artists may use such a computerized tool to create images quickly as a kind of preview for their own work to save time.

2.3.1 Automatic Methods

Stippling relies on an even, but random, distribution of dots. To create such a distribution automatically, several methods are possible. A common approach is to regard the target density distribution of the dots as a surface where the desired density is mapped to the height of that surface (varying between zero and one). The starting point for the so-called rejection method is an appropriate random distribution of dots. Each of the dots is then tested in the following way: choose a random number uniformly between zero and one, and test if this random number is less than the height of the surface at the given point. If this test is true, keep the dot; otherwise, discard it. In this way, more dots get discarded in regions where the desired dot density is low (and thus the intensity surface is low), and more points are kept in regions with a high desired density. This is exactly the behavior needed for stippling. An approach could thus be to treat the target image as a piecewise-continuous surface with each piece being a flat plane covering a pixel and the height being proportional to the image intensity at this pixel (between zero and one).

The Intersection Method

Looking at those dots that are kept, a line drawn from the base plane up to that height, which is given by the chosen random number, would intersect the surface defined by the image intensities. Taking a randomly distributed collection of vertical lines of random heights and selecting only those lines that intersect with the intensity surface should yield a reasonably stippled image, if a dot is placed at the position of each selected line. Ideally, at an intensity value of $i = 1$, the distribution of dots should cover the plane completely, whereas at an intensity value of $i = 0.5$, the plane would be half covered, and at an intensity value of $i = 0$, there would be no points at all. Since each intersection point is converted into a small circular disc of radius r (the stipple), only a finite number of intersecting lines are needed. The general procedure to produce stipple drawings is as formulated in Algorithm 2.12.

The key point in this algorithm is to find a distribution of lines that has the following properties:

- The distribution should be defined on the unit cube in $\mathbb{R}^3$: $[0, 1] \times [0, 1] \times [0, 1]$ with the first two coordinates describing the position of the line in the plane and the third coordinate describing the lines' height.

- The final distribution of stipples should
  - have a linear intensity response; that is, the ratio between input intensity value and produced output intensity value is constant,
  - should not have overlapping stipples (with the exception that it might be allowed to have overlapping stipples to achieve very high intensities), and
  - should not produce any visual patterns.

1 convert S to a piecewise function $S' : [0, 1] \times [0, 1] \to [0, 1]$ by scaling
2 generate a distribution of lines in the unit cube of $\mathbb{R}^3$
3 intersect each line with the surface defined by S'
4 display intersection points as stipples

ALGORITHM 2.12 Procedure to automatically create a stipple image from an input image S.

The first point is assured by an appropriate parameter selection when generating the distribution; the second point is somewhat more complicated. We will thus inspect some distributions to see which results can be achieved.

Distributions

The simplest distribution is just vertical lines positioned uniformly at random in the unit square with randomly chosen heights between zero and one. As can be seen in Figure 2.31, this distribution does not have a linear intensity response, nor does it ensure non-overlapping stipples. Choosing a quasi-random distribution that is based, for instance, on a Sobol sequence[3] does not dramatically improve the situation. The resulting images are quite similar to those created using a completely random distribution. However, the Sobol sequence offers a way to improve the result by taking advantage of its properties.

The Sobol sequence fills the given plane *in order* at increasingly finer resolution. This means that the first 10% of the dots are equally distributed on the plane and the second 10% of the dots fall nicely and evenly in between the first 10% and so on. It is now possible to treat the dots differently when testing against the intensity surface. The height of each line is no longer determined randomly but is set to n/N with n being the number of the current (n-th) line and N being the total number of lines. With this scheme, an intensity of 0.1 will select the first 10% of the dots (which are nicely distributed), and an intensity of 0.2 will select the second 10% (which fit nicely in the spaces), and so on. Although the point distribution now is much better (see Figure 2.32), the intensity response is still not linear.

3. The Sobol sequence is a quasi-random sequence that generates numbers between zero and one based on operations on the binary representation of numbers. For a detailed description, see, for instance, Chapter 7 of Press et al. (1993).

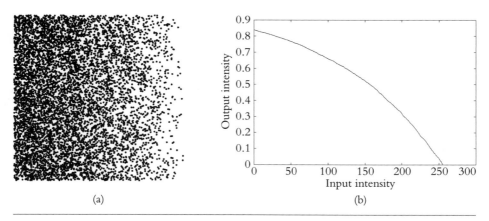

(a)

(b)

FIGURE 2.31 Uniform random distribution of 15,000 lines where 7,526 dots are kept: stipple drawing output (a) and intensity response diagram (b).

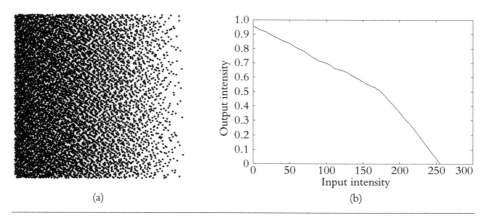

(a)

(b)

FIGURE 2.32 Sobol distribution of 15,000 lines where 7,529 dots are kept: stipple drawing output (a) and intensity response diagram (b).

Using the scheme as described, the heights of the lines intersecting the intensity surface are algorithmically determined, whereas the position of the lines is determined by using a pseudorandom number sequence. Going the other way around—determining the height of the lines by random numbers and placing the dots regularly—offers a more regular dot distribution. For this, the plane is covered with dots that are equally spaced in a way that they overlap just enough

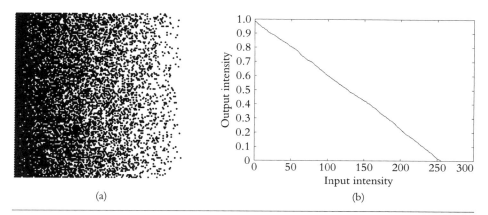

FIGURE 2.33 Osculating distribution without jittering: stipple drawing output (a) and intensity response diagram (b). From the initial set of 15,477 lines 7,749 dots were created.

to allow no gaps in between. These dots serve as anchors for the vertical lines with random heights. The resulting distribution is very regular in the plane but introduces visual patterns (see Figure 2.33). However, the intensity response is very good. To relieve the regularity and thus minimize the patterns, a jittering can be exploited, which has the disadvantage of resulting in a much worse intensity response.

As with any randomized method, jittering does not depend on the already achieved results or on any other input variable. However, an artist creates a stipple distribution by constantly observing the current results and adding stipples in a position so as to maintain spacing and desired density. Here, relaxation methods can be applied to approximate this behavior. Starting point is a uniform random distribution of dots that is then relaxed into a new distribution with better interstipple properties than the original. Borrowing from physics, a force on each dot is introduced to be

$$f = - \sum_{i=0}^{n} \frac{v_i}{d_i}$$

where v_i is the unit vector pointing from the dot to the i-th dot in the direction and d_i is the distance between these two dots. This yields a distance-based force that is highly repulsive at close distance. The movement of the dots under the influence of those forces is now simulated until the distribution converges into a

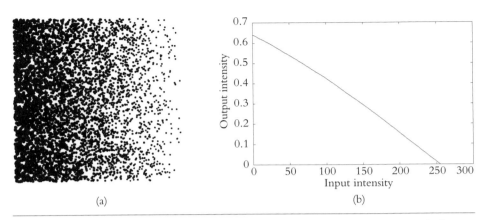

(a)

(b)

FIGURE 2.34 Relaxed distribution with 20,000 initial lines creating 4,972 stipples: stipple drawing output (a) and intensity response diagram (b).

local minimum of the related energy. Hence, the resulting distribution maximized the interdot distances. The intensity response of such a distribution is very good (as can be seen in Figure 2.34) but rather flat. By increasing the number of dots this can be overcome, although this will also increase the computational effort.

Compensating for a Non-Linear Intensity Response

As has been seen in the last examples, there are many methods of automatically distributing dots such that the initially stated properties are met. The shown techniques offer just a small selection of a vast variety of usable algorithms. The main problem is to achieve both an evenly spaced distribution of dots and a linear intensity response at once. If this is not possible, that is, if the intensity response is still non-linear, a compensation step can be introduced. To compensate automatically for the intensity response of a particular distribution, a map of input intensities to corrected intensities is calculated such that when using the corrected intensities, the resulting stipple image has a linear intensity response.

The map is constructed by rendering stippled images of constant intensities at several discrete intensity levels i_k. For each of these, the average output intensity o_k is computed by averaging the pixel intensities. If the intensity response of the distribution is linear, then $i_k = o_k$ for all k. If not, then the corrected intensity

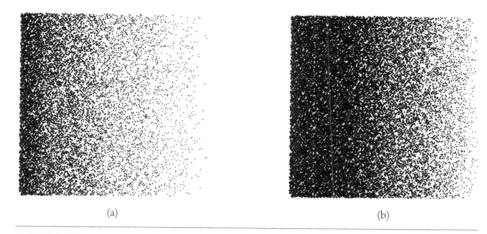

(a)   (b)

FIGURE 2.35 Uncorrected (a) and corrected (b) intensity response for a Sobol distribution.

i_k/o_k will produce i_k when rendered with this particular distribution. In this way, a correction table is produced containing input intensities i_k and corrected intensities i_k/o_k with which—in a preprocessing step—the input image is transformed. As an example, Figure 2.35 shows the corrected and the uncorrected version of a stippled image using the Sobol distribution to place the dots.

As can be seen in Figure 2.35, the intensity response is much better and comes closer to the original. In particular, the corrected image has an intensity closer to 0.5 in the middle than the uncorrected version. However, the correction map has stretched the dark regions of the image so that, in general, not only a correction for non-linear intensity response is needed, but also a correction of the intensity values of the input image to account for that intensity scaling. This means that automatic methods would need specially prepared input images in order to achieve good results. The resulting images from the algorithms described can still be used as input images for a further interactive treatment, which will be the focus of the following section.

2.3.2 Interactive Methods

Automatic methods for stippling are well suited if the only goal is to represent the distribution of gray values in an image by the placement of dots. They do not take into consideration any additional information or image features that might be present. Among these, edges in the image are of utmost importance for recognizing objects. To correctly represent such edges in a stippled rendition means to introduce discontinuities in the dot distribution that depend on features of the underlying image. Even though it is possible to determine the locations of these discontinuities algorithmically, a better visual result can be achieved by defining them manually. Further, in some cases a user wants to have influence on certain parameters of the dot distribution, so it is desirable to come up with interactive methods to locally or globally change an initially given dot distribution.

The Problem

The problem to be solved can be stated as follows: we want to approximate a given grayscale image S by a discrete, dot-based representation D that enables halftoning *and* fulfills additional geometric constraints. More formally, a two-dimensional intensity function (the input image) $S(x, y)$ is to be approximated by $D(x, y) = D(x, y, j)$, which consists of n discrete elements j (the dots that the stippled drawing consists of).

Let $C_{I,j}$ be the observable quantities of the input image at position j (for example, intensity or gradient), and $C_{D,j}$ the same quantities of the desired output $D(x, y, j)$, which are computed by a different algorithm since D is our discrete representation. By minimizing the penalty

$$E = \frac{1}{n} \sum_{j=1}^{n} \left(v_j E_D(j) + w_j E_g(j) \right) \tag{2.7}$$

we will find a representation that approximates the tonal values and fulfills the geometric constraints. In Equation (2.7), $E_D(j)$ is a function that describes the approximation error of the discrete representation at the position j, $E_g(j)$ describes the geometric error, and v_j and w_j are weights. It is quite simple to obtain the value for $E_D(j)$ by using the difference between the observable quantities in the input image and the discrete representation:

$$E_D(j) = \left(C_{I,j} - C_{D,j} \right)^2$$

Using the fact that, ideally, dots in the image should be spread out evenly, we can say that the geometric error $E_g(j)$ depends on the dot distribution. We could say that the deviation of the dot distribution should be as small as possible, and we can therefore use the variance of the dot-to-dot distances to define the geometric error as follows:

$$E_g(j) = \frac{1}{n_j} \sum_{i=1}^{n_j} \left(l_i + |p_i - p_j| \right)^2 \tag{2.8}$$

In Equation (2.8), l_i is the mean value of the dot-to-dot distances in the neighborhood of the element j, n_j is the number of elements in this neighborhood, and p_j denotes the element whose neighborhood is considered, while p_i are all other elements in this neighborhood.

If $E_D(j)$ and $E_g(j)$ are continuously differentiable, Equation (2.7) can be minimized globally by optimization methods like relaxation, gradient descent, or simulated annealing. However, we need more to find a globally optimal dot distribution. Some artistic features of stippled drawings require the movement or a change in the properties of the dots. Thus we need an interactive system where we can also optimize Equation (2.7) on the basis of a local dot subset.

Obtaining an Initial Dot Distribution

As we already stated, halftoning methods can be used to obtain a first distribution of the dots for stippling. Halftoning, however, only counts for the approximation of tonal values of the input image. Since the technique of stippling is actually stemming from art, there are a few considerations to be made that may modify the dot distribution gained by a halftoning algorithm. Some of these considerations are as follows:

- Dots should not be placed on white or very bright regions.
- Dots should always be inside the object to be stippled.
- Different tonal values can be achieved by distributing a different number of dots but also by changing the dot size.

Thus, given the result of, let's say, a Floyd-Steinberg error diffusion algorithm, additional interactive manipulations can be used to prepare this dot set for relaxation methods that will then lead to the final stippled drawing. Moreover, dot distributions that were used for the automatic stippling methods may be considered. In fact, using the algorithm from Section 2.3.1 provides very interesting starting points for an interactive manipulation of the dot set.

Minimizing the Penalty Function

Given an initial dot distribution, a minimization of $E_g(j)$, which is given in Equation (2.8), can be achieved by an iteration scheme. Given n dots p_j in a region, this scheme works as follows:

1. Compute the Voronoi diagram of the dots. This assigns a Voronoi region to each of the dots, the boundaries of which are (possibly open) polygons.

2. Intersect the Voronoi regions with the boundaries of the region to be stippled.

3. Move each dot to the center of mass of its Voronoi region.

This process is repeated until the dot distribution achieves its desired state. This process minimizes only one part of Equation (2.7), namely, the geometric quality. We need also to minimize the approximation error for preserving the halftoning property of the output image.

For doing so, we calculate C_D for each Delaunay triangle, in the following demonstrated with intensity values. By three dots, their sizes, and the area covered by the respective Delaunay triangle, the gray tone of this area is given. We can now enforce the dots to create triangles of the right size during the iteration process by moving them appropriately. If a triangle is too big, the dots have to be moved toward the center of the triangle. This process is unfortunately very time consuming since it requires the computation of the area of each triangle as well as the average gray level of the given image by calculating the weighted sum of each pixel value covered by the region.

To overcome this problem, a second possibility is to prevent the dots from moving into areas of different tone within the Voronoi iteration. The movement can be constrained by a grayscale image if during an iteration step dots are allowed only to move in areas that differ in tone below a given threshold. This results in dot distributions that preserve, for instance, edges in the input image much better than unconstrained dot movement would.

Interaction

The preceding method relies on the selection of relatively small regions of the input image on which the processes have to be performed. Even more, the strict enforcement of all constraints might result in images that are "correct" in the sense of fulfilling all necessary requirements but that show also a rather "synthetic" look. Therefore, user interaction is necessary and should be used. As a metaphor, the interaction techniques rely on painting with different brushes and are well known from image manipulation and paint programs. In the following, we will give a few examples of brushes that are useful for the creation of stippled drawings.

- *Selection brush*   This brush is used to identify larger regions of the image to which the application of other brushes can be constrained. This feature allows a faster application of a brush since the user does not need to take care of moving outside the desired region.

- *Relaxation brush*   This brush performs a local relaxation process within the area of the brush. By moving the relaxation brush over the image, the dots in the areas touched with the brush undergo the minimization process.

- *Jitter brush*   Using the jitter brush adds small random changes to the positions of the dots within the area covered by the brush. This helps to remove correct regions, where the dots are too evenly spaced.

- *Shape brush*   This brush allows to modify the shape of the dots. Different parameterizations lead to different results like enlargement or shrinking.

Figures 2.36 and 2.37 show how images look that are created with an interactive system covering all the techniques mentioned.

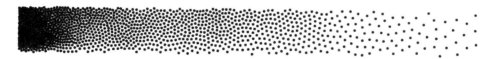

FIGURE 2.36   The intensity ramp based on stippling.

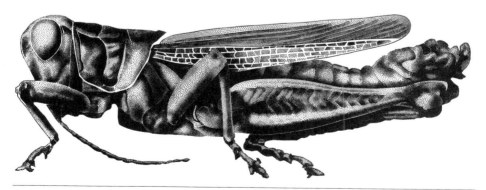

FIGURE 2.37   Stippled image of a grasshopper.

2.4 **Image Mosaics**

Incorporating shapes into renditions—as shown in Section 2.2.4—is one form of combining different information sources and formats in one image. Another way is to include several small images and, by doing so, also include the contents of these into a larger rendition. We will thus move on to *image mosaics*, which have become very popular in the last few years as a form of art used for advertisements, posters, and the like. In art, a mosaic is a surface decoration of small colored components—such as stone, mineral, glass, tile, or shell—closely set into an adhesive ground. The mosaic pieces together form a larger image.

An image mosaic is created from other smaller images that together portray a larger subject. The creation of image mosaics is somewhat connected with digital halftoning. An input image has to be replaced by an output image that is constructed from several "tiles" of a size larger than a pixel and that match the tonal values of the input image. In traditional halftoning, black dots of varying sizes are arranged in a regular grid to convey various shades of gray. Digital halftoning, however, uses dither matrices (screens) to replace parts of the image by patterns.

The creation of an image mosaic requires the four major steps that are given in Algorithm 2.13, which we will describe in turn.

2.4.1 **Choosing a Tiling Grid or Pattern**

The first step in creating a mosaic is to find a layout for the tiles. There are several ways to arrange the tiles, each of which has certain issues to be considered. Figure 2.38 shows the results of different strategies to choose a tiling grid. These strategies are described next.

One possibility is to use no regular tiling grid at all but place the tiles randomly on the target image. This *scattered layout* creates the impression of a huge pile of photographs that together form a larger image. This impression is even stronger if we allow the tiles to overlap each other. Here it is important to always compare the tile with the original image region so that the features of the target image do not disappear. In addition to this, it is also possible to rotate the tiles at random

---

1   choose images that are to be used as mosaic tiles
2   choose a tiling grid
3   find an arrangement for the mosaic tiles within the grid
4   possibly perform a color correction on the tiles to match the target image

---

ALGORITHM 2.13   The four major steps for producing an image mosaic.

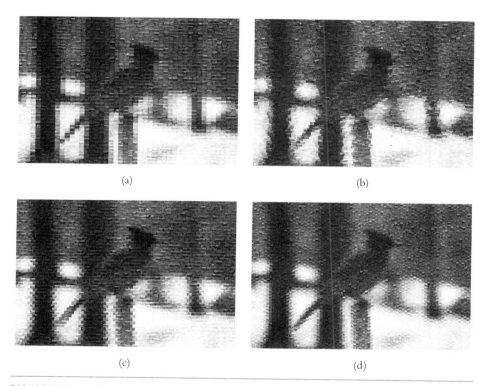

(a)

(b)

(c)

(d)

FIGURE 2.38 Different strategies for choosing a tiling grid lead to different mosaic structures: regular arrangement (a), scattered layout (b), angled alignment (c), and hexagonal grid (d). (See also color insert.)

angles to get away from the impression of a regular arrangement. Rotating the tiles, however, implies more computational effort.

When using a regular tiling grid, there are, again, several possibilities. Most often, rectangular grids are chosen, so we will discuss this case in more detail. Nevertheless, other tilings, like hexagonal grids, are also possible. For rectangular grids, it is advantageous if all potential tiles have the same aspect ratio as the grid region. If not, they have to be either cropped or non–uniformly scaled to fit in the target region, which will lead to unwanted effects. If they are not of the same size (but the same aspect ratio), a uniform scaling operation can be applied that makes the tile fit into the target region. Considering a rectangular grid, there are two ways to subdivide the image into regions:

1. A regular arrangement places all tiles in rows and columns next to one another.

2. An angled alignment creates a pattern like a brick wall.

Besides these rather simple tilings, we can also apply multiresolution techniques for mosaics. Normally (in the regular arrangements), all tiles and target regions have the same size irrespective of the detail of the target image. It would be desirable if more smaller tiles were placed in areas with high detail, and less but bigger tiles in areas with low detail. This keeps areas with high and low detail unchanged, whereas a regular distribution of the tiles somewhat equalizes the level of detail over the image.

To break up the target image into the desired regions, we can use a quadtree. The idea behind this is the subdivision of a (rectangular) area according to a given criterion. In our case, the criterion is the amount of detail being contained in a rectangular area of the target image. This amount of detail can be measured in different ways, two of which are as follows:

◆ Identifying the frequency content of the image region using, for example, a Fourier or wavelet transform. If a region contains much high-frequency content, then it can be regarded as being very detailed, and a further subdivision has to be performed.

◆ Determining the level of detail by computing the average value of an edge detection algorithm. A high value here means that many edges are present in the region that can be interpreted as high detail.

To create the quadtree, we start with dividing the target image into four quadrants. For each of the quadrants, we calculate the amount of detail in it and decide by a simple threshold if we need to divide any further (if there is much detail) or not. This procedure stops if the regions get too small or there are no longer any regions of high detail. Once the subdivision into different-sized regions is done, the image tiles are scaled appropriately and placed into the respective region.

Another quite simple way of creating multiresolution mosaics is to build the mosaic using only a few, but relatively large, tiles. This mosaic is then used as the new tile image in the second step to create a "mosaic of mosaics." Using this technique is possible only with color correction since the same image is used in different places.

2.4.2 Arranging the Image Tiles

Once we have agreed on a tiling grid and have subdivided the target image in the respective regions, we need to place individual images in these regions. There are a few ways of placing the tiles that significantly influence the final mosaic:

- *Using the same image everywhere* Here, only one image is needed as the tile image—usually, this is a small version of the target image. Color correction is necessary to make the tile match.

- *Choosing a random arrangement of tiles* The tiles are placed regardless of the matching of color to the target region. Color correction is necessary.

- *Arranging tiles manually by eye* This procedure is possible only with very small mosaics and thus will not be discussed any further.

- *Placing image tiles by matching their average color to the region of the target image they cover* This is by far the most used placement algorithm. For each target region, the average color is computed, and the tile whose average color matches best is chosen.

- *Placing image tiles by matching several different properties to the region of the target image they cover* Besides matching the average color, other properties can be used to make the image tiles fit better. One example are edges that are matched in the target image and the tile. This procedure yields the best results; however, the computational effort needed is rather high.

2.4.3 Choosing Tile Images

The choice of which images are to be used as tiles is a rather artistic one. There are no technical limitations or restrictions except that for the reproduction of color images, colored tiles are necessary. Images that are used as tiles should match the subject of the target image. Mosaics can be viewed in two ways. From a distance, the viewer only recognizes the target image, that is, the mosaic as one image. Getting closer reveals the details of the tiles. If the tiles match the subject, the viewer has the impression of revealing secrets from the image. For example, the movie poster for *The Truman Show* shows only the head of the main character. The whole poster itself is a mosaic of stills from the movie, so getting closer to the poster reveals images of other contributing actors, scenes from the movie, and so on.

In general, there are two ways of selecting images as tiles. First, a small version of the target image itself can be chosen. Here, a proper scaling of the image is necessary to make the subject in the tiles still recognizable. Further, this approach requires a color correction since all tiles have per se the same color. Second, different images can be chosen as tiles. Here also the scaling has to be performed in a way that the images remain visible and recognizable. Each of the tile images themselves should have a relative uniform brightness distribution that eases a possible color correction.

Normally, an image database is given, containing *many* images from which the tiles can be chosen. In this case, "many" means having far more images in the database than are needed for the creation of the mosaic. We still need an algorithm that helps in picking the correct image at a specific tile's position. For the sake of simplicity, we assume rectangular regions in the target image and rectangular tiles. In the following, we will represent the target image regions as well as the tiles by three matrices, one for each color channel R, G, and B. To find the best matching tile image, the target region T is compared to each potential replacement image I by computing the mean squared error $J(I, T)$ between the red, green, and blue channels. This computation is outlined in Equation (2.9) for $n \times n$ pixel regions and tiles of the same size:

$$J(I, T) = \frac{\sum_{x=0}^{n-1} \sum_{y=0}^{n-1} \sum_{c \in \{r,g,b\}} (T_c(x, y) - I_c(x, y))^2}{3n^2} \tag{2.9}$$

To replace the target region T, we chose the tile image I with the smallest $J(I, T)$. This comparison based on the color values is rather complicated and should be accompanied by a preselection based on other properties so that Equation (2.9) does not have to be calculated for each tile. Furthermore, other comparison methods are possible, either by calculating a different value or by choosing a different color model.

2.4.4 Color Correction

The last step in the creation of a mosaic is the correction of the tile's color. This is needed only if the tiles were not chosen in a way that they already match the target region's color. In the following, we will restrict ourselves to describing the color correction for gray-level images by considering the intensity of the pixels.

The actual task can be broken down into solving the following problem: Given an image tile T having an average color a_t and a target region R having an average color a_r, change the color of the tile's pixels in a way that after the adjustment the tile's average color is the same as a_r. To solve this problem, we use so-called color correction rules, which take as input an image tile and a desired average color *a*, and which generate a *color correction function* $F : \mathbb{R} \to \mathbb{R}$. Many families of functions can be used for this purpose:

- *The constant function* $F(x) = a$ Each pixel is set to the color *a* that yields a correct average color value of *a*. However, the original colors of the image tile are completely ignored. This function would yield a mosaic made of uniformly colored tiles.

- *A color scaling function*   Assume an average tile color a_t that is larger than the desired average color *a*. If we want to scale each pixel's color to achieve the correct average, the scaling factor would be a/a_t, which yields $F(x) = (a/a_t)x$ as the correction function.

- *A color shifting function*   Here we obtain a correction function that shifts the colors in the tile by the difference between a_t and *a*. This function $F(x) = x + (a - a_t)$, however, may shift colors out of the range of reproducible colors.

- *More sophisticated functions*   There are many possible ways of performing color corrections, for instance, taking into account gamma correction or other more accurate methods. These functions can also be applied if necessary.

For the purpose of creating image mosaics, a simple combination of scaling and shifting yields sufficient results, and is relatively easy to compute. Figure 2.39 shows a set of images to compare color scaling and color shifting. The respective histograms can be found in Figure 2.40.

(a)   (b)   (c)

FIGURE 2.39 Sample image and color correction functions applied: original image (a), color scaling (b), and color shifting (c).

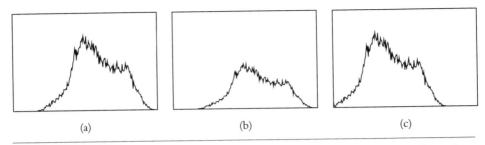

(a)   (b)   (c)

FIGURE 2.40 Histogram shapes for the images in Figure 2.39: original image (a), color scaling (b), and color shifting (c).

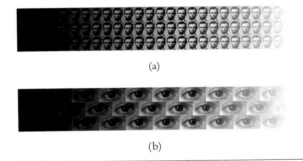

(a)

(b)

FIGURE 2.41 Mosaics created from only one tile image with applied color correction. In (a) the tiles are arranged regularly whereas in (b) the angled alignment was chosen.

For the combination of scaling and shifting, the following considerations can be made. If colors can be shifted without leaving the allowed color range, this shifting is applied; otherwise, we shift as far as possible and then scale the resulting colors until they match the desired color a.

To explain this in more detail, let's look at an example. Assume the average color a that we will achieve is smaller than the average color a_t in the given tile: $a < a_t$. If the minimum color m_t in the tile is greater than the difference $a_t - a$, then we can shift the colors using the function $F(x) = x + (a_t - a)$ without leaving the allowed color range. In the other case, if $m_t \leq (a_t - a)$, then we combine shifting and scaling in the function $F(x) = a(x - m_t)/(a_t - m_t)$. The formula for all other (symmetric) cases can be derived easily and is left as an exercise (see Exercise 2.11). In Figure 2.41, two gray ramps are shown where this color correction technique has been applied.

So far, the description was for grayscale images where the brightness was changed appropriately. Many mosaics, however, are constructed from color images where a simple change in brightness will not help to make the tile image match the target region. Here, the same kind of color correction can be performed on each color channel independently. Although most of the images use the RGB model to specify colors, other color models, like YIQ, HSV, or LAB, might be used in this process.

Exercises

2.1   How do the dither patterns that are generated from the matrices $D^{(2)}$ and $D^{(4)}$ look? Take a sheet of paper and draw the patterns for all intensity levels.

2.2   Design different sets of dithering patterns from the ones described in this chapter for 5, 10, and 17 intensity levels (2×2, 3×3, and 4×4 patterns). When designing the patterns think about reducing artifacts as well as deliberately creating artifacts.

2.3   Implement an ordered dithering algorithm using the patterns $D^{(2)}$, $D^{(3)}$, and $D^{(4)}$. Experiment with your own patterns (see Exercise 2.2).

2.4   Implement a Floyd–Steinberg algorithm and test it with different gray-level images.

2.5   Use your implementation of the Floyd–Steinberg algorithm to create images like the ones in Figure 2.9 by drawing short lines instead of single dots. Experiment with the parameters of the lines (slope, length).

2.6   Write a program to

    a. compute the histogram of a given gray-level image,

    b. display the histogram as a bar chart,

    c. perform a simple histogram equalization on the given image, and

    d. perform an adaptive histogram equalization on the given image and compare the result to the simple histogram equalization.

    Use this program to see if histogram equalization indeed yields a uniform distribution of the gray levels in a given image.

2.7   Implement the basic screening algorithm from Section 2.2.1 and experiment with your own dither screens. Which effect has a special treatment of the screens (Exercise 2.3) on the resulting images?

2.8   Implement text-based screening. Choose a string (for example, your name) and experiment with different fonts. Can you devise a method to automatically compute the dither rows for a given font (outline font or any other font description)?

2.9   Assume the given shapes for contour-based screening as in the example in the text. Find a way to design the jigsaw puzzle tile shapes so that neighboring screen dots nicely fit.

2.10   Implement procedural screening. Use different dither kernels, mappings, and displacement functions to create different renditions. Create an interactive program where users may select these functions.

2.11   Create different dot distributions for automatic stippling based on different probability distribution functions. Apply these distributions to gray-level images and evaluate the results.

2.12   Derive the complete set of color correction functions for mosaic tiles similar to the example given in the text.

2.13   Devise and implement a method for creating hexagonal mosaics (the tiles have a hexagonal shape).

2.14   Devise and implement a method for creating mosaics where round or elliptical tiles are arranged in a scattered layout.

Bibliographic Notes

Although this chapter deals with some operations that are very basic in image processing, it is not intended to replace an introductory text on image processing. We thus recommend any image processing literature, especially the book by Jähne (1997). For a quick overview and some basic techniques, the book by Foley et al. (1990) and the book by Watt and Policarpo (1998) are possible references.

Regarding digital halftoning, the book by Ulichney (1987) is by far the most complete work. Besides describing the algorithms, this book offers statistical data to evaluate and compare the different techniques. There is also a wealth of literature available on different halftoning techniques, for instance, Floyd and Steinberg (1976), Knuth (1987), Ulichney (1999), Ulichney (2000), Ostromoukhov et al. (1994), and Ostromoukhov (2001). The use of halftoning techniques in the field of NPR is mainly focused on by Buchanan (1996), Buchanan et al. (1998), Streit and Buchanan (1998), and Streit (1998). Texture-based screening is explored in depth by Veryovka and Buchanan (1999b), Veryovka and Buchanan (2000), and Veryovka (1999), whereas procedural screening and adaptive screening are presented by Veryovka and Buchanan (1999a). There are also other halftoning approaches like the one by Velho and de Miranda Gomes (1991), who use space-filling curves as a basis for their algorithms.

Screening as a basic halftoning technique is described in the books already mentioned. The artistic aspects of screening, especially the embedding of different shapes (be it letters or arbitrary contours) in a rendition is presented by Ostromoukhov and Hersch (1995). They concentrate on digital halftoning and image reproduction aspects, and thus also formulate ideas on constructing contours for contour-based screening (Ostromoukhov, 1998; Rudaz et al., 1998) and are interested in how to use the features of the resulting images (Ostromoukhov et al., 1996). An interesting comparison of the screening approaches with other techniques can be found in Ostromoukhov (2000).

The fascination of stippled images inspired Hiller and Deussen to develop an interactive system for the creation of stippled drawings. This system and the methods being used are described in Hiller (1999), Deussen et al. (2000), and Deussen et al. (1999b); an extension of the core algorithm (Voronoi relaxation) is presented in Hiller and Deussen (2001).

Finally, there exist many programs for the creation of image mosaics based on a smaller or bigger set of image tiles. The theory behind these programs is described by Finkelstein and Range (1998), as well as McKenna and Arce (2000).

3 | LINES, CURVES, AND STROKES

While the last chapter dealt exclusively with techniques that change single pixels in either their position or color, we will now explore how units extending over and above the size of a single pixel can be created, and we will consider how they will be used in non-photorealistic renditions. We have already seen examples for such techniques in the last chapter—stippling and image mosaics; they were, however, based on altering the pixels of a given image. Here, the main focus is on constructing new images from units that extend the size of a pixel. The reason we explore this area is that it is indeed one of the fundamental characteristics of non-photorealistic images that their basic "building blocks" are often markings that can be distinguished as image artifacts by the naked eye (see Section 1.3.1). Simon Schofield, one of the pioneers in the area of NPR, expressed that non-photorealistic rendering is actually defined by "the construction of images from indivisible pictorial subunits that are larger than the pixel, such as 'brush marks'" (Schofield, 1994). This chapter thus deals with such subunits and describes how they are constructed and rendered.

Schofield's definition is understandable when seen from the point of view that one aim of NPR is to mimic handmade visualization styles. Painters also construct their pictures by the subsequent addition of brushstrokes (for an oil painting) or lines (for a pen-and-ink rendition). Thus, to be successful in the creation of non-photorealistic imagery, it is of utmost importance to clarify how such pictorial subunits can be defined in terms of modeling their shape and attributes and how they can be rendered one by one. The question of how they are combined to create the desired visual impression at large is not the subject of this chapter; instead, we will examine this topic later on.

Here we will examine different approaches for the creation of *lines*. The introduced techniques can also be exploited for *marks* that can be regarded as very short lines. We will see that there exist a wide variety of methods starting from simple modifications of the line-drawing algorithm to sophisticated simulation methods that take into account the physical properties of the paper and the dye particles left behind by a drawing tool. Finally, a method is introduced to describe lines and strokes using a multiresolution representation. To round out the chapter we provide a comparison of the introduced methods.

3.1 Drawing "Incorrect" Lines

With the availability of output devices for computers that produce high-resolution output (like laser printers) or that are capable of transferring vector data onto paper (like plotters), these devices became popular especially in the area of computer-aided design (CAD) and computer-aided architectural design (CAAD). The "sterile" looking output of these printers is perfectly suited to show exact drawings, construction diagrams, floor plans, and so on. However, as studies (for instance, in Schumann et al., (1996)) have shown, especially in early design stages and for discussion with customers, handdrawn images or sketches are much more appropriate.

There are many different ways to include a "hand-drawn" effect in computer output. The historically first approach was to modify the output hardware (plotter) to introduce some "wiggliness" in the lines, followed by modifying line printing routines in computer programs or page description languages (basically PostScript). Finally, a common denominator was found with the introduction of multiresolution curves. We will study all these approaches in turn and also come to an extension of these algorithms to handle "artistic" lines.

3.1.1 Observations of Human Drawings

To be successful in creating more vivid line drawings (we will stick to line drawings at the moment), some observations of the specifics of human drawings will lead to the development of algorithms. The most striking feature of hand-drawn images is their "incorrectness." Lines drawn by a human artist are never completely straight (if the artist does not use any aids, such as a ruler); instead, they are more or less wiggly, their line width may change over the length, they tend to overshoot the line's correct endpoints, and so forth. We will investigate each of the features and their origins in turn to reveal characteristics that can be used to devise new line-drawing algorithms.

◆ *Wiggliness* Probably no human being is able to draw a completely straight line over a certain length without using a tool like a ruler. Small irregular movements of the hand cause the line to be more or less wiggly; that is, the line deviates from the intended "analytical" path. Moreover, depending on the drawing tool and the applied pressure, the paper structure may also create such deviations since the tip of a pen, for instance, may be "guided" along paper fibers and thus deviates from the intended straight path.

◆ *Line length* The inaccuracy of drawn lines increases with the "sketchiness" of the drawing. While more thoroughly executed drawings almost only show wiggly lines, one of the more prominent features of sketches is the overshooting at the line ends. This means that lines do not begin or end at the intended starting points but instead are somewhat longer or shorter.

◆ *Line thickness and brightness* The line width or thickness, as well as the line brightness, depends to a high degree on the pressure applied to the drawing tool. If a line is drawn with a rather fast hand movement, the pressure on the pen is rather low and thus the line thinner or brighter. On the other hand, a more slow and thorough hand movement results in pressing the pen on the paper slightly harder and thus in darker or wider lines.

◆ *Line ends* Depending on the drawing speed, the line ends may differ significantly. In some cases, a line ends in a small hook or in a dot. The dot stems from ink that flows out of the pen if it is held in place for a longer time when starting a line. These line ends give the drawing a certain appeal and have to be taken into account.

3.1.2 Drawing Wiggly Lines with a Computer

Based on the aim to mechanically produce drawings for architectural and engineering applications, a whole area of computer graphics has been developed: CAD and CAAD systems. The output of these tools, however, demanded precision and accuracy, and the "toolkits" being used for the development of CAD and CAAD systems were analogous to the traditional drawing tools that have been in use for a long time. So, for instance, the requirements for plotting hardware included speed, precision, and reliability, and soon these machines created better drawings in shorter time than a human draftsperson ever could do. The drawing quality reached a standard that was equal to the work of an expert draftsperson.

However, especially in the architectural domain, other types of drawings are needed. There are anecdotes of students in architecture who would buy a wooden ruler and bang it to an edge in order to create dips in the ruler's edge and so be able to draw "perfectly" wiggly lines. Or architects would take a computer-generated drawing and put tracing paper on top and "redraw" the image this way. They would show only the traced-over version to their customers since these more sketchy drawings do not imply that the plans for the portrayed building are finished and unchangeable. Instead—as the study performed by Schumann et al. (1996) shows—people are more likely to discuss design variations using such "sketches."

As the search for perfection in architectural drawings has driven the development of CAD and CAAD software, so did this need for imperfect drawings inspire the development of NPR algorithms to achieve the desired results.

A Hardware-Based Solution

The first solution to this problem was hardware based and used the properties of plotting devices. If the pen is detached from the grip of the plotter, deliberate wobbles into the pen motion are introduced. The pen starts to wobble and even skips sometimes, which produces hand-drawn effects. By closely observing these features, the variables that affect the character of the drawing can be identified: pen looseness, pen type, and pen speed. It is, however, relatively hard to control each of these variables independently since they strongly depend on each other. The more loosely the pen is held, the more wobbly the lines are. When the pen is not securely mounted in the plotter, the only pressure applied to the paper is the pen's weight. Thus it is important to select media with free-flowing inks (or very soft lead pencils). Free-flowing inks naturally lead to wider parts of lines where the plotter moves slower or even stops. The fluidity of the ink in connection with the plotting speed thus determines the line width and brightness. The plotting speed generally has influence on the amplitude of the wobbles and also on the occurrence and size of gaps in the line. Figure 3.1 shows an example drawing.

A Software-Based Solution

The hardware-based solution already outlined revealed interesting results although it is not generally applicable. The plotter that is being used has to be modified, and the parameter control is less accurate and intuitive than desired. Further,

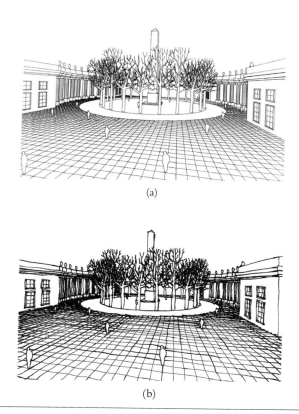

(a)

(b)

FIGURE 3.1 Freehand plotting: regular plotter output (a) and freehand plotter output (b). The image in (b) was generated using a modified plotter based on a CAD model.

with the development of output devices, laser printers started to rule out pen plotters as the standard device.[1] They are smaller, cheaper, and faster and thus very efficient for concept proofs and printouts in early design stages. These laser printers are controlled by page description languages like PostScript or PCL. A logical consequence was thus to change the line-drawing routines in these languages so as to produce sketchy instead of accurate lines. The following thoughts are not

---

1. However, for CAD and architectural drawings, plotters are still the choice of output devices for large and accurate drawings.

restricted in any way to page description languages but can be applied to any graphics package that contains line-drawing routines.

Again, the first step in producing wiggly lines is to identify variables that affect the character of the line. Here, the following three basic variables are chosen:

1. The *line thickness* describes how wide (thick) a line is drawn and how this thickness changes over the length of the line. Here, an *additional line end thickness* thickens the line ends and gives the illusion that the person drawing the lines is pressing harder or moving the pen slower at the beginning and end of each line. A *thickness dropoff* parameter enables the line thickness to change gradually or even abruptly.

2. To achieve the impression that the pen has come to rest at some line ends, a *line end dots* parameter is used. Here, the percentage of the lines can be adjusted at which line end dots should appear, the diameter of the dots, and the gap between the line end and the dot (if desired).

3. To control the wiggliness of the lines, the *line squiggle* variable is used. When drawing the line, it is divided into small segments, where the length is determined by the *average segment length*. The deviation of the given straight line can be controlled by setting a maximal amplitude of the wiggles. Within the parameter bounds for frequency and amplitude, random displacements are used to give the final line a vivid and non-regular look.

When printing (or displaying) the line, instead of creating a straight line (as the original code would have done), the new line-drawing routines jump in and modify the drawing accordingly. Each set of parameters is valid for the whole drawing, which leads to a uniform style throughout the drawing.

Viewer Response

This simple approach was one of the first ideas that dealt with producing non-photorealistic line drawings on the computer. A more thorough investigation led to more generalized models later on. But also the viewers' response to the drawings drove the development further. Besides being astonished that the images were done using computer hardware, viewers characterized them as being expressive, sketchy, rich, informal, or even freehanded. Although some of the viewers that were included in a survey (most of them architecture students) also gave "negative" comments, there was mainly attraction to the images. Some of the reasons for this apparent attraction might be as follows:

- The illusion that these images are hand drawn makes them stand out from the images being produced on a computer.

- As sketches permit interpretation, the incomplete quality of these images leads to a certain openness and encourages viewers to discuss the portrayed designs.

- The wiggly line drawings contain more complexity and therefore hold attention and interest more effectively than an image that is understood quickly.

- Fuzzy images are closer to reality, whereas the hard line computer plots appear more as an abstraction of the rounded corners and irregular forms in nature.

Although all these reasons are more or less hypotheses, studies have shown later on that indeed sketches are preferred to computer output in many areas, especially for design and planning.

3.2 Drawing "Artistic" Lines—The Path and Style Metaphor

The techniques mentioned include a random factor in the computation or the output of lines in order to make computer-generated drawings more "vivid" to achieve a more "handcrafted" look. Artistic techniques, however, do not use randomness alone as a source for parameters determining the final appearance of lines being drawn. Actually, every single line is carefully placed and parameterized by an artist in order to fulfill the artistic or communicative goal.

Observing the way human artists create a line drawing, there are two particular aspects to be taken care of. First, there is the placement of lines, that is, their position, which is to a great extent, determined by the scene to be portrayed. Second, there is the actual look of the lines or how they are drawn with respect to their width, brightness, color, and so on. Usually first a rough pencil sketch is drawn, which shows the overall characteristics of the lines to be drawn. This sketch is then refined using pen and ink or other pencils to work out the local characteristics of the lines in terms of their width and brightness.

Based on these observations, a model for rendering lines can now be devised. The pen is moved along a certain *path*. Depending on the shape of the pen and the pressure applied, the width of the line changes. The line's brightness is changed in accordance with the amount of ink available. In addition, the lines finally drawn do not correctly match the intended path due to irregular movements of the hand and to the unevenness of the drawing surface. These distortions of the path are described collectively as the *style* with which the line is drawn.

The path that determines the placement and course of the line on the display surface can be given in several ways. It might be specified interactively (using, for instance, a mouse or a pen on a pressure-sensitive tablet), given as a 2D model (a CAD drawing), or even created by a rendering program based on a 3D model. Let us first assume that the path is given as a piecewise polynomial curve or a polygon. We can then find several techniques to overlay this path by a style to create the desired effects.

3.2.1 Deforming Images

Many vector-oriented drawing programs still rely on the *constant thickness stroke* as the only tool to create an image. This, however, either limits the possibilities and thus the creativity of the users or burdens them with additional work since every "stroke" a user wants to apply to the paper has to be put together from other primitives. For larger drawings, this is a painstaking method, and there is enough room for improvement.

Stroke Definition and Skeletons

Drawing with *skeletal strokes* as a new type of stroke is an interaction technique that uses transformations of predefined pictures along a given path. These transformations may include bending, twisting, non-uniform compression, and stretching of the picture.

The basis for all this is the definition of a skeletal stroke, which is a picture placed around a single reference backbone, and a reference thickness line, which is perpendicular to the reference backbone and described by the maximum width of the stroke. Figure 3.2 illustrates this concept. The picture placed around the reference backbone is called the *flesh* of the stroke and might be composed of points, closed polygons, or Bézier curves. The reference backbone provides a reference x-axis for the points defining the flesh; the reference thickness gives a scale to specify the lateral distance of these points from the backbone (and might thus be considered a y-axis).

The stroke's definition is based on parametric coordinates. The reference backbone and the reference thickness specify the range of the parametric coordinate system of the stroke by defining the [0, 1] intervals in both directions.

Applying a Stroke to a Path

Once the stroke has been defined, it can be applied to any arbitrary path. There are no restrictions for the path's shape or description although it must be possible

(a)   (b)

FIGURE 3.2 Definition of a skeletal stroke around a reference backbone (a) (the black horizontal arrow) and a reference thickness (the vertical arrow in (b)).

to compute any position on the path using a parametric formula. To apply the stroke to the path, the reference backbone is aligned with the given path and the flesh is distorted accordingly.

In an interactive system, the user may specify the width of the stroke and the shear angle; otherwise, those parameters are determined from the stroke's definition. Within the mapping process of the reference backbone to the path, each position defining a feature of the stroke (a control vertex for the flesh) is mapped with respect to its position along the reference backbone. The distance from the path is determined from the lateral distance this particular point has from the reference backbone in the stroke definition. The process of applying a skeletal stroke along an arbitrary path is actually a coordinate transformation of the parametric space in which the stroke's definition is given such that the x-axis is aligned with the path and the y-axis points in the direction of the path normal at each position.

Controlling the shear angle with which the stroke is applied to the path offers another degree of freedom when using skeletal strokes. There are basically two possibilities, which are illustrated in Figure 3.3:

1. In *sausage style*, the shear angle is relative to the tangent of the path. Thus in this style, a more literal path is displayed with the skeletal stroke distorted accordingly. The stroke itself remains perpendicular to the path, turning as the path curves and turns.

2. In *ribbon style*, the shear angle is kept constant with respect to the global coordinate system. This style creates images something like what you get

(a)   (b)

FIGURE 3.3 Sausage style (a) and ribbon style (b) of stroke application.

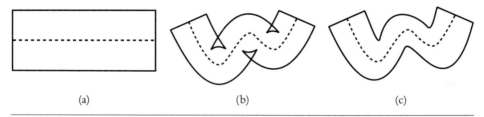

(a)   (b)   (c)

FIGURE 3.4 Problems associated with the bending of the stroke in areas of high curvature: stroke definition (a), wrinkled areas (b), correct deformation (c).

with a calligraphy pen. The stroke remains oriented along the y-axis or the paper as it was originally defined.

When bending a physical elastic object, the material on the concave side of the bend will be compressed axially while that on the convex side will be stretched axially. The amount of compression and stretching varies depending on the material properties. The elasticity properties of "real life" materials often cause local deformations in all three dimensions so that lateral compression and expansion is also possible and may yield buckles or wrinkles. When deforming the flesh of a skeletal stroke, similar problems may arise in either style of application. Such problems arise in areas with high curvature since they are also observable in the "hairy brushes" model (see Section 3.2.3). Simply drawing the flesh using the normal to the application path as the local y-axis yields areas in which the flesh wrinkles or even folds back on itself, as illustrated in Figure 3.4.

To overcome all these problems, a deformation model describing the behavior of the flesh especially in sharp bends is needed. Here, different approaches are possible—for instance, using finite element theory to calculate the deformation of skin around a complicated bone structure or using algorithms based on kinesiology. The deformation model proposed in the original literature on "skeletal strokes" (see Hsu et al., 1993) is based on modeling the deformation of the Cartesian space as a whole. As a reference model, an imaginary material is used that stretches like rubber and compresses like a piece of sponge. This idealized material is infinitely stretchable and compressible and no lateral changes are induced on axial deformation. The lateral deformation is handled by spatially constraining the material to the local center of curvature.

Extended Features

Besides the basic transformation of a stroke along a path, the skeletal stroke model also allows for more elaborate possibilities: higher order strokes and animation.

A stroke can be defined to consist of simple geometric objects like polylines, polygons, and curves. If a stroke definition includes other strokes as elements, this is called a *higher order stroke*. The substrokes can also be instances of the original stroke itself, which leads to recursive definitions. In both cases, special algorithms have to be devised in order to correctly render the final stroke (apply it to a path). For recursive strokes, which resemble in some way iterated function systems (IFSs), algorithms from this area can be examined for their use in our case. Here, special care must be taken on the termination of the drawing process, that is, on limiting the recursion depth.

Animation has always been an area of application for such computerized drawing techniques. For creating cartoon-like animation, 3D techniques are less practical than traditional 2D drawing techniques. Nevertheless, the animation of 2D shapes is still a tedious process if there is no further support by an animation system since each frame has to be drawn separately. Traditional keyframe techniques can be used with skeletal strokes where the artist defines the keyframes by directly drawing or manipulating the objects in the drawing. The in-betweens are then calculated by the system where only the paths have to be interpolated while for each frame the strokes are applied after calculating the new path. This reduces the design effort to drawing the keyframes. Since the defined paths are usually rather simple forms, a proper interpolation between the keyframes can be ensured. No interpolation has to be performed on the points belonging to the flesh so that bending and wrinkling will be handled automatically by the stroke application process.

3.2.2 Using Path Information—Line Styles

With the technique just described, the appearance of the lines is exclusively controlled by the style. However, the path can also carry information that may determine the visual parameters of a line. If we assume the path stemming from a rendering process, information on the light distribution in the scene is available and can be evaluated. Looking at hand-drawn images gives an idea of how such information is used. Very often—especially in illustrations—the line width varies with varying light intensities. Lines that lie in rather dark areas are drawn much wider and darker than those in brightly lit areas. Depth information, which is gained from a 3D model within a rendering process, can also be mapped onto the visual properties of the lines as we have already seen in Section 1.3.3 (see especially Figure 1.14).

Although the skeletal strokes model is very powerful and flexible, all changes in the line's appearance result from changes in style parameters. To make the line also depending on the path's properties, we will examine a slightly different model. Instead of deforming an arbitrary image over the length of the path, we will compute the superposition of two attributed curves.

The Model

Thus the model is based on two different curves:

1. the *path* describing the position and course of the line on the display surface and

2. the *style* describing the distortions of the path that leads to the characteristic appearance.

The path is simply given as a parametric curve. Here, several variants of splines can be used that all are specified by control vertices. The style describes how a straight line would be distorted (see Figure 3.5). The geometric distortion as well as the change of parameters such as the line width and its brightness over the length of the line are specified by polynomial functions (in spline representation). Here the following parameters for each control vertex are supplied:

*   the position (x- and y-coordinates),
*   a weight value (w) used by some interpolation methods, and

FIGURE 3.5 The style describes the distortions of a straight line.

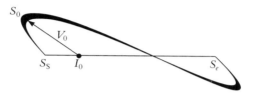

FIGURE 3.6 Calculation of the difference vector v_0 for a given parameter value t.

- values for pressure (p) and saturation (s) that determine the line width and brightness. The terms *pressure* and *saturation* are chosen since they are appropriate metaphors for describing the respective properties of the line.

Furthermore, a specification is required to describe how the control vertices are interpreted. The following options can be chosen:

- The control vertices are regarded as vertices of a polyline and as such interpolated linearly.
- The control vertices are approximated using (cubic) B-splines.
- An interpolation of the control vertices is performed using Catmull-Rom splines.

Further interpolation methods can be implemented easily.

Drawing the Lines

So far we have examined how the path and the style are defined. We now describe the mapping of the style onto the path and thus how to compute the output. To map the style geometry onto the path, we use the line segment from the style's starting point s_s to the endpoint s_e (see Figure 3.6). We then compute for a given parameter $t \in [0, 1]$ the point $l_0 = s_s + t(s_e - s_s)$. Furthermore, we calculate the point s_0 on the style curve for the same parameter value t and the *difference vector* $v_0 = s_0 - l_0$.

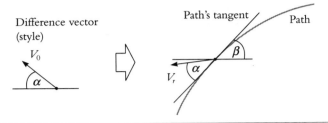

FIGURE 3.7 Geometrical superposition of path and style by using the difference vector method.

This difference vector is then added to the point p_0, which is the position on the given path for the parameter t, and we get the final point p. To do so, the path's tangent is calculated at p_0 and the difference vector is then added perpendicular to the direction of the tangent; that is, we first rotate v_0 by β and then add the rotated vector to p_0. In this case, the angle β is the slope of the tangent at p_0 (see Figure 3.7).

It should be noted that the scale of the difference vector is somewhat problematic. Since the path and the style might be defined in different scales, the length of the vector is not necessarily appropriate. Thus scaling is necessary. The ratio between the path length and the style length is used as the scaling factor. The user also has the possibility to specify a *style scale factor* that is applied before the mapping.

The mapping of the geometric properties leads to a *skeleton* of the curve to be drawn. The flesh that is attached to this skeleton is derived from the given pressure and saturation values, yielding a hull shape for the line. This is done by interpolating the parameter values over the length of the created skeleton curve. There are two ways in which the interpolation method can be defined:

1. Having a specific pressure and saturation value given with each of the style's control vertices results in interpolation of these values according to the interpolation method for the geometry given in the style's definition.

2. In addition, the change of pressure and saturation may be specified by an explicit interpolation function defined over the parameter range $0 \leq t \leq 1$. This function is then used to determine the actual brightness and width values for a given t. This method leads to very powerful control over the appearance of the lines.

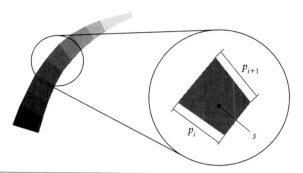

FIGURE 3.8 Drawing the line as a sequence of quadrilaterals. The width of each quadrilateral results from the pressure values at $t = t_i$ and $t = t_{i+1}$ (p_i and p_{i+1}). The brightness is the average value of the saturation values s_i and s_{i+1} at $t = t_i$ and $t = t_{i+1}$.

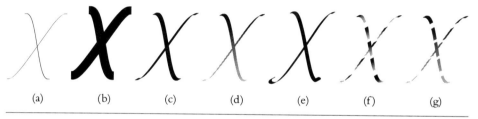

| (a) | (b) | (c) | (d) | (e) | (f) | (g) |

FIGURE 3.9 The character X drawn in different styles: the path geometry (a); changing the pressure, pen angle based on the tangent direction (b); like (b), but given a specific pen angle (c); change in pressure and saturation over the length (d); change in geometry and pressure (e); stroked style applied to each single stroke (f); and stroked style applied globally (g).

For drawing lines, the position, width, and brightness are computed for subsequent parameter values t_i. For each pair of value sets, a quadrilateral is drawn according to Figure 3.8. The width of those quadrilaterals is determined from the pressure values at t_i. This width is seen either with respect to the normal direction of the path or to a given *pen angle*. The effects resulting from a change of the pen angle are illustrated in Figures 3.9(b) and (c). In general, similar problems, as with the skeletal strokes model, arise in regions of high curvature when the step size (distance between two points for subsequent parameter values t_i) is small compared to the width. In this case, quadrilaterals with self-intersecting bounds may arise that have to be handled correctly.

Advanced Features

More advanced features for creating line drawings can also be derived. The method of mapping styles onto paths now pays off particularly lucratively in that information is readily available and manipulatable for post-processing, which allows customizable control over a variety of visual effects.

A line renderer creates a set of curves out of a 3D model and supplies a mathematical description of these curves on a 2D surface. Besides this, the renderer may provide further attributes based on lighting and depth information. For example, a line should appear darker in a shaded area than in a bright region of the image. Further, depth cuing determines the fading direction of lines. This means that the path provided by the renderer contains not only geometric attributes but also information about the lighting and depth coded as pressure and saturation.

A method for combining attributes defined with the path and the style addresses this topic. A *style dominance value d* $(0 \leq d \leq 1)$ describes the priority of the attributes given in the style over those given in the path. A value equal to zero means that the style has no influence on the final drawing; a value equal to one gives complete control to the style. Normally, path and style values are interpolated linearly, that is, $v = v_p(1 - d) + v_s d$. (Here v is the resulting attribute value interpolated between the path's value v_p and the style's value v_s.) Other interpolation methods are also possible and can be chosen by the user.

An observation of traditional drawing techniques reveals another task that can be tackled thanks to the separation of path and style. Often lines are drawn as a set of smaller *strokes*. Here the pen is lifted from the surface and then put back to draw the next stroke. The subdivision of a style into strokes is also possible in the model described earlier. It is specified with the following parameters:

- *strokeNumber* determines the number of strokes into which the curve is divided,
- *strokeGap* determines the size of the gap between two strokes, where a positive value creates real gaps and a negative value creates overlapped lines, and
- *strokeLength* determines the length of a stroke.

Depending on which value is given, either the length or the number of strokes is computed. As an example, the stroke length is calculated as follows:

$$strokeLength = \frac{pathLength}{strokeNumber + strokeGap(strokeNumber - 1)}$$

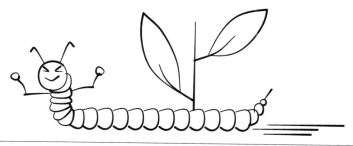

FIGURE 3.10 "The Little Worm." A cartoon character with styles.

Finally, a style must be parameterized with respect to the kinds of strokes used. Either the style definition is applied to each stroke independently or it is spread over all strokes, resulting in strokes nicely fitting together at the end in terms of line brightness and line width. These methods are illustrated in Figures 3.9(f) and (g).

Applications

This line model is suited for rendering line drawings that are created out of a 3D model within a rendering process. Other areas of application can be found in 2D visualization and drawing programs. Since the attributes are connected with the path, user interaction—for instance, using a pressure-sensitive graphics tablet—can also influence the final output. In the following, we show a few examples for images that have been created using the line styles described.

Figure 3.10 shows a cartoon character that was created based on the entered path shown in Figure 3.11. Even though the style used (Figure 3.12) is very simple, it results in a remarkable change of the image.

Figure 3.13 shows the bones of a foot rendered with an analytical rendering system out of a 3D model and drawn with different styles. Note in Figure 3.13(a) how a light source in the upper left corner affects the rendering, and in Figure 3.13(b) how geometric changes together with changes stemming from evaluating the lighting information can be used.

3.2.3 Simulating Watercolor

While the first two techniques using the path and style metaphor (skeletal strokes and line styles) work in a vector-oriented manner and are thus well suited for high-quality printouts, it is also possible to use this metaphor in a pixel-based

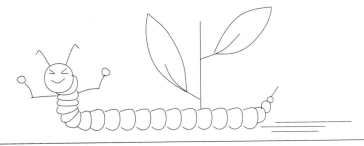

FIGURE 3.11 The path for Figure 3.10.

FIGURE 3.12 The style that is applied.

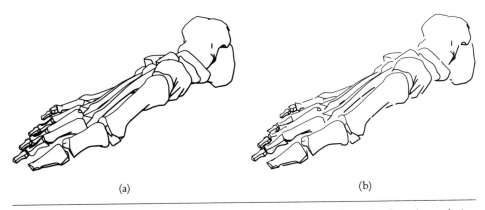

(a)   (b)

FIGURE 3.13 Illustrations of the bones of the human foot: lighting information from the rendering process was used to determine the appearance of the lines (a); this is combined with geometric deviations introduced via the style (b). In (b), the style shortens the lines so that the impression of "haloed lines" is given.

environment for the simulation of watercolor painting. The following technique is a simple simulation of the traditional Japanese art *sumi-e*, which is characterized by the composition of the image by placing only a very few strokes all in the same dark color. The basis for this approach is an object-oriented model consisting mainly of four parts: the *brush*, the *dip*, the *stroke*, and the *paper*. We will have a look at all four parts in turn to see what they represent.

♦ The *brush* can be thought of as a collection of bristles, each of which has its own amount of ink and its position within the brush. The brush is moved along the path and leaves a "footprint" at each position. For the sake of simplicity, the brush is defined as a one-dimensional array of bristles centered at the stroke. This simplification to a one-dimensional brush has several advantages over a two-dimensional approach:

1. It can be assumed that the brush is always perpendicular to the stroke. This eliminates the additional computations that arise when rotating a two-dimensional brush has to be taken into account.

2. The spreading of the bristles can be modeled by defining the width of the brush at any point as a function of the pressure applied to the brush at this point.

3. It is easier to predict the effect of a brushstroke in an image because no two bristles write over the same region of the paper.

4. The speed of the computation is increased significantly since fewer bristles are to be observed. Furthermore, the influence of neighboring bristles is also reduced (there are only two neighbors to each bristle).

In the sense of this section, the brush (in connection with the dip) can be thought of as the *style* that determines the final appearance of the brushstroke.

♦ The *dip* describes the state of the brush when it is dipped into the paint. The dip must carry enough information to restore the brush's initial state or a sufficiently similar state so that it becomes possible to repeat a stroke with an equivalent result. At the very least, the dip must set the initial color and amount of ink for each bristle and restore the positions of the bristles within the brush. This can be achieved by simple rules that set the parameters accordingly or by storing a snapshot of all parameters. The dip heavily influences the visual effects of the resulting brushstroke so by selecting the same brush and stroke, you can still experiment with different dips to create different effects.

♦ The *stroke* is a set of parameters that evolve as a function of an independent variable. The parameters in question are the position (x- and y-coordinates) and the pressure. The independent variable can be seen as the distance the brush has moved or the elapsed time from the beginning of the painting process. To be more specific, the shape of the stroke is determined by a 2D spline curve, where for each control point, not only the coordinates are given but also a value defining the pressure at this location. The stroke models the path along which the brush is moved and builds thus the second part of our general path and style model.

♦ The *paper* is responsible for rendering the ink as it comes off the brush. Each bristle that is about to leave an imprint on the paper sends a message to the paper object indicating its position and other relevant parameters. The paper object then renders the appropriate result—usually a single dot—at the appropriate position. Since the paper itself renders the result, all additional properties of the paper need only to be stored here. Hence an additional texture for the simulation of different paper types or qualities can be taken into account when rendering the bristles' imprints.

Algorithms

For drawing a line with this setup, first the stroke has to be defined by a user. The definition of a stroke consists of a list of position and pressure samples. Both position and pressure are later interpolated using cubic splines. This spline curve is then subdivided into sufficiently small intervals that are to be connected by line segments (see Figure 3.14). The size of the intervals can be chosen small enough so that the impression of a smooth curve is retained but large enough that it is not below the size of one pixel. After this subdivision, the stroke path is represented by a series of n nodes $(x, y, p, s)_i$ for $i = 0 \ldots n - 1$. The values x, y, and p represent position and pressure, whereas s is an approximation of the distance traveled along the curve. This distance can be computed using Equation (3.1):

$$s_i = \sum_{k=1}^{i} \sqrt{(x_k - x_{k-1})^2 + (y_k - y_{k-1})^2} \qquad \text{where } s_0 = 0 \tag{3.1}$$

To move the brush along this stroke, a discretized version of the line segment chain[2] is used to give the positions of the brush's center. To draw the whole brushstroke, each segment will be drawn in turn by covering the region between two consecutive nodes by a quadrilateral.

Assume a segment between the two nodes A and B (refer to Figure 3.14 for the following explanations). If this is not the last segment of the curve, the following point will be called C. For each segment, a quadrilateral (*EFGH*) is constructed that has the following properties:

---

2. Each line segment is discretized using Bresenham's algorithm (see Foley et al., 1990, pp. 72–80).

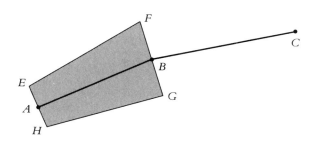

FIGURE 3.14 Construction of a quadrilateral on a given path segment.

- A bisects $\overline{EH}$,
- B bisects $\overline{FG}$,
- $|\overline{EH}|$ is the width computed from the pressure at A,
- $|\overline{FG}|$ is the width computed from the pressure at B, and
- $\overline{FG}$ bisects the angle $\angle ABC$.

In addition, keep in mind that for the first and the last point of a curve, $\overline{EH}$ and $\overline{FG}$ are perpendicular to the path in A and B, respectively.

Once the polygon's vertices have been found, it can be filled. However, a simple filling algorithm would not suffice since it does not take into account that a brushstroke has to be generated where the actual color distribution is defined in the brush's attributes (the bristles). By using bilinear interpolation, the actual "filling" works as described in Algorithm 3.1.

The overall algorithm thus moves the (center of the) brush along the discretized stroke, generating the appropriate quadrilateral for each segment, and then fills the quadrilaterals according to Algorithm 3.1. This basic procedure can be influenced in different ways to create special effects, which we will discuss in the following section.

Special Effects

By simply changing some of the parameters of the algorithms, it is possible to create various effects that are also derived from effects gained by painting by hand. When painting with a real paintbrush, there will be a point in time when the brush runs dry. This usually happens in a way that not all bristles at the same time

---

1   $P :=$ pixels' position in the output image (x, y)
2   $S :=$ pixels' position along the stroke by interpolating (S_A, S_B, S_B, S_A)
      on *EFGH*
3   $B :=$ pixels' position across the brush by interpolating $(1, 1, 0, 0)$ on *EFGH*
4   sort all generated data for each pixel by S
5   **foreach** pixel in order of S **do**
6   determine the nearest bristle to B
7   invoke the drawing process for this bristle
8   update the bristle's state
9   **od**

ALGORITHM 3.1   Filling a generated quadrilateral when drawing a brushstroke.

stop giving ink to the paper, yielding a scratchy breakup at the tail of the stroke. Within the model described earlier, the ink supply on each bristle is assumed to be a reservoir of a finite quantity of fluid that gets refilled each time the brush is "dipped" into the ink. When dipped, for each bristle the new amount of ink is defined and how long this ink will last. This might be specified either as a fraction of the stroke length (if the stroke length is known beforehand) or as an absolute distance (remember the parameter s in Algorithm 3.1).

Each bristle has an assigned color that, for the sake of simplicity, is a gray value between 0 and 1. All ink applied to a bristle has the same color; however, different bristles may have different colors. This color distribution over the brush has to be specified in the dip and thus gets applied when the brush is dipped into the ink. During the stroke, neighboring bristles may affect each other leading to a different color distribution each time the state of the bristles is updated. This evolution of the color distribution can be modeled in several ways; we will give a few examples:

◆ A color distribution is specified for the start and the end of a stroke. At any point in between, the actual color distribution is calculated by interpolating between those two distributions over the parameter s.

◆ From the starting configuration, diffusion may be simulated by smoothing the colors of neighboring pixels by partial interpolation. If C_{i_t} is the color of the i-th bristle at time t and D is a parameter between zero and one determining the speed of the diffusion (larger values mean faster diffusion) and if the bristles are assumed to be equally spaced, then

$$C_{i_{t+1}} = C_{i_t}(1 - D) + \frac{C_{i-1_t} + C_{i+1_t}}{2} D$$

is the new color of the i-th bristle at time $t + 1$.

- A general algorithm for distributing the color may also be specified.

Besides computing the ink's color over the course of the stroke, the color that actually appears on the paper is also of interest. Here, colored paper or previously colored spots on the paper may yield a color that distinguishes it from the one specified in the bristle. To achieve this effect, a color combination function has to be specified that creates the resulting color from the three sources: ink color C_i, previously drawn color C_o, and paper color C_p.

There are many more possibilities to influence the appearance of the brush-stroke that is finally drawn, and the exercises at the end of this chapter will encourage you to experiment with parameters and assess the effects. A few more ideas shall illustrate what can be done:

- transferring ink among neighboring pixels so that they not only affect the color of the ink but also the quantity,
- applying more pressure to the brush to either spread the bristles farther apart or bring more bristles in contact with the paper, and
- mapping textures onto the image of the stroke.

With the techniques and algorithms described, a simple but powerful tool for simulating real brushstrokes has been developed. Figure 3.15 shows an example of what is possible to create with this model.

The most important disadvantage of this approach is its speed. The state of the bristles needs to be updated in each step, and if the brush contains many bristles and if they influence each other in a rather complicated way, the method is very time consuming. What's more, the simulation does not take into consideration some of the more advanced effects that are achievable in watercolor paintings. In Chapter 4, we will take a closer look at some different techniques that strive for a physical simulation of such effects.

FIGURE 3.15 Hairy brushes use a simulation of the behavior of a wet brush on paper to create images like this. Note that this method is particularly well suited for the Japanese art *sumi-e* since here only a few brushstrokes form an image.

3.3 A Generalization: Multiresolution Curves

As we could see from the last section, the path and style metaphor is particularly well suited for this kind of application and can be used in many different ways to create images in different styles. However, a more general solution is desirable, and we will describe such a technique next. We will turn away from "artistic lines" and look at a representation of curves in general that supports a variety of operations, for instance:

- The ability to change the global shape of a curve while maintaining small details. This is similar to changing the path and applying the same style in our earlier model.

- The ability to change small details while maintaining the global shape. This resembles a change in the style being applied to one path.

- The ability to represent a curve on multiple levels of detail.

- The ability to fit a curve through a given set of points within a maximum error tolerance. This is particularly interesting if we wish to create a drawing by giving only a few points and having the lines computed by the computer.

For addressing all these issues, a multiresolution approach for representing the curve is well suited. Multiresolution techniques have developed within the last few years to become powerful tools in many areas of computer graphics. *Wavelets* have proved especially useful for representing curves on different levels of detail. The derivation of a multiresolution representation for curves requires some detailed mathematics, which we will not cover here. We refer you to the literature, for instance, Stollnitz et al. (1996).

3.3.1 Wavelet Representation of Curves

In short, consider a curve C^n being described by a set of control points $[c_1^n, \ldots, c_m^n]^T$. To create a representation with a fewer number of control points, say, m', we would apply some kind of filter or downsampling algorithm on C^n yielding a representation C^{n-1} having m' control points:

$$C^{n-1} = A^n C^n$$

The detail D^{n-1} being lost in this process can be computed using Equation (3.2):

$$D^{n-1} = B^n C^n \tag{3.2}$$

In these equations, A^n is an $m' \times m$ matrix, and B^n is an $(m - m') \times m$ matrix. Both matrices are related to each other and collectively referred to as the *analysis filter*. This process of splitting a high-resolution curve into a lower-resolution curve and the respective detail is called *decomposition*. The other way around, the *reconstruction* of a high-resolution curve from a given lower-resolution representation and a given detail is accomplished by a second pair of matrices, the *synthesis filter* as described in Equation (3.3):

$$C^n = P^n C^{n-1} + Q^n D^{n-1} \tag{3.3}$$

If the decomposition process is applied recursively to the result of the previous step, we get a hierarchy of lower-resolution curves and details, as can be seen in Figure 3.16.

FIGURE 3.16 Recursive decomposition yields a series of lower-resolution curves and respective details.

To recover the original signal C^n, the lowest-resolution curve C^0 and the sequence of all details $D^0, \ldots, D^{n-1}$ have to be known.[3] We can easily see that this representation technique fits into the path and style metaphor by treating the lowest-resolution curve C^0 as the path and the sequence of details added to that path in the different steps of the reconstruction process as the style.

3.3.2 Editing Multiresolution Curves

The path and style metaphor has been introduced to support two different types of editing operations.

1. Changing the "global" shape of the curve. This has been accomplished by changing the path and using the same style for the edited curve.

2. Changing "local" detail. Here, different styles are applied to the same path.

Both operations can be carried out on a multiresolution representation in a similar manner.

Changing the overall shape of the curve C^n means changing one of the lower-resolution representations C^j into $\widehat{C^j} = C^j + \Delta C^j$ (see Figure 3.17). Reconstructing the high-resolution curve is done by applying the reconstruction process to the *changes* in the lower-resolution signal:

$$\widehat{C^n} = C^n + \Delta C^n$$
$$= C^n + P^n P^{n-1} \ldots P^{j+1} \Delta C^j$$

Since on lower levels of the representation the curve consists of fewer control points, a change here means a change in a larger portion of the high-resolution curve.

On the other hand, changing local detail is also straightforward to derive. The style, that is, the deviations of the global shape, is expressed by the chain of details $D^0, \ldots, D^{n-1}$. Now, changing the local detail means replacing these details by a different chain $\widehat{D^0}, \ldots, \widehat{D^{n-1}}$. A reconstruction using these new details yields a curve having the same global shape as the original curve but different local detail (see Figure 3.18).

Even though editing the curve in a multiresolution representation is rather straightforward, a few issues are to be considered. In contrast to the other methods,

---

3. Note that the total memory size required to store the sequence $C^0, D^0, D^1, \ldots, D^{n-1}$ is the same as for the original curve C^n.

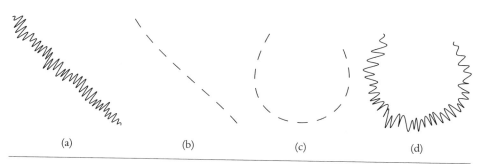

FIGURE 3.17 Changing the overall shape of the curve given in (a) means changing a lower-resolution representation (b) into what can be seen in (c) and then adding details again, finally yielding the curve in (d).

FIGURE 3.18 Changing local detail keeps the global course of the lines unchanged.

the curve can be edited on several levels; thus, to achieve the desired result, a thorough knowledge of the properties of the curve and the algorithms for creating the final high-resolution representation is necessary. Furthermore, this method is well suited to controlling the geometry of the lines being drawn. Controlling the visual attributes, since there is thickness, texture, brightness, or transparency, is rather difficult to include. These attributes might be considered additional dimensions in the line's description (more exactly in the data associated with each control point). The decomposition and reconstruction algorithm and thus the whole framework can then be applied to any value associated with the curve.

3.4 Comparison of the Line-Drawing Methods

In the last sections, some line-drawing methods were proposed that all rely on the path and style metaphor. Even though this common principle is shared by all the presented techniques, many differences result in different conditions for application.

By far the most general approach is the use of multiresolution curves. This technique offers the most possibilities to influence the geometry of the resulting line. One major drawback, however, is that other visual attributes such as line thickness or line color can not easily be integrated in the model. Hence the use of multiresolution curves is well suited for images where the geometry of the line may change but the line width is the same. This is actually the case for pen-and-ink renditions so that multiresolution curves are a perfect tool for simulating the appearance of this kind of drawing (see, for instance, Chapter 5 for an application).

Even though it seems limited at a first glance, the skeletal strokes approach offers a tool to create a wide variety of images that can be used for illustrations as well as artwork. The most challenging task when using skeletal strokes is the design of appropriate strokes for the application at hand. If a library of strokes is available to choose from, the character of an image can be changed rapidly by selecting a different stroke. The major disadvantage with this technique is that the path controls only the geometry of the line so no additional information that may be gained from a 3D model can be mapped onto line properties. This mapping is one of the inherent properties of the line styles model, so it is particularly well suited for illustrative images being rendered from a given 3D model. The achievable styles range from simple lines of uniform width to mimicking pen-and-ink drawings done with very different kinds of pens.

Finally, the painting simulation done with hairy brushes is more an artistic approach to use the path and style metaphor. It nicely demonstrates the possibilities of this rather general framework.

Exercises

3.1   Review graphical methods for drawing and rastering lines (for instance, the Bresenham algorithm). Which requirements are set for these algorithms and how are they achieved?

3.2   Implement a procedure for drawing incorrect lines by changing points on the line (or points in a parametric description of the line) based on random variations. Which problems arise and how can they be solved?

3.3   Implement an interactive drawing system that allows you to place lines on a plane. Use this system to experiment with different line-drawing methods (see the following exercises).

3.4   Implement the skeletal stroke line-drawing method. Design different stroke shapes, some of which should result in lines that appear to be drawn with pen and ink or a felt pen. Include this method in your interactive system from Exercise 3.3. How can the parameters of the lines be set?

3.5   Implement the painting simulation approach and include it in the interactive system from Exercise 3.3.

3.6   Experiment with several methods of how the bristles may influence each other and compare the results.

3.7   Based on your observations with your own implementations, collect ideas for interaction techniques that are suitable for such a painting or drawing system. How can a line's parameters be set (without using a dialog box)? Implement some of your ideas.

3.8   Implement the multiresolution representation of lines. You will need this representation in Chapter 5.

3.9   How can the multiresolution representation be extended to also handle line attributes like width or color (saturation)?

Bibliographic Notes

The theoretical basis of this chapter is built in the Ph.D. thesis of Schofield (1994). Here, the necessity of picture units of a size larger than a pixel is derived, and it is shown that the construction of images based on such "marks" is actually one of the main characteristics of non-photorealistic renditions. Schofield uses the theoretical principles in a system called Piranesi, which includes many aspects of NPR and which is also the topic of Lansdown and Schofield (1995) and Richens and Schofield (1995).

The technique for drawing incorrect lines was first introduced by van Bakergem and Obata (1991). Even though the hardware-based approach by modifying a plotter seems somewhat outdated from today's point of view, it has shown the principles behind the development in this area. Starting with the introduction of *random* variations in line-drawing routines, it becomes obvious that some kind of control has to be provided over and above pure stochastic deviations.

The topic of lines and how to draw them, especially in the context of illustrative images, has been studied by several authors. Dooley and Cohen used different line parameterizations for their interactive illustration system (1990a; 1990b). Elber explored different variations of lines to better communicate the spatial structure of geometric models (1995).

The path and style metaphor allows for this kind of control and is well suited to make line deviations depend on some variables given either with a 3D model or by user interaction. The latter is thus the key to skeletal strokes, a technique mainly based on the two publications on this topic by Hsu, Lee, and Wiseman (1993) and Hsu and Lee (1994). The technique described here has been included in a few commercially available drawing programs.

Line styles have been developed at the University of Magdeburg in the context of an analytic rendering system. They are based on the work of Schumann, which is briefly covered in Strothotte et al. (1994). The line styles are an extension thereof and have been developed by Schumann. For a detailed description, also of the analytic rendering context, see Chapter 4 in Strothotte et al. (1998) as well as Schlechtweg et al. (1998). An interesting application is described by Isenberg (2000). A similar approach to line styles can be found in Northrup and Markosian (2000).

Finally, the path and style metaphor also supports the simulation of brush-strokes, which is described for the first time in the master's thesis of Strassmann (1986b) and which was the basis for a SIGGRAPH article (1986a). Even though other paintbrush simulation methods have evolved (see Chapter 4 and Hertzmann 1998), the general concept of the path and style metaphor was proved useful.

Nonetheless, a general method of representing lines is given by using multiresolution curves in the context of NPR first introduced by Finkelstein and Salesin (1994). This representation method builds on wavelets, a technique from sampling theory; an in-depth study of wavelets can be found in Stollnitz et al. (1996).

4 | SIMULATING NATURAL MEDIA AND ARTISTIC TECHNIQUES

The approaches introduced in the last chapter served mainly one purpose: to build tools that are then used to enrich the expressiveness of computer graphics so as to create more vivid images. They are oriented on artistic techniques but are not seen as an actual simulation of human painting and drawing. Indeed, the goal to simulate artistic techniques is a rather questionable one. Simulating artistic techniques means also simulating human thinking and reasoning, especially creative thinking. This is impossible to do using algorithms or information processing systems. What computer graphics can do is to mimic the result of artistic processes and provide tools for doing so. Such tools are again a step toward an enrichment of the expressiveness of computer graphics techniques.

In this chapter, we will take a closer look at tools that aim to create images that resemble hand-drawn (or hand-painted) ones. The methods described here differ from the ones described in Chapters 2 and 3 insofar as they possibly try to simulate the physical processes connected with painting and drawing. They are a simulation in the sense of imitating the physical behavior of ink or paint on paper or imitating the distribution of graphite particles left behind by a pencil, but not in the sense of imitating the human drawing and painting process. The chapter concludes with two methods for the simulation of woodcuts and engravings. In contrast to the first two sections, here computer graphics techniques are used that do not simulate the real physical processes.

4.1 Simulating Painting with Wet Paint

Besides the artistic qualities of watercolor or oil paintings, such images also are a challenge from a physicist's point of view. We will concentrate on watercolor paintings since the relevant physical processes form the basis for any other techniques. A simulation of applying watercolor on paper includes, especially, the following:

- A simulation of the physical properties of the medium, namely, paper, brushes, and paint, including
  - the paper properties (fine or coarse paper, its fiber structure, and so on),
  - the peculiarities of different brushes, and
  - the consistency of the paint resulting from the amount of water and paint particles.
- A simulation of effects of the painting processes such as
  - the flow of paint on the paper,
  - the interaction between various brushstrokes (actually a simulation of mixing two fluids),
  - the adsorption of paint particles in the paper,
  - the adsorption of water in the paper,
  - the "aging" of paint, that is, the evaporation of water making the paint drier over time, and
  - other processes like the flow of paint on paper, which is not perfectly even.

Although all these processes are quite complex, they can be used by a skilled artist to achieve exactly the effects he or she wants. A simulation is rather complicated and will not include all aspects in a whole. Moreover, as in many of these cases in physics, an idealized model will serve the purpose of simulation well, so for our purposes a more empirically based model is used that incorporates physically based behavior.

The observed scenario is of continuous nature although the desired output on a computer screen or in a bitmap file is discrete. This imposes the first real limitation to the computational models that are being used. There are mainly two directions in which we can go:

1. choosing a discrete simulation model and
2. simulating in a continuous model and discretizing the simulation result.

We will examine both methods in turn, where in the first case cellular automata are chosen as the model, and in the second case fluid simulation is exploited directly. The described simulations work only on abstract models and do not include a visualization of the "computed image." Therefore, we will focus on this topic in a later section.

4.1.1 Simulating Watercolor Using Cellular Automata

The following model simulates the behavior of water and ink "particles" based on a 2D cellular automaton. Before we explore the model in more detail, we will introduce the concept of cellular automata as a model of computation. Then we will identify the main parts of the watercolor simulation model and discuss each part in turn.

Sidebar: Cellular Automata Basics

A cellular automaton (CA) is a model of computation, almost like a Turing machine. Formally, a CA is a 4-tuple (L, S, N, f) with the following components:

- L is a regular lattice of cells,
- S is a finite set of states,
- N is a finite set (of size $|N| = n$) of neighborhood indices such that $\forall c \in N, \forall r \in L : r + c \in L$, and
- $f : S^n \rightarrow S$ is a transition function.

More informally, a CA is a set of cells arranged in a regular grid (of any dimension) that are in a certain state at each point in time. With evolving time, a cell's state changes depending on the state of the cell itself and the state of neighboring cells. These state changes are described by the given transition function. We will restrict ourselves to 2D cellular automata; that is, the cells are arranged in a 2D grid. For practical reasons, we further assume the lattice to have a finite size. A cellular automaton is a discrete system in space and time since the space is divided into discrete cells and the evolution of the cells (the change of states) takes place in finite time steps. Probably the best known example of a CA is Conway's game of life, popularized in Martin Gardner's *Scientific American* columns (Gardner, 1983). We will provide a second example to clarify the concept.

The following cellular automaton models an excitable medium. Excitable media appear in different situations. An example might be a forest or prairie fire where each discretized part of the forest can be either burning, burnt down, or

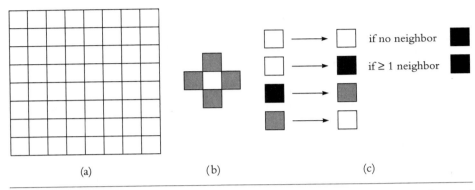

FIGURE 4.1 Visualization of the CA from the example given in the text: visualizes the lattice of cells (a), the used 4-neighborhood (b), and the transition rule (c).

recovering. Other examples include nerve and muscle tissue or many chemical systems. For our model, the lattice L is a regular 2D grid made of square cells (see Figure 4.1(b)). For each cell, we consider a 4-neighborhood as can be seen in Figure 4.1(b). S contains three states:

- 0, meaning the cell is in a resting state,
- 1, meaning the cell is in an excited state, and
- 2, meaning the cell is recovering.

The evolution of the cells is characterized by the following rules: a resting cell remains resting unless one neighbor is excited. In this case the cell becomes excited. An excited cell becomes recovering in the next step. A recovering cell becomes resting. To summarize, more formally, the transition function f is as follows:

$$f(0) = \begin{cases} 0 \text{ if no neighbor} = 2 \\ 1 \text{ if at least one neighbor} = 2 \end{cases}$$
$$f(1) = 0$$
$$f(2) = 1$$

The example in Figure 4.2 shows the development of a set of cells over ten steps.

Cellular automata provide an intuitive model to simulate water and paint distribution on paper as we will see in the next section.

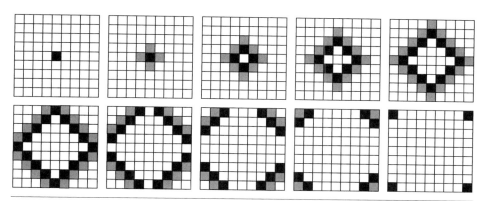

FIGURE 4.2 Configuration of the CA for the first ten steps (top left to bottom right).

Ink Transfer and Diffusion Model

To model the transfer of ink from the brush onto the paper as well as the distribution of ink on the paper, we will use a 2D cellular automaton with a finite grid size representing the paper plane. Basically, this is an array of cells, each of which has the ability to hold a certain amount of water and paint (dissolved in the water). The cell array can be thought of as an ice-cube tray where paint is filled into the single containers; if a container is full, paint flows into neighboring ones.

The cellular automaton that is used for the simulation is as follows:

- *Cells* For each cell P_{ij} the position on the grid is given by the two indices i and j.

- *States* The contents of a cell is described by two variables W_{ij} and I_{ij} representing the amount of water and ink, respectively. These numbers can be interpreted differently, for example, as percentage values or the number of "paint and water particles,"[1] depending on the model used for further computations.

- *Neighborhood* For our purposes it is sufficient to use a 4-neighborhood system (also called Neumann-neighborhood) where each cell has four neighbors,

---

1. The term *particles* in this sense has nothing to do with particle systems; it should emphasize only that a discrete model is used where the contents of a cell consists of W_{ij} indivisible "units" of water and I_{ij} "units" of ink.

namely, at the top, bottom, left, and right. Formally, the neighbors to cell P_{ij} are $P_{i,j+1}$, $P_{i,j-1}$, $P_{i+1,j}$, and $P_{i-1,j}$. It is also possible to use the Moore-neighborhood with eight neighbors to each cell (including diagonal cells), but this complicates the computations. In both cases, special care has to be taken with the cells at the grid boundaries.

◆ *State transition* If we denote the state of the cell P_{ij} at a given time t as $S_{ij}(t) = (W_{ij}(t), I_{ij}(t))$, then the transition function f translates this state to

$$S_{ij}(t + \Delta t) = f(S_{ij}(t), S_k(t) \mid k \in N).$$

We describe the concrete implementation of the transition function in more detail later.

Modeling Paper

The paper is represented as the grid of cells of the CA. Using no additional information would result in an ideal plane and unstructured paper that has no resemblance in reality. Real-world paper, however, is made out of fibers that give the paper surface its typical texture and structure. These fibers produce a capillary attraction that is responsible for the behavior of the ink and thus for the effects achieved when painting.

To model the fiber structure of the paper, the cells are modified in a way that each of them can hold only a limited amount of water and paint. We extend the state of a cell S_{ij} by adding two variables B_{ij} and C_{ij}, which are constants chosen initially proportional to the thickness of the paper. B_{ij} describes the height of the cell's "bottom," and C_{ij} describes the maximum capacity of the cell. Algorithm 4.1 creates a paper structure by means of modifying these variables (see Figure 4.3).

The fibers can be generated in a variety of ways; the most convenient is a procedure that creates randomly placed fibers, but an interactive placement is also possible. For special paper structures, a library of predefined fiber positions could be created and used. As a result of Algorithm 4.1, each cell is assigned a bottom height and a maximum fill height, which is then used in the painting process to limit the amount of water and ink being placed in this cell.

```
1   foreach cell P_ij do
2       choose C_ij and B_ij proportional to the paper thickness
3   od
4   for i := 1 to m do
5       generate a 2D line segment on the paper
6       foreach cell under the line segment do
7           (B_ij, C_ij) := (B_ij − ΔB, C_ij + ΔC)
8       od
9   od
```

ALGORITHM 4.1 Modeling the fiber structures of the paper. The constant m in the second loop corresponds to the number of fibers placed on the paper.

Modeling Brushes

The original intention behind the simulation was to produce images resembling *Suibokuga* paintings.[2] These paintings are made with brushes composed of bristles that are arranged in a cylindrical cone. The ink that is transferred to the brush is kept in the narrow spaces between the bristles due to capillary attraction. When painting, ink flows toward the tip of the brush until the brush runs dry. Additional effects arise from an unequal ink distribution in the brush or from the change of pressure or velocity with which the brush is applied to the paper. An unusual but effective way of simulating this behavior is to use a second CA that represents the brush.

For every cell in this first CA, the initial states are set appropriately. This involves the choice of two constants B_{ij} and C_{ij}, which describe the "thickness" of the brush. These constants are similar to the ones introduced for modeling the paper structure. At the brush tip, only a small amount of water (ink) can be held while at the end this amount is much bigger.

When painting with the brush, ink flows toward the tip, which can be modeled by changing the bottom height for each cell in an appropriate way: $B_{ij} = B_{ij} + \theta x$. In this equation, x is the distance of cell P_{ij} to the brush tip, and θ is a constant proportional to the gradient of the brush. Moreover, ink flows

---

2. Suibokuga is a style of traditional Chinese monochrome painting (usually black ink on white paper).

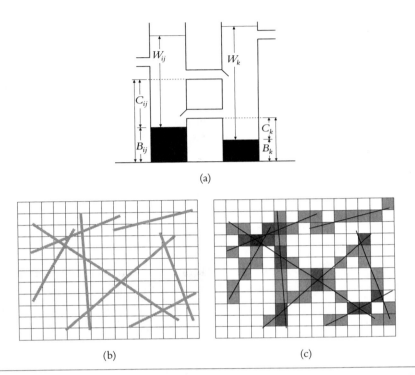

(a)

(b)   (c)

FIGURE 4.3 Paper model using cellular automata: variables describing the cell's state (a), placing line segments to describe paper fibers (b), and height field generated from the line segments (c).

unevenly within the brush, yielding many of the effects that can be observed in watercolor paintings. In the simulation, a 2D noise function F of the same resolution as the CA is added to the bottom heights of the cells: $B_{ij} = B_{ij} + F(i,j)$. Finally, the effect of bristles can be introduced in the model by a process similar to introducing fibers in the paper model. Line segments parallel to the bristle direction (typically toward the brush tip) are generated, and for all the cells lying under these line segments the bottom height and the maximum fill are adapted.

The steps described so far model a brush that is used to paint on the paper. When painting a stroke, a constant pressure is assumed that is applied to the brush. The paper contact side of the brush CA moves in the stroke direction while maintaining horizontal (or vertical) posture against the grid coordinates of the paper CA. Drawing a stroke means transferring ink from the brush to the paper. This causes the cells of the CA representing the brush to become empty and the cells of the CA representing the paper to be filled. After the stroke has been drawn, in both CAs the cells' states have to be updated. We will describe only the paper side of this process since this explains how watercolor effects can be simulated.

Modeling the Painting Process

The paint process starts with transferring ink and water particles from the brush to the paper. This adds a certain amount of water and ink to the cells, and the transition function is then responsible for distributing this among the cells. This is done in four steps, each of which deals with a certain aspect of water and ink distribution on the paper. In the following descriptions, we assume that the computations are carried out for each time step.

1. *Transfer and diffusion of water particles*   If a cell P_{ij} is filled with water, it will overflow, and water is transferred to the neighboring cells. At the same time, overflowing water from the neighboring cells is transferred to the cell P_{ij}. Thus the resulting amount of water in P_{ij} is computed as the sum of water flowing into P_{ij} (denoted as $\Delta W_{k \to ij}$) reduced by the amount of water flowing out of P_{ij} (denoted as $\Delta W_{ij \to k}$).

$$W_{ij}(t + \Delta t) = W_{ij}(t) + \sum_{k \in N} (\Delta W_{k \to ij} - \Delta W_{ij \to k})$$

If these calculations result in $W_{ij} < 0$, then $W_{ij} = 0$ is assumed. The flow of water between neighboring cells can be computed from the properties of the involved cells, especially their bottom heights, their fuel capacity, and the actual fill.

2. *Transfer of ink particles accompanying water particles*   With the transfer of water, ink is also transported from one cell to another. The number of ink particles depends on the concentration of ink in the transferred water:

$$I_{ij}(t + \Delta t) = I_{ij}(t) + \sum_{k \in N} (\Delta I_{k \to ij} - \Delta I_{ij \to k}) \tag{4.1}$$

In Equation (4.1), the amount of ink flowing either into P_{ij} (denoted as $\Delta I_{k \to ij}$) or out of P_{ij} (denoted as $\Delta I_{ij \to k}$) is computed from the amount of transferred water and the ink concentration as follows:

$$\Delta I_{k \to ij} = \Delta W_{k \to ij} \frac{I_k(t)}{W_k(t)}$$

$$\Delta I_{ij \to k} = \Delta W_{ij \to k} \frac{I_{ij}(t)}{W_{ij}(t)}$$

3. *Transfer of ink particles to balance the concentration*   After water and ink have been transferred to and from neighboring cells, the ink concentration has to be balanced out since solutions of two fluids tend to balance the concentration to the most stable state.

$$I_{ij}(t + \Delta t) = I_{ij}(t) + \sum_{k \in N} \Delta I_{dk \to ij}$$

The change in ink concentration $\Delta I_{dk \to ij}$ depends on the diffusion coefficient of ink in water (β) and the water concentrations in the two cells where the balancing takes place:

$$\Delta I_{dk \to ij} = \beta \left(I_k - W_k \frac{I_{ij} + I_k}{W_{ij} + W_k} \right) = \beta \frac{I_k W_{ij} - I_{ij} W_{ij}}{W_{ij} + W_k}$$

4. *Evaporation of water*   In each time step, a certain amount of water evaporates so that the paint gets drier. This is modeled by subtracting a quantity of water from the cell's contents, that is, $W_{ij}(t + \Delta t) = W_{ij}(t) - \Delta W$. If all water is evaporated, the ink particles I_{ij} remain in the cell P_{ij} as dry ink.

These four steps describe the local transition function f of the CA and are carried out in each time step. The model is rather complex and takes into account several properties of watercolor when applied to paper. Nevertheless, it is a compromise between a complete simulation that would include many more steps and that would extend over and above the observed local behavior, and a simple, much idealized approach. Given the CA model from earlier, almost any complexity of a transfer and diffusion model can be realized by choosing an appropriate transition function f. As with any CA-based model, this painting simulation is particularly well suited for a parallel implementation that reduces the computation time but creates other bottlenecks since communication between the processors has to be taken into account.

4.1.2 Computer-Generated Watercolor Using Fluid Simulation

In the first approach, the CA was used as the basis for the development of the simulation. We will now describe a second, empirically based way of creating the effects of watercolor on paper. Here also, CAs play a certain role, but more as a tool for doing the calculations in a discrete, pixel-based plane. The combination of the CA with a more physically based paper model and a fluid simulation leads to more effects such as edge darkening, backruns, and glazing. An effective watercolor simulation does not study only the physical properties of the medium but also the characteristics that make artists use this technique.

Watercolor Effects

Watercolor is a very interesting artistic technique since it allows for many effects that are impossible with other media. The most important property of watercolor that has to be taken into consideration when developing a simulation is that watercolor paint only spreads freely when the surface (the paper) is wet. This is the reason for the development of two different painting techniques: *wet-on-wet*, where the paint is applied to already wet paper and thus can flow freely, and *wet-on-dry*, where the paint is applied to dry paper causing a variety of effects. The following list contains some of the most important of these effects:

- *Edge darkening* If watercolor paint is applied to dry paper, the surface tension of the water (which is also applied to the paper since the paint is actually a solution of paint particles in water) does not allow the paint to spread freely over the area of the paper. While drying off at the border of the wet areas, water evaporates and has to be replenished from the interior of the wet area. This also moves pigment to the borders, causing these areas to be darker than the interior.

- *Backruns* When water from a brushstroke flows back into a still damp area from an earlier stroke, it pushes pigment along, creating shapes that are the result of an uneven water flow depending on the dampness of different parts of the paper.

- *Flow patterns* In a similar process, patterns are created when using the wet-on-wet technique where the surface allows the paint to spread freely. Because of the decreasing water pressure and the paper structure, feathery shapes are created that follow the direction of water flow.

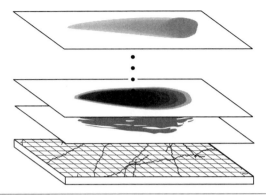

FIGURE 4.4 An image is regarded as a stack of layers or *washes*. Each wash contains a different simulation process and, when combined, yield the image.

Artists deliberately use these effects when creating watercolor paintings by adding plain water to the painting or by letting the brushstrokes run into each other. Since all these effects can be described physically by fluid dynamics, the simulation process described in the next section is mainly based on this technique.

The Fluid Simulation Setup and Algorithms

To produce the effects mentioned, an approach like the one in Section 4.1.1 can probably be chosen, but the needed transition functions would be very complicated to develop and compute, resulting in very time-consuming algorithms. Instead, the model consists of several layers, so-called washes, over a more or less rough paper surface as can be seen in Figure 4.4. Such a wash can be thought of as a layer of paint (and water) added one after another to create the painting. In each wash, a *wet-area mask* limits the area where the simulation process takes place. This mask is simply a bitmap where a value of one indicates that the paper is wet; otherwise, the respective bit is set to zero. The fluid simulation is carried out in each wash independently; at the end, all washes are combined to yield the image.

At the bottom of this "stack" of washes lies the paper surface. Modeling the paper and the paper structure is done in a similar manner as in the CA approach. Each cell of the paper surface (represented as a lattice in a CA) is assigned a height that limits the capacity of the cell and thus creates the paper structure.

FIGURE 4.5 A wash is composed of three layers, each of which is responsible for a different part of the simulation.

For the fluid simulation, each wash itself comprises three layers as shown in Figure 4.5:

1. *Shallow water layer* In this layer, water flows across the paper in the areas indicated by the wet-area mask. Pigment is lifted by the water, transported, and deposited in a different location. To model this water flow, especially the velocity of the water, the pressure of the water, the concentration of pigment, and the slope of the paper (the gradient of the paper's height) have to be taken into account.

2. *Pigment deposition layer* The processes of adsorption and desorption control the transfer of pigments between the shallow water layer and the pigment deposition layer.

3. *Capillary layer* Within the capillary layer, water transport through the pores of the paper is simulated. This allows the wet area on the paper to expand. Based on the water saturation or fluid-holding capacity of the paper, the wet-area mask is manipulated here.

As mentioned, all quantities observed in the simulation are discretized over the paper and can thus be regarded as the "state" of the cells of the underlying CA.

The simulation itself takes as input for each wash the initial wet-area mask, the velocity and pressure of the water, and the pigment concentration. All these values can be obtained from a brushstroke with which wet paint is deposited on the paper. The simulation main loop iterates over a given number of time steps and performs basically four different steps (see Algorithm 4.2). We will investigate each of the steps in turn.

1. *Moving water in the shallow water layer* To obtain realistic results, the physical properties of the water flow must be obeyed as well as the effects that occur in

```
1  foreach time step do
2      move water in the shallow water layer
3      move pigments
4      simulate pigment adsorption and desorption
5      simulate capillary flow
6  od
```

ALGORITHM 4.2 Main loop for the fluid simulation within one wash.

watercolor paintings. Thus, several conditions must be satisfied in this step. First of all, the water flow has to be restricted to the wet-area mask, and any water flow has to lead to a concentration equilibrium; that is, water flows from areas of high concentration to areas of low concentration. This condition is satisfied by implementing the basic shallow water equations.[3] For doing so, these equations have to be discretized in time and solved, for instance, using Euler's method. Another condition to be satisfied is that water flow is influenced by the paper texture, which is done by adding respective conditions to the fluid simulation.

Finally, an observational quality of watercolor painting is that pigment tends to flow toward the edges of the wet area over time. This so-called edge darkening effect is indeed one of the most striking features of watercolor paintings, and artists make deliberate use of this effect. There is also a physical explanation for this, which was already given. In the simulation, this effect can be gained by increasing the water pressure near the edges.

2. *Moving pigments*   The transport of pigments within the shallow water layer depends on the local velocities of the water. Since these velocities are computed in the first step of the simulation, these values are now used to determine how much pigment has to be moved from one cell to its neighbors.

3. *Pigment adsorption and desorption*   In each time step, a certain amount of pigment is adsorbed by the pigment deposition layer and also a certain amount

---

3. The equations that can be found, for instance, in Vreugdenhil (1994) are of the form
$\frac{\delta u}{\delta t} = -\left(\frac{\delta u^2}{\delta x^2} + \frac{\delta uv}{\delta y^2}\right) + \mu\nabla^2 u - \frac{\delta p}{\delta x}$ and $\frac{\delta v}{\delta t} = -\left(\frac{\delta v^2}{\delta y^2} + \frac{\delta uv}{\delta x^2}\right) + \mu\nabla^2 v - \frac{\delta p}{\delta y}$.

is desorbed back into the fluid. This transfer of pigment between the shallow water layer and the pigment deposition layer simulates the deposition of pigment on the paper, a process that can be described by three variables, namely, the adsorption and desorption rate and the granulation. The latter determines how the paper height (and thus the paper structure) affects the pigment desorption.

4. *Capillary flow*   The wet area on the paper after a brushstroke (the area covered by the wet-area mask in the simulation) can slowly expand by capillary flow. Damp areas are created either by drying water or by moving water from wet areas into dry areas in the capillary layer. In contrast to the shallow water layer, where water flow is caused by momentum, here the flow of water is dominated by capillary effects. To simulate these, water is transported from one cell to its neighbors. If the capacity of a cell is exceeded, the wet-area mask is expanded to include this cell.

As can be seen from the preceding description, the simulation using fluid dynamics is more complicated than the first approach where all algorithms are coded directly in the transition function of the CA. The cellular automaton also plays an important role in the second approach; however, it can also be used independently from the actual simulation. The fluid simulation can also be carried out in the continuous domain and then be discretized to fit in the cells.

After carrying out the simulation, in both approaches the result is a two-dimensional array of "numbers" (namely, the states of the CA's cells), which has to be visualized correctly to finally create the image.

4.1.3 Rendering the Simulation Results

To actually create an image that represents the results of the painting simulation, the cell's states have to be visualized. Since the CA is based on a 2D grid of cells, they can be mapped directly onto color values in a bitmap.

For the first technique, where the cell's state consists only of two values (the amounts of water and ink "particles"), this mapping is a straightforward procedure. Since all ink particles have the same color, the concentration of ink in the water can be translated directly into color saturation values. If, for instance, we assume a bitmap where each pixel color is described in terms of the HSV color model, the hue value is determined from the color used for painting. The values of saturation and brightness are then free to be chosen depending on the water-to-ink ratio to be visualized. In summary, the CA-based technique is well suited for monochrome paintings as they appear in traditional Japanese art.

The second approach where different layers (washes) that can hold differently colored paint have to be combined is more challenging. We cannot perform a physically based computation of the resulting color since in real watercolor paintings brushes are not independent from each other placed one atop another. To compute the color for each pixel (CA cell, respectively), an optical composition of the layers is performed. There are several methods for composition of glazing layers, such as the Kubelka-Munk model.

This model is a theory describing the optical properties of a medium that transmits visible radiation largely by diffuse transmission such that objects are not seen distinctly through it. Each pigment is assigned a set of *adsorption coefficients K* and *scattering coefficients S*. These coefficients control the amount of energy (light) adsorbed or scattered back in the layer of pigment. The appropriate coefficients have been determined experimentally and, since they depend on the wavelength, differ for the red, green, and blue color channel.

Given the coefficients K and S as well as the thickness of the layer, the reflectance and transmittance through the layer can then be computed. Using the Kubelka-Munk model, we can then determine the overall reflectance and transmittance of two abutting layers. Successive computations yield the desired overall transmittance and reflectance for all layers and from this the respective color value.

These two approaches should suffice to demonstrate the simulation of watercolor paintings. It should be noted that—even though the results of both approaches are very promising (see Figure 4.6)—they resemble more a printed reproduction of a watercolor painting. This would be even more the case if you try to simulate oil paintings. The reason for this lies in the fact that real paintings are actually three dimensional. Many of the visual sensations when looking at a painting in a museum stem from reflections and shadows of small three-dimensional features that are created by adding layers of paint to the image. Nonetheless, this section has shown that astonishing results are possible when combining physical simulation with computer graphics methods. Besides physical simulations, it is also interesting to observe the physical properties of the result of a drawing or painting process, which will be the topic of the next section.

(a)   (b)

FIGURE 4.6 Examples of computer-generated watercolor paintings: (a) was created using the CA approach, whereas (b) is the result from the fluid simulation technique. (See also color insert.)

4.2 Simulating Pencils Drawing on Paper

A straightforward approach to the generation of line drawings by computer is to use line-drawing primitives offered by standard graphics packages and to tune them to account for parameters of hand-drawn sketches such as was shown in Chapter 3.

Another approach is to examine the physical pencils and the paper more closely at the level ascertainable with a microscope and to model the drawing process on this level. The results of such a simulation are then compared to real, handmade images to determine the extent to which the simulation goals have been met.

4.2.1 The Microscopic Level

Every pencil has a writing core (or "lead") that is made of a mixture of graphite, wax, and clay. The marks that a pencil makes on paper are due to the graphite; the wax acts as a lubricant; and the clay is used as a binding agent. The hardness of the lead depends on the ratio of graphite to clay and varies from about 90:4 by weight in very soft pencils to 4:5 in very hard ones. The wax is generally fixed in amount (5% by weight). The data for the different kinds of pencils and their composition is shown in Figure 4.7. The thickness of the lead can be approximated by a linear interpolation of the thickness of the hardest pencil (2 mm for 9H) and the softest pencil (4 mm for 8B).

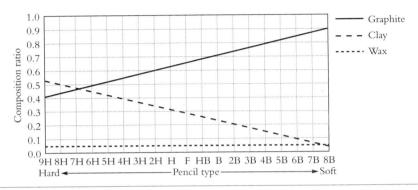

FIGURE 4.7 Relationship between graphite, clay, and wax in the composition of different kinds of pencils. Hard pencils have roughly equal proportions of graphite to clay, whereas soft pencils are made mostly of graphite.

While pencils can be modeled in such a straightforward manner, paper is more involved because it comes in a great variety of weights and textures. The weight of the drawing paper determines its thickness and is measured in grams per square inch (gsi), ranging from 48 gsi to 300 gsi. Paper textures for pencil work (categorized as smooth, semi-rough, or rough) have "teeth" forming peaks and valleys that enable lead material from pencils to adhere to the paper.

Paper can be studied with an electron microscope to see what effects different pencils have when applied to the paper. Our example uses moderately toothed paper of medium weight. Figure 4.8 shows images taken with an electron microscope. In the left column, three top views are given, enlarged 200 times. They show empty paper and the effect of drawing with a soft and a hard pencil, respectively. The right column shows cross-sectional views that are enlarged 2,000 times for the same kinds of pencils. In the images of paper that has been drawn on, lead deposited on the paper appears dark. Note how the hard pencil leads to sharper edges of areas in which the lead is deposited compared to the soft pencil. Indeed, the paper fibers are in fact *damaged* by the pencil.

4.2.2   A Model

We will now turn to an abstraction to model the observations made in the real drawing situation. We will treat this model in three parts corresponding to the pencil, the paper, and the interaction between these.

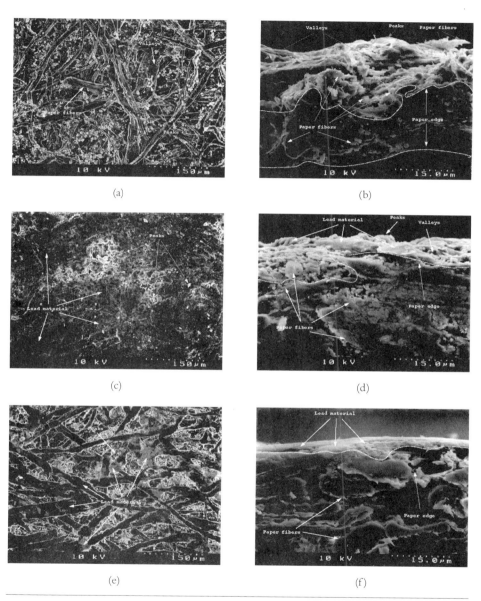

FIGURE 4.8 Different levels of magnification of a top view and a cross-sectional view of paper without marks (first row), paper shaded with a soft pencil (second row), and paper shaded with a hard pencil (third row): (a) enlargement ×200, empty paper; (b) enlargement ×2,000, empty paper; (c) enlargement ×200, soft pencil; (d) enlargement ×2,000, soft pencil; (e) enlargement ×200, hard pencil; (f) enlargement ×2,000, hard pencil.

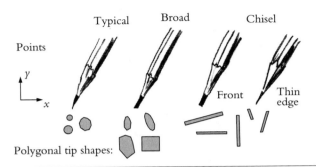

FIGURE 4.9 The model treats pencil tips as convex polygons with three or more edges.

Pencil Model

For this model, important aspects of a pencil are first to what extent and how it has been sharpened, and second, how much pressure the user applies. For the first aspect, we consider pencils to be sharpened with a particular shape. We will define three such shapes (typical, broad, and chiseled) and treat a pencil tip as comprising a convex polygon with three or more edges. The different shapes are then modeled by adjusting the shapes of the polygons accordingly. Examples are shown in Figure 4.9.

The amount of lead deposited on the paper depends in part on the pressure that the artist applies to the pencil. Computationally, this pressure is treated as a set of coefficients c that (can) vary over the pencil tip. For a pencil tip defined by a polygon with n vertices $v_1, v_2, \ldots, v_n$, we consider that there are $n + 1$ pressure coefficients $P_c = \{c_0, c_1, \ldots, c_n\}$, where c_0 is the coefficient at a primary location within the polygon (usually at its geometric center) and the other c_i are the coefficients at the respective locations of the vertices v_i. The values of the pressure coefficents at other locations on the pencil tip are defined by linear interpolation. A higher c_i, means more surface area of the pencil is in contact with the paper.

Figure 4.10 illustrates this concept by showing the distribution of lead on paper as a function of the pencil tip's geometry. In the top, a sample polygonal tip shape is shown in a top view. In the second row, three different sample cross-sectional views are shown. A value of $c_0 = 1.0$ is used, whereas in (a) $c_1 = c_5 = 0.2$, in (b) $c_1 = c_5 = 0.5$, and in (c) $c_1 = c_5 = 0.9$. Note how a higher pressure broadens the bottom surface of the pencil and thus enlarges the contact area with the paper.

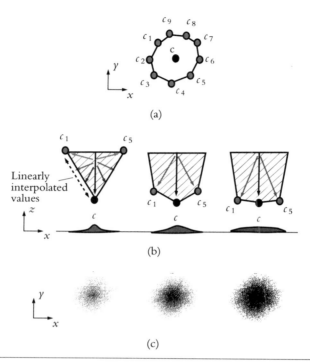

FIGURE 4.10 Distribution of lead on paper as a function of the pencil tip's geometry: top view of tip shape (a), three possible cross sections between c_1 and c_5 and the resulting pressure distribution (b), and visualization of lead deposited on paper (c).

In general, the pressure coefficients represent the ratio of the pencil tip's surface that has contact with the paper. The third row in Figure 4.10 shows the respective pressure distributions over the cross section, while the last row shows the respective marks deposited by the lead. From this illustration, the effect of varying the pencil tip geometry and pressure coefficients on the mark left behind is evident.

Paper Model

Paper can be modeled as a height field ranging between zero and one, that is, $0 \leq h \leq 1$. This height field either can be generated procedurally or can be generated by extracting it from a digitized paper sample.

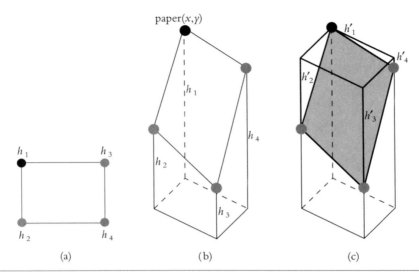

paper(x,y)

(a) (b) (c)

FIGURE 4.11 A paper grain, seen from above in (a), is defined as a volume (b). The empty volume above the grain (c) can be filled with lead.

The smallest element of the paper's rough surface is the *grain*. It can be regarded as a container that is then filled with lead material from the pencil. A grain itself is defined by giving the paper heights at the four corners h_1, h_2, h_3, and h_4, where h_1 is at the paper location (x, y), and the other coefficients are its three neighbors as shown in Figure 4.11(a). We assume that each such grain can be filled with at most an amount T_ν of lead, a value that is to be determined beforehand. Two cases can occur.

1. If for a grain $h_i = h_j$ $\forall i, j : 1 \leq i, j \leq 4$, that is, all heights defining the grain are equal, then T_ν is a constant F_s, which is the maximum amount of lead necessary to fill the flat surface of the grain. Basically, only a bit of lead gets deposited forming a thin layer. For the sake of clarity, we can assign F_s a specific value like 500 lpu (lead particle units).

2. If there exists at least one grain height such that $\exists i, j : h_i \neq h_j$, we define V_g to be the volume bounded from below by the top of the grain, and from the top by the lowest possible horizontal plane not cutting the grain (Figure 4.11(c)) (see Exercise 4.4 for how to compute V_g). Now the maximum amount of lead

that can be deposited in the grain is $T_v = V_g \cdot F_v$. Here F_v is the maximum amount of lead material necessary to completely fill a grain's volume (for $F_v \in [1{,}000, 3{,}000]$ lpu). F_v corresponds to a maximal lead absorption rate based on the type of paper being used. In principle, this means that lead gets deposited on uneven parts of the paper, and the amount of lead deposited here depends on the heights of the respective paper "teeth" (given the grain's height coefficients).

The proposed values for F_v and F_s are based on the observations of real drawings and can be changed to model different paper properties.

Finally, we can compute the distribution of lead T_v among the paper locations at h_k in the grain. The higher the height h_k, the more lead will stick to the location. Each of the locations has assigned a variable L_k, which is the local lead volume for k. For the location k in one grain g, we set

$$L_{k_g} = \frac{h_k}{\sum_{i=1}^{4} h_i} \cdot T_v \tag{4.2}$$

Since each h_k is shared by at most four grains, the final value for L_k is the sum of the values for the (up to) four grains sharing h_k.

Model of Pencil-Paper Interaction

With the two models, we now have a basis for exploring the interaction of the pencil with the paper. The pencil hardness and the pressure applied on the pencil are the main variables that influence the final drawing. For each grain in the paper, the amount of lead has to be computed that sticks to this particular location. Before we can compute this volume, the grains that are touched by the pencil's tip have to be identified, and an average pressure value (P_a) for each of them has to be computed. The amount of lead is then determined in the following four steps:

1. *Compute the depth of lead in the grain*   The depth D_l to which lead penetrates the height field is proportional to the pressure P_a applied to the pencil (although it cannot penetrate deeper than h_{min}):

$$D_l = \max(h_{min}, P_a \cdot h_{max}) \tag{4.3}$$

This means geometrically that a plane is determined that cuts the grains at the height D_l.

2. *Compute the volume bitten* Some of the lead is "bitten" by the paper's surface fibers, meaning that it is deposited in that part of a grain's volume above the clipping plane defined by D_l. More precisely, this value B_v corresponds to the volume of the rectilinear polyhedron with four rectilinear sides of heights $D_l - h_i$, respectively. Note that if all heights of the grain are above or equal to D_l, then the whole grain "bites" the lead and is filled completely, that is, $B_v = T_v$.

3. *Scale the volume according to the pencil type* The amount of lead deposited in a grain is scaled according to the hardness of the pencil. A scaling factor s is used for $0 \leq s \leq 1$, where a low value corresponds to hard pencils, a high value to soft pencils. This scaling factor can be modeled as a constant, but more precise results are achieved when making it depend on the applied pressure. Hence, the scaled volume computes as $B_v = B_v \cdot s(P_a)$.

4. *Compute the lead's distribution among the grain's heights* The higher a grain is, the more lead will stick to it. Hence, the amount of lead deposited at a position of height h_k is defined to be proportional to L_{k_g}.

Putting it all together, the final volume of lead bitten is distributed proportionally to the heights h_k in each grain:

$$B_k = B_v \cdot \frac{h_k}{\left(\sum_{i=1}^{4} h_i\right)} \cdot s(P_a) \qquad (4.4)$$

Finally, the intensity of light at each grain must be determined. The more graphite at a grain k, the less light I_k is reflected. The amount of graphite in the pencil is modeled with the pencil itself by giving the ratio between wax, graphite, and clay as described in Section 4.2.1. Given an amount of graphite G_k at a particular grain k, if the total amount of lead needed to completely cover the paper's flat surface (including filling the grain's volume) is $F_t = F_s + F_v$, then the reflected intensity I_k can be approximated by

$$I_k = 1 - \frac{G_k}{F_t} \qquad (4.5)$$

which is the portion of the reflected intensity at the given grain k.

(a)

(b)

| 4B pencil | 4B pencil | 6B pencil | 6H pencil |
| Medium pressure | Heavy pressure | Medium pressure | Light pressure |

FIGURE 4.12 Handmade pencil shading (a) compared to simulation results (b) using a medium-weight, moderate-tooth paper.

4.2.3 Results

Figure 4.12 shows some results of this simulation. The top row is hand-drawn, and the bottom row shows the corresponding simulation. Note that there is a large correspondence between the handmade drawings and the simulation. The tone or intensity of the simulated images especially resemble the original ones, which leads to the conclusion that the lead material distribution over the paper's surface is modeled appropriately. Further, the roughness of the paper is well represented since it is nicely comparable with the hand-drawn samples. Figure 4.13 shows

(a)   (b)   (c)

FIGURE 4.13 Simulation results made by automatically sketching predefined images: 3B pencil (a), 6B pencil (b), and 6H pencil (c).

some other examples of renditions of objects made with the simulation described in this section.

4.3 Simulating Woodcuts and Engravings

The basis for the development of a model for the simulation of watercolor as well as pencil drawings was an observation of how the real-world tools work. A respective model was derived by taking into account either physical processes (like fluid dynamics) or the behavior of the tools on a microscopic level. This often results in computationally expensive models since the underlying physical processes are quite complicated. Computer graphics, however, offers a different approach that mimics the *results* of artistic techniques. If we can modify well-developed (standard) computer graphics techniques such that the rendered results visually resemble handcrafted images, there would be no need to perform physical simulations or computations on a microscopic level. In the following, this approach will be demonstrated for the simulation of woodcuts and copperplate engravings.

Both woodcuts and copperplates are engraving techniques and can be traced to the Middle Ages. Before other reproduction techniques were devised, copperplates especially were often used for technical illustrations. Later on, both methods became well known as artistic techniques. One of the best-known artists in this field is Albrecht Dürer. Engravings are made by cutting lines into a metal sheet (for copperplates) or a wooden block (for woodcuts) with some engraving tool. These engraved lines are then filled with paint and finally transferred to a sheet of paper when pressing the plate onto it. This process could be modeled directly by modeling the engraved plate, the filling with ink, and the transfer process of ink to the paper. Indeed, this has been done by various authors (see the Bibliography for further information). Another possibility that will be discussed here is determining the characteristics of the resulting images and reproducing these characteristics. We will study two of these reproduction techniques. The first uses a three-dimensional description of the scene to be portrayed and uses a modified raytracing algorithm to achieve a copperplate impression. The other one is based on procedural screening and thus works completely in 2D.

A typical copperplate is a drawing that consists of lines of varying thickness and single dots. Furthermore, copperplates and engravings are bi-level images, that is, they do not contain gray values. For presenting the scene objects, contour lines play an important role; they are usually somewhat overemphasized. Shading is done using hatching lines in various thicknesses, distances, and orientations.

4.3.1 A Raytracing Approach for Copperplates

To modify a raytracer in such a way that the resulting images resemble copperplate engravings, the geometry processing routines are kept and changes are introduced only in the computation of the intensity values for each pixel. The basis for raytracing in general is a so-called ray query, where for each pixel p in the output image a ray is shot in the scene. The starting point for the ray is the pixel position p, which travels along the direction r and finally hits a scene object. The result of the ray query is the first intersection point $t = (t_x, t_y, t_z)$ of the ray with the scene.

For this intersection point, the object being hit as well as different parameters such as the object's material, the surface normal at the intersection point, and the intensity values according to a local or global illumination model are determined when performing standard raytracing. To mimic copperplates, especially the last point—the computation of the intensity value at the intersection point—has to be modified.

In general, the copperplate rendering process is performed in four steps after determining the intersection point, as is shown in Algorithm 4.3. The five steps given in the algorithm are performed for each image. Since the first three do not differ from the general raytracing technique, we will not go into details here. We will concentrate instead on the remaining two steps.

---

1   $t =$ intersection point as a result of a ray query
2   determine material properties at t
3   determine color (intensity) value at t for a given illumination model
4   compute geometric and intensity parameters for hatching lines
5   post-processing to achieve the optical properties of copperplate images

---

ALGORITHM 4.3   General procedure for copperplate rendering using raytracing.

Creating Hatching Lines

Looking at copperplate images reveals that in most cases each object is hatched separately with a slightly different hatching. This means that hatching parameters can be stored together with material properties for each object. In the most simple case, a new value a_0 is introduced in the material description of an object, and after the ray query, for each intersection point a value l is computed as

$$l = (\lambda \bmod a_0)/a_0 \qquad (4.6)$$

These values are calculated for each pixel and yield circular patterns. These circular patterns are well suited for some objects, but the repertoire of copperplate images is not limited to these. The use of straight hatching lines will widen the expressiveness and also give in many cases a better method to convey shape and illumination. For the creation of straight hatching lines, the objects in the scene are overlaid with a set of parallel and equidistant planes in 3D space. Each plane set is described by the plane coefficients e_1, e_2, e_3, e_4 for the first plane and an offset parameter a that models the distance between the parallel planes. Let $t = (t_x, t_y, t_z)$ be the intersection point of the ray with an object. If we compute f as the distance of the intersection point from the first plane

$$f = e_1 t_x + e_2 t_y + e_3 t_z + e_4$$

the normalized distance b from a plane with offset a is given by

$$b = \begin{cases} (f \bmod a)/a & \text{if } f \geq 0 \\ a - (f \bmod a)/a & \text{if } f < 0 \end{cases} \qquad (4.7)$$

Plotting the values of b for each pixel creates a structure of parallel lines that is seen on the object's surface (see Figure 4.14).

We can combine several hatching patterns generated this way by using several sets of planes and computing the values of b_i for each set i separately. A combination of the patterns is achieved by a weighted sum $b = \sum_i c_i b_i$, where the weight

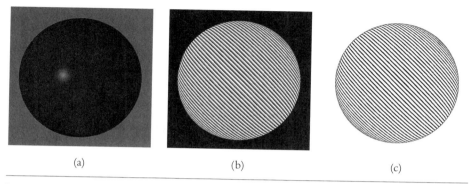

(a) (b) (c)

FIGURE 4.14 Plotting the distances from the planes reveals hatching patterns: image generated using standard raytracing (a), image generated using the procedure outlined (b), image generated after post-processing (threshold quantization) (c).

parameter c_i, again, depends on the surface material of the objects being rendered. Summing up two different hatchings results in a triangle pattern, which is not always desirable. The operator $\cup$ defined in Equation (4.8) avoids this behavior. Given two hatchings x_1 and x_2, an overlay of these hatchings is computed by

$$x_1 \cup x_2 = \begin{cases} \max(x_1, x_2) & \text{if } x_2 \geq 0 \\ \min(x_1, -x_2) & \text{if } x_2 < 0 \end{cases} \qquad (4.8)$$

For successfully mimicking the copperplate look, the thickness of the generated lines in the hatching patterns depends on the lighting conditions. The raytracing approach gives the correct lighting calculation for free so that we need only to modify the hatching calculation with that respect. To take different properties of different object materials into account, we introduce two more parameters—h_f and h_b—to the material description. The line thickness is then modified using a term $(h - h_b)h_f$ with h being a weighted sum of the RGB components of the computed color value for the given pixel.

For finishing the third step in the generation of a copperplate image, we connect the preceding computations such that for each pixel value in the output image a value κ is calculated using

$$\kappa = \bigcup_i c_i \cdot b_i \cup l \cdot c_0 + \sum_i d_i \cdot b_i + l \cdot d_0 + (h - h_b) \cdot h_f \qquad (4.9)$$

This requires the introduction of two more weight factors c_i and d_i that are to be defined for the object's material. This equation combines hatching lines stemming from different plane sets and uses Equations (4.6) and (4.7) for calculating l and b_i, respectively. Note that this equation explicitly includes the circular patterns from Equation (4.6).

Adding Edges and Optical Effects

The image generated in the previous step has to be manipulated in two ways to finally yield a copperplate look-alike image. First, a discretization has to be performed, and second, additional information has to be brought into the image. This additional information pertains especially to edges that greatly enhance the visual perception of the portrayed objects and that are an integral part of any copperplate image.

Edges in the sense we are using this term are sudden changes in the image domain with respect to certain properties. What we are looking for are edges that describe geometric changes rather than changes in color values as they would appear in photorealistic rendering caused, for instance, by textures or lighting conditions. Finding these edges can be done using image processing operators, but instead of working on the rendered image these operators work on pixel-based representations of geometric values. This technique is quite common in non–photorealistic computer graphics and will be covered in depth in Chapter 6. For the time being, consider an image where for each pixel the z-value of the intersection point t is stored. Then, applying an edge detection operator on this image will reveal edges that represent sudden changes in z-depth, which are almost always associated with object silhouettes. Another possibility is to apply the same technique on an image that represents the normal vector coordinates at the intersection point or even the angle between the normal vector and the query ray.

Raytracing offers several ways to include optical effects in an image that range from reflection and refraction to special transmission functions and caustics. Reflection and refraction are computed by considering second or higher order rays that emanate from the computed intersection point and can be followed in the same way as the rays shot from the pixel position. Considering these higher order rays in photorealistic image generation means adding the color value computed for them to the color value for the initial ray's pixel position. Even though reflection and refraction are seldom included in handmade copperplates, the proposed method allows for a visualization for such properties. Instead of computing the RGB values in a recursive manner by following higher order rays, the value κ is computed. Let κ_i be the value for the current (i-th) depth according to Equation (4.9), and κ_{ij} the value for the j-th ray[4] emanating from the intersection point in depth i. If we further assume c_{ij} and d_{ij} are proper weighting factors, then the value of $\kappa_{i,\text{total}}$ computes as

$$\kappa_{i,\text{total}} = \kappa_i \cup \bigcup_j \kappa_{i-1,j} \cdot c_{ij} + \sum_j \kappa_{i-1,j} \cdot d_{ij}$$

When computing these values from higher order rays, it is necessary to make some design decisions so that reflection and refraction are actually distinguishable from the hatchings that visualize the object's surface (and that are computed from first order rays). These design decisions are represented in the choice of the weighting factors c_{ij} and d_{ij}.

Computing the Final Image

The result of the computations from the last two sections are two images. The first one contains for each pixel the κ values, and the second one contains the results from the edge detection algorithm as stated earlier. To create a copperplate image, these two have to be combined in an appropriate manner. This post-processing step determines some of the optical properties of the copperplate images.

The first and most important step to be performed is a discretization of the pattern image. As already said, these images are gray-level images, where each pixel represents a value for κ. Computer-generated copperplates, however, are bi-level images, where each pixel represents either the presence or the absence of color (ink). The discretization can be performed using different techniques; mainly threshold operators or convolution algorithms are used here. As with any algorithms that discretize a gray-level image, aliasing problems may occur. This is already evident from the example images used throughout this section, where no anti-aliasing techniques have been used. The hatching lines are very sensitive with respect to aliasing so that—especially when creating low-resolution images—an anti-aliasing can yield better images.

The second issue that has to be dealt with in this final stage of the image generation is to combine the (at least two) intermediate images to yield a final rendition. Here, the computed edges are combined with the hatching lines by

---

4. j-th in this sense means that all $(i + 1)$th order rays that are considered here—reflected, refracted, and others—are enumerated and assigned an index j.

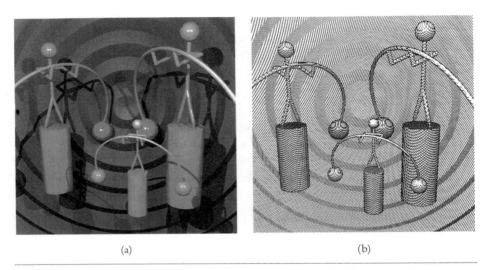

(a)   (b)

FIGURE 4.15 "Mobile" as computer-generated copperplate: standard raytracing (a) and copperplate (b). (See also color insert.)

merging the bitmaps pixelwise using an OR operator. If anti-aliasing techniques are used, the combination is somewhat more complicated but can also be done.

Altogether, this process of generating copperplate renditions depends highly on the resolution of the final image. Thus, the most crucial issue when using this raytracing approach is to find the correct parameters for the plane sets as well as the weighting factors in order to avoid moiré patterns. If these values are set properly, astounding results can be achieved, as can be seen in Figures 4.15 and 4.16.

4.3.2 An Image Processing Approach for Engravings

The raytracing approach for generating copperplates has several advantages but also some problems. One advantage is certainly the availability of three-dimensional information. Using raytracing means in this case that for any point in the image a wealth of information about position, normal vectors, surface materials, or lighting is readily available. The main drawback is that, at first, raytracing done at very high resolutions (which would be needed for copperplates) and with rather complex scenes can become quite time consuming. Furthermore, dealing with

(a) (b)

FIGURE 4.16 "Martian Bananas" as computer-generated copperplate: standard raytracing (a) and copperplate (b). (See also color insert.)

more complicated object shapes—for instance, human faces—makes raytracing not the method of choice. Such objects require fine-tuning and manipulating the parameters, which should even be possible in an interactive environment. What's more, objects like human faces are hard to model in three dimensions, and it would be desirable to work on a 2D image instead.

Taking this into consideration and looking back at the image-oriented techniques that were introduced in Chapter 2, we will find that (procedural) screening bears a high potential for reproducing the optical effects of copperplates. In the following, we will describe a technique that is based on screening using decomposition of the target image into several layers, each of which is treated with a different dither screen. These layers are then combined to yield the final image.

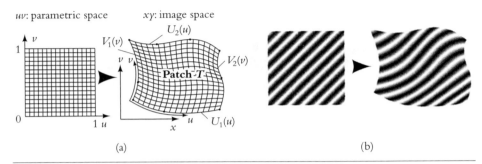

FIGURE 4.17 Warping a uniform grid (a) yields a transformation in the dither screen (b).

The Basic Engraving Layer

For this purpose, we define a *basic engraving layer* as a general dither screen that represents the basic building blocks for an engraving. Handmade copperplates or woodcuts are composed almost exclusively of lines with different widths. The line width depends on the light intensity at the respective surface points. To simulate this behavior, the basic engraving layer should be defined by a sequence of equidistant lines in such a way that—using it as a dither screen—wider lines are achieved in darker areas and thinner lines in bright areas. A dither screen like the one in Figure 4.17(b) serves this purpose well. It can be created by using a function like Equation 2.4 in Section 2.2.3, which was used for procedural screening. It is also possible to produce this screen as a bitmap beforehand.

This basic engraving layer is defined in its own *uv*-coordinate system over the range $[0, 1] \times [0, 1]$. To achieve different effects in copperplates that result from lines not being straight, the basic engraving layer is transformed by warping it such that the lines follow the intended direction. Using, for example, Coons patches (for details, see Farin, 1996) to model the transformation yields a simple and intuitive way of specifying the warping parameters. If the lines should follow a certain direction, then simply the borders of the patch have to be aligned properly.

Warping a regular grid defined in a parametric space *uv* yields a warped grid that is then appropriately filled with the basic engraving layer. Thus, a transformation of the *uv* unit block into image space also transforms the basic engraving layer accordingly. This process is illustrated in Figure 4.17.

Combination Rules

The basic engraving layers transformed in such a way have to be combined in order to create different effects like, for instance, cross-hatching. Since the

FIGURE 4.18 Two examples for engraving layers.

basic engraving layer is used as a dither screen, the combination of two or more such layers yields another dither screen with different properties. For the sake of simplicity, we will treat each pair of layers separately and so successively merge two layers until all layers are processed. The superimposition of two layers is done according to a set of *merging rules*.

To define these rules, we consider an engraving layer as consisting of three parts. First, there is the actual dither screen $T(x, y)$, which is defined as described earlier. This dither screen may undergo several range transformations to make it applicable in a concrete case. The grayscale values representing the dither screen (and thus the engraving layer) may be scaled by a function $S(x, y)$, and they may also be raised or lowered; that is, a range shifting operation $D(x, y)$ may be applied. These two functions S and D affect the pixel intensities depending on the pixel position (x, y) and are defined as two matrices with the same dimension as the dither screen $T(x, y)$. We can thus write

$$T'(x, y) = T(x, y) \cdot S(x, y) + D(x, y)$$

which yields a more detailed description of an engraving layer. Figure 4.18 shows two examples that will be used throughout the following explanations.

We will now define a set of rules to superimpose *two* layers. A subsequent application of these rules will ultimately lead to a superimposition of several layers. For simplicity of notation, we say that a current layer (*CL*) is merged into a resulting layer (*RL*) while both *CL* and *RL* are given as input and *RL* is the result of this operation. To initialize the engraving for the first merging operation, a special rule copy is defined that simply copies the values from the current layer to the resulting layer:

$$RL \text{ copy } CL : T_{RL}(x, y) = T_{CL}(x, y) \cdot S(x, y) + D(x, y)$$

Any other rule will alter *RL* based on the values of *RL* and *CL* by combining the values in a special manner. We will look at a few rules in detail although this number of possible rules is much bigger than the few ones introduced here.

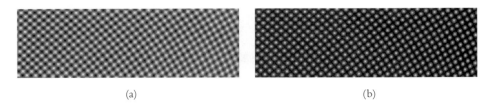

(a)   (b)

FIGURE 4.19 The merging rules add and multiply applied to the engraving layers given in Figure 4.18: *RL* add *CL* (a) and *RL* multiply *CL* (b).

(a)   (b)

FIGURE 4.20 The merging rules smaller and bigger applied to the engraving layers given in Figure 4.18: *RL* smaller *CL* (a) and *RL* bigger *CL* (b).

Using basic arithmetic operations on the two layers immediately yields the two rules multiply and add that can be seen in Figure 4.19. The first one multiplies the two screen intensities at each position (x, y), whereas the second one adds the two values:

$$RL \text{ multiply } CL : T_{RL}(x, y) \cdot (T_{CL}(x, y) \cdot S(x, y) + D(x, y))$$
$$RL \text{ add } CL : T_{RL}(x, y) + (T_{CL}(x, y) \cdot S(x, y) + D(x, y))$$

Two other rules smaller and bigger are based on the minimum or maximum of the two layers at the position (x, y) and defined as follows (see Figure 4.20):

$$RL \text{ smaller } CL : \min(T_{RL}(x, y), T_{CL}(x, y) \cdot S(x, y) + D(x, y))$$
$$RL \text{ bigger } CL : \max(T_{RL}(x, y), T_{CL}(x, y) \cdot S(x, y) + D(x, y))$$

These basic rules can be combined with different range shift or scale operations to achieve the desired result. Usually a combination of two layers will result in threshold values falling out of the range [0, 1] so that in such cases a trimming operation is needed. Unfortunately, there is another problem. The tone reproduction curve of two superimposed layers may show non-linear behavior even if the two original layers behave linearly. For the resulting engraving, this may mean that it appears locally darker or brighter than expected. A correction of this behavior is quite complicated and cannot simply be done by performing a histogram equalization. Instead, local changes have to be introduced that take into account the output medium and the properties of the human visual system. Basically, local histogram equalization is performed here such that the modified dither screen—when applied—must produce visually uniform gray for a uniform input signal. We refer you to Ostromoukhov and Hersch (1999) for details of this procedure.

Creating an Engraving

In the last paragraphs, we defined the basic building blocks for the creation of image-based digital engravings. We will now see how they are applied to create a rendition of a given gray-level image. The overall procedure is as follows:

1. Identification of regions in the image that have to be "engraved" differently.

2. Transformation of the basic engraving layer for each identified region such that the respective region is covered and the features of the engraving layer follow the image features. This will create a separate layer for each identified feature.

3. Specification of the range shift and range scale matrices for each layer. This can be done by "painting" these matrices interactively.

4. Superimposition of the engraving layers by subsequently merging two layers.

5. Correction of the superimposed dither screen as described earlier.

6. Application of the dither screen to the image.

We will demonstrate this procedure using the example in Figure 4.21. Figure 4.21(a) shows the placement and deformation of the basic engraving layers. For the creation of this particular image, five different layers are chosen. Note how the borders of the grids and thus also the lines are aligned to follow the key features of the face. Figure 4.21(b) is a visualization of the range shift matrices. Note that no range scaling is applied for this particular example. For the shifting matrices, black corresponds to $+1$, white to -1, and gray means no shift. As can be seen especially in the first layer, a transition between two layers can be achieved by a fading in the range shift matrix. Finally, Figure 4.21(c) shows how the layers are successively combined. In this case, after an initial copy operation to initialize the first layer, only one merging rule is used: smaller. This yields the following formula as a description of the combination process:

$(((L1$ smaller $L2)$ smaller $L3)$ smaller $L4)$ smaller $L5$

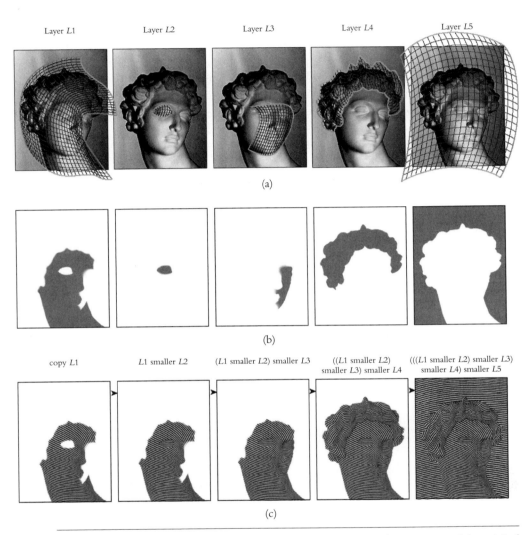

FIGURE 4.21 Creating an engraving: parametric grids for successive layers, on top of the original image (a), range shift matrices (masks) for successive layers (b), and succession of resulting engraving layers (c).

FIGURE 4.22 Resulting engraving from the process shown in Figure 4.21.

The resulting dither screen is then applied to the input image, which yields the rendition in Figure 4.22.

Exercises

4.1 Implement the basic concepts of cellular automata and extend your implementation so that it can be used for a simulation of wet paint on different paper surfaces.

4.2 Extend your implementation from the last exercise in order to be able to compare different transition functions. Compare the results. Which effects are the most important ones to be included in a simulation of watercolor?

4.3   Can the CA approach also be used to simulate oil paintings? Find the main characteristics of an oil painting and discuss how a simulation of these effects could be performed.

4.4   Show that if a paper grain (as introduced for the pencil simulation in Section 4.2) has a maximum height of h_{max} then the volume of a grain is $V_g = \frac{1}{4} \cdot \sum_{i=1}^{4} h_{max} - h_i$.

4.5   Investigate the model for pencils drawing on paper when pencil strokes are repeated more than once.

4.6   Extend the pencil-and-paper model to handle colored pencils or different kinds of pencils (crayons). Can this model also serve as a basis for charcoal or chalk drawings?

4.7   Develop a model for the effect of erasers and blenders on pencil drawings. Note that such drawing instruments can be considered to have an effect analogous to that of pencils.

4.8   What are the main drawbacks of the pencil-and-paper model introduced in this chapter and what are the advantages?

4.9   Develop a systematic method to assess the quality of a simulation model such as the one presented for pencil drawings.

4.10   If you have the source code of a raytracer available, extend the raytracer such that copperplate rendering is possible. Note that finding the correct parameters for aesthetically pleasing images is not intuitive. Experiment with the raytracer to find usable parameter sets.

4.11   Implement the merging rules and the deformation functions for engraving layers. Create simulated engravings with these methods and compare them to the ones obtained by raytracing.

4.12   Can the boundaries of the different regions be found algorithmically?

Bibliographic Notes

The simulation of wet paint on paper emerged very early in the history of NPR. Already in 1986, Strassmann tried to simulate the Japanese art *sumi-e* (Strassmann, 1986b; Strassmann, 1986a). He used the path and style metaphor as described in Chapter 3 to create single brushstrokes. An extension to this model was presented by Pham, which is also suited for animation (Pham, 1991).

The interaction of wet paint between strokes and between the paint and the paper was then introduced in a paper "Wet and Sticky: Supporting Interaction with Wet Paint" by Cockshott and England (1991; Cockshott et al., 1992). Here, for the first time, cellular automata were used to simulate the behavior of paint on paper. Even though their main interest has been on interaction techniques and exploiting parallelism, Cockshott and England have provided the basis for further research in this area.

The use of cellular automata for paint simulation enabled Zhang et al. to present a system for the creation of monochrome images resembling the traditional Chinese art (Zhang et al., 1999). They introduced interesting features like shade, scratchiness, and blur into a behavioral model of water and ink, and used this model especially to render images of trees.

Finally, Curtis et al. described the various effects of watercolor and showed how they can be simulated automatically (Curtis et al., 1997). Their model uses fluid dynamics in a set of layers to also simulate the mixing of color when several brushstrokes are applied on top of each other. Their model is so far the most complex and realistic one.

Some other authors have also spent considerable effort in simulating brush-strokes although they concentrated only on very specific effects. For instance, Guo and Kunii simulated the phenomenon of "Nijimi," a technique in traditional Chinese art, where ink is diffused into the absorbent paper. Their approach is based on the physical analysis of the phenomenon and uses the concept of disorder systems (Guo and Kunii, 1991). A highly parallel algorithm using CAs is also presented by Small (1991).

Significant work on the simulation of pencil drawings taking into account the microscopic level has been done by (Sousa, 1999; Sousa and Buchanan, 1999b; Sousa and Buchanan, 2000; Sousa and Buchanan, 1999a). This work is an excellent example of one direction in which such simulation approaches can be taken: analyzing the result of the real-world process and trying to build the same result on a computer.

The first attempt to simulate copperplate engravings was done by Leister using an extended raytracing method (Leister, 1994). The modification of this method, which was originally intended to produce highly photorealistic images, yields astonishingly good results; however, it needs a 3D model as input. Starting from a 2D image, pixel-based methods were developed by Ostromoukhov (1999). With this, he extends his repertoire of dual tone representation techniques for images that were already mentioned in Chapter 2 (see also Ostromoukhov and Hersch, 1995; Ostromoukhov et al., 1996; Ostromoukhov, 2000).

An area that is emerging and has not been covered in this chapter is the simulation of the woodcut and engraving process itself. In this area, the research work done by Mizuno et al. (1998) as well as by Sourin (2001) is of interest.

5 | STROKE-BASED ILLUSTRATIONS

Having seen in the last chapters how images can be manipulated on the level of pixels, how lines and strokes as basic building blocks for non-photorealistic imagery can be created, and how artistic techniques can be simulated, we now turn our attention to the question of how individual strokes and lines can be combined to build interesting images. In a certain way, this continues the simulation approaches described in Chapter 4 since the results obtained here may also resemble handcrafted renditions. The style of the images is thereby determined by the kinds of strokes that are used. It ranges from paintings, where paintbrush marks are distributed over an image, to pen-and-ink renditions, where lines are the basic building blocks.

5.1 Strokes and Stroke Textures

Stroke-based illustrations have a number of features that make them interesting for the creation of illustrative images but also for artistic purposes. Although the first application area ought to be in the center of interest in this chapter, the latter should be kept in mind when designing algorithms. The aesthetic quality of an image determines to a great extent how the image will be used and whether it successfully transfers the intended message.

Looking at pen-and-ink illustrations, the strokes from which they are built have two major properties:

FIGURE 5.1 Depicting shape and illumination by the placement of single strokes.

1. They depict both tone and texture *simultaneously*.
2. They work *together* to express tone and texture.

This means that, even though every single stroke is of critical importance for the image, it has to contribute to tone as well as texture. In the end, each single stroke is part of a texture that conveys both shape and illumination as can be seen in Figure 5.1.

Almost the same holds for other types of illustrations. Paintbrushes cover a surface and provide a sense of shape by depicting the lighting conditions via colored brushstrokes. Different shape features of the portrayed objects are conveyed by the use of different-sized strokes. Alternatively, only the object contours may be drawn by special kinds of strokes so as to depict different materials like fur, grass, or the foliage of a tree. In the following, we will see how such strokes are defined and drawn, and how they are used to cover larger areas.

5.1.1 Defining and Drawing Single Strokes

Each single stroke has to be designed carefully with respect to its own properties and its combination with other strokes. In the case of pen-and-ink-style strokes, lines with equal thickness are a good starting point. The strokes have to be irregular; otherwise, a rather synthetic, mechanical look of the illustration would be the result (see Section 3.1). The procedure to create one stroke thus starts with a straight line that is then subdivided to yield a chain of line segments. The positions of the joints between these segments are perturbed randomly in order to introduce irregularities. Finally, this line segment chain can act as the control polygon for a free-form curve to make the stroke more smooth. As an alternative, multiresolution curves (as described in Section 3.3) can also be used.

Drawing such a stroke requires not only the rasterization of the line or curve but also the clipping of the stroke. In typical pen-and-ink renditions, several situations arise where strokes do not cross specific features in the image. These features include:

1. the edges of the overall image,
2. tonal edges in the image, that is, abrupt changes in intensity due to lighting, shadow, or material, and
3. object contours.

Many algorithms for clipping have been developed and have become standard in computer graphics.[1] For the purpose of clipping a stroke, however, a much simpler approach will suffice. When drawing the stroke, we simply stop at the respective position (edge) but add a random offset so that we achieve a ragged edge and thus prevent too much regularity.

For different types of applications, different strokes may be needed. Pen-and-ink-style strokes are well suited to cover larger regions of the image in a certain style. Other styles require "marks" to be placed along the contour of the objects or footprints of a paintbrush (see Figure 5.2).

The Dr. Seuss-like strokes from Figure 5.2(a)—also called *graftals*—are defined in different levels of detail such that they can be drawn differently:

◆ as a complete stroke with outline and interior fill if high detail is required,

◆ as just the interior fill and parts of the outline, or simply the outline for medium detail, or

◆ as just a part of the outline (basically, one line) if very little detail is required.

---

1. See, for example, Rogers (1998).

(a)   (b)

FIGURE 5.2 Different strokes to create different styles of illustration: marks placed along the object contour (a) and filling regions with paintbrush strokes (b). (See also color insert.)

Drawing a stroke in this case simply means to scale the graftal accordingly and draw those parts of the graftal that are needed in the current situation. Clipping is not performed here because, on the one hand, these strokes do not fill larger areas in the image, and on the other, scaling and the level of detail replaces the need for clipping.

Finally, paintbrush-like strokes can be created in a variety of ways. For covering a surface, the most promising way is to use prerendered brush images. These are color bitmaps that contain an additional alpha channel for storing transparency values. In such a way, the shape of the brushstroke can be defined. The application of such a stroke is a copy operation that transfers the stroke image into the frame buffer while observing orientation, color, and scale. For orienting the strokes, a reference coordinate system is established that describes the stroke and that is then transformed in 2D for the final rendering. Paintbrush strokes are also not clipped but scaled accordingly so that they resemble original paintings. Instead of "stopping" to paint at an edge, smaller strokes are used. As opposed to pen-and-ink-style renditions, where no color information is used, paintbrushes rely on color. Thus, either the correct stroke has to be selected from a set of strokes with different colors or the stroke color itself has to be adjusted before rendering the stroke.

Rendering single strokes is the first step for stroke-based illustrations. Only a combination of many strokes will cover a surface or depict the outline of an object. We will see in the following how strokes can be combined and which additional requirements will arise.

5.1.2 Building Stroke Textures

Given a method of defining and drawing single strokes, these strokes have to be combined to fill a surface region of the image. We will refer to sets of strokes that fill a certain area as *stroke textures*. In general, using stroke textures, it is important to represent *texture* and *tone* appropriately. Texture suggests the material properties of the surface in question and thus yields the impression of, for instance, a brick wall, a sandy beach, or the foliage of a tree. Tone is important to visualize lighting information especially, and both are indispensable tools for conveying the shape of the depicted objects. Thus, the key to the composition of individual strokes into complete renditions lies in finding a way to convey information about

- the *form* of the object and perhaps also the *material* of which it is made and
- the scene, in particular (but not necessarily limited to) the *effect of light*.

Equally important is the realization that not only must the underlying geometric model be considered, but also the size of the paper (or the size and resolution of the computer screen) on which the resultant image is to be displayed. A small drawing of a scene cannot, in general, be obtained by photoreducing a large drawing, or vice versa. Instead, small drawings tend to be made with fewer strokes though the width of a stroke may remain the same. This problem will be addressed in more detail in Section 5.3.

Regardless of any features of the underlying geometric model, to reflect the light intensity, the following naive algorithm might be considered. For each region in the image, compute the intensity of light v reflected toward the viewer from a point on the surface. We refer to v as the *tone* of the surface. In photorealistic rendering, this can be expressed in a pixel-by-pixel manner by choosing the color appropriately. In NPR, the same effect is achieved over an entire surface by adjusting the density of strokes. Given an area A of an image to be covered with non-overlapping strokes of width w, the total length l of the strokes is thus

$$l = v \cdot \frac{A}{w}$$

Note that strokes often actually do overlap one another though covering a surface with ink twice does not make it darker. Hence this factor must be taken into account (see also Exercise 5.1).

The procedure outlined works well for equally spaced strokes if a rather large area has to be covered with the same tone. However, these conditions are rarely encountered. More likely the tone will gradually change over a surface so that the preceding algorithm is not applicable. The basic principle behind texturing a surface in such cases is that more strokes have to be placed in darker regions while fewer strokes go to bright regions. This implies an adaptive distribution of the strokes based on the tone value of the underlying image. To achieve this goal, the tone of the created illustration has to be compared with the tone of the original (target) image.

To compare the stroke-based illustration with a gray-level image, consider a stroke to darken a region of the image when applied. After applying each stroke, it then remains to be determined how much darker the illustration needs to become in a specific region in order to match the tone of the target image. The following *difference image algorithm* (DIA) yields good results for this problem. Given a target (gray-level) image and an empty illustration, we would need an additional difference image buffer to actually perform the tone matching. This buffer is initialized with the contents of the target image. Each stroke is drawn in the illustration. After this has been done, a blurred version of the stroke is computed using adaptive averaging filters on the illustration. The filter radius is inversely proportional to the target tone of the image since in darker regions strokes are more closely spaced than in light regions. The blurred version of the stroke is subtracted from the difference image such that the remaining intensity difference is recorded. This difference between the target image and the blurred illustration is a measure for the "success" of achieving the desired tone. The location where the next stroke will be placed is then selected from this last "difference image" by choosing the position with the largest value. This procedure is more formally outlined in Algorithm 5.1.

```
1   create an empty difference image
2   foreach stroke S do
3       P = position in the difference image with the highest value
4       draw S in the illustration at position P
5       create a blurred image of S
6       subtract this blurred image from the difference image at position P
7   od
```

ALGORITHM 5.1 Difference image algorithm for placing strokes.

This algorithm stops placing new strokes when the difference image contains only values that are below a given threshold. There is no way to reach a difference image that contains only zero values since the stroke-based illustration is only an approximation of the target image. This method of placing strokes matches the tone of the target image but does not take into account texture or material properties. It works well for textures where the placement of single strokes depends only on the target tone. For introducing textures, the strokes have to be placed in a certain arrangement (so as to draw, for example, a brick wall). To match tone *and* texture, the strokes in these arrangements have to be drawn in a certain order such that for light tones only the most significant strokes are drawn and less important strokes are filled in for darker regions.

To model this behavior, we need to refine the definition of the stroke textures. Normally, a stroke texture is a collection of strokes that are given relative to a reference coordinate system and that are chosen in random order for drawing. To predefine the drawing sequence, a priority value is assigned to each stroke. This will yield a so-called prioritized stroke texture. As an example, for a brick wall, the lines defining the outlines of the bricks are most important to convey the type of material (see Figure 5.3). If the image gets darker, then the individual bricks may be shaded using horizontal or vertical lines. Finally, in very dark regions, the whole texture might be covered with diagonal strokes.

These stroke textures—prioritized or not—can easily be stored for later use. When using stroke textures, Algorithm 5.1 is affected only in the generation of

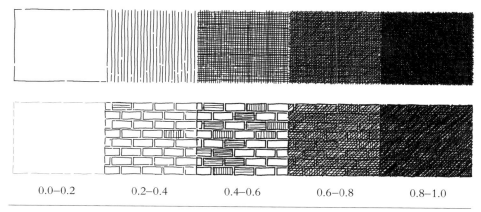

| 0.0–0.2 | 0.2–0.4 | 0.4–0.6 | 0.6–0.8 | 0.8–1.0 |

FIGURE 5.3 Examples of prioritized stroke textures. Each field represents a tone v in the range [0, 1] increasing from left to right.

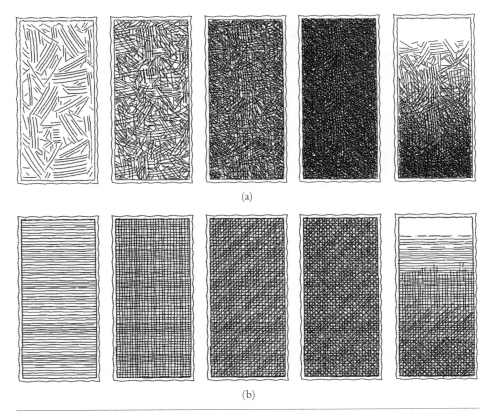

(a)

(b)

FIGURE 5.4 Comparison of standard and prioritized stroke textures. In the first case (a), strokes are drawn in random order, whereas in (b) prioritized textures determine the drawing order by assigning priority values to the strokes.

prospective strokes. They are now no longer computed randomly by choosing a certain position and testing if it needs darkening, but are selected from the stored texture. For a prioritized stroke texture, the candidates are tested in priority order, and if a candidate fails the tone test, no lower prioritized strokes are drawn. For a standard stroke texture, candidates are chosen in random order (see Figure 5.4).

For monochrome images, where only gray levels have to be handled correctly, this general approach has proved to work well. If the strokes are colored (for example, when simulating paintbrushes), this additional complexity has to be taken into account. The base color of the stroke can be determined from the target image, and a blurred version of the applied stroke is then subtracted from the target image, to yield the entries in the difference image. However, since three color channels have to be observed, a distance metric has to be established. One option for this is a comparison based on the red, green, and blue color channels, or on some combination of these.

A simple coverage of areas having different tonal values with some kind of texture that creates the required tone and texture is in most cases not sufficient for illustrative purposes. Some features of the image have to be highlighted in order to enhance the perception of the objects' shapes. On the other hand, the orientation of the stroke also plays an important role for recognizing shape features. We will thus focus on these two issues in the next section.

5.2 Detail and Orientation

Besides covering an area with a texture in order to provide a sense of shape, there are also other indications for form and shape that ought to be included in an illustration. Surface detail and orientation of the strokes especially aid the perception of objects in a scene. Though strokes should be oriented along prominent features, they also have to convey surface detail. Textures can be used even though they are in many cases not sufficient. Outline strokes are a very natural means of subdividing an image into regions and thus separating objects from one another. Finally, lighting conditions, which are already portrayed by the chosen texture, can be greatly enhanced in their perception by drawing shadows differently. Shadows themselves are a well-established medium for depicting lighting direction and intensity.

5.2.1 Outlines and Shadows

Outlines come in two varieties. *Boundary outlines* surround the visible polygons of the image. They must be drawn in such a way that the textures of both the surrounded and the adjacent regions are clearly separated from one another. By contrast, *interior outlines* are used within polygons to suggest shadow directions or to give view-dependent accents to the stroke texture. Each of these must be treated with care.

◆ *Boundary outline line style*   Each stroke texture has an associated outline boundary of a particular *line style*. This must be chosen carefully so as to match the

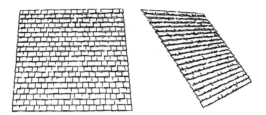

FIGURE 5.5 Viewer dependence of outlines. Fewer lines are used when the surface is tilted so as to maintain the original tone.

texture to be indicated. Examples were already shown in the leftmost column of Figure 5.3.

♦ *Minimizing outline* Outlines are drawn only if the surfaces that they divide are not sufficiently different in their tone to be disambiguated by their shading alone. If a boundary edge is in fact drawn, it uses the boundary outline style of the texture that belongs to the surface closer to the viewer.

♦ *Viewer-dependent outlines* Outlines are very sensitive to the viewing direction. Viewed from above, in most cases, all edges are visible and thus all outlines are drawn. Viewed from an angle, however, objects tend to blend together and, hence, not all outlines should be drawn (see Figure 5.5).

Many of these principles can be addressed in an illustration system. However, the intuitive way in which painters use outline strokes cannot be modeled in general.

A similar challenge exists when drawing shadows. Up to now, the algorithms have assumed that light falls in an unobstructed manner onto the surfaces. However, shadows in fact provide important depth cues for viewers and hence are generally added to illustrations. The most simple procedure uses cross-hatching to darken the regions lying within shadows. These regions have to be determined from the 3D model (if available) or given by user interaction. The cross-hatching can then be chosen so as to orient the lines in the direction of the light source. As an alternative to cross-hatching, shadows can also be indicated by making lines denoting the edges of objects thicker if these edges cast shadows. Examples of a combination of these techniques are shown in Figure 5.6.

Figure 5.7 shows the results of applying the techniques that we have introduced in this section. The object is a house in which the textures were chosen a priori for each surface. Note that in Figure 5.7(a), the strokes vary nicely over the image, but the fact that all objects are entirely covered by strokes leads to a

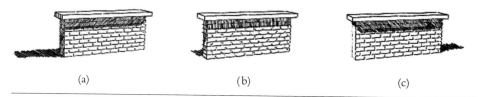

FIGURE 5.6 Examples of indicating shadows by cross-hatching and by thickening lines representing edges that cast shadows. In (a), the light source is in the upper right of the wall; in (b), it is above the wall; in (c), it is to the upper left of the wall.

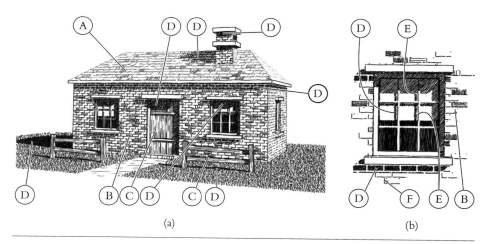

FIGURE 5.7 Examples of automatic pen-and-ink renditions. The letters indicating interesting parts have the following meanings: A-texture to indicate shingles, B-texture to indicate bricks, C-texture to indicate wood, D-cross-hatching added to indicate shadow, E-outlines used to differentiate surfaces of like tone (window and crossbar), F-indication of shadow by drawing edges of bricks casting shadows.

certain monotonicity. We will address this issue in the final section of this chapter. Figure 5.7(b) shows an enlargement of the left window and illustrates the application of the various rules for outlines. The choice of stroke textures for illuminated surfaces and those with shadows yield an image with many different stroke combinations.

5.2.2 **Orientation**

Orienting strokes is one of the keys for illustrators to provide the viewers with a sense of shape of the portrayed objects. To successfully create illustrations, two questions have to be solved: how is the orientation of the strokes computed and how are the single strokes finally aligned?

The computation of the stroke directions depends on the way in which the images are produced. If the stroke-based illustrations are the result of some kind of rendering software where the three-dimensional model is available, then this data will be used. On the other hand, if only image data is available,[2] then user interaction might be necessary. In this case, the user "paints" the direction vectors over the given image. The directions are represented as a vector field where for each pixel (or each group of pixels) a value is stored. The basic operation is thus to change the directions of the vectors to match the motion of the painting tool. The length of the direction vectors is not important, so a regular mouse-based interface is sufficient. Painting over a complete image to match every single pixel is a tedious task, and irregular movements of the hand might negatively affect the desired result. Therefore, filling operations—much like gradient fills in paint programs—help to set the direction in larger areas. The following operations are some of the possible ways:

* *Region fill*   The user selects an image region and a direction, which is then filled in the selected area.

* *Interpolation fill*   The user specifies two curves and the system interpolates between them. The direction vectors are then the tangents to these interpolated curves.

* *Source fill*   The user specifies a region of the image and a "source pixel." The direction vectors are then computed to always point away from this source pixel.

While using these tools, a visual feedback should be given to control the success of the operations.

Given three-dimensional information, the direction field can be computed almost automatically. In most cases, strokes are aligned to the curvature of the object to be drawn. These curvature values are relatively easy to derive. However,

---

2. This limits the available data to color or intensity information stored on a per-pixel basis.

1   pick a random control point P_i from the stroke
2   map P_i to the target point X in the illustration
3    $\theta_i =$ angle between $v_i = P_{i+1} - P_i$ and the vertical in the stroke texture definition
4   **foreach** point p along the curve segment P_iP_{i+1} **do**
5   let the angle between the tangent at p and the direction field be θ_i
6   **od**

ALGORITHM 5.2   Determining the orientation and bending of a stroke based on a direction vector field.

the question here is whether the strokes should follow the maximum, minimum, or average curvature. The visual result depends strongly on this decision so that in such cases, user interaction should, again, be considered.

For pen-and-ink-like textures that cover a certain area, this direction field is the basis to align the strokes properly. For this purpose, the procedure to draw a stroke is changed. Instead of simply placing the stroke in the image, it has to be rotated and bent. Since the strokes are given as curves via control points, the technique in Algorithm 5.2 can be used to align a single stroke along the given direction vectors. In this algorithm, the original points P_i and P_{i+1} are given in the stroke texture, and new positions for these points are calculated.

This algorithm effectively bends the stroke based on the given direction field. It aligns the tangent of the strokes (in line 5) in such a way that the angle between the tangent and the direction vector is approximately the same as the angle between the tangent and the vertical in the predefined stroke texture. As an additional constraint, the arc length of the curve between the new computed positions P_i' and P_{i+1}' should be approximately the length of v_i. This makes the computation somewhat complicated; effectively, a set of differential equations has to be solved.[3]

For strokes that are built as graftals (as described in Section 5.1.1), such a complicated procedure is not necessary because these strokes rarely cover a complete area. They are placed along the contour of an object (see, for instance, the tree image in Figure 5.2), and they are oriented such that they always point outward from the object. To do so, the surface normal at the target position,

---

3. Refer to Salisbury (1997) for details.

(more specifically, the angle between the surface normal and the view direction) can be consulted to compute the graftal's rotation.

This strategy is also feasible for paintbrushlike strokes. If three-dimensional information is available, then such values as curvature and normal vector directions are used to determine orientation and scale. Furthermore, such strokes are well suited for an interactive approach, where location, size, and direction are obtained from user interaction. The challenge is to map user actions while interacting with the computer in the context of the underlying rendition onto parameters of these attributes.

The attributes and their parameters can be selected as follows:

- *Location and color* As the user moves the cursor over the image to be manipulated, the image is continuously sampled at the tip of the cursor. The color of the pixel under the tip is used as the color of a stroke originating at that point. Variations are to use the color in the middle of the cursor instead of at its tip or to use a stochastic distribution around the sampled pixel for the start of the stroke.

- *Size* The speed with which the user moves the mouse while drawing can be mapped onto the length of the stroke. If the mouse is moved quickly, the strokes are long and coarse, whereas if the mouse is moved slowly they are shorter. This enables the overall structure of the image to be painted quickly, while finer detail can follow.

- *Orientation* The direction of movement of the cursor can be used to derive the orientation of the strokes. Alternatively, the system can allow the user to enter a special mode (for example, by pressing the middle mouse button) to record the direction of a mouse movement; this direction can be used as the orientation of all subsequent strokes.

- *Shape* The stroke shape can, for example, be selected from a menu. Examples of stroke shapes include lines, circles, or cones; each of these needs another parameterization that might be fixed for a given image.

Figure 5.8 shows an example image that can be produced with this method.

5.2.3 Abstraction of Detail

One of the key features of NPR is the possibility of constructing an image without touching its every pixel, and without covering every surface with strokes or other image artifacts. Instead, a significant amount of "real estate" can be left

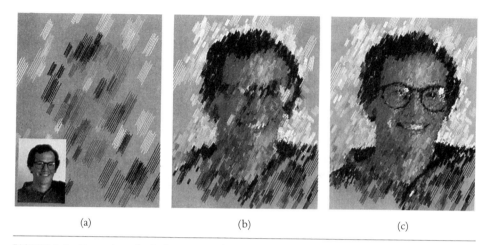

(a)   (b)   (c)

FIGURE 5.8 Examples of painting over a photorealistic image with the mouse. The inset shows the original image; (a) shows the results when a small number of fast strokes are made over the original. In (b) and (c), the strokes have become successively finer. (See also color insert.)

untouched, that is, can be left with the background color. This process has been called *abstraction* or *indication*. Besides arousing curiosity about those areas left blank, the technique has the convenient side effect that the underlying geometric models can be incomplete. The psychological process by which viewers "fill in" the blank spaces with artifacts of their choice or imagination is called *projection*.

There are basically two ways in which such an abstraction can be carried out algorithmically. The first is to have some way to compute which of the parts of an underlying geometric model ought to be drawn, or alternatively, which parts can in fact be left out. The other way is to enable a user to select interactively the parts to be left out.

Of course, it is possible to give a user a kind of eraser brush like those common in the usual paint programs in order to "rub out" those parts of an image that should be removed. This approach has the problem that it will be difficult to enable smooth transitions between blank and rendered regions of an image. Moreover, the approach is not particularly systematic and can lead to self-contradictory results.

More direct, however, is the approach to give a user tools to express what is important in an image. Recall, for example, the image in Figure 5.7(a), which contains all details encoded within the underlying model that are visible from

(a)   (b)

FIGURE 5.9 (a) Sample interactive placement of detail segments; (b) result of applying the detail segments to (a).

the vantage point of the camera. A user is now given a tool to place thin rectangular widgets (called "detail segments") on the image to indicate regions of interest. These detail segments emit a field that affects each region in the vicinity. This can be computed according to the following scheme: let $w(x, y)$ be a field that is generated by the detail segment l at a point (x, y). In texture space, $w(x, y) = (a + b \cdot \text{distance}((x, y), l))^{-c}$, where a, b, and c are non-negative constants that are used to change the effect of the field. When several detail segments affect a single point, a good approach is to define the field at point (x, y) to be determined by the closest detail segment. So as not to create patterns that are too regular, the field $w(x, y)$ can also be perturbed by a small random value.

Textures with building blocks such as bricks evaluate the strength of their fields at the center of the respective element. The set of strokes for that element is generated only if the field is above a certain threshold. An example of this approach is shown in Figure 5.9.

Graftals, on the other hand, which are placed only along the contour of an object and thus already follow the abstraction paradigm, can be varied in detail on the level of a single stroke. To determine the amount of detail, the orientation of the stroke can be used as a criterion. Depending on the angle between the viewing direction and the surface normal, more or less detail is drawn. The definition of the strokes has to include different detailed versions that are then chosen appropriately. Besides the orientation, the distance of the object to the camera is also a valuable criterion to determine the level of detail for the strokes. This behavior is illustrated in Figure 5.10.

FIGURE 5.10 Different levels of detail when drawing graftals. Notice the differences among the grass tufts in the three images but also among the trees.

5.3 Rescaling Stroke-Based Images

One of the problems encountered with stroke-based illustrations is that they cannot readily be changed in their scale without significant changes in their overall appearance. For example, Figure 5.11(b) shows an image that was made smaller to yield Figure 5.11(a) and enlarged to yield Figure 5.11(c). In each case, the stroke endpoints were recalculated based on the resize operation, and then the strokes were redrawn. The result is that the tone of the images changes significantly, which presumably is an unwanted side effect.

Some alternatives for solving this problem are as follows:

1. *Resize stroke width*   It is possible to resize the stroke width along with the overall image. Larger images are rendered with proportionally wider strokes, smaller ones with thinner strokes. This enables the tone to be maintained; however, it ultimately yields unusual stroke widths that change the character of the image.

2. *Rescale gray-level image and apply new stroke textures*   The problem with this approach is that sharp edges in the original tend to get washed out (see, for example, Figure 5.12).

3. *Replay painting history on the rescaled image*   This approach depends heavily on the details of how the image was painted. It is unlikely that this approach yields good results each time. Further, the size of the representation depends mainly on the number of editing operations, which does not necessarily correspond with the image complexity.

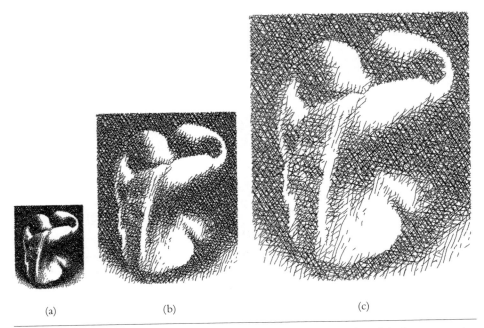

(a)   (b)   (c)

FIGURE 5.11 A stroke-based illustration at three different scales: (b) is the original, represented as a set of individual strokes; (a) and (c) demonstrate changes in tone and character of the illustrations.

5.3.1 Goals for a Rescaling Operation

To develop a method for changing the size of illustrations, we will borrow from signal and sampling theory. What is really happening when rescaling a gray-level image is that the image, which is available at one scale, consists of uniformly spaced discrete samples, while the new image needs samples at different places in the plane (see Figure 5.13).

The following two requirements must be met by a rescale operation in order to be of use in the scenario observed here:

1. Maintain the character of the original.

2. "Sharp" features in the original should remain "sharp", "smooth" features should remain "smooth."

Abrupt changes in intensity along predefined boundaries are regarded as "sharp" features and are to be maintained. These boundaries are also referred to as

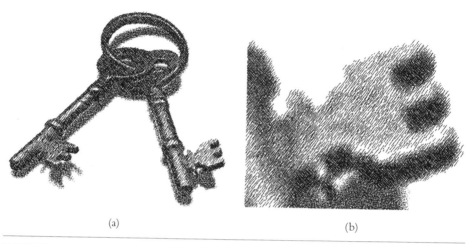

(a) (b)

FIGURE 5.12 Stroke-based image (a) based on a gray-level image that was selectively enlarged about seven times and new strokes applied (b). Notice how the crisp edges of the original have been washed out in the enlargement.

discontinuity edges. Besides keeping the character of already present image features the same, the rescaling operation must also not introduce any new discontinuities.

More formally, the problem can be stated as follows:

Given a set $\{x_i\}$ of uniformly spaced discrete sample locations (pixels), a set $\{f_i\}$ of corresponding intensity values, and a set $\{l_i\}$ of (non-overlapping) discontinuity edges as line segments.

Find a function $f(x)$ that is smooth everywhere except across the discontinuity edges, such that $f(x)$ interpolates the values f_i.

The reconstruction function $f(x)$ can then be resampled at a different rate than the original input data. If resampling is done at a higher rate, then the original image is magnified. Resampling at a lower rate means to minify the original although, before doing so, the bandwidth of the given image has to be lowered.

5.3.2 Approximating the Input as a Continuous Function

The reconstruction of a continuous signal $f(x)$ from a set of uniformly spaced discrete samples (x_i, f_i) may be performed by convoluting with a reconstruction kernel $k(x)$:

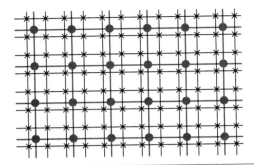

FIGURE 5.13 Rescaling means converting from one set of uniformly spaced discrete samples (circles at the crossing points of a grid represented as gray lines) into another such set (x's at the crossing points of the grid represented as thin black lines).

$$f(x) = \sum_i f_i k(x - x_i) \tag{5.1}$$

It is important that the function $f(x)$ yields the original value f_i for $x = x_i$, that is, when it is evaluated exactly at the position of an input sample. Figure 5.14(a) illustrates the situation. Although many different convolution kernels are available to solve this problem from the signal processing point of view, experience has shown that a 4×4 cubic convolution kernel as in Equation (5.2) works well.

$$k(x) = \begin{cases} 1.5|x|^3 - 2.5|x|^2 + 1 & 0 \le |x| < 1 \\ -0.5|x|^3 + 2.5|x|^2 - 4|x| + 2 & 1 \le |x| < 2 \\ 0 & 2 \le |x| \end{cases} \tag{5.2}$$

Figure 5.15 shows a plot of this kernel function. Notice that the values close to $x = 1$ contribute the most, whereas values between $x = 1$ and $x = 2$ contribute negatively to counterbalance this. The reconstruction of a value at point x is done using Equation (5.1) if no discontinuity edge crosses the area of the kernel (the 4×4 region). Otherwise, these discontinuities have to be taken into account, and a different kernel has to be chosen.

5.3.3 Discontinuity Edges

We now assume that there are discontinuity edges anywhere within the 2D image space; these edges may be either computed by edge detection software or defined through user interaction. Figure 5.14(b) shows such a situation, where discontinuity edges are present within the 4×4 area of the kernel. Intuitively, we would now expect point a not to make any contribution to $f(x)$ because it is contained within

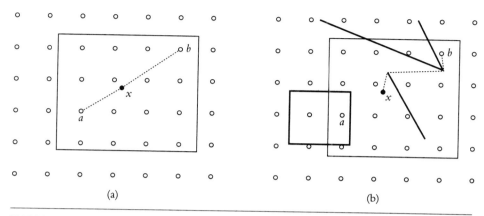

FIGURE 5.14 Reconstruction function to be evaluated at x. All pixels in the 4×4 neighborhood of x contribute to the value of $f(x)$ at x (a) and the same neighborhood in the presence of discontinuity edges (b).

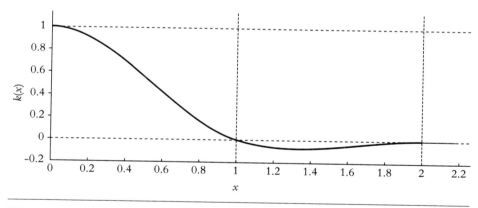

FIGURE 5.15 Kernel function $k(x)$ versus x.

a kind of cage whose intensity values ought not to spill over into the other regions. By contrast, the point b would be expected to make a contribution to x, albeit a smaller one than if there were no edges disrupting the view from x to b. Indeed, b's contribution should reflect the "ease" with which you can move from b to x.

In order to preserve discontinuities in the reconstruction function $f(x)$, we replace the reconstruction kernel k with a modified kernel $\tilde{k}$ that attenuates k by a factor α according to each entry's "reachability":

$$\tilde{k}(x, x_i) = \alpha(x, x_i)k(x - x_i)$$

To compute this attenuation, the distance between x and a respective point has to be computed in both cases, with and without discontinuity edges. Let $d(x, x_i)$ be the Euclidean distance between x and x_i, and let $sp(x, x_i)$ be the length of the shortest unobstructed path between the two points (recall Figure 5.14(b)). We define the *detour cost* between x and x_i as

$$\text{detour}(x, x_i) = sp(x, x_i) - d(x, x_i)$$

This detour cost defines the attenuating function $\alpha(x, x_i)$ as follows:

$$\alpha(x, x_i) = \begin{cases} 1 & \text{if } \text{detour}(x, x_i) = 0, \text{ that is, if } x_i \text{ is visible from } x \\ 0 & \text{if } \text{detour}(x, x_i) \geq r, \text{ that is, if } x_i \text{ is too "far"} \\ 1 - 3t^2 + 2t^3 & \text{if } \text{detour}(x, x_i) < r, \text{ where } t = \frac{\text{detour}(x, x_i)}{r} \end{cases}$$

If a sample is too far away from the given position x, then it should have no effect. This is ensured by the constant r in the above equation. Experience has shown that a value of $r = 1$ works well for the 4×4 kernel. The cubic polynomial in the third case ensures that $\alpha(x, x_i)$ is C^1 continuous and as such does not introduce any more discontinuities.

Now, the modified kernel k no longer has the property that the value of $f(x)$ equals the input sample value when x corresponds to an input pixel. To compensate for this, a *weighted average convolution* as given in Equation (5.3) can be used:

$$f(x) = \frac{\sum f_i \alpha(x, x_i) k(x - x_i)}{\sum \alpha(x, x_i) k(x - x_i)} \tag{5.3}$$

A slight complication occurs in this last equation when the denominator becomes very small. This has the effect of amplifying any noise in the reconstructed image, causing visible bright "speckles" in the reconstructed image. To overcome this difficulty, a threshold value is introduced. If the denominator falls above this threshold, then the kernel as defined earlier is used. However, if the denominator falls below this threshold, it has been recommended to switch to an entirely nonnegative B–spline kernel. The definition for this kernel is given in Equation (5.4), and a plot can be seen in Figure 5.16.

$$k(x) = \frac{1}{6} \begin{cases} 3|x|^3 - 6|x|^2 + 4 & 0 \leq |x| < 1 \\ -|x|^3 + 6|x|^2 - 12|x| + 8 & 1 \leq |x| < 2 \\ 0 & 2 \leq |x| \end{cases} \tag{5.4}$$

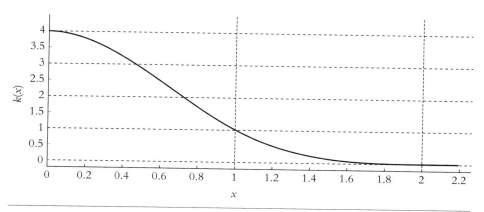

FIGURE 5.16 B-spline kernel function $k(x)$ versus x.

The switching between two kernel functions bears another potential problem. If the threshold value is reached and the switch occurs, unwanted discontinuities could be introduced. We shall thus blend smoothly between both kernels as the denominator approaches zero.

The resampling method described so far is optimized for a regular arrangement of the intensity samples (the pixel grid). Discontinuity edges can be defined at arbitrary positions and in any arrangement. This gives a framework in which the original goal, namely, the rescaling of stroke-based illustrations, can be carried out.

5.3.4   Creating and Reconstructing Renditions

Any gray-level image can serve as input to the algorithm being described. Discontinuity edges can be placed either by hand by a user, or automatically by an edge detection filter.[4] The image can then be changed in scale by the following steps:

1. *Compute a sample value for each pixel*   Usually, the actual pixel value will serve as the sample value. Around discontinuity edges, however, the sample value should be computed from nearby unobstructed pixels.

2. *Reduce the resolution of the sample grid*   This process yields large regions of almost equal tone when the sample grid is enlarged. Such regions are common

---

4. For example, algorithms that can be used here are presented in Canny (1986).

to pen-and-ink illustrations. The reduction process should stop if just enough detail remains to yield satisfactory results.

3. *Assign appropriate stroke textures to each image region*   This will define the appearance of the final illustration. The image is separated into several regions, each of which is—at the end—filled with the assigned texture. For an easier handling, each region should be defined in a separate layer and then also handled separately. All layers are overlaid for the final illustration.

4. *Assign outline strokes*   If possible and desired, let a user choose to include outline strokes for selected regions. In particular, discontinuity edges should be considered as possible positions for the placement of such outline strokes.

5. *Rescale the sample grid to the desired size*   Now, the rescaling operation, as described earlier, is applied to the sample grid. This yields a grayscale image of the desired size where the sharp features are maintained. In order to avoid a mechanical look of the final illustration, a little blurring can be introduced in this step. This is done by first scaling the sample grid to half the desired size using the method described. This intermediate image is then doubled in size by a standard filter.

6. *Apply the textures to the scaled image*   In this final step, the same approach as introduced in Section 5.1.2 is used. The defined image regions are filled with the assigned stroke textures. The strokes are clipped against the outlines of the regions. Finally, the layers holding the different image regions are merged to yield one single illustration.

Recalling the illustration in Figure 5.11, we will now see how the tone of the image stays the same when the preceding method is used. Figure 5.17(b) shows the same original image that was also used in the naive approach. The other two images show rescaled versions of the original. Note how the overall tone does not change regardless of the scale in which the image is presented.

The rescaling and rendering techniques are mainly applicable to pen-and-ink-style illustrations. For other types of brushes, several new challenges arise, which have to be mastered. Nonetheless, this algorithm offers a high potential for further development. One example might be the device-dependent rendering of such illustrations. The device in question—be it a web browser or a PostScript printer—gets the desired gray-level image and the set of stroke textures that are to be applied to certain image regions. The output is then produced in the highest possible quality by using drawing primitives offered by the device. This might also include a rescaling of the illustration in order to achieve the device's resolution. Another

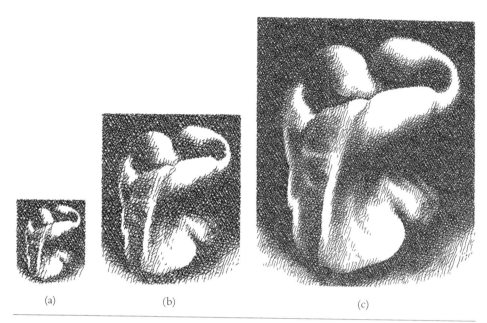

(a)   (b)   (c)

FIGURE 5.17 Rescaling the same image as in Figure 5.11 using the described method. Note that the images in (a) and (c) now show almost the same tonal value as in (b).

direction for further development is given by the definition of the textures itself. The techniques described in this chapter employ the same texture whatever the resolution or size of the image. This is not completely appropriate for textures with high structural detail. Here, multiresolution textures are needed, which change for different scales and resolutions of the target image.

Exercises

5.1   To compute tone accurately, it is important to take into account the overlap between strokes that cross one another. Suppose a surface of tone v is to be represented by bi-directional hatching and that the strokes in each direction deposit a total amount of ink x on the paper. Show that x can be approximated by $x = 1 - \sqrt{1 - v}$.

5.2   Design stroke textures to indicate wood, plastic, and water. Show that your stroke textures yield reasonable results by using them in the rendition of a simple scene.

5.3   Experiment with the formula $w(x, y) = (a + b \cdot \text{distance } ((x, y), l))^{-c}$ to determine good combinations of the constants a, b, and c.

5.4   We wish to devise an efficient algorithm for applying prioritized stroke textures:

    a. Design and implement a 3D BSP tree to compute visible volumes and shadow volumes. The result should be a set of convex polygons that can easily be ordered in depth with respect to the viewpoint.

    b. Design and implement a 2D BSP tree to describe a 2D image and show how it is to be generated from the 3D BSP tree. The 2D BSP forms a partitioning of the image space in normalized display coordinates with each cell in the partition corresponding either to a unique frontmost polygon in the 3D scene or to the background. Show how this data structure can be used for fast clipping of strokes.

    c. Design and implement a planar map (Mäntylä, 1988). Show how this data structure can be used to efficiently generate outline strokes of surfaces.

5.5   Design and implement a data structure to manage the collection of strokes that together form a painting. The following operations are to be supported and are to be implemented efficiently:

    a. Find all strokes that overlap a given stroke.

    b. Find the stroke nearest to a given pixel.

    Show how to use these operations to delete a stroke in an image. (Hint: You may find it useful to try a k-D tree and then to modify it.)

5.6   Devise a way of applying stroke textures to a region over which the intensity varies slightly. See Salisbury et al. (1994) for a possible solution.

5.7   Design and implement an interactive painting program where a user places paintbrushlike strokes over a given image. The speed and direction of the mouse movement influences the size and orientation of the strokes.

Bibliographic Notes

The most important papers in the area covered by this chapter are Salisbury et al. (1994) and Winkenbach and Salesin (1994). They introduce algorithms and data structures for pen-and-ink illustration, in particular, prioritized stroke textures and outlines. The first paper by Salisbury, Anderson, Barzel, and Salesin introduces stroke textures for a 2D illustration system. The second paper by Winkenbach and Salesin uses this technique to create illustrations of 3D models. The main focus here is on providing different levels of detail as well as a correct sense of illumination. In both papers, the drawing of single strokes is based on Finkelstein's work on multiresolution curves (Finkelstein and Salesin, 1994).

In Salisbury et al. (1994), the difference image algorithm to select stroke positions is introduced. It has been used and extended by Kowalski et al. They present a method to render fur, grass, and trees using *graftals* (Kowalski et al., 1999) as well as animating the resulting images in a frame-coherent way (Markosian et al., 2000) with different levels of detail.

Fundamental ideas for algorithms to leave out parts of a visualization were introduced in Winkenbach and Salesin (1994). The psychological background to explain the advantages of this approach was introduced by Weidenmann (1994), who worked on the use of images for knowledge acquisition (see also Schumann et al., 1996). More information on the psychological background for illustrations can be found in a collection of papers edited by Willows and Houghton (1987; Houghton and Willows, 1987).

The orientation of strokes along "painted" vector fields is the main focus of the paper by Salisbury et al. (1997). This work continues the research on pen-and-ink illustrations on the level of strokes. Winkenbach, at the same time, goes into a different direction and uses parametric surface models directly for rendering pen-and-ink illustrations (Winkenbach and Salesin, 1996). Here, new problems arise with respect to stroke spacing and line thickness. The treatment of these, however, lies over and above our introductory text. The orientation of strokes on such surfaces and its influence on the recognition of the shape of the depicted object has been examined by Girshick et al. (2000) and Girshick and Interrante (1999).

Seminal work on selecting strokes through mouse movements was carried out by Haeberli (1990) and called "paint by numbers." Another application of paintbrushlike strokes that is especially suited for animation was introduced by Meier (1996).

Finally, work on resizing images has been carried out by Salisbury et al. (1996). Ideas on replaying an edit history have been explored by Marshall (1995) and by Perlin and Velho (1995) in systems called "live pictures" and "live paint."

6 | WORKING WITH $2\frac{1}{2}$D DATA STRUCTURES

In the last few chapters—especially in Chapter 2—we have exclusively used two-dimensional information pertaining to light intensities. All algorithms work on the basis of altering images that encode light intensities on a per-pixel basis. These light intensities are created either by a (photorealistic) rendering program or in a real photographic process when we work with scanned images. We will now start our exploration of three-dimensional techniques. In this chapter, one of the most important concepts in NPR is introduced—the encoding of three-dimensional information in two-dimensional data structures.

These data structures are called *G-buffers*, and we will first define them and give some examples of how to create such G-buffers and of some operations defined on them. We will cover a few applications. The use of additional geometric information and the inclusion of this information in a rendition can greatly enhance the perception of an object's shape. The first application we will describe in detail thus pertains to such "comprehensible rendering" techniques. G-buffers can also be used in interactive applications and help to set the parameters for drawing tools. After studying such methods, we will finally see how G-buffers can be used in connection with dithering algorithms to create comprehensible and aesthetically pleasing images.

6.1 G-Buffers

All the images we have been using so far present information that is visible to the human eye and recordable with a photographic camera. Though the resulting

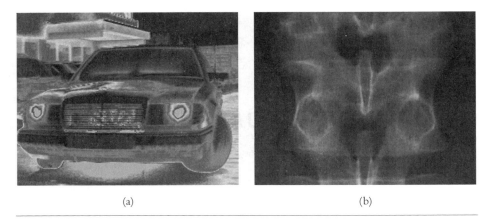

(a)   (b)

FIGURE 6.1 Special recording equipment allows the creation of images that show normally hidden properties: infrared image of a car showing regions of different temperature (a), x-ray image of a part of the vertebral column (b).

photographs are the most widely used kinds of images, there are also other "images" to look at. Even when we think about photography and take newer high-tech approaches into account, other information can be recorded provided we use the proper equipment. As an example, Figure 6.1 shows an infrared and an x-ray image being taken with highly specialized cameras. The x-ray image especially shows properties of the object that are normally hidden to the eye of an observer.

If we translate this to computer graphics, it should be possible to create images that show properties of the depicted geometric objects other than those we are used to seeing. For the remainder of this section, we will assume that we have a particular system that creates the images we need. For a closer look at the rendering process in general, we recommend the books by Foley et al. (1990) or by Watt (2000). Normally, a renderer creates a bitmap, where for each pixel a color value represents the actual color of the scene object at the position that projects onto the pixel's coordinates. This color value is computed using information about the geometry as well as information about the lighting in the scene.

In a similar process, special rendering techniques may now create bitmaps where each pixel represents, for example, one of the following values:

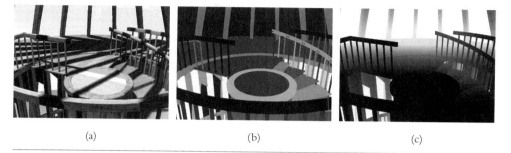

(a)   (b)   (c)

FIGURE 6.2 Images revealing different scene properties: color of scene objects (RGB-buffer) (a), object identifiers (ID-buffer) (b), and depth (z-buffer) (c). (See also color insert.)

- the ID of the scene object to which the pixel belongs,
- the distance of a given point on an object from the view plane (z–depth),
- the surface normal coordinates at the respective point, or
- the patch coordinates (u, v) for models consisting of spline surfaces.

These bitmaps should encode the respective values in an appropriate manner so that these geometric properties become visible to the human eye. In Figure 6.2, several images that are created this way show different scene properties.

Since such bitmaps store geometric properties of a scene, they are called *geometric buffers* or, for short, *G-buffers*. They themselves already reveal a great deal of information about the observed scene. Applying image processing operations to them makes it even more appealing to use such bitmaps as an additional source of input information for the creation of non–photorealistic renditions. We will look at a few examples to make clear which information can be collected and how it might be used.

6.2 Operations on G-Buffers

Let us start with a rather simple example. Assume we have an image, generated by a rendering system, where the projection of each scene object has been assigned a unique color (or gray value). With this image, we can easily determine the number of visible objects in the scene from a given viewpoint by simply counting the number of different colors (or gray values, respectively) in the image. Such an *object ID-buffer* also helps with selecting a specific object o in a rendered scene.

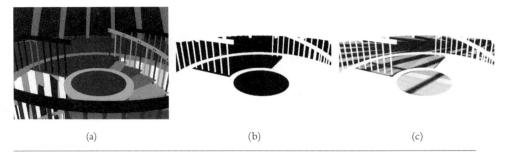

(a)   (b)   (c)

FIGURE 6.3 Using an object ID buffer (a) to create a mask (b). This mask is then used to select all parts of the image (c) that belong to that specific object (here the object itself consists of several parts).

We may set all those pixels to black that contribute to object o by selecting them based on the color o is rendered with. All other pixels do not belong to the desired object and are set to white. In this way, we yield a mask for filtering out exactly the area covered by o that can be applied to other renditions of the same scene if they are created with the same camera parameters and in the same size and resolution. Figure 6.3 shows an example of this technique.

Probably the best-known kind of G-buffer in computer graphics is the *z-buffer* although its use is mostly seen in a different context. A z-buffer contains for each pixel the z-part of the screen coordinates of the respective object's position. It is thus a representation of the distance of the object from the point of view, or— said in a simpler way—a depth map. What can this be used for? First, z-buffers are a common tool in photorealistic techniques to easily solve hidden surface removal problems. Second, they can be used to provide structural information of the scene.

Each pixel in a z-buffer represents the distance of the respective object's position to the view plane. Thus, two neighboring pixels that have the same value (color) tell that the points of the scene being projected on those pixels have the same distance to the view plane. Taking this further, a smoth transition between the values of neighboring pixels means that there is a face in the scene that gradually changes its distance to the view plane. A sudden change in the z-buffer can then be interpreted as a larger difference in the depth of two points in the scene. In most cases, such differences appear when an object's border is reached and a second object happens to be behind or in front of the first one. So,

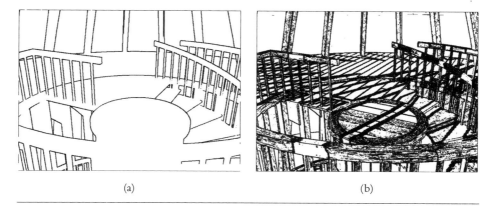

(a)   (b)

FIGURE 6.4 An edge detection filter applied to a z-buffer (a) and the actually rendered image (b). Note that in (b) not only the object's contours but also other color changes in the image are found that do not stem from geometrical properties but instead from differently lit areas or changes in the material.

detecting sharp discontinuities in the z-buffer helps to detect the contours of the scene objects.

There are several possibilities to algorithmically detect discontinuities in a bitmap. The most common one is to apply differential operators or edge detection operators to the image—a classical operation in image processing. One of the most widely used first order differential operators is the Sobel operator, as denoted in Equation (6.1). Here $G_{i,k}$ means the value of the pixel in line i and row k.

$$d1(G_{i,k}) = \frac{1}{8} \begin{pmatrix} |G_{i-1,k-1} + 2G_{i,k-1} + G_{i+1,k-1} \\ -G_{i-1,k+1} - 2G_{i,k+1} - G_{i+1,k+1}| \\ +|G_{i+1,k-1} + 2G_{i+1,k} + G_{i+1,k+1} \\ -G_{i-1,k-1} - 2G_{i-1,k} - G_{i-1,k+1}| \end{pmatrix} \tag{6.1}$$

If we now apply this operator to the z-buffer from Figure 6.2, we get the result shown in Figure 6.4(a). Applying the very same operator to the original rendered (RGB) image yields Figure 6.4(b). As it can be seen easily, the discontinuities detected in the rendered image not only have their origin in the *geometry* but also in changes in texture and lighting. Those few examples have already shown that G-buffers are a useful tool to obtain information about a scene that could otherwise not be communicated in an appropriate way (see the example given in

Figure 6.4). In the field of NPR, this kind of information is especially valuable since it can be used as input data for the image generation or modification. Some examples of this will be explored next.

6.3 Comprehensible Rendering

Many computer-generated images have problems concerning the *comprehensibility* of the portrayed scene. This is due to the image generation process that tries to mimic physical optical phenomena. This often yields images where certain features are hard to recognize or even completely missing. Such features include, for instance, the contrast between adjacent objects that have a similar color, a clear indication for surface shape or curvature, or indications for the internal structure of a complex object.

Illustrators use certain techniques to enhance such features in handmade illustrations that result in image artifacts that cannot be explained with physical laws. However, these image artifacts are a valuable tool to increase the comprehensibility of an image and help the viewer to "read" the illustration and extract the information the author wanted to communicate. As already stated, many of the features that need enhancement are pertaining to three-dimensional properties of objects in the scene. For example, the distinction between two almost equally colored objects can be enhanced by drawing silhouette edges of one or the other object. In a similar manner, curved shapes can be made more recognizable if curved hatching lines were added, possibly even to a shaded image. Hatching lines as well as contour lines can be computed from 3D information that is given in a G-buffer.

If we take the edges detected from the z-buffer, we can greatly enhance object boundaries, as can be seen in Figure 6.5. The given input data include a photorealistically rendered image that shows problems in differentiating between the nut and the background in low-contrast regions as well as estimating the form of the nut in the front part where the edge disappears in the highlight. Also given is a z-buffer that may be created within the rendering process. Applying a differential operator (for instance, the Sobel operator) to this z-buffer yields profile edges and internal edges (first and second order differential operator, respectively, see Figure 6.5(c)). Combining the resulting images from this operation with the input image enhances the edges and thus makes the distinction between the nut and the background more clear.

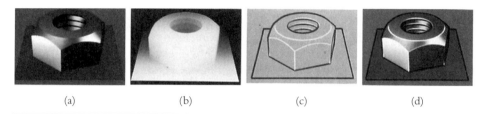

(a)	(b)	(c)	(d)

FIGURE 6.5 Given a rendered image (a) and a z-buffer (b), the image can be visually improved by including the discontinuities in the z-buffer (c) as edges in the rendition (d).

The second example that we will talk about in detail is connected to shape recognition of curved surfaces. Here, shading is already a strong cue, but wrong or insufficient shading can lead to inappropriate "imaginations" of the visualized surface. Looking in the area of line drawings, hatching is an even stronger shape cue that can be incorporated in shaded images to guide the viewer. Hatching lines usually follow the contour of an object and represent the curvature of the surface. To create hatching lines, we need different G-buffers than just for enhancing the contour. If we are working with free-form surfaces as geometric models, we can derive G-buffers that are particularly well suited to create hatching lines.

Free-form surface models are based on a parametric description of the surfaces; we can thus save the coordinates (u and v) of these parametric descriptions on a per-pixel basis in a bitmap and create two G-buffers. In these two buffers, pixels having the same color value represent the same value for one parameter direction. It is now possible to connect pixels with the same color and in this way to create lines that represent equal parameter values. These lines can be used as hatching lines in two different directions. Without further processing, the hatching would be equally dense and cover the whole surface. If we combine these hatching buffers with the photorealistic image by varying the intensity of the hatching image based on the light intensity, we can create images where the surface shape is clearly communicated by hatching lines (see Figure 6.7). Furthermore, a combination with the first and second order derivatives from a z-buffer enhances the contours and makes the image even more comprehensible. An overview of this technique is given in Algorithm 6.1 and shown schematically in Figure 6.6.

1   generate a shaded image S
2   generate G-buffers for u and v parameter directions
3    $U :=$ hatching lines for the whole image in u direction
4    $V :=$ hatching lines for the whole image in v direction
5   combine U and S for vertical hatching
6   combine V and S for horizontal hatching
7   combine $U, V,$ and S for cross-hatching

ALGORITHM 6.1   Generating curved hatching lines using G-buffers.

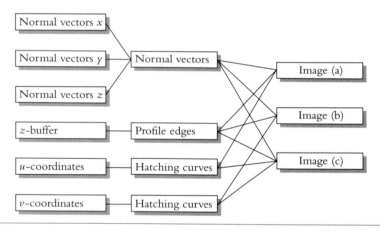

FIGURE 6.6   Combination of different G-buffers to create hatching lines.

These two examples have shown that including three-dimensional information in a rendition may enhance the perception of the portrayed scene. There are many more possibilities to create such renditions while the basic approach is usually the same—create certain G-buffers, possibly manipulate them to extract additional features, and finally combine them with the photorealistic image. As we will see in later sections of this chapter, G-buffers can also be used to choose and parameterize rendering algorithms based on three-dimensional properties of a scene.

FIGURE 6.7 Results to Figure 6.6.

6.4 **Interactive Painting**

While the last sections focus more on automatic image processing, G–buffers offer possibilities to enhance interaction with images or even create new interaction facilities. Simon Schofield, one of the pioneers in the field, dealt with this kind of question and set the stage for further development.

Standard painting and drawing systems place geometric elements—like dots (even pixels), lines, shapes—or brush marks in a bitmap such that these elements cover a certain region on the image. The placement is simply a *copy* operation; that is, the color values from the element's or mark's description are copied at the appropriate pixel positions regardless of what the contents of that particular position is at that time. Further, painting programs in that sense are inherently two dimensional; all effects that create the impression of 3D have to be created manually by the user. This is very often a difficult task if a certain kind of realism is required since many of the dependencies between features in the image and the three-dimensional position of the respective object part are hard to estimate. An incorporation of 3D information in such paint programs would be highly beneficial.

The key to using 3D information in interactive systems lies in the employment of G–buffers. An interactive painting system can then be built as a "post-processing" application to a photorealistic renderer if this renderer supplies the necessary data for each pixel. Among others, the following G–buffers are particularly useful:

- *ID-buffer*   Object identifiers are used to distinguish between model parts and to selectively apply certain algorithms.

- *z-buffer*   The z-buffer contains the z-coordinate of the respective object point, that is, depth information.

- ◆ *n-buffer* The *n*-buffer contains the surface normal at the object's point. Usually the normal vector's *x*-, *y*-, and *z*-coordinates are encoded in the three color channels of an RGB image.

- ◆ *material-buffer* Here, material attributes are encoded in a way that different materials can be distinguished. More detailed buffers, where distinctive features of the materials might be treated separately, also fall into that category.

- ◆ *shadow-buffer* Shadow masks that are generated for each light source separately or for all light sources in one mask are stored so that lighting conditions can be evaluated later on.

As an extension, there are also buffers that contain user-supplied values, for instance, regions of interest or more subjective descriptions of the model.

Since all these values are stored on a per-pixel basis, they can be combined in the (extended) bitmap that serves as a background for the following painting and drawing operations. This makes all data for all points quickly and readily available within an interactive environment. We can now paint on this "canvas" and make use of the data that is stored therein to manipulate the painting tools or painting operations. For these painting operations, we will use an extended definition of brush marks such that they can be parameterized in a variety of ways (color, size, shape, and so on).

The extensive description of the scene's geometry within a bitmap makes some new algorithms possible. Brush marks can change their size with respect to the *z*-depth so that they get smaller with increasing distance from the viewer. Further, lines can be made thinner this way, achieving the effect of depth cuing. The most interesting application for the *z*-values, however, comes with perspective texturing of an area. Imagine a painting tool with which areas can be filled with a certain kind of texture. If this texture does not change the size of its structural elements (for example, bricks) with the distance from the viewer, then the resulting images look "wrong." Making the fill algorithm depend on the *z*-value will prevent this problem.

For such filling operations, the selection of the area to be filled is a crucial operation. In standard painting programs, this selection is often placed into the responsibility of the user who identifies a specific area by explicitly providing the geometry of this area or by giving a color where all pixels sharing this color are selected. We can now select regions based on more appropriate information. It is—especially in architectural illustrations—often the case that several areas have to be selected that lay in one plane, even if these areas are not connected to each other. Such a selection can be performed based on the normal buffer values since all pixels referring to points lying in the same plane have the same normal vector coordinates. Further, area filling based on material properties or object IDs is supported by selecting areas with the same object ID or material ID.

Finally, we can place additional bitmaps in the image while maintaining the correct perspective and the correct depth sorting. For this, an interaction tool is needed with which the bitmap can be moved through the scene in z-direction. While doing this, the bitmap is appropriately scaled and only drawn in places where no other object is in front of it. (This is calculated by evaluating the z-buffer.) This technique is nicely applicable for architectural illustrations to place trees or other additional elements in the image.

We will illustrate these methods with a number of examples. The scene in Figure 6.8(a) is rendered from a 3D model and then displayed by showing only contour lines. The user then selected a few different paintbrushes to achieve this rather pointillist style. More interesting is Figure 6.8(b), where the effect of placing additional bitmaps (in this case, the trees) can be studied. They get smaller the further away from the viewer they are placed. Note also the brick texture at the columns, which changes according to the perspective.

The second example (Figure 6.9) shows different stylistic variations that can be created from one and the same model by choosing different painting tools. In Figure 6.9(a), the output of a simple photorealistic renderer is given. This will be used as a reference image for the following renditions. First, some additional bitmaps showing trees or persons are placed in the scene that change their size according to the perspective (Figure 6.9(b)). Moreover, these bitmaps are planes that are added to all underlying G–buffers such that they are treated as scene objects in subsequent operations. Besides that, the building is textured in a certain style and the resulting image can easily be used as an architectural illustration. In Figure 6.9(c), the textures are changed to a more pen–and–ink style that is also applied to the trees in the background. (This means the textures are drawn on the planes that are inserted in the G–buffers for the trees.) Note that these trees are partially occluded by the building in front even though they are not part of the 3D model. Finally, Figure 6.9(d) employs a different set of paintbrushes, giving the image a more painted appeal.

(a)   (b)

FIGURE 6.8 Interactive painting based on G-buffers. The paintbrush strokes in (a) are parameterized based on properties of the underlying geometric model. The trees in (b) are additional bitmaps with placement based on the z-buffer. Note how they change in size and how correct occlusion is achieved. (See also color insert.)

As can be seen from the examples, adding three-dimensional information to painting programs and building tools to use this information in the painting process can help to create highly illustrative images. Even more, creating these images in an interactive session has the advantage that the user can manipulate the rendition exactly as he or she wants and hence create images that exactly fit to the application at hand (see Figure 6.9(b)).

6.5 3D Parameters for 2D Dithering

In the final section of this chapter, we come back to a class of algorithms that can make extensive use of provided additional information: halftoning algorithms as explored in Chapter 2. In this earlier chapter, the goal was to reproduce a given color or grayscale image using just two colors. The resulting bi-level images should come as close to the original as possible in terms of tone reproduction. Since we are working only on the given image, no additional information is available that pertains to three-dimensional features of the underlying model. Our goal now is to enhance the display of three-dimensional scenes using halftoning textures. This is useful for displaying rendered images on a bi-level display or for the preparation of

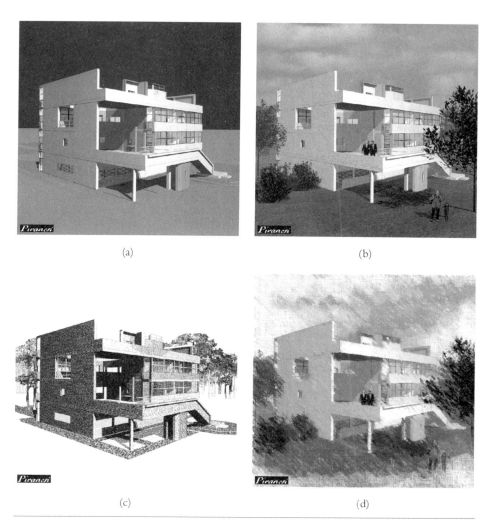

FIGURE 6.9 Different stylistic variations achieved by using different drawing tools: photorealistic rendition (a), added environment (b), pen-and-ink style (c), and painted style (d). (See also color insert.)

rendered images for printing. In particular, we will aim at enhancing the depiction of geometry, illumination, and user-defined features.

An obvious way to render three-dimensional objects differently depending on their geometry or other 3D information is to work directly in 3D since it is the case with many photorealistic approaches. Here, texture mapping plays an important role since the parameters of the mapping process can be controlled by the objects' geometries, and the appearance of the mapped texture depends on the lighting conditions in the scene. We will not, however, go into detail for this approach since using G-buffers in this area opens up a different and promising way to exploit two-dimensional techniques for the display of 3D features.

The image-based approach to the halftoning of 3D scenes constructs the dither screens by two-dimensional texture control techniqes as they are described in Section 2.2.3. The depiction of geometric information can be enhanced by determining the parameters for the dither screen generation based on G-buffers. In the next paragraphs, the following G-buffers are exploited:

- ID-buffer containing object IDs,

- normal-buffer containing normal vector coordinates,

- lighting-buffer containing scene illumination information, for instance, shadows, direct and indirect illumination intensities, and

- z-buffer and its derivatives.

These G-buffers are given in Figure 6.10 for a sample scene.

The simplest technique to distinguish visually between different objects in a scene is to render them differently either by using a distinctive texture for each separate object or by making the parameters for the texture creation depending on the object's ID. If we generate the dither screens (textures) based on the method proposed in Section 2.2.3, then a selection of a different function set consisting of the displacement functions D_S and D_t, the control function C, and even the dither kernel τ and the mapping function $\mathcal{M}$ for each object is possible. This can be seen in Figure 6.11(a), where the ID-buffer controls the scale and direction (both mapping), and the waviness (displacement) of the texture.

The enhancement achieved with the application of this technique results in a better discernibility of the scene objects. However, the recognition of such geometric features like curvature is still rather poor. Thus, the direction of the

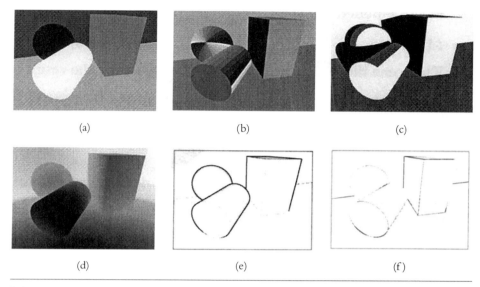

FIGURE 6.10 Different G-buffers used for the techniques described in this section: ID-buffer (a), normal-buffer (b), lighting-buffer (c), z-buffer (d), first derivative (e), second derivative (f).

texture should be aligned with some value that describes the geometry. The normal vector direction can be chosen here, which is seen in Figure 6.11(b).

If we take this last image as a starting point for further enhancements, the following changes will be rather subtle but nevertheless a contribution to the comprehensibility and perception of the depicted scene. Illumination is a key issue in illustrative images since many of the perceptual processes involved with human vision rely on such visual cues that are generated by light and shadow. The lighting buffer contains information about whether an area of the image is directly lit, indirectly lit, or lying in shadow. One possible use for this information is to apply a different texture in the shadow areas that unifies all those surfaces in the image that are not illuminated by a light source (see Figure 6.12(a)).

Finally, depth perception and depth cues are very often problematic in computer-generated images. Photorealistic computer graphics often employs fog effects to make distant objects appear farther away. By changing the contrast of the generated halftoning texture (dither screen), a similar effect can be achieved in NPR, as can be seen in Figure 6.12(b). Here, the error diffusion process is

(a)   (b)

FIGURE 6.11 The ID-buffer is used to control texture waviness, scale, and direction for each object (a) whereas the normal-buffer controls the direction of the texture (b).

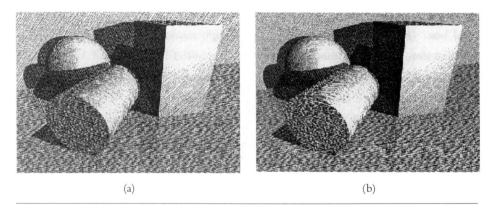

(a)   (b)

FIGURE 6.12 The lighting-buffer is used to unify the texture in areas that are in the shadow (a) whereas the distance from the viewing plane (z-buffer) controls the error diffusion algorithm and thus the contrast in the image (b).

guided by the z-buffer so that the contrast in the image is reduced the farther away a depicted object is from the viewer.

As an additional enhancement of the scene, edge lines generated from the first and second order derivatives of the z-buffer can be included in the rendition yielding the final illustration in Figure 6.13.

FIGURE 6.13 The final illustration shows all techniques together and incorporates geometric information.

Besides pure geometric information, user-supplied values also can be used to guide the image generation process. In a similar way as it is done for the generation of G-buffers, the user creates a buffer where each color or gray-scale value represents a certain feature. These features can be important values or additional classification schemes that are then expressed graphically by choosing different rendering (halftoning) methods and parameters. We have already seen an example for this method in Section 2.2.3 (recall Figure 2.19). Here, an object ID-buffer was used to select a specific object that is then treated with a certain rendering style (dithering).

Exercises

6.1 Use your favorite geometric modeling and rendering software and find out whether it is capable of creating G-buffers. If not, find software that has this capability. Create a few different G-buffers from one model and see how the different geometrical properties are represented.

6.2 Take a set of different G-buffers (created with a rendering program as described in Exercise 6.1) and use a painting program to manipulate a photorealistic rendition based on masks that are obtained from the G-buffers. Use different image processing filters on different regions of the image.

6.3   Extend your implementation of the procedural screening methods (see Chapter 2) in such a way that G-buffers are included in the image manipulation process. Find different ways of influencing the kernel, mapping, and displacement functions.

6.4   Use the techniques introduced in this chapter to create illustrations from a 3D model that clearly visualize the shape of the scene objects as well as illumination features. Which methods are useful for illustrations?

6.5   Implement an interactive system to "paint" with parameterizable brushstrokes. The size and orientation (and possibly other parameters) of the strokes should be computed from G-buffers.

6.6   Extend your program from Exercise 6.5 to place bitmap images in the created rendition that can be moved back and forth in z-direction.

6.7   Which user-defined buffers do you think are useful for illustrations? Create such buffers and test your assumptions.

Bibliographic Notes

G-buffers as a term and as a concept for the creation of more "comprehensible" renditions were introduced in the paper by Saito and Takahashi (1990). G-buffers have been used, however, before and after this time under different terms. Schofield, one of the NPR pioneers, has chosen the term *enriched pixel matrix*. The interactive system Piranesi that Schofield introduced in his Ph.D. thesis (Schofield 1994) used G-buffers to select regions of an image that are then interactively changed by a user via painting operations. This technique is also described in Lansdown and Schofield (1995), where it is put in the context of other NPR techniques. Richens and Schofield (1995) have been using Piranesi for architectural designs and thus report quite extensively on the users' responses.

G-buffers in connection with halftoning techniques are exploited by Buchanan and Veryovka. Their paper (1999a) made a big contribution to research in the area of G-buffers. Based on earlier work on halftoning in general (see Buchanan et al., 1998, Veryovka and Buchanan, 1999b) and on procedural halftoning (Veryovka and Buchanan, 1999a), they introduce the concept of *comprehensible halftoning*, also in (Veryovka and Buchanan, 1999a). The key for comprehensible halftoning is to make the functions for the generation of the (procedural) dither screens depending on the contents of G-buffers.

Since then, many authors have been using this technique to achieve different effects. Among these are Deussen et al., who developed hatching methods that fall back on G-buffers (1998). The exploitation of G-buffers in the context of lighting models and illustrative images is presented in more detail in Chapter 8. This topic is based on the work of Hamel (Hamel, 2000; Hamel et al., 1998; Deussen et al., 1999a).

7 | GEOMETRIC MODELS AND THEIR EXPLOITATION IN NPR

Whereas in the first few chapters of this book techniques are shown that are independent of the geometry behind a rendition, we will now move on to methods where geometric properties of the objects being portrayed in a rendition are used to determine parameters of the visualization. Geometric models are basically mathematical descriptions of a scene in terms of shape and other properties. This chapter explores how different types of models are constructed and what kind of information can be taken out of the geometric model to be employed in NPR.

In this sense, this chapter continues the line of reasoning from Chapter 6. There, G-buffers are explored as one way of representing three-dimensional information. This information is encoded in a two-dimensional data structure (an image) and used by exploiting image processing and image combination algorithms. Such G-buffers can be produced with modeling and rendering packages and are in most cases a by-product of the rendering process. Nevertheless, they offer a wide range of possibilities for non-photorealistic image generation techniques.

Going one step further and looking directly into three dimensions, there are basically two different types of models from which renditions can be created—surface models and volume models. While the first concentrate on the description of an object's surface, the latter are a description of the contents of the volume occupied by the object. We will concentrate on surface models since most current applications of NPR draw on such models. We will discuss the description of the models and derive their main characteristics. Our goal will be to see how those characteristics are used in NPR to create effects that were classified as *model artifacts* in Chapter 1. The present material, however, only scratches the surface of the topic. Many possibilities to extend the research here are still open for future work.

The chapter starts with a general discussion of geometric models as data types. The description of the geometry together with operations defined thereon can be regarded as one entity and thus compared with the concept of abstract data types. Nevertheless, a special treatment is needed for the different kinds of models since the algorithms depend heavily on the underlying data structures. This dependency leads to a separate exploration of polygonal models and free-form surface models. We describe possible data structures and a few algorithms that come in handy for the creation of non-photorealistic renditions. For polygonal models, these operations are the classification of edges, the computation of intersections, and the determination of the global shape of a given model. These together form a basis to create and place hatching lines. For free-form surfaces, the computation of lines or points on the object's surface is treated in detail. Finally, an algorithm is presented to transform free-form surface models into polygonal meshes.

7.1 Geometric Models as Data Types

The classical view on geometric models—taken in the area of photorealistic computer graphics—considers a geometric model to consist only of the description of an object's *form*, that is, a polygonal, free-form surface or other description of the shape of the object's surfaces. In addition, certain information pertaining to the surface material properties can also be assumed to be available. In photorealistic computer graphics, such information suffices to describe objects to be rendered. With the addition of lighting information and camera settings, final renditions can be created. However, as we will demonstrate in this section, there is in fact more to modeling for NPR than this.

Certainly, geometric modeling for NPR can be carried out using conventional tools that are available commercially. However, NPR requires a shift in the emphasis in geometric modeling. This can be summarized by noting that NPR requires more *context information*, that is, information pertaining to the geometric model that normally would have no bearing on its appearance in a photorealistic rendition. This information influences both how users can interact with geometric models themselves, and which external data sources can be drawn into the process of rendering and interaction. Indeed, in the end we will see that while we are aiming at modeling for NPR, photorealistic rendering systems can benefit, too, from systematically paying more attention to these aspects.

To motivate further the need for such context information, recall some of the techniques discussed thus far in this book, and consider from where the information is to come that is required to use them effectively. In Chapter 1, we have already seen that different data sources are possible. To combine these data sources with the rendering process, we want to make full use of *presentation variables*. A presentation variable in this context is a value connected to an object being visualized where changes of this value have a direct influence on the visualization of this object. Presentation variables are, for example:

- *Visualization style* What is the overall visualization style (shaded, hatched, stippled) of the rendition or the visualization style used for single objects?

- *Color* Which color is to be used to render an object in a certain context (normal, highlighted, unimportant)?

- *Dithering* Which dithering technique is to be used or which dither patterns should be exploited?

- *Painting* Which stroke texture is to be used for a given surface or which stroke style for a specific line?

- *Abstraction* Where should blank spaces be left in the rendition?

Other examples pertain to some of the techniques that will be presented in the remainder of this book:

- *Level of detail* How much detail is to be presented?

- *Distortion* By how much is the scaling factor of individual objects changed?

- *Annotations* Which objects are to be labeled by texts giving their names or information on other aspects of the model?

Much of this can be decided interactively by users. Nonetheless, users will require a significant amount of support in the form of visualization and editing tools to be able to make appropriate decisions.

Moreover, NPR is also used in applications in which decisions on the design of an image have to be made by other programs (we will come to this when talking about applications of NPR in Chapter 10). This implies that data from other applications must be linked up with objects, attributes, and parameters of the geometric models used as a basis for rendering. For example, a system for computer–aided learning (CAL) may draw on an NPR system for illustrating certain concepts. The presentation variables come in handy in such an application for helping users to focus on the topic at hand.

These considerations are relevant for photorealistic rendering, but they are absolutely essential in NPR. In particular, NPR systems have a much greater range of presentation variables than systems for photorealistic rendering because the former are not bound to obeying the laws of physics. Hence geometric models for NPR need to be more than only descriptions of what objects are to look like when rendered photorealistically. In particular, they need to provide access to the information that is used to decide on the values of presentation variables.

We will now treat geometric models in the sense of data type theory so as to formalize the requirements placed on them. An *abstract data type* T is defined as a mathematically specified collection of data-storing entities with operations to, for example, create, access, and change instances of these entities. For short, T is a collection of data and operations defined thereon: $T(D, O)$. In the following, we will apply this theory to geometric models. We will start with a rather general treatment of geometric models with this regard and then continue to specific kinds of models. In what follows, we emphasize the issues relevant to NPR, so it might be a good idea to derive a description of an abstract data type for your geometric model as an exercise.

7.1.1 **Data**

The data portion of an abstract data type describing a geometric model contains as a minimum a mathematical description of the objects' shape or volume.[1] In addition to this, there has to be information that is needed to define the appearance of the object in the rendered image. Both types of information are typically available in geometric models for the purpose of photorealistic image generation although they are not sufficient for NPR. Geometric models for NPR need to contain the following components:

- *Geometric information G* consists of the mathematical description of the object's geometry.

---

1. In the following, we will concentrate on surface models although most of the issues also apply to volume models.

- *Graphical information R*   consists of all the information needed to define the individual appearance of the geometric objects. Elements of R are, for instance, surface properties, color, transparency, smoothness, and so forth.

- *Context information C*   contains all the information over and above that needed to model the object's material properties, which nonetheless are needed to enhance the rendering process itself or support interaction with an image.

The third point in this list is one that is optional in photorealism but essential in NPR. All three information sets are interconnected to one another and form together the data portion for the abovementioned abstract data type. It is possible to differentiate further within these data sets, which yields different types of models, as is demonstrated for polygonal models in Section 7.2 and free-form surface models in Section 7.3. The graphical information and the context information are rather independent of the way in which the geometric information is defined. Thus, they can be treated in a more general manner.

We will not go into detail here about the graphical information. The elements of this set are well known from photorealistic computer graphics. For the context information, the following two elements are of particular importance:

- *External references*   This is data that makes it possible to establish and access links to external data sources. In particular, knowledge bases and databases can be accessed by treating symbols used as external references or links. Such external references can also represent links to the end user's knowledge. Examples are the object and subobject *identifiers* C_{ID} as well as records for other information (keywords, individual annotations provided by users, and so on).

- *Internal references*   This is information that is generally not accessed from outside the geometric model but used primarily for internal structuring. The most important example of such information is a *hierarchical structure* C_s of the geometric model. Such a structure describes a partial order among the objects in the model, using geometric primitives as the leaves and object identifiers as the internal nodes of a (sub)object hierarchy.

Given the information space formed by the abovementioned data sets, operations on this data have to be defined to complete the definition of an abstract data type for a geometric model. Since operations on the geometric data rely to a great extent on the actual definition of the geometry—be it a polygonal model or a free-form surface or a volumetric data set—they cannot be dealt with in a general way. In the following, the focus is mainly on general operations that are to be performed on the overall information space.

7.1.2 Operations on the Data

One of the fundamental characteristics of NPR is that not every individual artifact encoded within a geometric model is actually represented within the resultant images. Instead, a process of abstraction is used to determine *which* features will actually be encoded within the image, and *in what way* these features will be encoded. This is in stark contrast to photorealistic rendering where there is an a priori one-to-one correspondence between features of the model and pixels in a rendition.

Indeed, NPR algorithms rely on the one hand on a *selection* of features within models to determine which features will have a direct bearing on the image. This implies the design of appropriate algorithms for *searching* for distinctive elements in geometric models. These distinctive elements need to be defined, and the results of the search operations need to be stored in data structures offering efficient access to them. In general, ways for *exploring* a model have to be defined. On the other hand, often several features of a geometric model need to be changed or refined for the particular application at hand. Thus, sophisticated algorithms for *editing* geometric models are required. In summary, the primary operations that are to be carried out on geometric models are *viewing*, *exploration*, and *editing*. We will discuss these in turn.

Viewing of geometric and graphical information can generally be carried out in unison, much as is done for photorealistic rendering. Not so obvious, however, is how to view this geometric-graphical information in combination with context information. In some situations, it is possible to blend these into one view (like labeling a rendition with the object identifiers). In other situations, this is not feasible and the method of choice is to separate the views on the geometric-graphical information in one window and the context information in a second window. Considerable care must then be taken so that users recognize the correspondence between objects in the different windows.

Perhaps the most important concept in this kind of viewing is that of providing "detail in context." Particularly when dealing with two entirely different kinds of information (geometric and graphical versus context) describing the same objects, it is of vital importance for the usability of the system to give users clues to help them assess what is being visualized. Fisheye techniques in visualization are one way of dealing with this topic.

Exploration requires that high-quality navigation tools are available within and between the geometric-graphical view and the context view. The crux here is the visibility and the recognizability of objects in one window as a reaction to navigation actions in the second window. Consider, for example, the situation that a rendition of an object is shown in one window and the hierarchical structure in the second window. If the user selects an object in the hierarchy, you would expect this object to be accessible in the other window. If it is not directly visible, changes must be carried out. For example, the object can be rotated, obscuring objects can be made transparent, or they can be cut away. In any case, smooth transitions, for example, through animations, must be carried out so as not to confuse the users with changes they did not affect directly themselves.

Furthermore, it is not sufficient that an object is visible; it must also be recognizable. This means that it must be discernible, and the viewer's attention should be drawn to it in an appropriate manner. Highlighting, enlarging, or labeling are possible options to achieve this goal.

Editing facilities are finally required so that users can maintain their geometric models. The most important aspect here is to provide tools that enable users to deal with the very large number of objects that are generally involved in editing operations. A common operation in editing is to *group* many objects together into a single object and to deal with attributes of the group. For example, when developing the hierarchical structure of a geometric model, it may be necessary to combine hundreds of geometric primitives (like polygons). It is entirely infeasible to expect users to choose all the primitives individually. Instead, for example, "growing" algorithms should be provided to assist the user in such an operation.

These operations have to be implemented in a way that they can be used *together* as well as *independent* from each other. Some of the operations (like editing) change the model, and these changes have to be reflected in the visualization so that viewing and exploration are always carried out on the most current state of the model. Most modeling and rendering programs that aim to photorealistic image production include selected facilities for managing data in the sense described earlier. However, there is still considerable room for improvement, as the following description will show.

7.1.3 Implementation

In the field of computer graphics editors, geometric and structure information is integrated in modeling systems. However, not every kind of non-graphical contextual information can be managed with these systems. Often, even in high-end systems, the structuring of a model during the modeling process is not implemented or only in a very rudimentary manner. Often, the user can define a hierarchical linking only for selected animation techniques. If a structure editing tool is available, the actual tasks that can be performed on the structure view are rather limited. In many cases, the creation of new geometry is possible only in the three-dimensional model views.

One of the main concerns when working with the provided tools for editing the model structure and possibly also the assigned graphical and context information is the integration of the different views. Usually, hierarchical structures (such as C_s) are visualized as a tree. These trees can become fairly large, thus methods of visualizing the details of a node within the context of the complete tree are necessary here. Furthermore, a bidirectional coupling between the different views has to be established. For example, in the structure view, the tree is collapsed automatically to include the node selected in the model view. What's more, the model view should highlight the selected node in the structure view—this may include making other occluding objects transparent or rotating the model.

Finally, changes in the graphical or context information should be supported by special "attribute editors" that are accessible from both the structure and the model view. These editors represent the more traditional way of providing values for the presentation variables. More interesting in our context, however, are novel approaches to set presentation variables based on user interaction. So, for example, textures might be painted directly on the three-dimensional surface of the model, or drawing styles could be transferred from example paintings.

Summarizing, we can conclude

- Tools for structuring models in commercially available systems are provided in rudimentary manner. The navigation facilities of structure browsers are insufficient, however.

- The coupling between structure and geometry view alone is of limited value. An object selected in one view may be selected in another one, but it may not be visible or it may be too small to be recognized. Users have to struggle to find the selected object and perform a variety of navigation operations (for example, scrolling, rotating).

- Orientation and navigation in large models (and corresponding large structures) often is not sufficiently supported.

- Only graphical information that is directly related to the rendering process (for example, material description of object surfaces) can be managed. Context information, such as special textual information, cannot be managed at all.

- For NPR, special approaches to define graphical and context information are possible. These include "texturing by example," where the user either paints a texture directly on the object or selects an example image for texture and style transfer. Such methods can also be used to actually create the 3D geometry.

The support for visualizing and manipulating geometric information is highly developed; a variety of tools for creating, navigating, and editing in geometric information sets are provided. Support is limited for modeling tasks on a different level than the direct manipulation of the geometry.

The discussion of geometric models in general did not include the actual geometric data. Operations on this data portion depend heavily on the way this data is defined. Further, depending on the actual geometry definition, different operations are possible. Since polygonal models are the most common type of geometry representations, they are the focus of the following section. Many, if not all, other types of geometry representations can be converted into polygonal descriptions; an example of such a conversion process is illustrated in Section 7.3. Hence, any operations described in the following section are applicable to any kind of geometry after an appropriate transformation.

7.2 Polygonal Models

We will start our discussion of three-dimensional models with the most commonly used types of models, namely, *polygonal models*. A polygonal model consists of any number of *polygon meshes*, which describe in their entirety the scene to be modeled.

On an abstract level, a polygon mesh itself is a collection of vertices, edges, and polygons connected to each other in a way that

- each edge is shared by at most two polygons,
- each edge connects two vertices,
- a polygon is a closed sequence of edges, and
- a vertex is shared by at least two edges.

Polygon meshes can be represented in different ways, each of which has its pros and cons where the main criteria for evaluating a representation are space and time to perform operations. Typical operations on a polygon mesh are

- finding the edged incident to a vertex,
- finding the vertices connected by an edge,
- finding the polygons sharing an edge or a vertex,
- finding the edges of a polygon,
- finding the polygon enclosing a given point on the surface,
- simplifying the mesh by reducing the number of edges, vertices, or polygons while roughly maintaining the shape of the surface being described,
- displaying the polygon mesh, or
- evaluating the polygon mesh in terms of identifying errors in the representation.

As we will see, NPR algorithms make heavy use of such operations, more so than standard algorithms for photorealistic rendering where pipeline processing of polygons and vertices has come to dominate commercially available systems. Hence for NPR, considerable care must be taken when deciding on the representation so as to be able to produce better space- and time-efficient algorithms.

7.2.1 Description of Polygonal Models

We will show some of the common representations for polygon meshes here and leave it to you to decide which of them best fits the needs of the application at hand (see also Exercise 7.1).

In the *explicit representation*, each polygon P is given by a list of vertex coordinates: $P = ((x_1, y_1, z_1), (x_2, y_2, z_2), \ldots, (x_n, y_n, z_n))$. The vertices of a polygon are stored in the order in which they would be encountered traveling around the polygon. Edges are created between two consecutive entries in the list as well as between the last and the first entry. The surface normal is computed from the vertices.

For a single polygon, this is a very efficient representation. However, considering a mesh of many thousand polygons, this representation yields several problems—especially the spatial efficiency decreases quickly with increasing polygon count in the mesh since shared vertices are stored multiple times. Further, when displaying the mesh, shared edges are drawn twice since they are not modeled explicitly.

Many graphics packages (like PHIGS and OpenInventor) use *pointers to a vertex list* to represent polygons. Here, each vertex is stored just once in a vertex list V containing *all* vertices of the mesh: $V = ((x_1, y_1, z_1), (x_2, y_2, z_2), \ldots, (x_n, y_n, z_n))$. A polygon P is defined by a list of indices (also known as pointers) into this list: $P = (i_1, i_2, \ldots, i_m)$. This representation is much more space efficient than an explicit representation since each vertex is stored only once. However, finding shared edges is still a problem.

Thus, taking a second level of indirection into account yields a representation of a polygon mesh by *pointers to an edge list*. Again, we have the vertex list V as before, but each polygon is defined as a list of pointers to an edge list E. In this list, each edge occurs just once and is itself defined as a pair of pointers to the vertex list. Even more, the description of an edge may also contain pointers to the polygons to which it belongs. Hence, we describe a polygon $P = (e_1, e_2, \ldots, e_n)$ and an edge $E = (v_1, v_2, p_1, p_2)$. Note that an edge does not necessarily belong to two polygons. In those cases, either p_1 or p_2 is set to zero. In this representation, we have several levels of indirection that help save space and that should make it easier to carry out special operations.

The three representations discussed earlier fit the needs of general applications. For special cases and other requirements, more elaborate representations have been developed.

7.2.2 Operations for Polygonal Models

Polygon meshes are, in general, an approximation of the objects being modeled. This is rather obvious since modeling round objects is impossible by just using polygons. To get a more exact representation, you may be tempted to create the model using smaller polygons, thus making the approximation error smaller. However, this may dramatically increase the polygon count and the storage capacity needed for representing the mesh; it will thus increase the processing time for any operation on the model or for display.

We can see how to exploit these approximation "errors" in NPR by studying them in somewhat more detail. First, there are unwanted lines and edges in the rendition. This is even the case in photorealistic images when using certain shading algorithms. Interestingly enough, computer graphics practitioners put great effort in developing algorithms to eliminate these artifacts. All those algorithms work on the assumption that the vertices of a polygonal model lie on the original

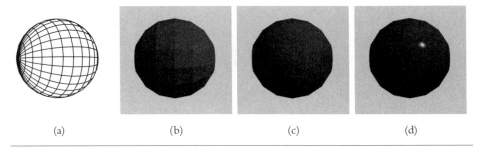

(a)   (b)   (c)   (d)

FIGURE 7.1 Different shading models try to cover the approximation error in a polygonal model: wireframe (a), flat shading (b), Gouraud-shading (c), Phong-shading (d).

surface (that is approximated by the polygon mesh). Thus, for these vertices a correct position is given and correct lighting attributes can be calculated. For all other points, those illumination values have to be interpolated. Here, several methods have been developed to make a polygonal surface appear smooth again (see Figure 7.1).

These photorealistic techniques try to hide information that is not needed in the context of creating a visually pleasing image and of creating the same visual stimulus as the original scene. However, this information is of interest to the viewer, and by using NPR techniques we are now in a position to deliver more information to the viewer than is possible with photorealism.

7.2.3   Edge Classification for NPR

Shading models generally interpolate over multiple polygons in the mesh and thus information on the internal structure of the model (or the scene objects, respectively) is lost. This information is determined by edges in the model. We can differentiate between four basic types of edges (illustrated in Figure 7.2):

1. *Contour edges*   These edges segregate an object from its environment and thus give an impression of the general shape of the object. They are considered to be most significant.

2. *Sharp edges*   These edges represent discontinuities between neighboring faces and give a strong indication of the internal structure of the model.

3. *Smooth edges*   These edges (typically perceived as curvature) indicate the internal structure at a finer level than the sharp edges.

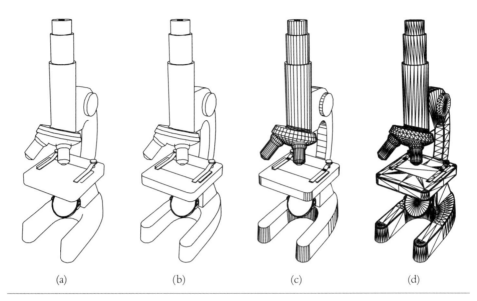

(a) (b) (c) (d)

FIGURE 7.2 Different edge types to visualize different structural information: contour edges (a), sharp edges (b), smooth edges (c), triangulation edges (d). Each image contains the edges of the images to its left in addition to those mentioned in the caption.

4. *Triangulation edges* Although only temporary, these edges can be presented to show the triangulation of the object. (This is needed only for illustrating and documenting geometric models.)

Edge Classification Using Normal Vector Information

The classification of the edges can be done automatically by inspecting the mesh and taking into account the viewer's position. As a first step, all polygons pointing away from the viewer have to be removed (backface culling). The dot product between the polygon's normal vector N and the line of sight V (a vector from the polygon to the viewer's position) determines the visibility of the polygon in question. If this dot product is positive, that is, if $N \cdot V > 0$, the polygon is facing the viewer and is thus visible (see also Exercises 7.4 and 7.5).

The contour edges together represent the border of an object to its environment, that is, either to other objects or to the background. Hence, contour edges separate visible polygons from ones that are hidden. Since in the previous step all hidden polygons are removed, contour edges can be identified easily as those edges not being shared between two polygons. The distinction between sharp and smooth edges is more subjective and depends also on the model. As the distinctive feature between those two classes, the angle between the normal vectors of the faces sharing the edge in question is used. The larger this angle, the sharper is the "peak" between the adjacent faces. Thus, to classify edges as being sharp or smooth, for each edge the angle between the two faces is calculated and all those edges that have an angle above a certain threshold are classified as being sharp.

Smooth edges are typically perceived as curvature, and the degree to which this curvature is visualized can also be controlled by the angle between two adjacent faces. Displaying edges only up to a certain value makes the curvature visible up to a certain degree.

Finally, if two faces of a polygon mesh lie in one plane, the edge in between typically is a triangulation edge. Such edges are introduced when subdividing polygons into triangles. This is done automatically by most modern modeling software. Displaying these edges does not, in general, reveal any new information to the viewer unless the goal of the visualization is the documentation of the geometric model.

Putting it all together, the model structure can be exploited in NPR by classifying model edges appropriately and drawing those edges with respect to the visualization goal. Algorithm 7.1 summarizes this procedure. As can be seen in Figure 7.3, modifying the maximal angle up to which edges are drawn yields different effects on the visualization and thus different amounts of information being conveyed.

Algorithm 7.1 works on the visible part of the model even though it is not restricted to only this model part. Indeed, information about hidden parts of the model may be of vital importance for the understanding of the object's exact form and structure. If the same algorithm is applied to these hidden parts of the model, it is possible to visualize also this information. Visualizing both visible and hidden model parts using the same style, however, may distract the viewer. In CAD drawings, hidden edges are often drawn using dashed lines (indeed, there are standards requiring this kind of drawing). Considering the hidden polygons and drawing the edges shared by two of them as dashed lines leads to this kind of image. Although tempting to do, not all the hidden edges should be included so as not to clutter the image with unnecessary detail. Drawing contour edges and sharp edges in the hidden part usually suffices to communicate enough structural information to enable easy recognition of the object's form. An example for such a visualization can be viewed in Figure 7.4.

```
1   foreach polygon p ∈ M do
2       compute the normal vector n_p for p
3       if n_p · V > 0 then mark p as visible
4                       else mark p as invisible
5       fi
6   od
7   M' := all polygons marked visible in M
8   foreach edge e ∈ M' do
9       if e belongs to only one polygon
10          then
11              mark e as being a contour edge
12          else
13              α_e := angle between adjacent faces to e
14          if α_e > α_max
15              then mark e as sharp edge
16              else if α_e = 0 then mark e as triangulation edge
17                              else mark e as smooth edge
18              fi
19          fi
20      fi
21  od
22  draw model according to visualization goals
```

ALGORITHM 7.1 Algorithm to classify edges based on the angle between adjacent faces in the model M.

Fast Edge Classification

When rendering objects in a non-photorealistic style (like the kinds of images that were used throughout this chapter so far or, for instance, in a cartoonlike style), the distinction between contour edges and internal edges is highly important. Since many modern rendering systems that work on polygonal models process *all* polygons of a given mesh and perform a front and back facing computation, this can be used to derive an efficient algorithm that uses these features and adds a minimum overhead to the image generation.

The following algorithm works on an additional data structure called the *edge buffer*. For each edge in the model, it stores a bit field that contains several flags. The first two flags are a front facing flag (F) and a back facing flag (B). To build

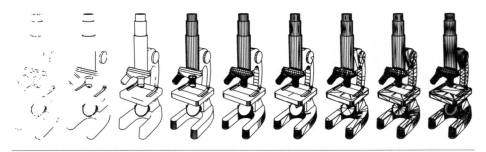

FIGURE 7.3 The angle between two adjacent faces in the model is used to determine the level of detail in the presentation.

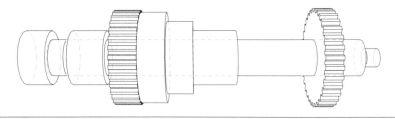

FIGURE 7.4 Explicitly drawing hidden edges to clarify the structure and form of an object.

the edge buffer, we create a table as can be seen in Table 7.1 for the example in Figure 7.5 where each edge is accessed using the lowest valued vertex index. The algorithm assumes that the polygonal mesh is stored as an indexed vertex mesh representation. The second vertex index is part of the edge's entry in the table. As an example, edge (3–5) is stored in the third line (for vertex 3) in the second position since for each vertex the edges are sorted by increasing index of the second vertex. Note that with this arrangement, the lower half of the table is completely empty.

The F and B flags for each edge are initially set to 0. The edge buffer is updated on a per-polygon basis. If the respective polygon is a front facing polygon, the F flag for each edge is XORed with 1; if it is a back facing polygon, the B flag is XORed with 1. After having done this for each polygon in the model, the edge buffer can be processed to determine the edges that form the silhouette of the object. For the given example, the final state of the edge buffer is illustrated in Table 7.2. All those edges that have set both the F and the B flag are silhouette edges and can be rendered accordingly as can be seen in Figure 7.6.

Vertex	VFB	VFB	VFB	VFB
1	200	300	400	500
2	300	500	x00	x00
3	400	500	x00	x00
4	500	x00	x00	x00
5	x00	x00	x00	x00

TABLE 7.1 Edge buffer setup for the model given in Figure 7.5. Note that each edge is accessed using the smaller vertex index.

Vertex	VFB	VFB	VFB	VFB
1	211	300	411	500
2	311	500	x00	x00
3	411	500	x00	x00
4	500	x00	x00	x00
5	x00	x00	x00	x00

TABLE 7.2 Edge buffer after having processed each polygon in Figure 7.5.

This approach works well for closed objects; however, there are problems if we deal with "open" objects, that is, meshes that do not completely enclose a certain volume. An example would be an open box, for example, a cube with one side missing. We will then get entries in the edge buffer where only one of the two flags is set. Those entries result from edges that belong to only one polygon. In our initial approach, these would not be drawn, although they clearly belong to the object's silhouette. If we change the algorithm to drawing all edges whose *FB* flag combination is not identical to 00, then we correctly render the boundary edges for the object.

Sometimes, however, it is necessary to render more than just the object boundaries, especially if an additional edge would make the drawing clearer. As can be seen in Figure 7.7, the most comprehensible rendering of the open cube would be the rightmost image where two edges are included with an *FB* flag combination of 00. Which edges have to be rendered to make an image comprehensible cannot be determined algorithmically, so user interaction is needed. In order to allow a user to define which edges *always* have to be drawn, an additional flag *A* is introduced in the edge buffer. This flag is set to 1 if the respective edge has to be drawn in any case. Now the decision about which edges

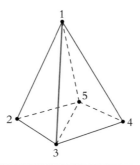

FIGURE 7.5 Closed polygonal model defined by five vertices and six edges.

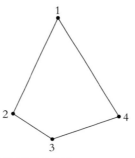

FIGURE 7.6 Resulting rendition if only the edges are drawn that have set both the *F* and the *B* bit.

to draw depends on three bits, and the edge is drawn if the *AFB* flags are not equal to 000. This method can be extended to decide whether an edge that has the *A* bit set is shared by two back facing polygons and thus does not have to be drawn. We leave the derivation of this extension to you (see Exercise 7.6).

This example of an open cube is not a particularly good example for the necessity of such an algorithm. If we consider this cube in an interactive or animated environment where it can be seen from each possible direction, then we quickly realize that *all* edges of the cube have to be marked as artist edges in order to render it correctly in any view. A better example might be a cylinder modeled as an *n*-sided prism where only those edges are marked as artist edges that define the top and bottom polygon. Now, if such a model were viewed from

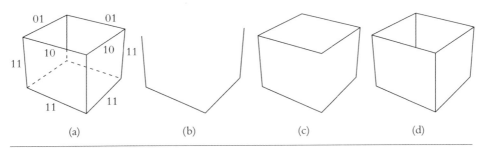

FIGURE 7.7 Images of a cube, different flags being used to draw the edges: F and B flags for the model edges (a), all edges drawn where $FB = 11$ (b), all edges drawn where $FB \neq 00$ (c), more comprehensible rendition (d).

any angle, these edges would have to be shown together with the two edges that form the contour along the sides of the prism. These two are detected using only the F and B flags; for the top and bottom edges, the artist bit is indeed necessary.

The edge buffer method is a simple technique that can be inserted into the graphics pipeline if in this pipeline *all* polygons are processed, the model is stored using indices into a vertex list, and front and back facing computations are performed anyway. Then it adds very little overhead since all operations to be performed are bitwise XOR or OR operations. It can be implemented very efficiently using a hash table as in the earlier examples, but other representations are also possible. Correct visible line determination is not part of the algorithm; even if an edge is halfway hidden, it will be handled as a complete edge. Thus, the edge buffer algorithm has to be combined with a polygon filling algorithm that overpaints occluded parts of edges.

Classifying edges and drawing them depending on the applied classification scheme greatly enhances the perception of the geometric forms of rendered objects. However, visual perception is more than just recognizing forms, and hence we will investigate which perceptual phenomena can also be supported by applying NPR techniques in the rendering process.

Enhancing Depth Perception

As can already be seen from Figure 7.4, graphical cues for depth in an image are important for the understanding of the model, especially for larger scenes. Besides distinguishing between visible and hidden edges and drawing them differently,

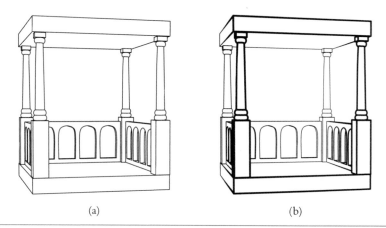

(a)   (b)

FIGURE 7.8 Simulating depth by changing line style parameters. In (b), the line width decreases with increasing z-distance. Depth perception is much better than in (a) where constant line widths are used.

there are more techniques to enhance depth perception when rendering a polygonal model. What we are aiming for is just the visualization of the model artifacts; more elaborate rendering techniques are introduced later on in this chapter.

In general, depth perception is supported by visual cues that simulate the human's normal depth perception. Examples of these are

- perspective foreshortening,
- displaying correct object-object occlusions, and
- atmospheric effects (light, fog, and so on).

Perspective foreshortening is achieved by using perspective projections for rendering. Atmospheric effects can be simulated in wireframe drawings by evaluating the z-value of each vertex and parameterizing the line width or brightness in accordance to this (see Figure 7.8). Furthermore, calculated light intensities can also be used to parameterize the line styles (see Figure 7.9).

The question remains how occlusions can be displayed in a manner that is easy to understand to the viewer and that does not require sophisticated shading techniques. A common technique used in handmade illustrations is to leave a gap at an intersection; the (partially) hidden edge is slightly trimmed at the intersection point. An extension of this technique to the display of 3D wireframe models is

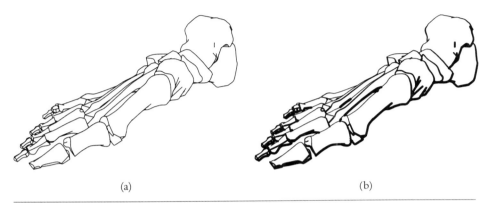

(a)   (b)

FIGURE 7.9 Two renditions from the same model: the "plain" drawing without further attributes (a), lighting information included and mapped onto the width of the line style (slightly overdone) (b).

---

1   I := all intersections of the given line segments
2   **foreach** valid intersection $i \in I$ **do**
3   δ := angle between intersecting edges
4   trim edge further from the viewer by $(t/\sin\delta)$ on both sides of i
5   **od**

ALGORITHM 7.2 Algorithm for creating the haloed line effect.

known as *haloed lines*. This technique is based on finding all intersections of the line segments that are calculated as the projections of the model edges. This can be done effectively with a plane sweep algorithm (see Exercise 7.7). However, only so-called valid intersections are of interest, that is, intersections that occur in the interior of a (projected) edge. For each valid intersection point, the edge further away from the viewer is trimmed by an amount t at the intersection. This can either be a fixed, prescribed value or be calculated depending on the angle δ between the two intersecting line segments (edges). The procedure is summarized in Algorithm 7.2.

Figure 7.10 shows the result of applying Algorithm 7.2 to a polygonal model. With haloed lines, the model structure becomes immediately clear to the viewer, especially the hidden parts of the model, even without sophisticated shading algorithms.

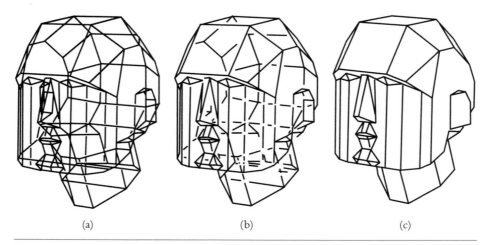

(a)   (b)   (c)

FIGURE 7.10 Drawing haloed lines reveals the model structure much more clearly: no haloed lines (a), thin halos (b), thick halos (c). Note that in (c) the halos are drawn so wide that hidden lines are completely removed.

We will now turn our attention to a fundamental operation on geometric data that has far-reaching implications for NPR: that of computing the intersection between a geometric model and a plane in object space. This is a fundamental operation deserving special treatment because in practice such intersection curves turn up very often in NPR.

7.2.4 Computing Intersections

The intersections of a geometric model and a plane in space are of special interest if it comes to drawing more than just edges of the model. Many methods for creating hatching lines rely on the computation of curves that result from intersecting a model with a set of planes. Depending on how the actual computation of these curves is performed, intersection calculation can be very time consuming. We shall thus introduce an approach that works in image space and that can make use of hardware accelerated graphics libraries.

An image-space approach is lucrative over and above analytic approaches because of its generality. Even though working in image space means that precise results cannot be obtained, the results of such a method are generally sufficient for NPR. The key to an algorithm implementing such an operation is to be able to

1   render model using a conventional shader and take a snapshot
2   extract the pixels on the boundary ($I_{contour}$)
3   display model with an additional clipping plane and take another snapshot
4   extract the pixels on the boundary ($I_{cutcontour}$)
5   generate $I = I_{contour} - I_{cutcontour}$
6   convert I to line segments

ALGORITHM 7.3   Computing intersections between a geometric model and a plane.

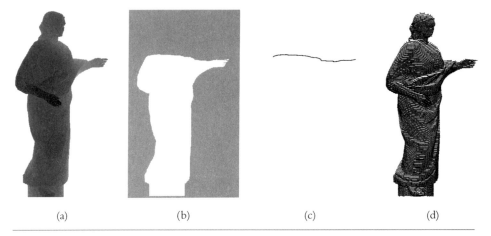

(a)   (b)   (c)   (d)

FIGURE 7.11   Image-based generation of intersection lines: z-buffer image of the model (a), image with additional clipping plane (b), resulting curve after subtracting outline of the complete model (a) from (b) (c), and the whole set of intersection curves (d).

make use of graphics hardware for at least certain parts. Another aspect to consider when working in image space is to avoid aliasing problems.

Algorithm 7.3 shows the procedure for computing intersections between a geometric model and plane in object space. This plane is introduced as an additional clipping plane and only the part of the model lying on one side of that plane is kept; the other part is clipped.

We will illustrate this algorithm using the model of the statue shown in Figure 7.11. The first step can be implemented by drawing the object in white on a black background. Steps two and four are performed on a pixel–by–pixel basis by determining the pixels that have a black neighbor. The results of steps

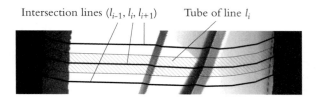

FIGURE 7.12 For halftoning the appearance of each intersection, line l_i is responsible for approximating the grayscale values belonging to a tube around the line.

three and four are illustrated in Figure 7.11(b) and (c), respectively. To avoid fat diagonal lines, it is useful to use only the 4-neighborhood of the pixels. Step five is a simple image operation that can be performed in an accumulation buffer, if available. The conversion from pixels to line segments is done by any standard method, for example, least square fitting.

The rendition can be improved further by carefully drawing long hatching lines. Each line l_i is responsible for a tube t_i (see Figure 7.12). The overall intensity of line l_i equals the average intensity of the pixels in t_i. A simple method is to modulate the width of l_i according to the intensities along the line. Two example results are shown in Figures 7.13 and 7.14. Note that in both cases, the geometric model was decomposed into subobjects. For each such subobject, the orientation of the cutting plane was decided upon manually by the user. In the next section, we will see a method of computing such directions automatically for certain cases.

7.2.5 Determining Global Shape

There are a variety of situations in which the style chosen for the rendition of an object depends in part on its global shape. Long skinny objects may be drawn differently than more chubby ones. Moreover, details of the parameterization of the chosen style may also depend on the global shape. For this purpose, it is often useful to reduce a geometric model down to a simpler data structure from which the global shape can be assessed.

Topology of a Geometric Model

Our goal is to devise algorithms for extracting information about the *topology* of a geometric model. Topology describes the neighborhood relationships between objects on an abstract level. Often the topology can be represented through a graph whose edges are labeled with such descriptions as "in front of," "behind," or "above." Also of interest in this connection is the *topography* of the geometric

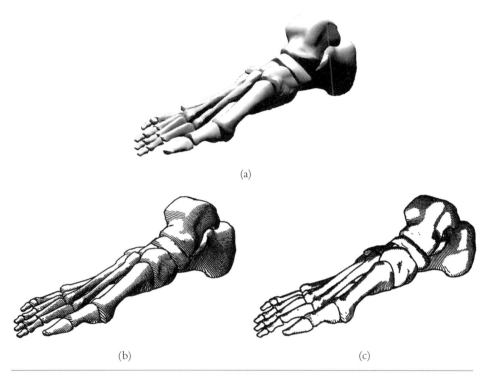

FIGURE 7.13 Example of applying the intersection operator to the model of a foot: (a) shows a shaded image, and (b) and (c) show two computer-generated copperplates.

model; this describes the concrete spatial relations, like size and distance between objects. Changes in topology imply changes in topography, but not necessarily vice versa.

We want to learn about the topology of a geometric object so that we can exploit this information in NPR. This will enable us to relate the attributes of a rendition to the overall shape of an object or to the shape of some of its parts. For example, Figure 7.15(a) shows the outline of a tube (like the inner tube of a bicycle). If the surface of the object is to be hatched, it would likely be inappropriate to apply simply vertical or horizontal hatching (Figure 7.15(b)); instead, hatching that accentuates the cylindrical and circular shape is a possible method of choice (Figures 7.15(c) or (d)). However, it is not obvious how to determine the global shape of the object so as to derive which kind of

(a) (b)

FIGURE 7.14 Example of applying the intersection operator to the bust of Beethoven (a), yielding a computer-generated copperplate (b). Note that several sets of hatching lines are used and that the line thickness is varied according to the illumination of the model.

hatching can be applied best. Although in some situations such hatching may be ascertained as a by-product of the method of modeling, this is not the case in general.

Indeed, a simplification of the geometric model must be carried out. The problem is akin to that of model simplification that has been studied extensively. Figure 7.16 shows an example of three models of the same object (a car), each with a different tessellation. The primary goal of most simplification algorithms in this area is to reduce the number of polygons (so as to reduce the rendering time) while making as few sacrifices as possible with respect to the visual quality of the renditions. Though our goals here are quite different, in the following we will show how an algorithm for model simplification can form the basis of algorithms for determining the global shape.

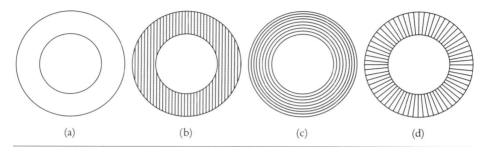

FIGURE 7.15 Visualizing the shape of an object by shading: (a) shows the outline of a tube and (b) a simple but inappropriate vertical hatching; whereas in (c) and (d) the hatching is applied according to the curvature.

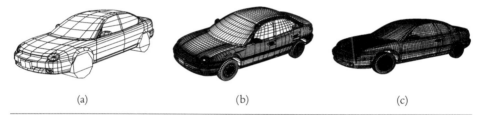

FIGURE 7.16 Example of polygonal models of a car in three different resolutions: 1,137 polygons (a), 22,935 polygons (b), 46,582 polygons (c).

Edge Collapse

We assume that we have a polygon mesh $M(V, F, E)$, where V is a collection of vertices v, F a collection of surfaces f, and E a collection of edges e. We further assume—without any limitation—that each $f \in F$ is a triangle, that is, $f = f(v_1, v_2, v_3)$. Edges are characterized by their vertices and their neighboring surfaces, that is, $e = e(v_1, v_2) = e(f_1, f_2)$.

The process of simplifying a geometric model is built around simple operations that are applied over and over again until the desired level of detail is reached. One approach in this sense uses the *edge collapse* operation for that purpose. We define the edge collapse operation e_{col} as follows. Two vertices v_1 and v_2 connected by an edge $e(v_1, v_2)$ can be merged into one new vertex v^* (Figure 7.17). In homogeneous coordinates, we can compute $v^* = v_1 + v_2$, which is an associative operation, that is, $v^*(v_1, v_2, v_3) = v_1 + v_2 + v_3 = (v_1 + v_2) + v_3 = v_1 + (v_2 + v_3)$.

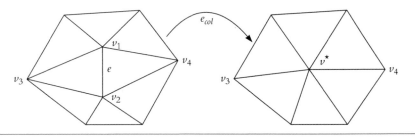

FIGURE 7.17   The edge collapse operation e_{col}.

The most important property of v^*, however, is that it is a good approximation of v_1 and v_2, that is, that $|\, v_1 - v^* \,|$ and $|\, v_2 - v^* \,|$ are minimal.

Now we can see that this e_{col} operation has several useful properties. It reduces the number of

- vertices by one,
- surfaces by at least one (usually two), and
- edges by at least two (usually three or more).

However, the edge collapse operation in itself does not solve our problem. Given a polygonal geometric model, the essential further questions to be answered are

1. Which edge should be collapsed next?
2. How many edges in total should be collapsed?

Computing Skeletons

We will define a skeleton as a data structure represented as an undirected, possibly cyclic graph that describes the global shape of a geometric model. Each node in the graph also has a position in three-dimensional space. We will use the aforementioned edge collapse operation, but for the purposes of producing the skeleton, we must show how it can be applied and developed further. In particular, we must answer the preceding questions as follows:

1. *Which edge should be collapsed next?*   Always the shortest edge is collapsed, and as soon as an edge e no longer has a surface attached to it, e is removed from the model M and added to the skeleton S.

2. *How many edges in total should be collapsed?*   The procedure is continued until M is empty. This is different from most approaches to polygon simplification

```
1   while there are faces in the model M do
2       sort all edges by length
3       foreach edge e (from shortest to longest) do
4           if either start or end vertex are marked then
5                   mark other vertex
6               else
7                   collapse edge e
8                   mark the new vertex
9           fi
10      od
11      move all edges without valid faces attached to it to the skeleton S
12  od
```

ALGORITHM 7.4 Computing the skeleton of a polygon mesh.

algorithms, which terminate much earlier and where the decision when to stop is much more difficult to make.

Conceptually, we can use the following strategy to build the skeleton. First, we construct a data structure H of all edges of M such that we always have fast access to the shortest edge e_{min}. H can be implemented, for example, as a heap (a min-heap, to be exact). Next, we collapse the successive shortest edges; every time this potentially yields one or more edges e_s, each of which is no longer associated with a surface. In this case, we remove e_s from M and add it to S. In each iteration, H is updated appropriately.

This algorithm optimizes local detail but in practice does not yield a good enough approximation of the global shape. Instead, it has been found better initially to collapse edges that are disjoint from one another. Short edges are then collapsed only if their endpoints have not been involved in an edge collapse operation. Once there are no more edges to collapse, the whole procedure is repeated. Extending this strategy in this sense yields Algorithm 7.4.

The worst case complexity of this algorithm is $O(n^2 \log n)$. However, in practice a positive fraction of the edges are removed in every iteration of the outermost loop so that a running time of $O(n \log n)$ is generally achieved. Examples of applications of the algorithm are shown in Figures 7.18 and 7.19.

An Application to Hatching

The skeletonization operation can now be used as a preprocessing step in NPR. Consider Figure 7.20(a) showing a tube with a knot in it. Given that the knot

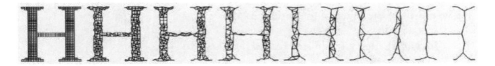

FIGURE 7.18 Computing the skeleton for a two-dimensional object.

FIGURE 7.19 Examples of computing the skeleton of various polygonal geometric models.

is modeled as a polygon mesh describing its surface (Figure 7.20(b)), we wish to produce an image with hatching lines that indicate curvature and that are drawn according to the lighting conditions (compare with Figure 1.17). After having computed the skeleton of the model, this skeleton is then converted into a spline curve. This curve approximates the skeleton nodes and guarantees a smooth progression of the skeleton, which is important for the following steps (see Figure 7.20(c)).

We now apply the intersection operator (recall Section 7.2.4) at regular intervals by moving the clipping plane along the generated spline curve, keeping the plane always perpendicular to it. Using the original skeleton here would yield artifacts where two line segments meet since the direction does not change continuously. The result of this operation is shown in Figure 7.20(e). The hatching lines themselves still have to be modified to better convey the shape of the knot (and the tube as well). This can be done via G-buffer operations. A standard shaded image like the one in Figure 7.20(a) gives all necessary information to shorten hatching lines or even make them more sparse.

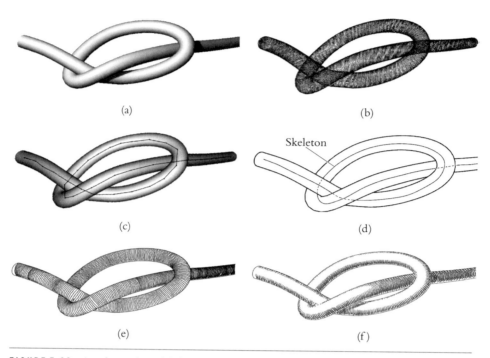

FIGURE 7.20 A polygonal model that is to be rendered with hatching: the shaded image (a), the underlying polygonal model rendered as a wireframe (b), the knot and its skeleton as computed by the algorithm presented (c), the skeleton approximated by a spline through its nodes (d), the hatched image without taking into account lighting information (e), and the final illustration (f).

7.3 Free-Form Surfaces

While polygonal models are an approximation of the object to be modeled, other ways of describing an object's surface are more accurate in terms of representing the exact geometry. However, the price for more accuracy is a more complicated description. Free-form surfaces are the tool we will describe next.

7.3.1 Description of Free-Form Surface Models

The geometric description of free-form surfaces is based on a given number of so-called *control points* or *control vertices*. In contrast to polygonal models where those vertices are connected by straight lines (called edges), free-form surfaces use interpolation schemes to compute all other points belonging to the actual surface.

The control vertices do not have to be part of the surface; instead, they define the surface's properties based on the used interpolation scheme.

In computer graphics, many different interpolation schemes have been developed and are used nowadays. Because of this diversity, we will not attempt to describe *all* representations here; see, for instance, the book by Bartels et al. (1996) for a comprehensive source for information on free-form curves and surfaces.

This section concentrates on a widely used kind of surface description, namely, *tensor product surfaces*. Tensor product surfaces can be regarded as "curves of curves," that is, a curve c_1 is moved along a second curve c_2 and all points that are touched when carrying out this movement belong to the surface defined by c_1 and c_2.

In mathematical terms, we denote a piecewise polynomial curve $F(u)$ of degree n by

$$F(u) = \sum_{i=0}^{n} C_i N_i(u) \qquad u \in [0, 1]$$

and a second piecewise polynomial curve $G(v)$ of degree m by

$$G(v) = \sum_{j=0}^{m} C_j N_j(v) \qquad v \in [0, 1]$$

The tensor product $S(u, v)$ of these two curves is then

$$S(u, v) = \sum_{i=0}^{n} \sum_{j=0}^{m} C_{ij} N_i(u) N_j(v) \qquad u, v \in [0, 1] \tag{7.1}$$

It describes a surface over the given control vertices C_{ij}. Equation (7.1) can also be rewritten as

$$S(u, v) = \sum_{i=0}^{n} N_i(u) C_i(v) \quad \text{with} \quad C_i(v) = \sum_{j=0}^{m} N_j(v) C_{ij}$$

which nicely demonstrates the concept of curves of curves. In all these equations, the C_i, C_j, and C_{ij} are the control vertices of the surface, while $N_i(u)$ and $N_j(v)$ are the base function of the polynomials of degree n and m, respectively.

To represent such a surface as a geometric model by means of data structures and algorithms, similar considerations for polygonal models can be made. Since the control vertices describe the surface, they have to be present in the model.

(a)

(b)

(c)

(d)

FIGURE 2.38 Different strategies for choosing a tiling grid lead to different mosaic structures: regular arrangement (a), scattered layout (b), angled alignment (c), and hexagonal grid (d).

FIGURE 4.6(b) Example of computer–generated watercolor painting using the fluid simulation technique.

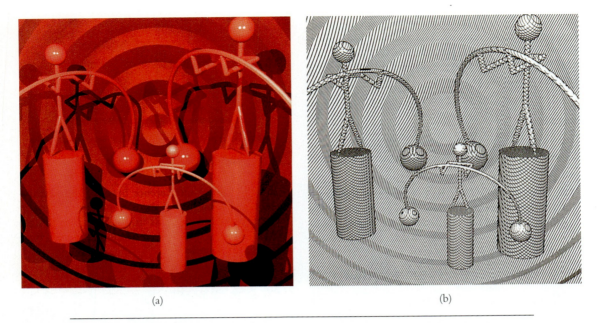

(a)   (b)

FIGURE 4.15 "Mobile" as computer-generated copperplate: standard raytracing (a) and copperplate (b).

(a)   (b)

FIGURE 4.16 "Martian Bananas" as computer-generated copperplate: standard raytracing (a) and copperplate (b).

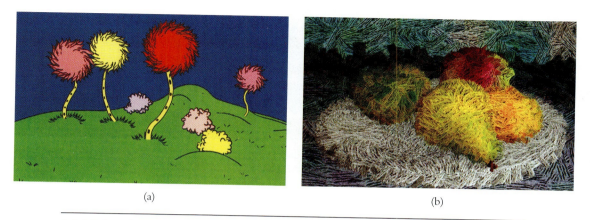

FIGURE 5.2 Different strokes to create different styles in illustration: marks placed along the object contour (a) and filling regions with paintbrush strokes (b).

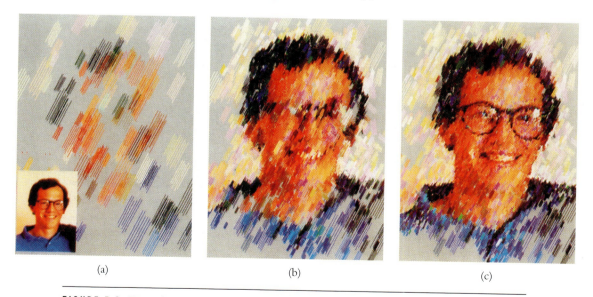

FIGURE 5.8 Examples of painting over a photorealistic image with a mouse. The inset shows the original image; (a) shows the results when a small number of fast strokes are made over the original. In (b) and (c), the strokes have become successively finer.

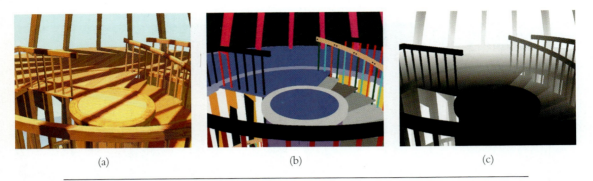

(a)　　　　　　　　　(b)　　　　　　　　　(c)

FIGURE 6.2 Images revealing different scene properties: color of scene objects (RGB-buffer) (a), object identifiers (ID-buffer) (b), and depth (z-buffer) (c).

(a)　　　　　　　　　　　　　　(b)

FIGURE 6.8 Interactive painting based on G-buffers. The paintbrush strokes in (a) are parameterized based on properties of the underlying geometric model. The trees in (b) are additional bitmaps with placement based on the z-buffer. Note how they change in size and how correct occlusion is achieved.

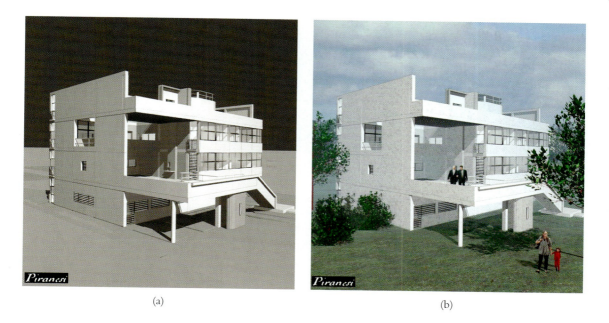

(a)

(b)

(c)

(d)

FIGURE 6.9 Different stylistic variations achieved by using different drawing tools: photorealistic rendition (a), added environment (b), pen-and-ink style (c), and painted style (d).

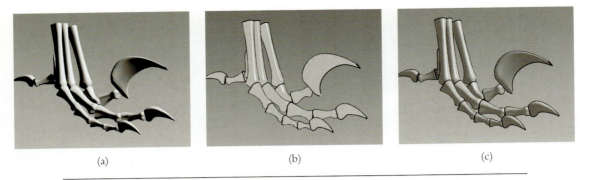

(a)   (b)   (c)

FIGURE 8.7 Using the Phong model as a starting point for illustrations reveals some shortcomings of the model: areas not directly lit appear with constant color ($k_d = 1$, $k_a = 0$) (a), shape information is lost, especially in regions of high curvature when rendering only highlights and edge lines (b), and details are lost when including edge lines in a Phong-shaded image ($k_d = 0.5$, $k_a = 0.1$) (c).

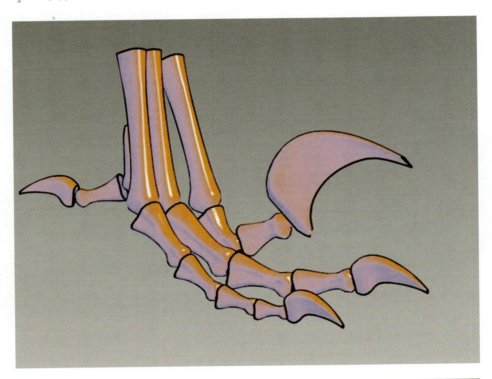

FIGURE 8.8 Approximately constant luminance tone rendering. Edge lines and highlights are clearly noticeable. Some details in shaded regions are also visible. The lack of luminance shift makes these changes subtle.

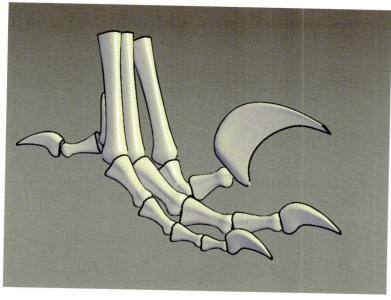

(a)

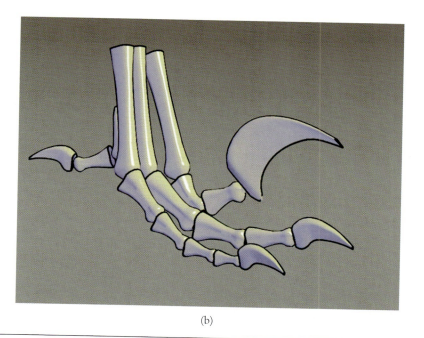

(b)

FIGURE 8.9 Images created with the introduced shading model: $b = 0.4$, $\gamma = 0.4$, $\alpha = 0.2$, $\beta = 0.6$ (a) and $b = 0.55$, $\gamma = 0.3$, $\alpha = 0.25$, $\beta = 0.5$ (b).

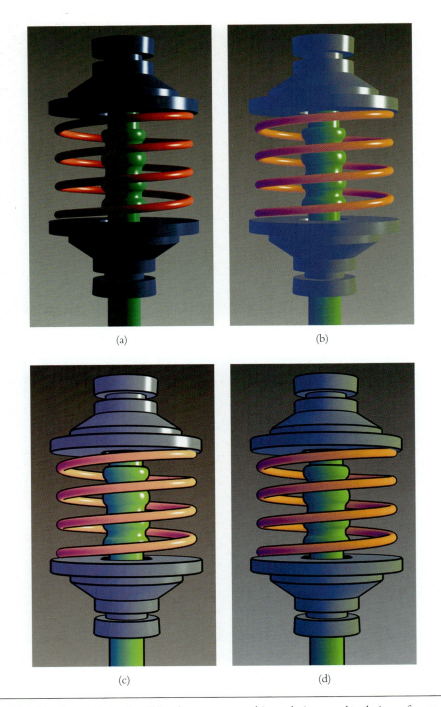

(a)

(b)

(c)

(d)

FIGURE 8.10 Comparison of traditional computer graphics techniques and techniques for creating technical illustrations: Phong shading (a), new shading model without edge lines (b), new shading model with edge lines and highlights (c), and approximation of the new model using Phong shading (d).

While in polygonal models the connectivity between the vertices is denoted explicitly by edges and polygonal faces, for free-form surfaces this connectivity is established via the interpolation scheme being used for computing points on the curve (or surface). Thus, unlike for polygon meshes, part of the model is represented in the form of algorithms, namely, as the definition of the basis functions.

7.3.2 Operations on Free-Form Surface Models for Rendering

When rendering free-form surface models, a simple projection of the control vertices and applying the interpolation scheme would not yield the desired result. Thus, several other methods have to be used to depict such models. In the context of non-photorealistic rendering, the use of G-buffers is particularly well suited to portraying the geometric properties of free-form surface models since this modeling technique is especially chosen for curved surfaces where a visualization of the curvature will help in recognizing the object and its features. In the case of free-form surface models, we can use the hatching technique described in Section 6.1 where u- and v-buffers are used to generate hatching lines.

For creating non-photorealistic renditions of free-form surface models, several approaches have been investigated and used. Line drawings especially can be rendered by following some of the inherent features of such a model. But as it is the case with polygonal models, operations on the data given with the model's description lead to more possibilities. In the following, we will first see how curves on the given surface can be used to produce images. Then, point coverage as an operation will be treated in more detail before we finally see that all operations defined for polygonal models can also be used for free-form surface models after they have been translated into a polygonal representation.

Rendering Using Curves on the Surface

An approximation of a free-form surface with polygons usually results in a vast amount of data. The surfaces have to be approximated by many small polygons to correctly model its curved character. If the mathematical description of the curves from which the surface is built can be used directly to render an image, the amount of data necessary is reduced. The trade-off, however, is a much higher complexity of the operations. This complexity results from the need for handling usually cubic polynomials and their derivatives. We will not go into the mathematical details here; instead, we point out the main principles behind the algorithms.

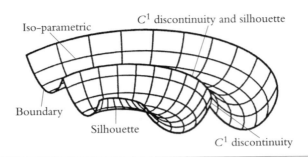

FIGURE 7.21 Four types of curves on a surface.

To visualize the shape of the model, curves can be extracted from the surface that correspond to important features. These are, among others, boundary curves, iso-parametric curves, curves along C^1 discontinuities, and silhouette curves (see Figure 7.21). Whereas the first three types are viewer independent, the silhouette curves can be computed only if a viewing setup is available.

Boundary curves are the most simple case. These are the surface boundaries and can be computed by inserting zero or one into the surface equation for each parameter direction u and v. They are important for any visualization since they mark the spatial extent of the surface in question. *Iso-parametric curves* are curves that contain all points having the same parameter value in either u- or v-direction. Thus, for a fixed $u \in [0, 1]$, all points computed by evaluating the surface equation for *all* $v \in [0, 1]$ lie on an iso-parametric curve.[2] The same computation can be done for a fixed v- and all u-values. These curves, in general, follow the boundary of the surface and can thus be used as initial lines for hatching. *Curves along C^1 discontinuities* represent creases or edges in the surface that can occur when the surface is put together from continuous patches. The discontinuities are then at the boundaries of the patches and can be computed in the same manner as boundary curves—treating each patch separately.

Although the curves mentioned all have in common that they are iso-parametric and independent of the viewing direction, this is generally not the case for *silhouette curves*. They are the boundaries of the front facing portion of the surface. In the following, we suppose a viewing setup in a way that the view point

---

2. In this sense, boundary curves can be seen as special iso-parametric curves for $u = 0$, $v = 0$, $u = 1$, or $v = 1$.

is on the positive z-axis at infinity and the image gets projected onto the xy-plane. Note that all other views can be transformed in such a setup. A silhouette point is then a point p on the surface whose normal has a zero z-component. Surface parts with a positive z-component of the normal are front facing; those with a negative z-component are back facing. Hence, at silhouette points this property changes. A silhouette curve is then an ordered set of silhouette points forming a continuous curve. Their computation cannot be done analytically; thus, they have to be approximated.

This approximation, however, does not introduce any new problems for rendering free-form surfaces. A direct rendering by projecting the control polygon and then reevaluating the surface is not possible, so any rendition has to be an approximation. To render a surface with hatching lines being computed from iso-parametric curves, for example, a number of points on the curves are evaluated and then projected onto the viewing plane. How to connect those points can be derived from the original curves. Here, the line styles from Chapter 3 come in handy. Polylines (from connecting the projected points) are connected and converted to a parametric description. An applied line style then creates the impression of a smooth curve.

Depending on the parameterization of the surface, such curves do not always visualize the shape of an object in the most appropriate way. Thus, we look for other ways of rendering free-form surfaces. One of them is to cover the surface with points that are then anchors to strokes; the other way is to convert the surface to an appropriate polygonal representation and render it using one of the methods described earlier.

Point Coverage

Using special curves on the surface and their properties limits the possibilities for rendering. First, there is a limit of stroke position and direction if we consider that strokes can only be placed along these curves and that the strokes' directions are parallel to them. Further, the position of the lines depends heavily on the surface's parameterization scheme. Finally, although the methods indicated have proved useful for creating relatively long lines, the coverage of a surface with small strokes is not easy to achieve.

In the following, we introduce a method to compute positions on a free-form surface where strokes can be placed. This method can be compared with stippling, a technique described in Section 2.3. The major goal in the development of stippling algorithms was to cover a 2D plane with dots that are distributed uniformly but randomly in the plane. The number of dots and thus their spacing is used to represent intensity values. A random and even distribution of dots on a surface allows the computation of positions for strokes that are then drawn in 3D.

The operation to create such a distribution of dots is referred to as *point coverage*. Since a surface $S(u, v)$ is defined over two parameters $u \in [0, 1]$ and $v \in [0, 1]$, a first attempt would be to generate a uniform point distribution in the area $[0, 1] \times [0, 1]$ in parameter space. This will not yield the desired result. In general, parametric surfaces are not isometric, or length and area preserving. In practice, this means that a small rectangular area in parameter space can be mapped onto an arbitrary small or large area on the surface. Thus, if the parameter space is uniformly covered with dots, the surface itself does not necessarily have to be uniformly covered.

Consider a small (differential) rectangular area in parameter space given by $[u, u + du]$, $[v, v + dv]$. The size of this area is $A_p = du\, dv$. The size of the corresponding area on the surface is

$$A_S = \left| \frac{dS}{du} \times \frac{dS}{dv} \right| du\, dv$$

Computing the ratio between A_s and A_p yields $R = \left| \frac{dS}{du} \times \frac{dS}{dv} \right|$. If R is less than one, the area on the surface is smaller than the area in the parametric domain and thus fewer points should be placed here. Conversely, if R is bigger than one, more points should be distributed in the respective area. To create a point coverage for the surface S, we start by computing a uniform distribution of points in parametric space. For each of the created points, a decision has to be made to keep the point or to discard it. The procedure is similar to that in Section 2.3.1 where an intensity value of a 2D image was chosen as the decision criterion. In the case of covering a surface with points, the decision criterion is the ratio between the value of R at the current position and the maximum value R_{max} for the whole surface. This ratio describes the probability with which a point should be kept. If $R = R_{max}$ then the point needs to be kept; that is, the probability for a point to be placed there equals one. If $\frac{R}{R_{max}} = 0.5$, the point should be kept with a probability of 50%. Using an additional random value (uniformly distributed in $[0, 1]$) aids in this decision, as can be seen in Algorithm 7.5.

Given a point set as computed (see Figure 7.22), this can now be used for stroke-based illustrations (recall Chapter 5). Some additional requirements arise; for instance, the direction or the size of a stroke has to be computed. Strokes can

```
1    P = ∅
2    n = number of points to cover the surface
3    calculate R_max for the given surface
4    i = 0
5    do
6       (u, v) = randomly generated coordinates in parameter space
7       r = random number between zero and one
8       if  R_(u,v)/R_max > r  then
9            P = P ∪ {(u, v)}
10           i = i + 1
11      fi
12   while (i < m)
```

ALGORITHM 7.5 Creating a point coverage of a surface. The algorithm computes m coordinate pairs in parameter space that are stored in the set P.

be aligned along iso-parametric lines as well as based on the local curvature at the strokes' position. Indeed, research has shown that aligning strokes along the principal directions of curvature will greatly enhance the perception of shape.

Nonetheless, in photorealistic computer graphics, free-form surfaces are often transformed into some kind of polygonal description since these can be treated easily with well-optimized algorithms. Thus it is reasonable to explore this process of going from a free-form surface representation to a polygonal representation in more detail.

Representing Free-Form Surfaces as Polygon Meshes

It is often more appropriate to first convert the free-form surface into a polygon mesh that approximates the original model and then to render this mesh. As we have already seen in Section 7.2.1, this yields model artifacts stemming from the approximation error being introduced in the translation process. Minimizing these artifacts is one of the goals when producing photorealistic images, and it applies to NPR in a slightly different manner. In non-photorealistic images, the primary goal is to *control* the artifacts and thus control the image generation process.

One way of controlling the creation of artifacts is to use a reparameterization scheme to generate polygon meshes from free-form surfaces. We will next describe one such reparameterization, called *normalization*. When modeling free-form surfaces, typically regions of higher curvature are modeled by using more

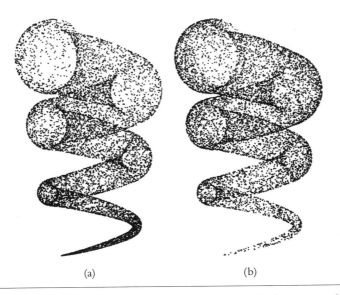

(a)   (b)

FIGURE 7.22 Uniform distribution of points in parameter space leads to non-uniform point distributions on the surface (a). Computing a point coverage using Algorithm 7.5 yields the image in (b).

control vertices than in rather flat areas. Algorithms that rely on the parameterization and thus visualize the density of the control vertices will create images with unwanted side effects. A usual way of converting a free-form representation into a polygonal mesh is placing the vertices of the mesh along the knot vector of the given surface. An example of a polygon mesh created this way can be seen in Figure 7.23. Note that from the top view the curvature is not recognizable and that this image thus leads to a wrong impression of the surface shown.

When presenting surfaces of high curvature, it would be convenient if the wireframe adequately suggested the curvature of the surface. One solution that we will present next is the presentation of the wireframe as an evenly spread mesh. Evenly spread means that the vertices in each row and column have approximately the same distance from one another *in 3D*. Figure 7.24 shows an evenly spread polygon mesh that was generated from the same surface as in Figure 7.23.

To create such a polygon mesh, we start with an *iso-parametric net* generated from a given free-form surface $S(u, v)$ with the assumption that $u, v \in [0, 1] \times [0, 1]$. An iso-parametric net I being constructed for S is a polygon mesh of size

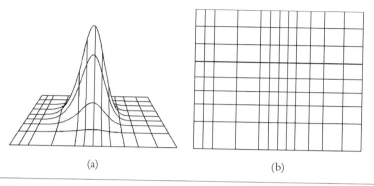

FIGURE 7.23 Regular wireframe created from a given surface: perspective view (a), top view (b).

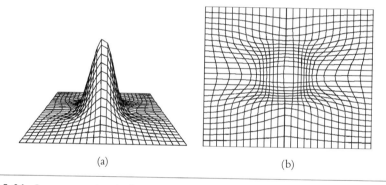

FIGURE 7.24 Iso-parametric wireframe created from a given surface: perspective view (a), top view (b).

$k \times l$ $(k \in \mathbb{N}; l \in \mathbb{N}; k, l > 1)$ with vertices

$$V_{ij} = S\left(\frac{i}{k-1}, \frac{j}{l-1}\right) \qquad 0 \le i < k, 0 \le j < l$$

Geometrically, this equation means that we subdivide the parameter range in both directions (along u and v) into k, respectively, l intervals. In the preceding equation, k and l are thus the overall number of intervals, and i and j the index of one of the intervals. With these vertices, we can now form 3D polylines for each value of i and j, respectively. The polyline that connects the vertices $V_{0j}, \ldots, V_{(k-1)j}$ is called the j-th column of I, and the one connecting $V_{i0}, \ldots, V_{i(l-1)}$ we call the i-th row of I.

While these polylines are equidistant in parameter space, they are not equidistant in 3D. A polygon mesh is called *fully evenly spread* if adjacent vertices of the same row (or column, respectively) are equidistant from one another in 3D space. For the creation of non-photorealistic renditions, it is sufficient to have an approximation of an evenly spread mesh; that is, we no longer require that adjacent vertices of a fixed row have equal distances but rather require them to be *approximately* equidistant. In the following, we will describe how such an approximately evenly spread mesh for a free-form surface S is created. This algorithm will result in a polygon mesh of size $n \times m$.

The algorithm requires the construction of an iso-parametric net I of size $s \times t$ as a first step. Considering the j-th column of I, this polyline P_j is an approximation of the curve defined on the original surface S by

$$
C_j(u) = S\left(u, \frac{j}{t-1}\right)
$$

Let l_j be the length of the polyline P_j. This length approximates the length of the curve $C_j(u)$. To get an evenly spread mesh, the distances between vertices in each row and column have to be approximately equal. Thus the distances of the vertices on some column that is placed near $C_j(u)$ can be estimated by

$$
d_j = \frac{l_j}{m-1}
$$

By choosing m vertices on each curve $C_j(u)$, an auxiliary net N is constructed in such a way that the vertices on each curve have a distance of d_j from one another. To approximate the distance, the initial iso-parametric net i is used. The resulting net N has the size of $s \times m$ vertices.

The rows of N approximate curves on S that are equally spaced on S with respect to the Euclidean distance in 3D space. This is due to the reparameterization in the last step. The final net is obtained by repeating this last step for the rows of N. This is done by placing n vertices in the neighborhood of each row R_i where adjacent vertices have a distance of about

$$
d_i = \frac{l_i}{n-1}
$$

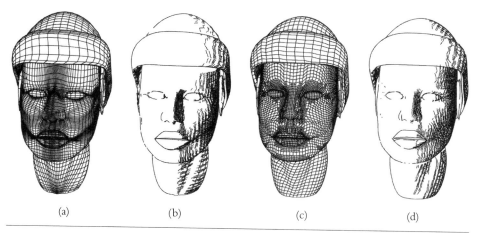

FIGURE 7.25 Comparison of iso-parametric and regular meshes and their implications to, for example, the application of hatching algorithms: wireframe, iso-parametric (a), hatching, iso-parametric (b), wireframe, regular mesh (c), hatching, regular mesh (d).

In this equation, l_i is the length of the curve R_i, which is again obtained by approximation from the iso-parametric net I.

Connecting the vertices created in this process yields a *normalized polygon mesh* where vertices have roughly the same distances from each other in 3D space. An example is shown in Figure 7.25.

Exercises

7.1 Give an overview of how the operations on polygon meshes identified in Section 7.2.1 can be performed on the different types of representations for polygon meshes. Compare the efficiency of each representation for the different operations.

7.2 Develop a few algorithms that check a polygon mesh for consistency.

7.3 Develop a program that displays a polygonal model as a wireframe drawing. Use an efficient data structure to store the polygon meshes also with respect to the operations to be performed on the edges of the mesh.

7.4 Given a polygon mesh with explicitly stored normal vectors at the vertices, how can the polygon normals for each face be computed? How can you compute normal vectors for the polygons of a mesh if there are no given normals at the vertices? What is the biggest problem with this method considering the definition of the model?

7.5   Implement Algorithm 7.1. Let your implementation be based on the assumption that the normal vectors given in the model (if any) are not correct; that is, in a first step recalculate the normal vectors for each polygon in the mesh.

7.6   Implement the edge buffer algorithm for fast edge classification. Extend the algorithm such that it also handles back facing polygons.

7.7   Given a polygon mesh M, projecting the edges of the mesh yields n line segments that intersect each other k times. An algorithm proposed by Preparata and Shamos (1985) needs $O((n + k) \log (n))$ operations to compute all intersections. Implement this algorithm and visualize all intersections.

7.8   Given the procedure for normalizing a free-form surface, how are the positions of the new control vertex computed?

7.9   Implement the algorithm for normalizing a given free-form surface. Visualize both the original surface (by cleverly approximating it with a polygon mesh) and the resulting mesh.

7.10   Experiment with normalization of free-form surfaces and prioritized stroke textures as a shading technique.

Bibliographic Notes

Polygonal models, their representations, and renditions have been studied extensively since the beginnings of computer graphics (see, for example, Foley et al., 1990). The classification of edges of a polygon mesh into contour, sharp, smooth, and triangulation edges was first suggested by Raab (1998); see also Schlechtweg and Raab (1998). For several years, it was considered a difficult open problem to render a geometric model with only a small number of lines; Raab was the first to provide a useful solution to choosing which lines are to be drawn. The algorithm for constructing haloed lines goes back to the pioneering work of Appel et al. (1979) and Elber (1995), and was developed further by Schönwälder (1997).

Saito and Takahashi (1990) first suggested to produce line drawings by following the u- and v-parameters as encoded in special G-buffers. Godenschweger, Strothotte, and Wagener (1996) were the first to use the edges of polygonal meshes stemming from free-form surfaces as the starting point for choosing lines in a rendition, and they also suggested the process of normalization of a polygonal mesh for this purpose; see also Godenschweger and Wagener (1998).

The direct rendering of free-form surfaces is still a hard problem and offers many facets. The use of different curves on the given surface for displaying model properties has been studied by Elber (1999; 1998; Elber and Cohen, 1990).

Data management in the context of geometric modeling has been discussed in detail by Preim and Hoppe (1998). They provide a thorough treatment of this topic. Early work in this area, particularly with regard to demonstrating the need for non-geometric data in geometric models, was reported by Schleich and Dürst (1994). Plaisant et al. (1995) give an extensive survey and classification of image browsers that are needed in this context.

The algorithm for carrying out the intersection operation was suggested by Deussen et al. (1999a); see also Deussen (1998). Methods of converting a sequence of pixels into line segments are presented in detail by Parker (1988) and Sklansky and Gonzalez (1979).

Thinning algorithms for two-dimensional images have been studied since the beginnings of image processing. Seminal work on so-called medial axis representations was reported by Blum (1967). An introduction to the topic is given by Pavlidis (1980), while a comprehensive survey is given by Lam et al. (1992). More recent literature uses the term *skeleton* as a generalization of the medial axis.

Polygon simplification has also been studied extensively, in particular over the 1990s (Hoppe et al., 1993; Luebke, 1998). A survey of methods and tools has been collected by Luebke (2001). The e_{col}-operation as discussed in this chapter stems from Hoppe (1996). The algorithm for constructing a skeleton from a 3D polygonal model presented here was developed by Raab (1998) and first used in connection with the intersecting planes by Deussen et al. (1999a).

8 | LIGHTING MODELS FOR NPR

In this chapter, we will explore lighting or illumination models as a method to modify systematically the appearance of images. By way of motivation, we will start by looking at sample images that were drawn by hand by scientific illustrators and artists. We will see that though the lighting effects are not straightforward, many of the effects that can be observed can be traced to a handful of effects that can be incorporated in a lighting model for NPR. While in photorealistic rendering the lighting models are based on physically determined relations between light sources, objects' positions, and surface materials, we have more liberty in NPR to obey the laws of physics or not. Nonetheless, well-established lighting models, which are used in photorealistic computer graphics, form the basis for the development of new models. They include aspects from perceptual psychology, arts, design, and so forth.

In the following, we will explain some of these design basics before we turn our attention to the development of alternative lighting models. We will start with an overview of the Phong lighting model. For colored technical illustrations especially, we present a lighting model that includes techniques borrowed from artists—such as cool-to-warm shifts and color undertones. Since such effects would require changing the possibly built-in lighting model of a rendering systen, we will then show how we can make use of a traditional lighting model instead of changing or replacing it. This yields a component-based model that is particularly well suited for line illustrations.

8.1 Conveying Shape Versus Illumination

Scientific illustrators see the world and the objects they portray through their own eyes, and re-create images such that viewers will be able to construct their own mental models of the objects in question. In doing so, scientific illustrators often accentuate important objects by using auras, or deaccentuate the background by lighting it up behind dark foreground objects. What immediately becomes clear is that the resultant images cannot simply be reproduced by a computer placing only a single light source in a standard location.

There is a physiological reason why a scientific illustrator has great liberties with respect to the use of light. Indeed, the human visual system is able to adapt locally to brightness so that no eye ever sees a scene as it is represented by a camera. Consider, for example, the photographs shown in Figure 8.1. In Figure 8.1(a), the photographer reported having been able to discern the details of the dark region to the left, but these details were not recorded on the film. The photographer's own visual system adapted locally to the illumination, enabling the details to be discerned. As soon as a flashlight was used, objects in the foreground were brightened (Figure 8.1(b)). This phenomenon turns up in many situations so that it may not be possible to capture on film and thus in a single photograph what a person can see at any given time.

Even more, a scientific illustrator will examine an object in detail from all sides and with various different arrangements of lights and subsequently synthesize these different views in one image that is passed on to a viewer. Hence, a hand-drawn image is quite naturally *not* restricted to encoding any one lighting condition. This procedure of mixing and matching the illumination of various parts of an image is often what makes a scientific illustration so much more informative than a photograph. Obviously, the varying positions of lights are generally not irritating to viewers; the contradictions, for example, due to impossible configurations of shadows, do not deter viewers from using such images as sources of information.

Moreover, there is also a pragmatic reason why the illumination of an illustration is often very different from the illumination of the original scene. This deals with the history of art. The art historian Rudolf Arnheim argues that historically and in the development process of an artist, shading is introduced at a late stage, while contour lines and local coloring are the first features to be mastered—and indeed are used initially to convey the roundness of objects, not the illumination. One reason for this order in which the skills are mastered lies in human cognition, which is focused primarily on objects and their attributes like shape and color. By

(a)   (b)

FIGURE 8.1 Two snapshots of a scene. The photographer reported seeing details of the boat while taking picture (a) on the left. His vision system had adapted to the local intensity, while the camera had not, leaving the entire region dark. Picture (b) shows the same scene photographed with a flash, revealing the detail.

contrast, light sources and illumination are secondary effects, and their relation to our ability to see things at all is generally underrated by human cognition, if not even ignored. Instead, light is considered an independent entity.[1]

Even when shading is introduced into an image, it is generally used to add depth to an otherwise flat medium, but not necessarily to express illumination. For example, the shading in Figure 8.2 is used to express layers of objects within the image, rather than the effects of light. Nonetheless, shading used in this manner may still be interpreted as a result of illumination.

Because of the way human perception works with respect to light sources and orientations, though, this shading does not even have to be consistent over a single illustration. For example, it is easy to verify that in Figure 8.3 the light

---

1. Recall that even the Bible reports that light was created on the first day, while objects (sun, moon, and stars) only followed later on the third day!

FIGURE 8.2 Shading used to present different layers rather than illumination.

FIGURE 8.3 Inconsistent shading used in a hand-drawn image.

reflecting off the upper telescope and the shadow cast by the box on which the person is standing cannot possibly stem from the same light source.

In general, reviewing illustrations in technical manuals, illustrated textbooks, or encyclopedias reveals a wealth of conventions that have developed over time and that are quite different from standard computer graphics models. The following list, although not exhaustive, presents the most common of these conventions. Note that here color is considered an integral part of the rendition although many of the principles also apply for grayscale images or even line drawings.

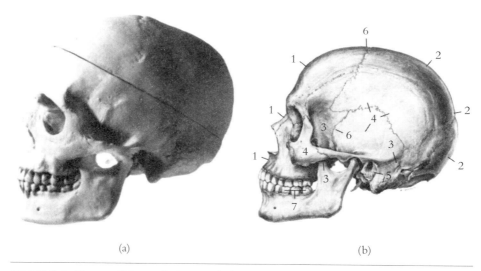

FIGURE 8.4 Two renditions of a human skull: a photograph with light from the front (a), a handmade scientific illustration (b).

- Edge lines are drawn with black curves.
- Matte objects are shaded with intensities far from black and white. (This limits the range of usable colors for shading.)
- Warmth and coolness of color usually indicate the surface normal.
- Shadows are rarely used. If shadows are used, they are placed in a way that they do not occlude important details or object features.
- Special lighting conditions are assumed in areas where important details have to be shown.
- Usually the objects are lit by *one* light source in standard position (upper left-hand corner in front of the object).

We will now study two images in detail to see how lighting affects the graphical details that can be conveyed. Both images are of a human skull; Figure 8.4(a) shows a photograph of the skull illuminated from the front, an image that could also have been rendered using the Phong illumination model described later. Next, Figure 8.4(b) shows a handmade illustration of the same object. It is easy to see that the second of these images does a better job of conveying the shape of the details than the first.

We will examine the differences between the two images with the goal of being able to derive algorithms for computing the non–photorealistic rendition. The following observations can be made:

1. *Rim shadow lighting* (Figure 8.4(b), label 1) Along the edges of the object facing almost perpendicular to the viewing plane, so-called rim shadows have been added to highlight the edges.

2. *Plateau lighting* (Figure 8.4(b), label 4) Large, quite flat areas of the object are given a high brightness.

3. *Back lighting* (Figure 8.4(b), label 2) Although the light clearly comes from one given direction, surfaces facing the other way are sometimes given some light effects to enhance the 3D appearance of these parts.

4. *Curvature lighting* (Figure 8.4(b), label 3) Areas of high curvature are drawn with more shading than areas with little curvature.

5. *Transmission and transparency* Special care is given to situations in which light travels through a medium. For example, in some illustrations it may be desirable to highlight the region through which light travels in a dark room (*volume lighting*). Furthermore, the medium through which the light travels may be something other than air (such as water, which need not be clear) or glass (such as when drawing an object behind a window pane).

In the following, we will study how these conventions can be simulated using computer graphics techniques and hence how effective illustrations can be generated from 3D models. We will draw on research that has been done in the area of photorealistic rendering, especially pertaining to lighting models. We will show how photorealistic illumination models, in particular the Phong model—which is explained in the following section—can be extended over and above a pure simulation of the physical processes involved.

The development of a lighting model for NPR will be our focus after describing the Phong model as our general basis. We will examine two different situations and directions. First, a model for colored illustration is presented. The main idea here is that for effectively using color in an illustration, it is not sufficient to derive the color values from the illumination situation alone. Instead, some techniques that artists would use have to be taken into account. Second, as we have seen in the illustration of the skull, one light source in standard position is often not enough to emphasize shape features of the object. Thus we will show

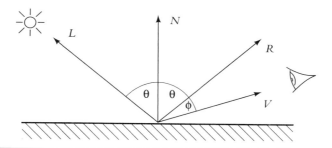

FIGURE 8.5   Vectors used in the Phong model of reflection.

how different light sources with specific parameters can be introduced in the scene to achieve certain effects.

8.2 A Basic Lighting Model

Practically all rendering tools available today make use of a lighting model named after a Vietnamese graduate student, Phong Bui–Tuong (1975). According to this model, the intensity of light I that is visible at a given point on a surface can be calculated as the sum of intensities due to several components of light. All identifiers used in the following refer to the diagram in Figure 8.5.

1. *Ambient light:* $I = I_a k_a$ This component models light of uniform brightness throughout the image caused by multiple reflections of light from many surfaces present in the environment. Each object is thus displayed using an intensity intrinsic to it. The intensity of the ambient light is referred to as I_a and is assumed to be constant for all objects, while k_a, the ambient reflection coefficient, is a constant related to the material being modeled. This coefficient is an empirical value that does not correspond to any physical property of real materials.

    Taking into consideration only ambient light, each object appears as a monochromatic silhouette since the intensity does not depend on geometric properties such as surface orientation or viewer distance.

2. *Diffuse reflection:* $I = I_i k_d \cos \theta = I_i k_d (L \cdot N)$ Light reflected by dull matte surfaces is referred to as diffuse reflection. It is scattered in all directions with an equal intensity that is proportional to the cosine of the angle between the incident light I_i and the surface normal N. Following Lambert's law, for matte

surfaces, the viewing angle has no influence on the light intensity; hence we do not need to consider the vector V in computing the diffuse reflection. For different surface materials, the reflected light intensity is furthermore modulated by a factor k_d, the diffuse reflection coefficient. In order to have any effect on the surface, the incident rays have to fall on the surface in an angle θ between $0°$ and $90°$. The cosine of this angle can be computed as the dot product of the two normalized vectors L and N.

3. *Specular reflection:* $I = I_i k_s \cos^n \phi = I_i k_s (R \cdot V)^n$ This models light reflected from a shiny surface. As such, the intensity can be expected to drop off with the angle ϕ between the reflected ray R and the viewer V since shiny surfaces reflect light unequally in different directions. On a perfectly shiny surface, light is reflected *only* in the direction of reflection R. The speed of the intensity dropoff from that given direction where $R = V$ to the edge of the resulting highlight region is modeled by taking the n-th power of $\cos \phi$, where n depends on the surface material. The specular reflection, too, is modulated by a constant k_s, the surface material's specular reflection coefficient. It is selected experimentally to produce aesthetically pleasing results.

Putting it all together, the intensity I_{Phong} of a point on an object's surface can be calculated according to Equation (8.1). Note that in this equation all vectors are unit vectors and the reflection coefficients all fall in a range between zero and one.

$$I_{\text{Phong}} = I_a k_a + I_i k_d (L \cdot N) + I_i k_s (R \cdot V)^n \tag{8.1}$$

Figure 8.6 shows a visualization of the relative intensities of the three components under different conditions. Note that Equation (8.1) can also be used to treat colored light and materials. For doing so, all light intensities as well as the reflection coefficients are vectors describing the color components (usually red, green, and blue).

We will now explore how the Phong model can be extended to create technical and medical illustrations that fulfill partially the requirements stated earlier. We will focus on color illustrations and see how an artistic handling of color yields images that emphasize the shape of objects. We will then see how the requirements from the list that are not met with this particular model can be fulfilled, especially in the context of line drawings.

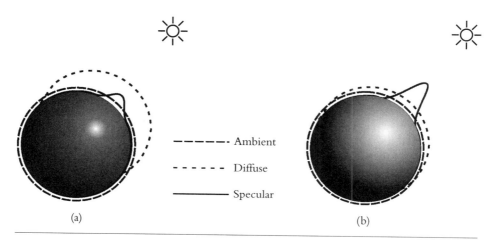

FIGURE 8.6 Phong lighting on a sphere with different coefficients: $k_d > k_s$ (a) and $k_d < k_s$ (b).

8.3 Colored Illustrations

Two of the main observations from handmade illustrations, especially from those done with airbrush and pen, relate to edge lines (contour lines), which are almost always drawn in black and to the limited range of colors used for shading. To use these techniques in a computer graphics model, we will first examine the artistic techniques a little closer in order to derive possible parameters for a technical realization.

Colored illustrations make use of variations in hue and luminance to communicate shape. In order to create color *tones*, artists can mix in black or white to darken or lighten a given color. Tones created by adding gray to a given color usually vary in hue but not much in luminance. This makes different tones useful if there is only a limited range of intensity values to choose from. This, however, is the case in the kind of illustrations that we are considering.

Another important concept for illustrators is the *color temperature*. Colors are classified as being cool, warm, or temperate. Cool colors include, for example, blue, violet, and green, whereas warm colors include red, orange, and yellow. Temperate colors, finally, are red-violets or yellow-greens. The human visual perception is very sensitive to color temperature; it can generate depth impression and hence be used as a depth cue. Objects with a cool color are percieved as being farther away than objects with a warm color. This effect appears when two

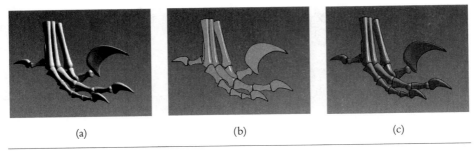

FIGURE 8.7 Using the Phong model as a starting point for illustrations reveals some shortcomings of the model: areas not directly lit appear with constant color ($k_d = 1$, $k_a = 0$) (a), shape information is lost, especially in regions of high curvature when rendering only highlights and edge lines (b), and details are lost when including edge lines in a Phong-shaded image ($k_d = 0.5$, $k_a = 0.1$) (c). (See also color insert.)

surfaces of different color are close together and can be employed in the design of illustrations.

The Phong model is a good starting point for illustrative images, although it has some disadvantages that we have to circumvent. The main problem when using the Phong model lies in areas that are not directly lit by the given light source. Here, the angles between the two vectors that are used to determine the diffuse as well as the specular reflection are both out of the valid range and hence only the ambient term in Equation (8.1) influences the intensity calculation. Since the ambient term does not depend on any light or viewing direction, the resulting intensity is constant over the respective area that results in images where shape features cannot be ascertained (see Figure 8.7(a)).

Edge lines and highlights are invaluable tools for visualization; however, the pure Phong model makes it hard to incorporate these features into illustrations. Figure 8.7(b) shows edge lines and highlights that can be created, whereas Figure 8.7(c) shows their incorporation into a Phong shaded image. For creating this image, the parameter values for k_a and k_d have to be hand-tuned to achieve this result. Moreover, in this illustration, the lack of shape information for indirectly lit areas is noticeable.

We will now explore how color temperature and color tones can be incorporated in the Phong model. We will restrict ourselves to the diffuse component since our goal is to come up with a lighting model for matte objects. Such objects are considered to be ideally diffuse reflectors, that is, they reflect incoming light equally in any direction. We will use the diffuse term of Equation (8.1), more

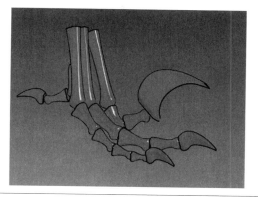

FIGURE 8.8 Approximately constant luminance tone rendering. Edge lines and highlights are clearly noticeable. Some details in shaded regions are also visible. The lack of luminance shift makes these changes subtle. (See also color insert.)

specifically the dependency between the intensity of the reflected light and the relation between the two vectors (surface normal and vector to the light source). As a first approach, blending between a cool and a warm color is examined. We can, for example, formulate

$$I = \left(\frac{1 + L \cdot N}{2} \right) k_{\text{cool}} + \left(1 - \frac{1 + L \cdot N}{2} \right) k_{\text{warm}} \qquad (8.2)$$

which yields an interpolation between k_{cool} and k_{warm} if we consider the full range being possible for the term $L \cdot N$, namely, -1 to 1. To make sure, however, that the full variation in this interval is used, the lighting should be set up properly. The light vector L should be perpendicular to the gaze direction. The best position for the single light source, which we use in that model, would be up and to the right, which can be explained psychologically. The human visual system assumes that light comes from above, and many of the ways in which we perceive shape from shading are related to this assumption. Using Equation (8.2), we can achieve results as in Figure 8.8 where luminance does not vary much over the image but tone does. Some details are recognizable now, however, in a very subtle manner. This subtlety comes from the lack of a strong cool-to-warm shift as well as from the little variety in luminance.

To bring more luminance variation in the image, the following two ways are possible:

1. Creating color scales by interpolating between two extreme colors, for instance, blue and yellow.

2. Creating color scales by scaling object color shades.

We will combine both approaches in one model as follows. If we create the scale from a fully saturated blue ($k_{cool} = k_{blue} = (0, 0, b)$ with $b \in [0, 1]$ in RGB space) to a fully saturated yellow ($k_{warm} = k_{yellow} = (y, y, 0)$, with $y \in [0, 1]$ in RGB space), it is again independent from the object's diffuse reflectance. On the other hand, if we consider creating the scale based on the object's diffuse reflectance, it would range from pure black (for k_{cool}) to the object's color defined by $k_{warm} = k_d$. The effect gained herewith resembles the traditional shading except that luminance also varies in areas where $L \cdot N < 0$.

A combination of these two strategies would combine the tone scaled object color and a cool-to-warm shift. This cool-to-warm shift creates an undertone in the color that can be compared to some effects that artists achieve when mixing their paints. A linear blend between both tones is achieved using the follwing equations:

$$k_{cool} = k_{blue} + \alpha k_d \qquad \qquad (8.3)$$
$$k_{warm} = k_{yellow} + \beta k_d$$

which are then inserted into Equation (8.2). To tune the image, the four variables α, β, b, and y can be set to different values to create several effects. Here, b and y determine the temperature shift by giving the maximum "blueness" and "yellowness." The other two values, α and β, determine the amount of which the actual object color is visible. Since one of the rules for illustrations requires that the colors that are used for shading are far away from white and black, we will choose some intermediate values here. Two images with different parameter settings can be found in Figure 8.9.

If it comes to implementing such an alternative lighting model, it would be desirable to use already existing libraries and possible hardware acceleration. The Phong model is well supported by almost any graphics library so that an approximation of the new shading model using the Phong model would save time in development and also execution time since we can rely on hardware-accelerated implementations. The key for an approximation is the use of negative colors for light sources that are possible in most systems (for instance, OpenGL). We can imitate the results of Equation (8.2) by placing two light sources in directions L and $-L$ and adjusting the light intensities to $(k_{warm} - k_{cool})/2$ for the first one and to $(k_{cool} - k_{warm})/2$ for the second light source. If we assume the object color to be

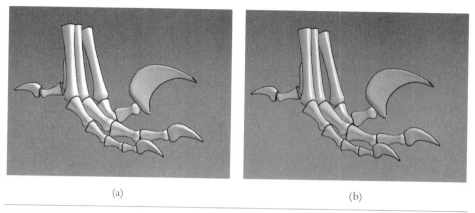

(a) (b)

FIGURE 8.9 Images created with the introduced shading model: $b = 0.4, y = 0.4, \alpha = 0.2, \beta = 0.6$ (a) and $b = 0.55, y = 0.3, \alpha = 0.25, \beta = 0.5$ (b). (See also color insert.)

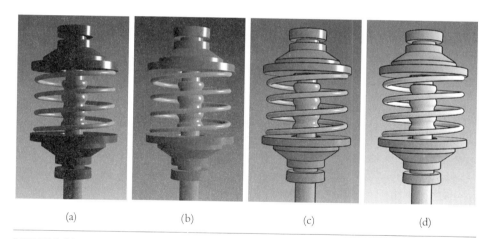

(a) (b) (c) (d)

FIGURE 8.10 Comparison of traditional computer graphics techniques and techniques for creating technical illustrations: Phong shading (a), new shading model without edge lines (b), new shading model with edge lines and highlights (c), and approximation of the new model using Phong shading (d). (See also color insert.)

white, the ambient term should be set to $(k_{cool} + k_{warm})/2$. Because of the second light source, this approach will not create highlights; however, some artifacts may occur if the highlighting of the Phong shading is turned on. Figure 8.10 shows a comparison between the different models mentioned in this section.

8.4 A Component-Based Lighting Model

We will now build on the Phong lighting model to derive a new model that is particularly well suited for NPR. We will concentrate on the intensity value of a light source regardless of what color the emitted light has. This makes the model particularly well suited for its application for line drawings as well as other continuous tone illustrations that do not require color. However, the model can be extended for color by treating each color channel separately or even including the model for colored illustrations from above. The presented model is component based; that is, we will consider the intensity of a given point to be composed of the sum of the intensities of five components: standard lighting with shadows, rim shadow lighting, curvature shading, transparency, and illumination volume lighting.

8.4.1 Standard Lighting and Shadows

As already stated, illustrations, especially technical and medical illustrations, are created following a set of rules that have been developed over time. One of these rules pertains to the placement of the main—in many cases, single—light source. Generally, a standard position for this light is chosen at 45° to the object in the image plane and 45° to the viewer. This ensures that shape cues that we are used to from our daily experience with objects being lit by the sun are also usable in the illustration. The human visual system is very sensitive to such shape cues and assumes light coming from above. For computing the intensity of each point, the Phong lighting model is used, taking shadows into consideration. The computation of shadows will not be discussed here. For the purpose at hand, standard shadow calculation algorithms are being used, for instance, shadow volumes, shadow z-buffer, or even raytracing.

8.4.2 Rim Shadow, Plateau, and Back Lighting

Rim shadow lighting was introduced to highlight edge lines by rendering them as if they would be in the shadow. This effect can be modeled with a light source in front of the object to render. This makes it possible to reuse standard rendering techniques. Placing the light source at the camera position, as shown in Figure 8.11, and using just the diffuse term in the Phong lighting model, renders surface parts with large angle to the viewing plane dark, while rendering others bright. Hence, I_{rim} can be derived from Phong's model in Equation (8.1) by setting $k_a = 0$, $k_s = 0$, and $L = V$:

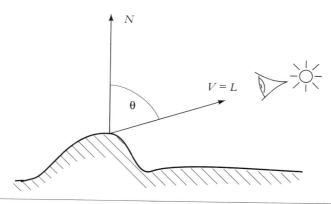

FIGURE 8.11 Vectors used for rim shadow lighting.

$$I_{\text{rim}} = k_d(V \cdot N) \tag{8.4}$$

Back lighting can be modeled by placing a light source in the same place as for rim shadow lighting and calculating I_{back} by using a negative value for the intensity:

$$I_{\text{back}} = -I_{\text{rim}}$$

In the same manner, in fact, *plateau lighting* can also be modeled by placing the light source at infinity instead of at the camera position. This yields Equation (8.5), which on first glance, does not look different from Equation (8.4). However, since the light source has moved into infinity, all vectors from the light source to the object (the light rays) have the same direction and are parallel to each other. Furthermore, all vectors are infinitely long. Hence, L is no longer a unit vector, nor can it be expressed by a unit vector so that the angle between this vector and the surface normal can no longer be computed by using the dot product.

$$I_{\text{plateau}} = k_d \cos\theta \tag{8.5}$$

8.4.3 Curvature Lighting

In *curvature lighting*, the effect to be achieved is to shade surfaces with a high curvature dark, while surfaces with a low curvature are to be bright. The dark shading is motivated by the shadow cast by raking light. Instead of placing different light sources at the appropriate positions, it is more convenient to use the value of the curvature κ directly. If not given directly, the curvature at a given pixel can

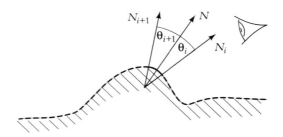

FIGURE 8.12 Computing the curvature from surface normals of adjacent surface patches.

be approximated using the surrounding surface normals (see Figure 8.12). Since we want to shade surface parts of high curvature dark, we can use the inverse curvature as intensity value:

$$I_\kappa = 1 - \kappa$$

This equation shows that curvature lighting is independent from the actual lighting condition since no incoming light intensity is considered. This seems to be not appropriate for calculating the intensity, but keeping in mind that curvature lighting is just one component of a more complex model and that it is evaluated on a per object basis makes this approach usable in the context at hand.

We are now in a position to see how rim shadow lighting and curvature lighting interact with each other. Figure 8.13 shows a wavy surface and illustrates the rim shadow lighting and curvature lighting analogous to the convention of Figure 8.4. Note that surface parts that are slanted away from the viewer are emphasized by rim shadow lighting (the curve is closer to the surface to indicate dark shading). The curve of the curvature lighting, in contrast, is closest to the surface in strongly curved areas, indicating that these areas are to be made dark.

8.4.4 Transmission and Transparency

The transmission of light through a transparent or translucent surface should also be possible to model since it would allow the inclusion of materials like glass and the proper display of objects that would otherwise be hidden behind such a surface. In most hand-drawn illustrations, a correct treatment of the laws of transmission and refraction is not completely considered. Instead, a technique called *ghosting* is often used. In a strong sense, ghosting means to reveal the interior parts of an object by rendering the outer surfaces as if they were transparent. In these cases as

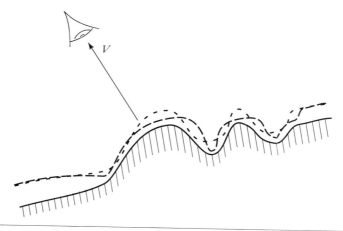

FIGURE 8.13 Comparison of rim shadow lighting and curvature lighting on a wavy surface. The surface is shown in a thick line, the relative intensity of the curvature lighting in the dashed line with small spaces between the dashes, while the rim shadow lighting is shown in the dashed line with larger spaces between the dashes.

well as in cases where a "real" transparent surface covers an object part, illustrators often violate the physical laws by treating the index of refraction as having the unit value. Hence, if a transparent surface f is in front of an opaque surface b, the intensity of the front surface I_f must be mixed with the intensity value of the back surface I_b. This is done by introducing a parameter α to help compute the resultant light intensity I_t:

$$I_t = \alpha I_b + (1 - \alpha) I_f \qquad (8.6)$$

As can be seen in Figure 8.14, an intensity value for both the front and the back surface is computed using the same viewing vector. The value α then determines how both values are combined, that is, how transparent the front surface is. This approach is also often called *non-refractive transparency*.

Studying hand-drawn images has shown, however, that the intensity of light of the object behind a transparent surface is generally not uniform. For example, Figure 8.15 shows a hand-drawn image in which the intensity of the object behind the transparent surface actually increases with the distance to the edge of the transparent object. By contrast, if the object actually progresses beyond the transparent object, its intensity is very high close to the edge but decreases with the distance from the edge.

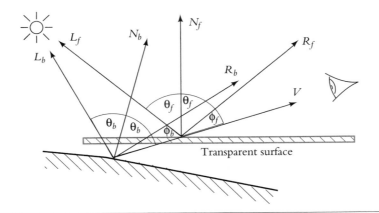

FIGURE 8.14 Mixing the reflection of the front surface with that of the back surface according to Equation 8.6.

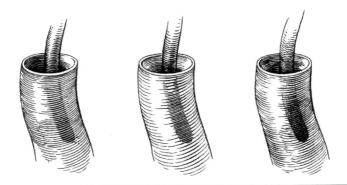

FIGURE 8.15 Example of a hand-drawn image. Notice how the contrast of the object hanging in the tube varies toward the edge of the transparent surface.

Hence, the value of α changes with the distance of the current surface point from the edge, and this must be considered by adding such a dependency, that is,

$$I_t = \alpha(d)I_b + (1 - \alpha(d))I_f \tag{8.7}$$

An implementation like that proposed in Equation (8.7) will actually change the perceived transparency of the surface depending on the value of d. Certainly other variants are possible that depend on the intended rendering style as well as on the used algorithms. A few example images that mimic the renditions from

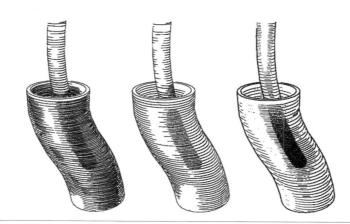

FIGURE 8.16 Example of a rendered image mimicking the effect portrayed in Figure 8.15.

Figure 8.15 are given in Figure 8.16 and show that this approach is indeed feasible and yields appropriate results.

8.4.5 Overall Intensity

After having dealt with all components of the lighting model separately, we will now see how to compute the overall intensity for a given surface point taking into account all the different components from before. The intensity I_{NPL} (for non-photorealistic lighting) of a given point in the image can be calculated as the sum of the components according to the equation

$$I_{NPL} = w_{Phong}I_{Phong}$$
$$+ w_{rim}I_{rim} + w_{back}I_{back} + w_{plateau}I_{plateau} + w_{\kappa}I_{\kappa} + w_{t}I_{t} \qquad (8.8)$$

The weights w have a function similar to that of the fractions k in the Phong lighting model. As the fractions k determine the amount of energy that is reflected from a surface via diffuse, specular, or ambient reflection, and thus determine the influence of the respective terms, the weights w determine the influence of the new aspects. Just like the fractions k, the weights w sum up to one. Since the values for w can be negative, the precise formulation would be

$$\sum |w| = 1$$

Finally, it has been found to be opportune to add controls for brightness b and contrast c to enhance Equation (8.8) yielding the final equation

$$I'_{NPL} = (I_{NPL} + b - 0.5)c + 0.5$$

---

1 $S :=$ compute image using the Phong model with a light source in standard
    position

2 $R :=$ compute image using the Phong model with a light source positioned
    for rim shading

3 $K :=$ compute curvature image

4 $T :=$ compute transparency image

5 determine values for the weights $w_{\text{Phong}}, w_\kappa, w_t$

6 combine $S, R, K,$ and T according to the weights pixel by pixel

---

ALGORITHM 8.1 Implementation of the component-based lighting model via G-buffers.

8.5 Implementation Issues

If it comes down to implementing such a component-based lighting model, it appears that there have to be many changes to the intrinsics of the actual graphics system. Most of today's graphics systems and libraries rely on the Phong model, which is tightly integrated into the rendering pipeline where parts of it are often implemented in a way that hardware support can be used. Replacing these functions with ones based on the component-based lighting model described earlier would destroy all advantages gained with using standard libraries. Most important, rendering speed would be dramatically decreased and since for an adequately rendered image possibly many parameter combinations have to be tested, the creation of a usable illustration would be very time consuming.

Hence, it is desirable to *use* standard libraries instead of *replacing* them. The components of the lighting model are all independent from each other and can thus be computed separately using either special rendering algorithms or the standard graphics pipeline. As a result, a set of G-buffers is obtained that can then be combined using the weighted sum of the pixel values (see Algorithm 8.1).

The given algorithm is incomplete since it does not contain all aforementioned components. Further, there are other possible components that can be incorporated. To do so, only the respective G-buffers have to be created and a weight value has to be assigned. It can then be incorporated into the combination in the last step of the algorithm. For creating the buffers that involve the evaluation of the Phong model, a proper lighting setup is required prior to the rendering.

For rendering the curvature buffer, several methods are possible depending on the given model type. For free-form surfaces, an analytic curvature calculation is the method of choice. Here the *principal curvature* values $\kappa_{\min}$ and $\kappa_{\max}$ as well as the *Gaussian curvature* $K = \kappa_{min}\kappa_{max}$ or the *mean curvature* $K = 0.5(\kappa_{min} + \kappa_{max})$ can be used for our purpose. We will not go into detail here. For polygonal models, there is generally no curvature defined and hence no straightforward way to determine curvature values. However, since the change in the size of the angle between the surface normal and a vector pointing toward the viewer's position can be interpreted as curvature, there is a way to approximate curvature values from a special G-buffer. Remember that the definition of rim shadow lighting in Section 8.4.2 yields an image where each pixel intensity represents the cosine of the aforementioned angle. Applying a first order differential operator on the rim shadow image thus yields the changes in the size of this angle and can be interpreted as the *average curvature*.

Exercises

8.1   Find a number of technical or scientific (medical) illustrations in books or journals. Find out which conventions the illustrators have been using to depict lighting conditions. Which of these conventions are rather general, and which can be seen as "personal style" of the respective illustrator?

8.2   Review the Phong illumination model and its components. How do the different vectors influence the final rendition? How can certain lighting effects be achieved by placing additional light sources at a particular position?

8.3   Implement the lighting model for colored illustration and experiment with your implementation. Which combinations of color and which parameter settings yield the most promisig results?

8.4   Try the lighting model for colored illustrations with models of different object classes (mechanical parts, organic shapes, parts of the human body). Can you use the same parameter settings for all different kinds of models?

8.5   Implement the component-based lighting model introduced in Section 8.4. Are there any other components that can be derived from your observations in Exercise 8.1?

8.6   Extend the component-based model by the parts you have identified in the previous exercise. Render a few images with different weighting factors to see how they influence the final result.

Bibliographic Notes

The topic of illumination in illustrations has been studied extensively in the literature. In particular, books by Arnheim (1984) provide valuable insights into the point of view of art history. The books by Hodges (1989) and Martin (1989) are excellent sources of inspiration on scientific and technical illustration and contain extensive material on illumination.

Lighting models in computer graphics are dealt with in practically every basic computer graphics book. Particularly good surveys can be found in Watt (2000) and Foley et al.(1990). The original paper on what has come to be known as the Phong reflection model is Phong (1975). Enhancements to the Phong model were presented by Gooch et al. (1998; Gooch and Gooch, 1999a; Gooch and Gooch, 1999b; Gooch et al., 1999; Gooch, 1998). Here, the Phong model was used and extended by color and tone shifts to yield effects as they are known from technical illustrations. Hamel (2000; Hamel et al., 1998) introduced the notion of a component-based illumination model that is introduced in this chapter. He also made use of G-buffers (see Chapter 6) to make the computations within such a component-based model more efficient.

Besides actually changing the way lighting calculation is done in a rendering system, some authors also map light intensities to stylistic changes in the image. Thus, the results of a standard lighting calculation are taken and interpreted not as pixel intensities but, for instance, as line width (see Schlechtweg et al., 1998; Schlechtweg and Raab, 1998). These methods work together with the path and style metaphor for drawing lines as introduced in Chapter 3. A unified approach in this sense is presented by Hall (1999). He introduces a texture mapping technique where the textures adapt to the light intensity.

9 | DISTORTING NON-REALISTIC RENDITIONS

NPR entails not only adjusting the rendition style to the communication needs at hand, but also tuning the final image or even the geometric model itself so as to ensure that the space available for the final image is well used. Indeed, we had observed that practically all renditions made by hand (like pen-and-ink drawings, pencil sketches) are not drawn strictly to scale. As the style of art called *photorealism* illustrates, the reason for such deviations is not that the artist cannot draw any better, that is, that the artist may not be able to draw to scale, but rather that in a conscious or unconscious process, such images are drawn to imply that certain objects are more important than others. This, in turn, suggests drawing important objects more prominently by enlarging them and making less important ones smaller.

Distortions not only serve the purpose of making certain (enlarged) objects appear more important, they also serve several other purposes. Making objects or parts of an image smaller makes room to display other information that may otherwise not have "fit." While presenting objects smaller means that less detail can be shown, objects drawn somewhat enlarged have the potential for having more detail.

The act of changing the scale of an object or a presentation can also be animated. Rather than showing only the final magnification, this enables users to see what has happened to their original image. It can be observed that if many objects in an image get larger or smaller all at once, viewers can ascertain the overall structure of the objects at a glance. Indeed, viewers of such an animation can see which objects are held together and which ones can be separated from one another.

In this chapter, we will approach the topic of distortions from three points of view. In the first, the distortion will pertain to the 2D plane of the rendition. We will show how selected regions can be enlarged at the expense of the rest of the image, particularly at the expense of such parts that lie in the immediate vicinity of the enlarged portions.

The second method of distortion is one that works in object space. We will discuss how geometric objects can be scaled selectively. When objects get too large to fit into the space available in world coordinates without violating certain contraints, the surrounding objects get appropriately smaller to make room. An important characteristic of the algorithm discussed here is that it can be applied to data structures of any dimension.

The term *distortion* for such changes in shape has a negative connotation. Indeed, selectively changing the scale of an image or of certain objects within an image also means that the presentation may become misleading. Viewers may interpret a distorted object verbatim and think that in reality it actually has the perceived shape. In the terminology of Chapter 1, a distortion is misleading if the viewer mistakes the change in scale for an object artifact rather than it being a model artifact or even only an image artifact.

To help viewers to interpret distorted images correctly with respect to their varying scale, information can be added to an image to indicate the location and nature of such changes. We will introduce some techniques to make distortions comprehensible. Among these is also animation that makes the changes in the image explicit to the viewer.

Conversely, in the context of animation, distortions play an important role as a means of communication. They help to clarify shape and form, give spatial cues, and give the animation an interesting and vital character. In the last section of the chapter, we will thus turn our attention to distortions in an animated context and see which methods can be used there.

9.1 Image-Space Distortion

The first method of distorting renditions that we will introduce works completely in image space. Its effect is much like that of placing a magnifying glass over an image, except that shape, magnification characteristics, and transition to regions that are to remain to scale can be adjusted by the user.

The method in its basic form works independent of the image being displayed. Hence it can be applied to scanned images or as a post-processing step in a renderer. In the exercises, we will examine how the basic method can be integrated into a rendering system. This way, the level of detail or even the aspect of the underlying information space displayed within a magnified region can be adjusted.

An image-space distortion uses a function $f : \mathbb{R}^2 \to \mathbb{R}^2$, which converts a 2D image into another 2D image. That is, each point p in the input image is mapped onto a point p' in the output image. While it is possible to define such functions and to work with them, recent work has shown that it is computationally effective to think of a distortion in 2D as a concatenation of two functions. The first function g maps every point in 2D onto a surface in 3D:

$$g : \mathbb{R}^2 \to \mathbb{R}^3$$

Subsequently, the resultant 3D surface is rendered to produce a new image in 2D using a rendering function

$$r : \mathbb{R}^3 \to \mathbb{R}^2$$

Thus, the image-space distortion is regarded as the concatenation of the two preceding functions, yielding $f = r \circ g$. In the following, we will see how this concatenation can be interpreted geometrically, which also leads to a possible way of implementing such image-space distortions in an efficient manner.

9.1.1 Fundamental Algorithm

Consider the construction of Figure 9.1. An image to be distorted is placed on the *base plane*, while a camera is placed at the position of the *reference viewpoint*. To effect a distortion, the surface is treated as though it were elastic. Selected points on this surface are raised somewhat in the positive z-direction, while the positions of all other points fall into place according to the elasticity of the surface. Finally, the surface is rendered as seen by the camera in the *reference view plane*. This rendition represents the distorted image. The placement of the original image on the base plane together with the elastic deformation of this plane represent the function g. Each point in the image is assigned a position and a z-height, yielding a 3D description of a surface. The rendering function r is realized by the viewing transformation of that surface, which includes a projection to get back to two-dimensional coordinates.

We will study this method in detail using a single focus point placed at the center of the image. Consider the cross section of the construction of Figure 9.1

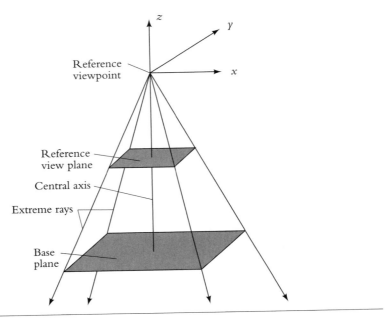

FIGURE 9.1 Basic setup with reference viewpoint and reference view plane.

as shown in Figure 9.2. The *focus point f* has been raised by an amount h_f. Around the edges, part of the surface, called the *context*, is pinned down to the base plane. The rest of the surface connects the focus point to the context.

Since the focus point has been moved closer to the view plane, it will appear magnified in the final image, while the context will appear in the final image as it did before the manipulation of the surface. Those parts of the image connecting these two will be compressed. What this compression looks like has a marked effect on the overall image and is determined by the specific dropoff function being used. Indeed, for a dropoff function $D(r)$, a point p on the surface to be distorted is raised to a level h_p with

$$h_p = h_f \cdot D(r). \tag{9.1}$$

Here, r is the radial distance from the original focus point f to p in the base plane. This construction is illustrated in Figure 9.3. Figure 9.3(a) shows a focus point and another point whose height is to be calculated, Figure 9.3(b) shows the

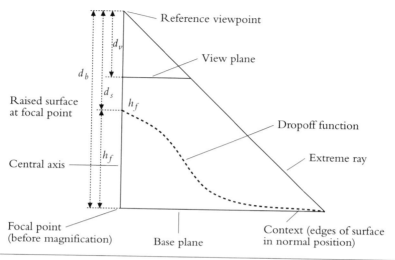

FIGURE 9.2 A cross-section diagram showing the raised central focus point, the profile of the dropoff function, and the edge of the surface in normal position.

z-translation of each of these points according to a dropoff function, and Figure 9.3(c) shows these two points in a final rendition on the viewing plane.

We are free to choose any dropoff function defined in the range [0, 1] such that $D(0) \cong 1$ and $D(1) = 0$, for example, the Gaussian function

$$D(r) = e^{-r^2/\sigma}$$

for $\sigma = 0.1$. This function is illustrated in Figure 9.4. Figure 9.4(a) shows the Gaussian function in 3D applied to a regular grid lying on the base plane, Figure 9.4(b) illustrates the same function in a cross-sectional view, and Figure 9.4(c) shows the rendition of the distorted surface as seen from the reference viewpoint.

These examples show that raising the surface to be displayed has the effect of distorting it. The higher a point is raised, the larger it gets. The more sloped the surface becomes, however, the more it gets compressed. As long as all parts of the surface are visible from the reference viewpoint, all the original surface will be visible in the distorted image. We will now study various aspects of this basic construction to see how it can be generalized.

9.1.2 Regions of Magnification

In the preceding construction, we showed how to magnify a focus point placed at the center of the surface that is to be distorted. Often it is not a single point we

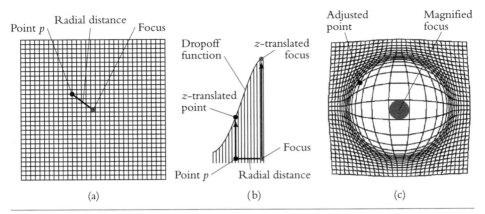

FIGURE 9.3 The process of creating a single central focus: the selected focus point (a), curve of the Gaussian dropoff function (b), resulting distorted rendition (c).

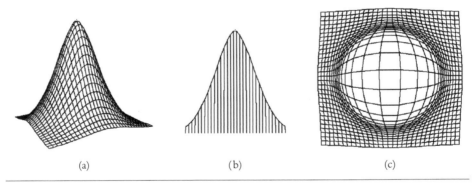

FIGURE 9.4 Single focus at the center of the field of view: 3D side view (a), cross-section view showing projection vectors (b), the resulting distorted image (c).

wish to magnify, but a larger part of the surface that we want to enlarge uniformly by a magnification factor m. We will refer to this larger part as the *focus region*. The focus region may typically be a circle (emulating a magnifying glass), a rectangle, any other (concave or convex) polygon, or even a polyline.

To extend the basic algorithm to include focus regions, we must further define the height h_p to which any point p on the original surface is raised. We raise all points f within the focus region to height h_f as necessary to achieve the desired magnification. To do so, a point-in-region test is needed that determines for each point p if it lies within the focus region or not. These tests may considerably slow down the algorithm since they might not be trivial for arbitrarily shaped focal regions. Any other points are raised as described earlier depending on the dropoff function. The distance to the focus region is typically the shortest distance to the closest edge of that region.

9.1.3 The Dropoff Function

The specific characteristics of the dropoff function being used are important when it is important to see how the focus region is connected to the context. Which dropoff function is best depends on the application at hand. This choice has influence on the final rendition with respect to controlling how much distortion is introduced, where the distortion is introduced, and how the distortion changes over the image. Several classes of functions have different characteristics in this sense. A few examples for such dropoff functions applied to a single focus point can be seen in Table 9.1. In order to classify these and other functions, they are compared to one another with respect to the following criteria:

- *Focal magnification*   The extent to which the actual focus point is magnified
- *Adjacent focal magnification*   The magnification of the regions near the focus point
- *Focus integration*   How well the focus point is visually integrated with the region affected by the dropoff function
- *Location of maximal compression*   Where the area is in which the visualization appears most cramped
- *Context integration*   How well the context blends into areas affected by the dropoff function

These criteria can then be used to select a class of functions that offers the best properties for the application at hand. All these and other functions are further parameterizable by finding constants to get a specific function out of the selected class. As an example, a linear dropoff function would create a cone-shaped surface. The slope of this cone can be adjusted by selecting appropriate parameters for the linear function.

Another way in which the effect of a dropoff function can be changed is to alter the calculation of the radial distance to the focus point or region. As can be seen in Equation (9.1), this distance in connection with the dropoff function

Dropoff functions

Assessment	Linear	Hemisphere	Cosine	Hyperbola	Gauss
Focus type					
Graph					
Image					
Focal magnification	Good	Minimal	Fair	Fair	Great
Adjacent focal magnification	Minimal	Great	Good	Good	Modest
Focal integration	Sharp	Good	Good	Good	Good
Location of maximal compression	Context connection	Context connection	Context connection	Context connection	Mid-distortion
Context integration	Abrupt	Poor	Abrupt	Abrupt	Good

TABLE 9.1 Assessment of dropoff functions based on certain criteria. Note that whole classes of functions are described by one column of this table; the actual function to be used is specified by additional parameters.

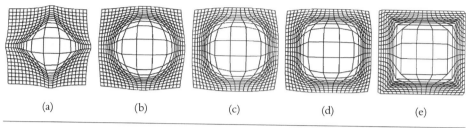

(a) (b) (c) (d) (e)

FIGURE 9.5 Varying the L-metric for a focus point: L_1 (a), L_2 (b), L_3 (c), L_4 (d), L_∞ (e).

directly affects the magnification. To describe the distance of any point on the surface to the focus point more exactly, the concept of so-called L_p-*metrics* is used.

Given two points $p_1(x_1, y_1)$ and $p_2(x_2, y_2)$, a general expression of the distance between these points is

$$L_p = \sqrt[p]{|x_1 - x_2|^p + |y_1 - y_2|^p}$$

It should be noted that the Euclidean distance is just one example of such an L_p-metric, namely, the L_2-metric. The Euclidean distance of two points is defined as

$$L_2 = \sqrt{|x_1 - x_2|^2 + |y_1 - y_2|^2}$$

Using $p = 1$ yields the so-called *Manhattan distance* $L_1 = |x_1 - x_2| + |y_1 - y_2|$, which is the sum of the distances in both coordinate directions. This resembles the walking distance in a city assuming a regular street layout.

In the limit, $L_{(\infty)} = \max(|x_1 - x_2|, |y_1 - y_2|)$. The higher the p, the more rectangular becomes the distorted portion of the grid around the focus point. Figure 9.5 shows several examples.

Of course, any other concept for measuring distance of a given point in the image to the focus point can be applied as well. This includes also "conceptual" distances, for instance, computed from given degrees of interest. As can be seen, the dropoff function as well as the distance metric offer a flexible way of controlling the distortion of an image. However, so far the focus point was only considered as being in the center of the image. Further, only one focus point was present. In the following, techniques are presented, which deal with an extension of the algorithm to multiple and possibly off-center focus points.

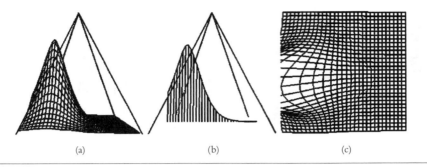

FIGURE 9.6 Single off-center focus point: view of the off-center perpendicular focus (a), the cross-section view showing perpendicular vectors and the view volume (b), and the projected view showing that the focus region cannot be seen (c).

9.1.4 Off-Center Focus Points and Multiple Foci

Up to now we have assumed that the manipulation of the surface to be distorted is carried out such that it is visible in its entirety from the reference viewpoint. However, if, for example, the focus point is not in the middle of the surface, even the Gaussian dropoff function will yield a situation in which this constraint no longer holds. An example is shown in Figure 9.6.

As can be seen, the region of the image that surrounds the focus point is no longer visible. The reason for this lies in the construction of the image. Moving an off-center focus point straight upward may cause the final position to fall outside the view volume and thus to be clipped within the rendering process. The translation vectors that are calculated for each point on the surface are always perpendicular to the base plane. A solution to the problem of moving parts of the surface outside the view volume is to use what is called *viewer-aligned focus*. Instead of raising the focus point f by an amount h_f straight upward, it is raised by this amount along a vector v_f pointing toward the reference viewpoint. Now, all other points are raised by a distortion vector v_p whose magnitude is the amount computed earlier (recall Equation 9.1) and whose direction is parallel to v_f. The result of applying this procedure to an off-center focus point is shown in Figure 9.7.

Note that using this technique, any point on the surface may now be selected as the focus point. Further, we are now equipped to deal with the situation when multiple foci are to be used. Suppose two such points on a surface are treated as

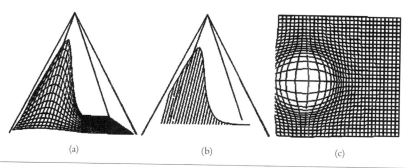

FIGURE 9.7 Viewer-aligned focus: 3D side view showing the focus directed to the viewpoint and inside the view volume (a), side profile view showing parallel vectors with the central vector directed to the viewpoint (b), and the top view of the projected image (c).

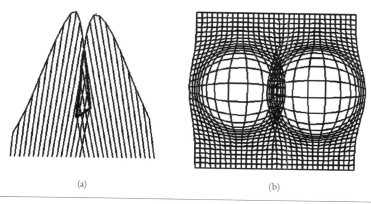

FIGURE 9.8 Buckling: the cross-sectional vector view, clearly showing the surface buckle (a) and the top or projected view showing the surface buckle (b).

focus points and thus raised by a certain amount. If these two points are close to each other, a situation can be encountered that we will call *buckling*. If in an area the two viewer-aligned vectors intersect, a self-intersecting area of the surface is the result. This creates visual discontinuities since the saddle between the two focus points may be hidden between parts of the surface. Figure 9.8 illustrates this situation.

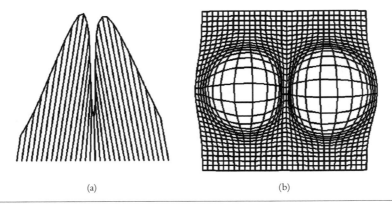

(a)   (b)

FIGURE 9.9 A blended interfocus region shown in a side profile view (a) and in a top view (b).

The solution would ideally be to interpolate the viewer-dependent vectors given at the focus points over the interfocal regions by maintaining the features defined by the dropoff functions. This "interpolation" happens by adjusting the alignment of the translation vectors so that they do not change abruptly. The key here is to compute the distortion vector v_{p_i} for each point p on the surface and for each focus region i. The final displacement of the point p is then given by a weighted sum of the contributions from each focus region,

$$v_p = \sum_i \omega_i v_{p_i}$$

The weights are computed from the final heights to which the respective points would be raised. This ensures that a more dominant focus point also affects these special regions more than a not so dominant one. This procedure finally leads to a blending of the effects of different focus points, as Figure 9.9 shows.

At the end of this section, an example should show what pixel images (in this case, a photograph) look like if the distortion algorithm is applied. Figure 9.10(a) shows a photograph of the campus of Simon Fraser University in Vancouver, Canada. You might recognize that there are people walking along one of the paths, but it is already hard to tell how many of them are there. Enlarging the respective point in the image (see Figure 9.10(b)) yields a detailed insight while keeping the overview character of the image.

(a)   (b)

FIGURE 9.10 Application of the image-space distortion algorithm to a photograph. Note in (b) that the persons are discernible.

9.2 Object-Space Distortion

While image-space algorithms like the one just shown are very good at yielding relatively smooth and predictable transitions from magnified parts to the context, a significant drawback of such methods is indeed that the actual distortion does not take into account the underlying geometric model. There are many situations in which applications rather call for the magnification of specific *objects* than for the magnification of *2D regions*. For example, the user of an online medical book may want an illustration of the heart with specific parts enlarged. At the same time, other objects that are not of particular interest may be made smaller. Their presence, irrespective of their scaling factor, may enable the viewer to recognize the visualized objects and the camera location, as long as the topological correctness is maintained.

To employ image-space distortion algorithms in such situations would require a segmentation of the image into such regions that contain exactly one object. As a result of applying the dropoff function, objects will get distorted. This may also be unwanted in certain situations since a non-uniform scaling can make objects unrecognizable.

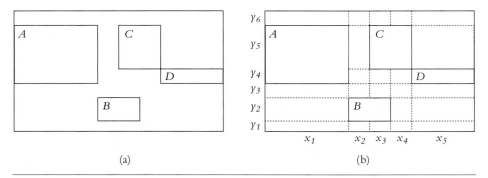

(a)　　　　　　　　　　　　　　　　　(b)

FIGURE 9.11 Rectangles to be zoomed (a) and their interval structures (b).

We thus call for object-based distortion techniques that circumvent such problems. Algorithmically, we shall rely on the context information (recall Chapter 7) of our models. In particular, the geometric model needs to be structured into the objects that the user wants to magnify. We can apply scaling operations in object space to change the magnification of the objects directly. Rendering the distorted objects should then produce the intended illustrations. The key for the development of an object-space algorithm is to derive the scaling factors from the original objects, the intended magnification, and the space being available.

9.2.1 Interval Structures

Consider the case of a collection of non-overlapping rectangles on a two-dimensional display as illustrated in Figure 9.11(a). We wish to be able to enlarge one rectangle (say, B) while maintaining its shape. Once the white space between the objects and between the objects and the edge of the viewing area have been used up, any further enlargements of B should result in A and C being made smaller.

The first step in the algorithm that we will devise is to establish data structures to work with. In the following, we will work with axis-aligned rectangles that can be seen as actual objects. More important, however, these rectangles can also be regarded as bounding boxes that enclose the actual objects. This makes the algorithm independent from the specific geometry of each object. To describe the arrangement of objects in the scene, so-called interval structures are established. These are constructed by computing the extremal values of each object in each dimension and projecting each of these onto the corresponding axis.[1] For the case of the rectangles in Figure 9.11(a), the interval structure is shown in Figure 9.11(b).

For defining the interval structures, each interval I_i is characterized by its bounds p_{i1}, p_{i2} and is represented by an interval descriptor

$$I_i = (p_{i1}, p_{i2}, s_{i0}, s_i, X_i)$$

where s_{i0} is the initial size of the interval, s_i is its current size (which will be changed in the algorithm), and X_i is a set of names of those objects falling within the interval. For the sake of simplicity, in the following derivation of the algorithm, the interval bounds are no longer considered. They can easily be computed from the sizes of the respective intervals. Hence, each interval descriptor is a triple

$$I_i = (s_{i0}, s_i, X_i)$$

The following object-space distortion technique works completely on this interval structure and is based on a resize operation that is described next.

9.2.2 The Resize Operation

We assume the display to have some defined size D. This size may or may not be limited (that is, $D = \infty$). The unlimited case leads to interesting applications and will be discussed later. For now, D has a finite value. We first define the *empty space* L within a given interval structure as the sum of the sizes of intervals with no objects:

$$L = \sum_{i: X_i = \lambda} s_i$$

We now assume that an object k is to be scaled by a factor $f > 1$. To do so, a list of scaling factors f_i for each interval is defined as follows:

$$f_i = \begin{cases} f & \forall i : k \in X_i \\ 1 & \text{otherwise} \end{cases}$$

In this way, the scaling factor for each interval containing object k is set to the scaling factor for the object. All other intervals are to remain unchanged, and their scaling factor is thus set to one.

---

1. Note that this implicitly includes the construction of the bounding boxes. Projecting the extremal positions of an object in each dimension onto the coordinate axes yields the coordinates for an axis-aligned enclosing box.

The first step in the algorithm is to use up the space of any empty intervals. For this purpose, the amount of space S required to carry out the magnification is computed as

$$S = \left(\sum_{i:\, k \in X_i} f_i s_i \right) - L$$

Now if $S \leq 0$, the necessary space S to magnify object k can be obtained by collecting it from the empty intervals. If not, more space is needed, which will be claimed from other objects. In any case, if $L > 0$, then empty space is available and is used as follows. The order in which the space is taken away is chosen so as to make the object being magnified move as little as possible. Space is taken away as evenly as possible from either side of the object, starting with the empty intervals closest to it.

If $S > 0$, we have the case that more space is required than is available in empty intervals. We now scale every interval that contains any object with its respective scale factor. This may yield a final size of all objects that exceeds the display size D. Thus, an adjustment is needed, which can be achieved by an additional uniform scaling. Both steps, the actual scaling of the intervals and the correction, yield the final interval size

$$s_i = f_i s_i \left(\frac{D}{\sum_i f_i s_i} \right) \tag{9.2}$$

Note that this equation includes the empty intervals that are already used up. Their size is zero so that no new changes are introduced in these cases. For an n-dimensional model, Algorithm 9.1 summarizes the procedure of object–space distortion for selected objects.

In the following, a specific example is given that will illustrate the preceding steps in detail.

9.2.3 An Example

For the sake of simplicity, we will demonstrate the algorithm using a one-dimensional example shown in Figure 9.12. This corresponds to the x-axis of Figure 9.11.

The scene consists of four objects and five intervals. The interval structure for this example is described by the following entries:

```
1   foreach dimension d do
2      set up the interval structure I^d
3      compute the maximum display space D^d
4   od
5   while there is a scale request for an object o do
6      foreach dimension d do
7         calculate the scaling factors f^d in each dimension d
8         multiply the interval sizes with the scaling factors
9         correct the interval sizes with respect to the display space
10     od
11  od
12  calculate the new object coordinates
```

ALGORITHM 9.1 Object-space distortion.

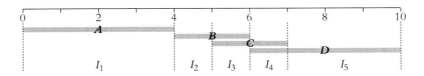

FIGURE 9.12 Details of an interval structure for the x-axis in Figure 9.11.

$$I_1 = (4, 4, \{A\})$$
$$I_2 = (1, 1, \{B\})$$
$$I_3 = (1, 1, \{B, C\})$$
$$I_4 = (1, 1, \{C, D\})$$
$$I_5 = (3, 3, \{D\})$$

Of particular relevance are the current sizes s_i, which for convenience of notation, we represent by a vector s:

$$s = (4, 1, 1, 1, 3)$$

The overall display size $D = 10$ corresponds to the sum of the interval sizes in s. In this case, there are no empty intervals that can be used up in a first step.

We now assume a request to enlarge object B by a factor of two. This object is present in the second and the third interval. Hence, the scaling factors f_2 and f_3 are set to 2; the others are set to 1. This yields the following factors f_i, one for

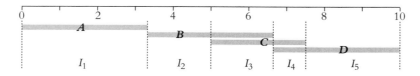

FIGURE 9.13 Final interval structure for the above example.

each interval, again, represented as a vector f:

$$f = (1, 2, 2, 1, 1)$$

The magnification is performed by scaling all intervals with the respective scale factors, that is, by multplying all s_i and f_i, yielding the vector $(4, 2, 2, 1, 3)$. This is the first part of Equation (9.2) giving the new interval sizes *before* the correction. Note that the sum of the sizes is 12, which exceeds the value $D = 10$. Hence, each interval must be scaled down by a correction factor of $\frac{10}{12}$, that is,

$$sf \frac{10}{12} = \left(3\tfrac{1}{3}, 1\tfrac{2}{3}, 1\tfrac{2}{3}, \tfrac{5}{6}, 2\tfrac{1}{2}\right).$$

This vector represents the final interval sizes after the resize operation. The resulting interval structure is illustrated in Figure 9.13.

9.2.4 Discussion of the Algorithm

Quite a number of issues must be dealt with before the algorithm as indicated earlier can be implemented. The most important point that should be noted is that the algorithm does not perform an *absolute* magnification. The display size has to be taken into account and must not be exceeded. The algorithm thus realizes a *relative* scaling compared to the other intervals. We shall explain this using a simple example. Given an interval structure consisting of three intervals of sizes $s_1 = \tfrac{1}{4}$, $s_2 = \tfrac{1}{4}$, and $s_3 = \tfrac{2}{4}$, and an overall (display) space that is limited to $D = 1$, doubling the size of the second interval with the algorithm yields the new interval sizes $s_1 = \tfrac{1}{5}$, $s_2 = \tfrac{2}{5}$, and $s_3 = \tfrac{2}{5}$. The second interval is not actually doubled in size, but its size has doubled *relatively* compared to the other intervals. The size ratio between intervals 1 and 2 was initially 1:1. After the performed magnification, it is 1:2, that is, interval 2 is twice as big as interval 1. Further, the ratio between intervals 2 and 3, which was 1:2 before, is now 1:1 (or better 2:2). This means that interval 2 now has the same size as an interval that had initially the double size—the second interval has doubled its size relatively.

Some other issues that have to be considered are as follows:

1. *Reversibility*   Interestingly enough, it can be noted that the algorithm is *reversible*. If a magnification of a factor α is carried out, and immediately thereafter another magnification of $1/\alpha$ is carried out, the original image is reproduced. Even more, the same holds for a series of magnifications. In this case, the order of the application of the inverse operations does not matter.

2. *Recognizability of objects*   It is useful to define a lower limit on the size that an object can take on. Otherwise, objects may become too small to be recognized. This can be implemented quite simply by observing the sizes of the intervals. Magnification requests need to be fulfilled only up to that point where the first object that is made smaller to "give room" would fall below the size limit.

3. *Deformations*   Since the algorithm works independently on each axis for two- or three-dimensional data, the case may arise that the scaling factor is different for each dimension. Several strategies are imaginable, which can be applied here. Using the computed scale factors in each dimension will change the aspect ratio of the objects. This will lead to deformations of the objects, which in many cases are not wanted. It is more apt to scale objects uniformly. Hence, only one scale factor for all dimensions has to be applied to the objects. We choose the minimum of all factors so that the space request can be fulfilled in all dimensions.

Finally, it should be pointed out that the introduced algorithm works for data with any dimensionality. This makes it applicable not only to 1D, 2D, and 3D geometries but also in the context of visualization of n-dimensional data.

Within an NPR system, object-space distortions are carried out before rendering begins or, at the latest, during rendering. Hence, the renderer can adjust the level of detail to the available space. The algorithm, which has a complexity of $O(n)$ for n objects with a preprocessing time of $O(p)$ for p polygons,[2] runs in real time for all but extremely large models or outdated computers. Although it is used within a renderer, the algorithm is designed to be used interactively for exploring an information space of which the geometry is a part. One such method to explore the geometry of a given model is the creation of explosion

---

2. Preprocessing is needed to compute the bounding boxes of the objects and thus the interval bounds.

diagrams. Used in an interactive context, explosion diagrams help to understand the internal structure of a model. Aside from this, they are a widely used tool for illustrating technical devices in manuals and documentations.

9.2.5 An Application to Explosion Diagrams

The method just described can be used to generate explosion diagrams automatically directly from a geometric model. Considering a resize operation, it is noticeable that actually only the interval sizes are enlarged within the algorithm. The objects enclosed by the intervals are rendered within the resized intervals, filling them completely. Besides computing a new size, the preceding algorithm also *moves* the interval bounds relative to other intervals. This behavior can be used to move objects apart in the model and so create explosion diagrams. The key in the application of the resize operation lies in resizing the intervals but rendering the objects in their original sizes in those cases when an interval has been enlarged. If an interval gets smaller, then the object is rendered smaller because there is not enough space available. This together yields objects that are repositioned with larger distances from each other. To achieve larger distances, more space should be available. Thus, the limit in display size (D in the algorithm) has to be loosened. It is even possible to work with unlimited display size ($D = \infty$), which will result in pure object displacement since no objects have to be made smaller to give room.

The prerequisite for the generation of explosion diagrams in this way is that the model is structured into objects and that it includes a description of its structure. This structural description is in this case a hierarchy, which we will call an *explosion hierarchy*. Parts of the model (objects and subobjects) that are to be explained together are grouped. Either the resize operations can be limited to an explosion group or the explosion groups can be treated as one object when scaling on a higher level in the hierarchy. The first approach keeps the complete model together except for the objects belonging to the selected group. They are scaled and moved according to the algorithm. The second approach changes the model (or a part of it) without breaking the group in its components. Both techniques, when used in connection with each other in an interactive program, are very effective tools.

Figure 9.14 shows two examples of explosion diagrams generated with this approach along with the original renditions. Note in Figure 9.14(d) that several objects are connected to groups that are not broken up by the algorithm. This is

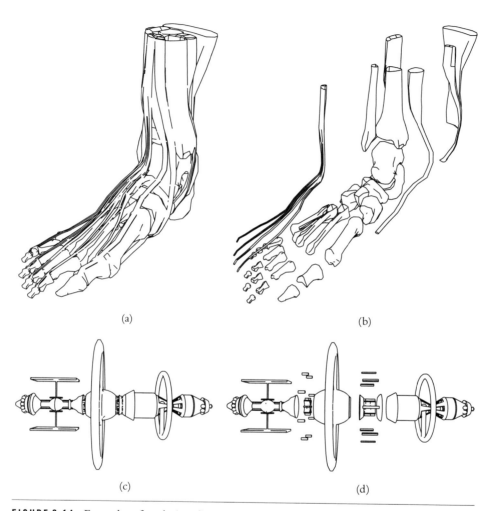

(a)   (b)

(c)   (d)

FIGURE 9.14 Examples of explosion diagrams: original rendition of the bones of a human foot (a), generated explosion diagram by moving *all* objects (b), original rendition of a space station (c), generated explosion diagram by exploiting an *explosion hierarchy* (d).

the case for the left and right part of the space station, which actually consists of several subparts.

Explosion diagrams in their own right are nothing particularly new. They have previously been made by hand, and CAD systems have the functionality to produce them, too. However, in such CAD systems additional information is generally included within the models, specifically on how the explosion diagram is to be generated. Thus, the projections of the objects during the explosion are precomputed and not as general as the method described here. The object-space distortion algorithm needs only geometric information to create explosion diagrams. If additional structural information is available, the resulting images can profit from this.

Explosion diagrams make the structure of a model comprehensible to a viewer by explicitly visualizing the parts that together form the model and their spatial relations. However, distortions themselves need to be explained to the viewer in many cases. We will see in the next section how changes in the image (which are introduced via distortions) can be made comprehensible to the viewer.

9.3 Making Distortions Comprehensible

A delicate aspect of carrying out distortions of objects, be they in image space or in object space, is that viewers may mistake features of the distorted image as being linear representatives of the underlying models.

In print media, scientific illustrators and others conveying information through images routinely work with distortions. They rely on their context to convey such information insofar as it is deemed necessary by the author. For example, some medical books include comments in figure captions such as "left ventricle slightly enlarged"; others include such disclaimers once and for all at the start of the book. More often than not, however, changes in scale go unmentioned because the authors consider that such changes do not adversely affect the message they are trying to convey with the image.

In interactive systems, changes to scale must be analyzed somewhat differently than in traditional media. On the one hand, images in interactive media are more likely to be used outside the context they were designed for. A distorted image may be used to illustrate a text without the person arranging the illustration ever having seen the surrounding text. Furthermore, such images may be tuned by application programs directly rather than by an author or by a user. Users may not want to rely entirely on the distortion by the system, but may wish to receive information pertaining to the distortion's parameterization. These scenarios suggest that it is crucial that a system carrying out distortions of images be able to convey such information to users.

On the other hand, in many interactive situations it is in fact even less important than in traditional media that the nature of a distortion be conveyed to a viewer. The reason is that a user's interaction may in fact have led directly to the changes in scale. In particular in such cases where the distortion is carried out continuously and visualized in an animation, observant users already know that a distortion has been carried out, and exactly what has been changed in an image. However, as soon as the image leaves the context in which the distortion was affected, for example, by being reused at a later point in time or by being passed on to another user, the potential for misinterpretations rises again.

In summary, a goal for visualization is to be able to convey information about a possible distortion without distracting from the primary information to be conveyed, and without taking away from it. We will call such information as pertains to the distortion a *viewing cue*, and classify such cues by the way in which they are perceived and the way in which they are integrated into a rendition.

9.3.1 Recognition Axis

One way to analyze how information pertaining to distortion can be conveyed to viewers is through their mechanisms of perception. The resulting axis is a cultural axis in that the distinctions between viewing cues are made primarily by which communities within society might be expected to be familiar with them. This axis considers human perceptual capabilities and education. They can be classified into the following four types:

1. *Precognitive skills*   Viewers' precognitive perceptual abilities can be harnessed for the purpose of communicating distortion information in a visualization. For example, it is well known that humans recognize the shape of objects from their shading using precognitive processing. Hence the challenge is to find a mapping of the distortion parameters onto such attributes of an image that can be recognized with precognitive processing. Care must be taken since there is not an agreed list of which perceptual skills are precognitive and which ones are not. There are, however, several skills for which arguments can be made for declaring them as precognitive. In this sense, we will concentrate on these.

2. *Acquired skills*   Certain skills of recognition are common to practically all members of society, even though they have to be acquired; humans are seemingly not born with them. For example, perspective foreshortening and depth cuing are examples of such skills. Thus, distortion parameters can safely

be mapped onto such image attributes with little risk that they will not be ascertained by viewers.

3. *Formalisms* Some skills for recognizing aspects of images can only be assumed to be known within small groups of users, for example, specialists within certain subject areas. For example, cartographic grids, orthographic projections, or the different kinds of lines used in CAD drawings can, in their generality, only be deciphered by appropriate specialists. Within such restricted domains, an encoding may be designable for conveying distortion information.

4. *Constructions* In some situations, specific image attributes may be designed for a specific purpose without any a priori knowledge about the users. These types of viewing cues are created to fit the particular information representation at hand and are a task to be accomplished by the viewers. It may not be immediately apparent how to create a useful viewing cue as a construction. Further, constructed cues need a large amount of cognitive processing to be understood.

There are a variety of ways in which users may perceive and recognize distortion information that is to be conveyed to them.

9.3.2 Dominance Axis

Another issue in conveying distortion information pertains to the certainty with which users will actually perceive it, or conversely, the probability with which the information may be overlooked by viewers. With this in mind, the following three methods of placing distortion information differentiate how the visual cues dominate the viewer's perception. The distinction between viewing cues is made primarily by their *location* with respect to the visualized model, and the classification can be established as follows:

1. *Integrated cues* These cues are actually part of a rendition and cannot be separated from it. For example, if the distortion information is mapped onto the color scale, the cues cannot be removed without destroying the entire image. In general, such integrated viewing cues can even be recognized by viewers without much conscious effort. In other words, an integrated viewing cue can be quite dominant.

2. *Augmented cues* These are cues that are added to an otherwise complete rendition so as to convey the extra information pertaining to the distortion

	Dominance axis		
Recognition axis	Integrated viewing cues	Augmented viewing cues	Accompanying viewing cues
Viewing cues as constructions	Transparency to indicate scale	*Motion to create groupings*	*Difference bitmap images*
Viewing cues as visual formalisms	Cartographic grids, *dashed lines to indicate hidden parts*	*Insets, wireframe backgrounds*	*Orthographic projections*
Viewing cues relying on acquired skills	*Perspective foreshortening*, depth cuing, *edge enhancement*	People in architectural drawings to indicate scale	Cursor to indicate point of interest
Viewing cues relying on precognitive skills	Occlusion, shape from shading	Spotlights	

TABLE 9.2 Examples of viewing cues according to the proposed classification.

parameters. An example is to use labels added to an image to provide information about specific objects. Another example would be an overlaid grid that shows how equal spaces get distorted.

3. *Accompanying cues*   These are cues that are presented separately from the image. For example, they may be encoded in the text that forms the context of the image. From the users' perspective, the recognition of an accompanying viewing cue is possible but optional since it can be skipped if this is desired. It can be examined for clues or easily ignored.

9.3.3 A Space of Viewing Cues

Both dominance and recognition axes form a 2D matrix where viewing cues can be characterized based on both criteria. Table 9.2 shows this matrix together with a few examples. The same characterization can also be applied to viewing cues other than the ones mentioned for the visualization of distortions. Such cues are indicated by italic type in the given table.

Note that the treatment gives only one possibility of a classification of viewing cues. On the one hand, more detailed classifications can be established by further subdividing the categories in Table 9.2. On the other hand, different criteria can be used to build the categories. In the following, a few examples are given that follow the classification in Table 9.2.

We will study the distortion of a rendition of a foot in which one part has been enlarged, resulting in most other parts being made smaller. Figure 9.15

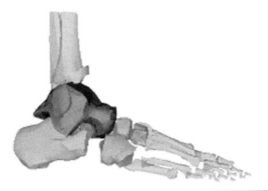

FIGURE 9.15 Example of a foot with the scaling factor mapped onto the degree of transparency for each object.

shows the foot rendered such that the scaling factor for each object is mapped onto the transparency factor. Large objects appear with little or no transparency, whereas objects with a small scaling factor have a high level of transparency. This is an example of a viewing cue as a construction (recognition axis) implemented as an integrated cue (dominance axis). Although no exact measurements can be made with respect to the distortion simply by inspecting the image, the viewer nonetheless can get a feeling for the distortion and assess it qualitatively.

By contrast, Figure 9.16 shows the distorted foot with a surrounding grid. The foot in its undistorted state has a uniform grid around it, while the spacing between the grid lines reflects the amount of distortion. This is an example of an augmented cue; the method is well known in some areas like cartography, hence it qualifies as a formalism.

Finally, figure captions can be generated and used to describe the distortion. The following would be an example:

> The face of a man from the ventral side. The skin and bones are rendered translucent. *Pars lacrimalis* is slightly enlarged.

This caption names the part of the face that was enlarged (also see Section 10.4.3) and refers to all other parts as having been reduced in size. Such captions can be generated automatically by having the system collect the relevant information during user interaction and using templates to produce the natural language sentences. It makes use of an acquired skill (since all literate members of society

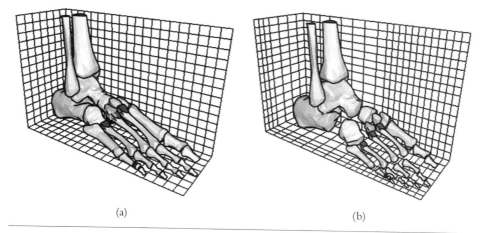

(a)   (b)

FIGURE 9.16 A distortion of the foot bones indicated by an augmented grid in the image: undistorted (a) and distorted (b).

know what a figure caption is and can work with them), which presents an accompanying cue.

9.4 Distortions in an Animated Context

While in the last sections the main focus was on the actual technique of how to distort an image or a model, the applications we have shown were limited to still images. Even though animation is needed to communicate *changes* in the scene while the distortion process is going on, we have not discussed the application of distortion techniques in animations. If we look at cel animation, for example, animated distortions are a widely used tool to give the animation itself a vital and interesting character. One example of this has already been mentioned in the introductory chapter. In every cartoon or animated movie, the ears of Disney's Mickey Mouse are almost always drawn from a front view, even if Mickey's head posture would normally require the ears to be drawn from the side. Another example is distorted buildings that are sometimes used in cartoon animations and that look much bigger and more detailed if seen from the front than from the side.

We will refer to distortions or deformations that appear in animations and that depend on the viewer's current position as *viewer-dependent distortions*. All these methods have in common that the observer's or viewer's position is taken into account when computing the distortion. In an animation, when the viewer's position changes over time, differently distorted images will result.

There are basically two different approaches to making distortions viewer dependent. First, we can include the distortion in the transformations of the model, and second, the model can be morphed according to previously specified shapes that are themselves calculated depending on a given viewer position. We will study both methods in more detail in the following.

9.4.1 Distorted Transformations

As we have seen throughout the book so far, many attempts are made to realize illustrative effects with the computer. However, changing the drawing style alone or simulating "natural" drawing tools is only one way of achieving these effects. Many illustrations are—as already stated—not drawn to scale. These distortions are not only applied to single objects or regions in still images but also very effectively used in animations. Depending on the viewer's position and distance from an object, distortions are introduced to emphasize the spatial structure of the scene. So, for example, a row of houses in a street "bends" backwards when moving along so that it creates the impression that the houses are really high.

To create this kind of distortion, we need better control of the transformation of the model. Normally, model transformations use static factors to determine the amount of rotation, scale, or translation. Further, the viewing transformation is not model dependent but instead depends on the parameters of the synthetic camera. The distortion is controlled by the distance of the viewing plane from the viewpoint and by the field of view. These constant factors should be replaced by *control functions* that themselves express the dependency of some viewer- or object-related feature. In order to make the model simple and controllable, the use of 1D control functions is preferable. This yields a technique known as *non-linear transformation* (and its derivatives).

For example, a regular translation of a three-dimensional point is expressed by the following transformation matrix:

$$M = \begin{pmatrix} 1 & 0 & 0 & 0 \\ 0 & 1 & 0 & 0 \\ 0 & 0 & 1 & 0 \\ t_x & t_y & t_z & 1 \end{pmatrix}.$$

The transformed point P' is computed by multiplying the original point P with this matrix: $P' = PM$. The translation vector (t_x, t_y, t_z) is a constant. Given a transformation M, a point (x, y, z) is tranformed into $(x', y', z') = (x, y, z)M$. As in the translation example, M is defined as a constant. We can now make the function M depend on, for example, the (changing) position of the viewpoint. This will turn M into a function of three variables $M = f(x, y, z)$. Such functions are hard to control; hence, usually one axis is selected that determines the change in the transformation. If we consider, for example, the z-axis, then M turns into $M = f(z)$. Applied to the translation example, a non–linear translation matrix would be

$$M = \begin{pmatrix} 1 & 0 & 0 & 0 \\ 0 & 1 & 0 & 0 \\ 0 & 0 & 1 & 0 \\ f_x(z_o) & f_y(z_o) & f_z(z_o) & 1 \end{pmatrix}.$$

Note that the translation vector now is a function that depends on the z-value of the observer's position (or viewpoint). In general, this introduces deformations in the image or model since not all points are transformed the same. The functions f_x, f_y, and f_z define how the parameters that control the deformation change. An example is given in Figure 9.17. The distortion effect is yielded by a combination of two transformations. The first is a non–linear zoom function that shrinks distant areas more than close areas. It is combined with another non–linear and non–uniform zoom that stretches the areas near the observer.

The use of non–linear transformations offers a way of introducing distortions in an image *without* directly changing the model. Instead, the rendering process is changed in a way that non–standard transformations are used. Most promising, the control functions for the distortions depend on the distance from the position of the viewpoint. The use of viewer-dependent control functions does not change the underlying geometry. It can be incorporated in the rendering process since it is actually only a change in the viewing transformation.

In some cases, however, a direct change of the geometry based on the viewer's position is desirable. This will introduce distortions in the model and thus in the final rendition as we will see in the following.

9.4.2 Morphing the Model

When creating cartoon-style animations, the first step is usually to hand–draw a set of reference drawings that then serve as the basis for the modeling process.

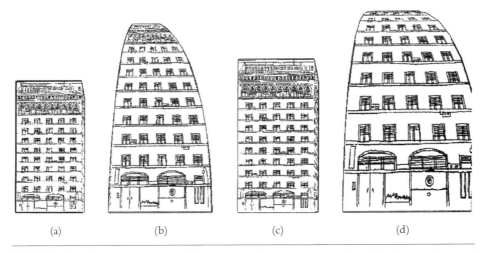

(a) (b) (c) (d)

FIGURE 9.17 Distance-dependent deformations of a house. Images (a) and (c) show undistorted renditions.

These drawings typically show the object in question from different viewpoints. However, in most cases, it is not possible to create a 3D model that matches *exactly* those drawings from every point of view. This may have several reasons, the most important of which certainly is that the artist wanted to achieve the best visual and aesthetical appearance of the object from the respective viewpoint. For the modeling, this would mean that many different models had to be created and used depending on the camera's position. Considering the modeling effort, this is not acceptable. More promising would be to use *one* geometric model and distort it according to the viewer's position.

In order to use this technique, a 3D geometric model as well as some reference drawings have to be given. These reference drawings show how the rendered image will look if viewed from a given position. By modifying the model in a way that rendering the modified model will yield images that correspond to the reference drawings, the viewer dependency is turned into an inherent model feature instead of a feature of the rendering process as described earlier. The model changes its shape according to the direction it is viewed from.

As already stated, to create such a viewer-dependent model, a conventional (in our case, polygonal) model of the object is needed as well as a set of *reference drawings*. These reference drawings together with the position of the viewer define

```
1  foreach reference drawing do
2      define camera position and orientation for key viewpoint
3      deform parts of the model to get the key deformation
4  od
5  save key viewpoints and key deformations along with the model
```

ALGORITHM 9.2 Extending the modeling process by these steps yields a view-dependent model.

FIGURE 9.18 Creating the view-dependent model.

a set of *key viewpoints* and *key deformations* that are created in an extension to the modeling process as described in Algorithm 9.2. Figure 9.18 shows an example for clarification.

We will now see how the two main steps in the algorithm can be accomplished. For defining the key viewpoints, we find a camera position and orientation where the projected image best matches the reference drawing. This is an interactive process where the user manually adjusts the camera until in his or her opinion the best fit is reached. Since the reference drawings are usually done by an artist who does not exactly match the features of the models, automatic alignment methods are not very promising. However, they are not necessary since a more exact match of the model's projection with the reference drawing will be achieved in the next step by deforming the model.

Once the key viewpoint is found, in the next step the given 3D model is deformed in a way that all features (or all important features) exactly match the reference drawing. In most cases, the main concern here is to match the features in this given viewing direction so that complete 3D deformations are barely needed.

1   find the three nearest key viewpoints to the current viewpoint
2   calculate blending weights
3   interpolate key deformations
4   render interpolated model

ALGORITHM 9.3   Rendering a view-dependent model.

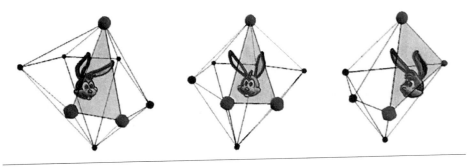

FIGURE 9.19   Finding the three closest key viewpoints.

Instead, the deformations are performed in 2D parallel to the image plane by selecting a set of vertices and dragging them in the right position. In some cases, an adjustment in the z-direction might be required since earlier deformation operations might create unwanted features in the polygon mesh.

Now that the view-dependent model is created, the rendering step consists of an interpolation between the key deformations and a final rendering. This can be expressed as in Algorithm 9.3.

In the following, we consider only the viewing direction; that is, we do not differentiate between different distances between the camera position and the object itself. Further, we assume that the view direction always points toward the center of the model. We now consider a sphere that encloses the model and that is intersected by the viewing direction vectors of all key viewpoints. For a given viewing direction that is to be rendered, the intersection point of this direction vector with the sphere is calculated, and the three closest key viewpoints are those whose spherical triangle encloses the calculated intersection point. This is equivalent to the corresponding planar triangle on the convex hull of sphere points as can be seen in Figure 9.19.

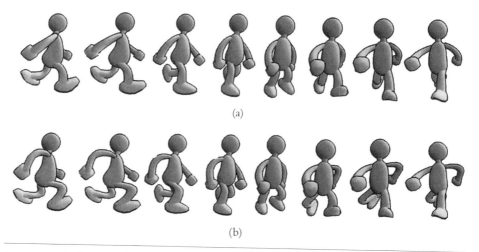

(a)

(b)

FIGURE 9.20 Example frames from an animation of an undistorted model (a) and a view-dependent model (b). The model is animated over time while the camera rotates around the character.

The distortion of the model for the given viewpoint can now be computed by interpolating between these three closest key viewpoints according to the distances from the intersection points. The blending weights for this interpolation are thus given by the barycentric coordinates of the intersection point.

Since the morphing operations performed to generate the key deformations do not alter the topology of the model, that is, the vertex connectivity is the same for all key deformations, an interpolation between corresponding vertices with respect to the blending weights yields the deformed model for the given viewpoint. Each vertex v is the linear interpolation of the respective vertices v_1, v_2, and v_3 in the three nearest key deformations.

$$v = w_1 v_1 + w_2 v_2 + w_3 v_3 \tag{9.3}$$

This interpolation scheme is certainly the most simple one, but it can be generalized. However, this scheme only interpolates between vertex positions without taking into account any possible changes that appear in a region of many vertices. There is a compromise between the quality of the resulting mesh and allowable deformations that needs to be observed. Figure 9.20 shows a comparison between an undistorted model and a view-dependent model in an animation. Compare, especially, the bending of the arms and legs of the character.

In an animation, this technique can be used without any changes. No changes are necessary in the distortion algorithm or in the rendering pipeline. This has the big advantage that properly distorted images can be created for every possible viewpoint. Considering this more thoroughly yields the observation that the key viewpoints and key deformations have to be specified and computed for every frame. This is a very tedious task and enlarges the risk for introducing errors in the animation model. In this case, a technique borrowed from standard computer animation can be used. Along with the undistorted model, key viewpoints and key deformations are specified only for a small number of frames (points in time in the animation). All deformations for the same viewpoint are interpolated over time such that finally the technique described earlier can be applied for the specific frame.

To summarize, the two techniques to introduce distortions in animations extend the possibilities of computer graphics and animation. If only traditional animation techniques are applied (regardless of the rendering method), part of the aesthetic appeal of hand-drawn animation is lost. Many of the astonishing effects that are well known from cartoon animations are based on physically incorrect behavior (especially deformations) of the animated objects. The introduced algorithms open up a new area to create interesting and aesthetically pleasing computer-generated animations.

Exercises

9.1   Given a magnification factor m, we wish to determine the height h_f to which a focus point must be raised to achieve this magnification. Show that

$$h_f = d_b - \frac{d_b}{m}.$$

Show also that, conversely, given an h_f, $m = d_b/(d_b - h_f) = d_b/d_s$.

9.2   Study how the image-space distortion presented in this chapter can be integrated into a rendering system based on raytracing. Assume that the geometric model remains to scale, but that the "rays" meeting the eye are no longer straight but curved as they shoot into the geometric model.

9.3   Does the usage of viewer-aligned focus have any effect on the magnification? If so, how can the magnification be computed in this case, and by how much must the height h_f be changed to achieve the same magnification as in the basic method?

9.4   Design and implement a graphical user interface for the image-space distortion algorithms.

9.5   Extend your implementation of the user interface to the image-space distortion algorithms to incorporate a standard renderer. Achieve the effect of having the renderer include more or other details in the focus region.

9.6   Integrate image-space distortion into a stipple rendering system (recall Chapter 2). Investigate alternative ways in which the distortion can or should affect the density of stipples in the image.

9.7   The approach to image-space distortion emphasizes regions of magnification by a factor greater than one. Suggest ways in which a magnification by a factor of less than one can be handled within the framework. This means that regions should be made smaller.

9.8   Design a dropoff function that guarantees that the final image will have exactly the same size and shape as the original. Note that as the algorithm was presented, this is not the case (see Figure 9.4 where the grid is slightly warped around the edges).

9.9   Discuss the use of the 2D method for enlarging stroke-based images (recall Chapter 5) within an image-space distortion algorithm.

9.10   Implement the object-space distortion algorithm and apply it to geometric models before rendering them. Compare the images with images that have been created by applying image-space distortions to renditions of the same model.

9.11   Show that the resize operation in the object-space distortion algorithm is reversible and that a series of operations can be reversed in any order.

9.12   How might the object-space distortion algorithm be applied to scanned images in 2D?

9.13   Implement different non-linear transformations that depend on the viewer's position as well as the distance and apply them to simple models. Describe how each distortion works. Create an animation and compare the effects of different transformations.

9.14   Build models corresponding to Figures 9.17(a) and (c). Determine the exact distortion function to produce Figures 9.17(b) and (d).

Bibliographic Notes

The method of image-space distortion presented in this chapter was developed by Carpendale (1999; Carpendale et al., 1995). It was Carpendale's idea to effect a 2D distortion by warping the object plane in the third dimension. Her method subsumes a variety of previous methods of carrying out such 2D distortions, like the methods of Sarkar and Brown (1992) and Keahey and Robertson (1996).

The algorithm for distortion in object space was developed by Rüger and Raab (1996) and is described in more detail in Raab's Ph.D. thesis (1998). Its origins are in detail-and-context visualization techniques that themselves originate in an article by Furnas (1986) on fisheye views. This work was extended by Shaffer, Bartram, Dill, and others (Schaffer et al., 1993; Schaffer et al., 1996; Bartram et al., 1995; Dill et al., 1994) to a 2D visualization and navigation method for large graphs.

The topic of making distortions comprehensible was studied independently by Carpendale et al. (1997) and Strothotte et al. (1998). The former developed the recognition axis described in this chapter; the latter, the dominance axis. The use of figure captions as viewing cues was studied by Hartmann et al. (1998).

Distortions in an animated context were investigated by Rademacher who also introduced the viewer-dependent geometry (Rademacher, 1999). The application of non-linear transformations to incorporate viewer-dependent distortions in images was proposed by Martín, García, and Torres (2000). The technique relies on work done by Alan Barr on global and local deformation of solid primitives (1984).

10 | APPLICATIONS FOR NPR

Throughout the book, the methods that have been introduced have also been illustrated directly using several different application domains. This has served to demonstrate the methods and at the same time suggest areas in which they are useful. This chapter now expands on selected applications and studies NPR in them per se.

We will start with animation, an area of application that is slowly emerging to a separate field of research in NPR. Indeed, animation data can be visualized either as moving images using NPR or even as still images with some additional markings to indicate movement. Next, we move to the area of visualization in architecture where handmade sketches are still being used extensively. Within this section, we also treat the problem of rendering trees and other plants. We then turn to two areas of application that take NPR further afield. First, we discuss illustrations in medical textbooks, where traditionally illustrations drawn by hand are used. The challange here is to coordinate images and the text that refers to them. Finally, we discuss a specific kind of graphical output in haptic form that is used by blind people.

10.1 Non-Photorealistic Animation

The word *animation* stems from the Latin word *animare*, which means to fill with life. In this sense, non-photorealistic animation makes use of aspects of NPR to bring still images to life, or non–photorealistic renditions themselves are changed

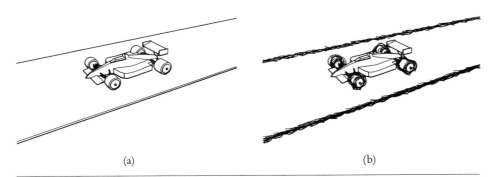

(a)   (b)

FIGURE 10.1   Using slight perturbations in the starting and endpoints of the strokes in this image yields to induced motion. In an animation, it looks like the car is actually moving down the street even though the geometric model does not change: start frame of the animation (a), intermediate frame of the animation (b).

over time to create the illusion of movement. In the following, examples of each will be given.

The major problem in this type of animation is that many algorithms for NPR to generate single frames have a non–deterministic element. For example, the "wiggliness" of an individual line within a line drawing is determined by a random number generator. When the random numbers are applied to each frame separately, the drawing elements like strokes jump around yielding a, presumably unwanted, disturbance in the image. Before going on, it is useful to note, however, that the lack of frame coherence can be harnessed to achieve special effects. For example, when the individual strokes of Figure 10.1 are allowed to vary even just slightly from frame to frame, motion is induced into the image. Watching this animation gives the impression that the car is actually moving down the street even though in the geometric model all objects (including the camera) remain stationary.

Another phenomenon to watch out for when generating non-photorealistic animations is the so-called shower-door effect. Imagine watching a person move behind a shower door that itself is filled with a pattern of squares. It quickly becomes obvious that it is not the person who is drawn, rather the door is; the latter is simply modulated in its gray level to account for the moving person. In the same way, when strokes are applied in screen coordinates to simulate a figure moving in model coordinates, an animation will look like the (static) screen has been textured rather than the (moving) object.

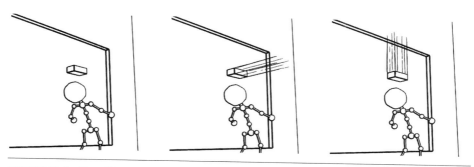

FIGURE 10.2 Speedlines can show the direction of movement. The three images are identical except for the speedlines.

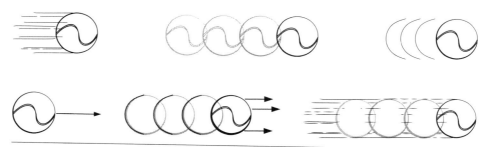

FIGURE 10.3 Alternative visualizations of a given movement.

10.1.1 Representing Motion in Still Images

Although the word *animation* is generally associated with moving images, it is noteworthy that still images can also convey movement. A classical example of this phenomenon can be found in cartoons where various techniques are applied to indicate movement. Figure 10.2 shows an example of three images that differ only in the direction in which so-called speedlines are drawn. These images illustrate the need for indicating the direction of movement.

Indeed, given a direction of movement, a number of techniques are used in comics to express movement in a still image, as can be seen in Figure 10.3. Note that such techniques can be used as a single stylistic element or that they can be combined.

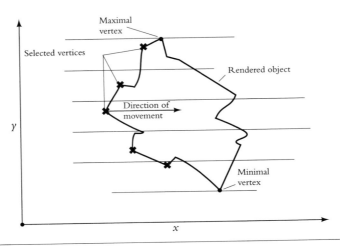

Maximal vertex

Selected vertices

Rendered object

Direction of movement

y

Minimal vertex

x

FIGURE 10.4 Geometric construction for computing the positions of speedlines.

Methods have been devised to compute automatically such visualizations of movement. In particular, it is possible to compute the positions of speedlines given a geometric model and the direction of movement of an individual object. Consider a three-dimensional geometric object moving in the positive x-direction. An algorithm must compute positions on the geometric object from which speedlines will emanate. The computation is done for a single frame in two dimensions. The three-dimensional coordinates of the points from which the speedlines emanate are determined by referring to the geometric model. This then enables the computation of speedlines for each frame in which they are needed, taking hidden line removal into account also for the speedlines. The variable controlled by the user is the number of speedlines to be used to visualize the movement.

Finally, an algorithm is needed to compute the actual positions from which speedlines are to emanate. For a movement in the positive x-direction, the extremal positions in the y-direction are used. This yields the positions of two speedlines. Now the y-extent of the image is divided up into n strips of like height, and one speedline placed near the middle of each strip on each trailing edge. In particular, for each strip, each trailing edge of the object is analyzed and the vertices are selected that lie closest to the middle of the strip. The situation is illustrated in Figure 10.4, whereas the actual procedure to compute the speedlines can be found in Algorithm 10.1. Examples are shown in Figure 10.5.

```
1   foreach moving object o in scene do
2       compute candidate points
3       if number of candidate points < desired number of speedlines
4           then
5               foreach stripe without candidate point do
6                   interpolate candidate point
7               od
8       fi
9       foreach candidate point c do
10          foreach animation frame do
11              c_p := projection of c
12              add c_p to the path of the speedline
13          od
14      remove hidden parts from the computed path
15      draw path with a certain style
16      od
17  od
```

ALGORITHM 10.1   Computing speedlines from a given animation.

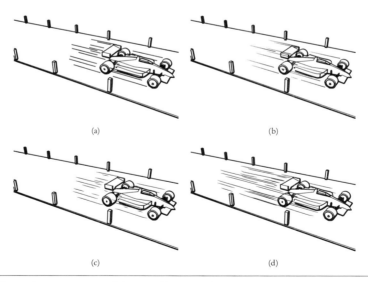

(a)

(b)

(c)

(d)

FIGURE 10.5   The appearance of the speedlines can be varied using line styles: to follow the algorithm (a), to make the speedlines fade away (b), to break up the speedlines to provide more variation (c), and to use more and longer speedlines (d).

10.1.2 Non-Photorealistic Animation Based on Particle Systems

Perhaps the most successful method of non-photorealistic animation is based on particle systems. In this approach, many points in the three-dimensional space of the geometric model are identified as positions of so-called *particles*. These particles serve as placeholders for drawing artifacts, such as strokes, marks, or dots. In the following, this approach will be demonstrated in an algorithm that simulates oil paintings on canvas. As opposed to real oil paintings, however, the algorithm that is presented enables walk-throughs of the underlying geometric model while maintaining frame coherence.

The algorithm is an elegant composition involving the idea behind the paint-by-numbers system (as described in Chapter 5) along with G-buffers (recall Chapter 6). The algorithm can be divided into three steps as follows:

1. *Generate particles* Any one of the many methods is used to populate the surface of the object to be rendered with particles. A simple method is first to triangulate the surface and compute its area S. Next, for each triangle t, compute its surface area $s(t)$ and derive that fraction $f(t)$ covered by t in relation to the overall area S, that is,

    $$f(t) = s(t)/S.$$

    Now if in total p particles are to be distributed over the entire surface, place $f(t)p$ of them randomly over t. Along with each particle, store additional parameters of the surface under it, like its orientation (normal vector). Each particle will ultimately contribute one stroke to the final image emanating from the position of the particle.

2. *Specify and apply stroke attibutes* For each frame in the animation, several G-buffers are generated from which stroke parameters are then derived. The parameters needed are in particular its color, size, and orientation. For example, the orientation of the stroke can be taken from the corresponding entry in the n-buffer (containing the normal vector coordinates). The size of the stroke can be computed by a combination of a standard size in x- and y-directions, modified by a value computed from the z-buffer (containing depth values). The color can be computed from a G-buffer for colors (for example, a photorealistically rendered image) by computing the average color under the stroke. Depending on the kind of stroke to be used, other parameters may be needed, too, and computed similarly from these or other G-buffers.

3. *Add randomness, render frames, and animate parameters* Given that the particle system is specified once and for all for the geometric model, and that the previous step of the algorithm is deterministic, frame coherence is achieved when repeating these steps for an animation. However, the resultant images will have a mechanical look, for example, because many strokes will be alligned perfectly. To alleviate this problem, parameters like the orientation of the stroke are perturbed slightly from frame to frame. For example, the user may specify that he or she is willing to have brush orientations fall within a range of -10 to $+20$ degrees from the orientation given in the *n*-buffer. To achieve coherence, a seed is associated with each particle so that the same random perturbations will be used for a particular particle throughout the animation and to ensure that the value changes only slightly from iteration to iteration.

Notice that it can happen that not all areas of the image are actually covered by at least one stroke. Hence, it is advisable to cover each area of the image with a base color before actually drawing the strokes. A different color is advisable for the background, ambient light, highlights, and shadows. This corresponds to a technique common in handmade paintings and yields good results.

Finally, all strokes are drawn in the order from back to front using the so-called *painter's algorithm*.

Note that even hidden particles must be rendered in practice. This is because while a particle itself may be hidden, the stroke that emanates from it may not be entirely hidden. This makes the algorithm run more slowly, but is unavoidable.

In general, the techniques for *stroke-based illustrations*, which have been described in Chapter 5, are well suited for an application in animations that are based on particle systems. An example of a sequence of images generated with the preceding algorithm is shown in Figure 10.6.

10.2 Architectural Illustrations

Perhaps one of the most important applications for NPR is in architecture. Indeed, this area was the one that provided the primary motivation for the early work in the area of NPR. The reason is that architects generally prefer to use handmade sketches to show the results of their work to their clients rather than polished, photolike images. Intuitively, it would appear that the motivation for this is

FIGURE 10.6 Four frames of a painterly animation.

that sketches are a good way of conveying to clients that the results represent "work in progress" rather than finished products. In this sense, NPR renditions accompany other developments in computer–aided architectural design (CAAD) since there are photorealistic rendering methods to show the building in its future environment or even virtual reality setups to "visit" the building before it is finished.

10.2.1 An Empirical Study

The area of NPR is one in which very little empirical work has been carried out. This section will provide a detailed account of what was probably the first such study. It was carried out in 1995 with architects in Germany. This is important to keep in mind because subjects' assessment of images is certainly a function of time and cultural conditioning. At the time of this writing (2001), some rendering software packages already contain a certain amount of functionality with respect to NPR. Its availability no doubt will change the attitude of professionals working with it over time.

One of the goals of the study was to determine in which situations an architect would use the various kinds of images. Since an architect's goal is in general to attract attention to the image, the following hypothesis was put forward:

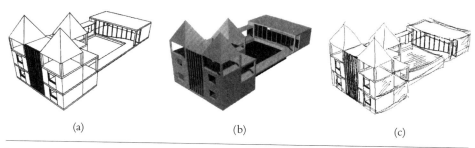

(a) (b) (c)

FIGURE 10.7 Three variants of rendering a design: CAD plot (a), shaded image (b), rendered sketch (c).

H_1: *For presentations of early drafts of architectural designs, sketches are preferred to CAD plots and shaded images.*

It was also assumed that there is a marked difference in the way the three images in Figure 10.7 affect their viewers. To structure the hypothesis, the possible effects of an image are divided into three groups:

♦ a cognitive group, pertaining to aspects like the understandability, clarity, or spatiality of the image,

♦ an affective group, to assess emotional aspects, like how interesting or imaginative an image seems, and

♦ a motivational group, measuring to what extent users are encouraged to participate in the design process.

The following was thus hypothesized:

H_2: *Sketches perform better in the communication of affective and motivational aspects, while exact plots and shaded images perform better in cognitive aspects.*

Finally, it was expected that the exact plot would arouse more interest in the actual design of the object being visualized. This leads to the following hypothesis:

H_3: *Sketches stimulate viewers more than shaded images to discuss and actively participate in design development.*

To test these hypotheses, an experiment was carried out in which a questionnaire was given to approximately 150 architects and architectural students in several cities in Germany. Of these, 54 (36%) answered the questions and returned it. Of those returning it, 67% said they regularly use CAD or CAAD software.

Subjects were shown three different images, each portraying the same object (see Figure 10.7). Subjects were then asked various questions. First, they should indicate which image(s) they would want to use to show a first draft to a client and which image they would use for a final presentation. They were also asked to provide a verbal justification of their choice. Next, subjects were asked about a number of (possible) effects of the images, classified according to the scheme mentioned. These were to be rated on a scale of 5 ("strongly disagree") to 1 ("strongly agree"). To test the third hypothesis, subjects were asked to say how they would make changes to the design being visualized. They were given four options to choose from:

1. using a verbal description,
2. gesturing or by pointing to the image,
3. drawing on another sheet of paper, or
4. drawing directly onto the image.

The results from the questionnaires were analyzed with regard to the following three issues:

1. *Use of images during the design process*   Of those subjects using CAD, 53% chose the sketch as a suitable way to present a first draft to a client. This is significantly more than those suggesting the shaded image (22%), or the exact plot, which was chosen by 33% of the subjects ($p < 0.05$). Those preferring the sketch generally argued that it best shows the preliminary character of the draft and does not focus on details that at this stage are not yet fixed. Many of those who chose the shaded image commented that they appreciated the ability to present the spatial concept of the design. Considering the development of NPR, there are now techniques available to put more emphasis on the spatial structure of a scene in the rendition (see Chapters 5, 6, and 8) so that a new study would confirm the obtained results.

   By contrast, only 8% chose the sketch to present a final result to a client, which is significantly less than those choosing the exact plot (50%) or the shaded image (42%) ($p < 0.05$). Subjects who chose the exact plot or the shaded image often argued that the selection committee or the client "wants to see exact renditions," while those few who chose the sketch commented on its originality and the desire to stand out against competitors.

2. *Impression made by the images*   Subjects were asked to assess the impression made by the three images in more detail. The results show that sketches were found significantly more interesting, lively, imaginative, creative, and individual, and less artificial than both the other media (affective group). Furthermore, they were found to stimulate significantly more discussions and active changes, in which shaded images performed worst. These results correspond to the observations made in early NPR projects, for instance, the freehand plotting as described in Section 3.1.

    In sharp contrast to these affective criteria, the CAD plot performed significantly better in the cognitive group, being more comprehensible, more recognizable, and clearer than both the other media. The shaded image was found to support spatial concepts better, but differences were not significant.

3. *Expressing changes in the design*   The observations so far were concerned with assessing the impression architectural presentations make on viewers, but it is an important goal of the communication between architects and their clients to explain ideas mutually and to develop them further. A major criterion in the assessment of the effectiveness of a presentation medium is its ability to provoke the active participation of the partners within a discussion.

    The results illustrate that in both the sketch and the shaded image, the methods 1, 2, and 3 were used almost equally often (the differences are not significant). However, drawing directly into the image was chosen significantly more often in sketches than in shaded images (69% versus 33%) ($p < 0.05$).

As far as the interpretation of the results is concerned, evidence has been gathered in support of all three of the hypotheses by the experiments carried out. To explain the results, let us look at them from a more theoretical point of view. The cognitive effort required by viewers would be expected to be greater for sketches than for the other two kinds of images tested. This is because sketches are more irregular in their form, which means that higher normalization demands are placed on a viewer deciphering an image. By this reasoning, these normalization demands and thus also the cognitive effort to understand the image is higher for sketches than CAD plots or shaded images. Normalization, on the other hand, is also linked to interest and creativity, resulting in a high level of motivation.

Going back now to the hypothesis H_2, the less favorable score of the sketch in the cognitive group can be explained because of the difficulty involved in deciphering the irregular forms; the resultant ambiguities are then responsible for the better scores in the affective and hence also motivational groups.

This reasoning also explains the results of H_1. In a first draft, architects reported they want to arouse interest in their designs, which according to our reasoning is higher with sketches. For a final draft, a good score in the cognitive group is more important; hence, the shaded images and CAD plots are preferred.

To explain H_3, a step to the theoretic background is necessary. Gombrich (Gombrich, 1977) speaks of the process of *projection* of our experience and expectations onto the phenomena seen. The empty spaces in the CAD plots and sketches can act as the required "projection screen." According to this argument, sketches and CAD plots provide more projection space than shaded images (because in these practically the whole area of the image is filled, and hence cannot act quite as well as a projection space). Sketches also provide more projection space than CAD plots because in the latter there is no room for interpretation of where and how lines (edges in the object visualized) meet. The larger projection space can thus explain the greater willingness of viewers of sketches to enter into a discussion about the design.

It is still unclear how far the results can be generalized to explain other observations. Furthermore, because of the rapid development in the field of NPR, more and different rendering methods are now becoming available. A new study of this kind should then include these methods to get more differentiated results and to add even more evidence for the application of NPR techniques in the field of architectural design.

10.2.2 Expressing Uncertainty in Designs

The use of NPR methods for architectural design has even more advantages than those being described in the last section. They are connected with the visualization of uncertainty in designs and with the visualization of design decisions. Architectural sketches are often drawn with relatively little detail. This is typically for one of the following three reasons:

1. *The architect may not have worked out more details yet.* A photorealistic rendition in this case would raise false assumptions at the client's side. Details being

shown in such renditions may stem from calculations within the rendering system (textures, and so on) and not from actual design decisions.

2. *The architect has more details but wants to focus on certain aspects of the design.* Here an abstraction process has to be carried out that emphasizes only those parts needed in the current project stage. Showing more would result in unwanted discussions about areas that are not relevant at the moment.

3. *The architect wants to present several design variants.* The client should then decide which of these variants would best fit his or her intentions. Nevertheless, all presented variants are to be visualized in the context of the whole building. A visualization might be helpful with respect to distinguishing these variants from those parts that were already discussed and where an agreement already exists.

Closely related to the third point is another area, namely, the visualization of reconstructions of ancient architecture. Here, also, photorealistically rendered images are rarely used. Instead, the archaeologists prefer hand-drawn illustrations to convey information over and above the pure geometry. This information pertains to the following:

1. *the certainty with which details are known* Archaeological reconstructions build on a (probably very small) set of findings and are to some extent speculative. A visualization of archaeological findings and of reconstructions derived from them should take into account the uncertainty of a reconstruction and communicate this uncertainty to the viewer.

2. *the reasoning process during an archaeological reconstruction* Design decisions for an archaeological reconstruction are based on different types of reasoning. Examples are artifacts that actually have been found, physical constraints that arise from structural properties of buildings, features of the architectural period in question, analogies to other buildings, as well as deductions. These different types of reasoning can also be visualized in order to make clear where the presented information comes from.

In summary, uncertainty in design should be visualized and can, in general, arise for two reasons:

- *imprecision*, which means that the existence of certain features can safely be assumed but not their dimensions or their actual details, or

◆ *incompleteness*, which means that certain information is not available.

NPR techniques are especially valuable for such tasks since many stylistic variations are available to render a given model. In this sense, the problem that has to be solved resembles the general approach to visualization. Given a (three-dimensional) geometric model and additional values that represent the level of uncertainty for parts of this model, a mapping of this additional data onto geometric or stylistic properties of the model is needed. Finally, a rendering process has to be carried out to create the image.

There are many possible ways to map levels of uncertainty to stylistic variations of a rendition. The methods and tools introduced throughout this book build a valuable repository that can be used here. Uncertainty (that is, imprecision or incompleteness) can, for example, be visualized by varying the

◆ sketchiness of lines in a line drawing: the more irregular the lines are, the more uncertain the shown part of the geometry,

◆ saturation of lines or textures: the less certain the visualized information is, the less saturated the image,

◆ texture: different levels of uncertainty are visualized with different textures, which implies discrete levels of uncertainty, or

◆ style of the rendition: different levels of uncertainty are visualized by using different rendering styles.

To use one of these methods, the geometric model has to be enriched by adding information pertaining to the desired stylistic changes. The encoding of this information can be either direct, by adding rendering-specific values (like line styles or textures) to the respective objects, or indirect, by adding numerical values that are then used to select or compute rendering-specific values from a database of styles. One example of such an indirect mapping is given in Section 10.4 for a different area of application. The theoretical principles are the same for both cases so that we show a case study here and refer you to the latter section for details of the implementation.

We will illustrate the visualization of uncertainty in archaeological illustrations by using as an example the virtual reconstruction of a building from the Middle Ages. Excavations performed around 1960 in Magdeburg, Germany have revealed the remains of a building that was said to be built by Otto the

FIGURE 10.8 Photorealistic rendition of the virtual reconstruction of a building of Otto the Great in Magdeburg (around 960–1207 A.D.)

Great, the first German emperor (912–973 A.D.). The findings were limited to parts of the foundations of the building, so a virtual reconstruction is very speculative. In cooperation with archaeologists, architects, and (art) historians, a model was created that represents the most probable variant of how the building would have looked. A photorealistic rendition of this model is shown in Figure 10.8.

This photorealistic interpretation leaves no room for speculation, even more, there is no evidence in the image that many of the properties of the building have been deduced from knowledge about buildings from the same time period or simply from logical reasonings. This information is included in the visualizations shown in Figures 10.9(a) and (b).

The connection between the actual findings and the "virtuality" of the reconstruction can even be made more explicit by combining photographs from the excavation site with NPR visualizations, as can be seen in Figure 10.10.

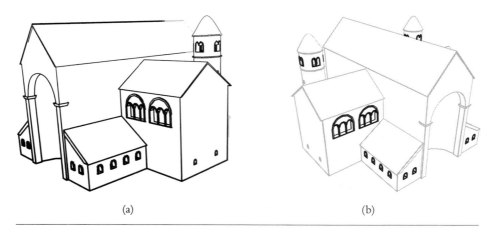

(a)   (b)

FIGURE 10.9 Visualization of uncertainties and drawn deductions: uncertainty rises with growing distance from ground; in addition, the back part of the building could not be proved to look like this from the excavation findings (a); the windows are likely to be in the same style as other windows from the same stylistic period—Romanesque (b).

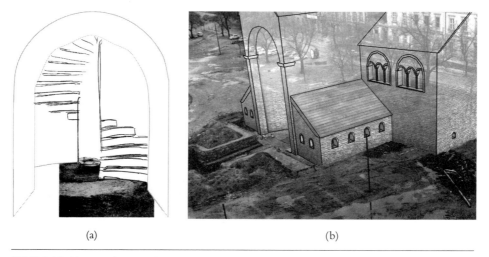

(a)   (b)

FIGURE 10.10 Combining photographs and NPR visualizations: the finding of the basis of a staircase leads to the deduction of how this staircase might have looked (a); combining an NPR visualization and a photograph of the excavation site clarifies size relations (b).

10.3 Rendering Plants

Plants—in particular, trees—are objects that are often needed in rendered scenes. On the one hand, they may be necessary because the viewers know of their existence. On the other hand, they can be used to convey size relationships to viewers who have a general idea of how big trees are and can thus judge the sizes of other objects with respect to them. For example, a viewer will have a general idea of the size of a fully grown sugar maple; an object lying beneath such a tree would be deemed to be much smaller.

The first step to create a tree illustration is to build a model of the tree using a conventional modeling system.[1] This will generally yield either a structured collection of polygons or some other geometric primitives like spheres and cylinders. Next, the model must be separated into two parts:

1. *the trunk, branches, and twigs*   If the model is too complex or large, it can be simplified by storing only first and second order branches. Higher order branches can be removed since they are generally hidden anyway.

2. *the leaves*   Each leaf is stored as a particle with a position and a normal vector. Some models have many more leaves (for example, several hundred thousand leaves) than are really necessary for producing sketches of trees. This number can be reduced by retaining only one leaf per twig. If there are still too many leaves, one leaf can be retained at each of the highest order twigs.

Once the model has been created in this manner, each of the two parts is rendered as described in the following section.

10.3.1 Rendering the Trunk, Branches, and Twigs

It can be assumed that the surface of that part of the model describing the trunk, the branches, and the twigs is more or less smooth. This enables the application of any algorithm for computing the silhouette of a geometric model. Perhaps the simplest method is in two dimensions: a G-buffer (with z-values, or object IDs) is computed and those pixels retained that separate the background from the foreground.

---

1. For example, currently the XFROG system from Greenworks Organic Software (*www.greenworks.de*) can be used.

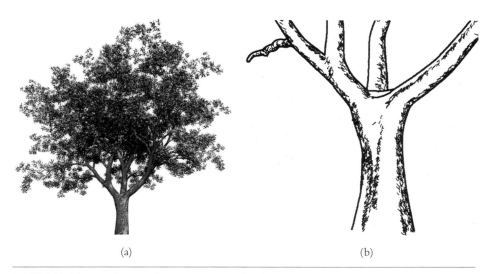

(a)   (b)

FIGURE 10.11 Renditions of a tree: a tree rendered photorealistically (a), rendition of the trunk of (a) using silhouette lines and cross-hatching (b).

Next, this part of the model, that is, the trunk and the branches, must be shaded. To shade the model using conventional gray levels, any one of the methods described in the earlier chapters can be used (see Figure 10.11).

10.3.2 Rendering the Foliage

The foliage of a tree differs from all smooth surfaces and must therefore be handled separately. Several thousand individual leaves must be combined visually into a single shape or a set of strokes. A method of solving this problem that comes to mind immediately is to define a texture for the foliage and to place it on the leaves of the model. This is a fast and simple method, but the images do not end up looking like drawings.

Instead, each leaf is represented by a geometric primitive (usually a two-dimensional disc); its visualization is computed on the basis of the silhouette of the primitive, its position is determined by the position of the leaf in the 3D model, and its size is controlled by the user. However, not the entire outline of every primitive is actually drawn, but rather a selection process takes place.

The strategy is now to consult an appropriate G-buffer on a pixel-by-pixel basis to determine which parts of the silhouette should be drawn in the visualization. Let $Z[x, y]$ be the z-buffer of the image rendered with conventional photorealistic methods. Let P be the set of pixels on the silhouette of each of the primitives representing leaves. For every p in P appearing at position (i, j) in the silhouette image, a pixel is drawn in position (i, j) if and only if the maximal difference in the z-value in the neighborhood of (i, j) is greater than a given threshold. Although this could, in principle, be done analytically, using the appropriate G-buffer is more efficient. Indeed, this method works at interactive rates. For printing purposes, a vectorization is performed to obtain stroke paths.

For the computation of the threshold value, it is convenient to express the depth of a point as a value z computed as in Equation (10.1).

$$z = \frac{\frac{z_1 z_0 (d_1 - d_0)}{z_1 - z_0}}{d - \frac{(z_1 + z_0)(d_1 - d_0)}{2(z_1 - z_0)} - \frac{(d_1 + d_0)}{2}} \tag{10.1}$$

Here, d_0 and d_1 are minimal and maximal values represented in the depth buffer, and z_0 and z_1 are the corresponding depth values of the near and far clipping plane in the camera model. Figure 10.12 shows two examples of varying disc size and depth thresholds. Note how small discs and a low threshold in Figure 10.12(a)

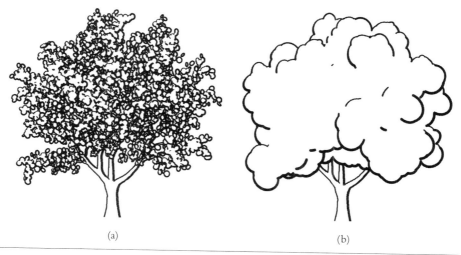

(a)   (b)

FIGURE 10.12 The tree of Figure 10.11 rendered with different disc sizes for the leaves and different depth thresholds. For (a), the disc size is 0.15 and the depth threshold is set to 1,000. For (b), these values are 0.7 and 2,000. In both images, $d_0 = 0$ and $d_1 = 65, 535$, $z_0 = 1$ and $z_1 = 11$.

(a)   (b)

FIGURE 10.13 The tree of Figure 10.12 rendered at three different distances to the viewer. In (a), the primitive size and threshold is held constant, and visual abstraction is already achieved automatically. This effect is enhanced in (b), where the primitive size is enlarged up to the factor two for the tree at the back.

yields a high level of detail, whereas if these values are enlarged, as in Figure 10.12(b), the resultant image is more abstract.

Interesting effects can be achieved by combining data sources. Figure 10.13(a) shows the difference in rendition as a tree is duplicated further back in the scene without changing the threshold or the disc size. In Figure 10.13(b), the disc size was changed gradually by a factor of two from front to back; notice how the shape of the tree at the back is more abstract in this case.

Some more examples of renditions of trees generated with the methods described here are shown in Figure 10.14.

10.4 Illustrating Medical and Technical Texts

Another highly important motivation for working on NPR pertains to medical illustrations. Recall the comments in Chapter 1 where it was noted that handmade illustrations dominate in many medical books. In digital books, such illustrations will ultimately have to be rendered from three-dimensional geometric models so as to provide the "added value" users expect from images on computer screens. This added value pertains to the possibility to interact with the image, to cut away parts, to have important parts labeled, and other such operations.

When examining such texts, it quickly becomes evident that the handmade illustrations are intimately related to the surrounding text. Such texts and illustra-

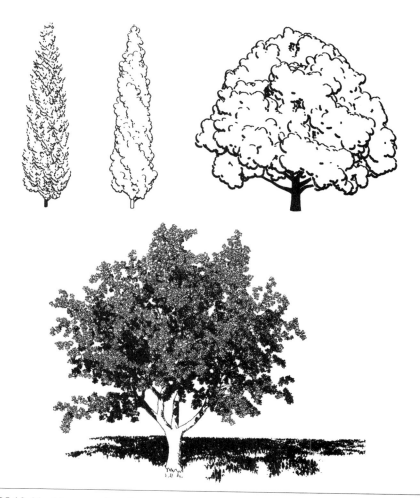

FIGURE 10.14 More samples of trees generated with the methods described. The examples use different primitives and vary their sizes as well as the threshold value.

tions are "formulated" in unison with one another; that is, the illustration makes those parts of the object in question visible and shows them in detail, which the text describes. Sometimes labels are used to point out objects that are important to understand the text. Finally, figure captions capture the essence of the image.

10.4.1 Generating Illustrations from Texts

We will now show how texts, labeled illustrations, and figure captions can be interrelated algorithmically. First consider the following problem: *Given a (medical) text, produce an illustration that can accompany the text.* It is safe to assume the following conditions:

1. *uniformity of terminology in the text*   For a systematic use of a given text, it is imperative that the subject-specific terminology of the area of application is uniform and used consistently. In the medical domain, this is generally the case; parts of the body are generally denoted by their Latin names. If these are not used exclusively, a thesaurus can be used to map common names onto the Latin ones.

2. *structured three-dimensional models*   An application system for producing illustrations to match a given text must have three-dimensional models from which they can be generated. Moreover, the models must be structured into the smallest units that are (to be) named in the text. Finally, the scientific (Latin) names of the geometric objects must be encoded within the model.

A method for generating an illustration for a given (medical) text segment S and a given geometric model G is given more formally in Algorithm 10.2. The main steps to be performed are the following:

1. *Match words*   Isolate all words in S and compare them to the labels on the parts of G. Use a thesaurus if necessary. Let $\mathcal{T}$ be the intersection of the two sets of words. $\mathcal{T}$ now contains a list of all words that appear in the text and that are present as objects in the geometric model.

2. *Compute importance of words in $\mathcal{T}$*   Just because a word is mentioned in a text does not mean that the corresponding object must be illustrated. Hence the text should be analyzed so as to assess the importance of the words. (For example, if an object is mentioned within parentheses, it is probably not as important as one mentioned within a chapter heading.)

3. *Compute illustration*   An illustration can now be generated on the basis of the importance values. An attempt must be made to make all objects in $\mathcal{T}$ visible if possible; in any case, visible objects in $\mathcal{T}$ are to be emphasized by using selected NPR techniques, like drawing them with thicker lines than other objects. Indeed, objects that are deemed to be more important can be made somewhat larger using the distortion algorithms presented in this book.

```
1    W = all words in S
2    L = all labels in G
3    𝒯 = W ∩ L
4    foreach t ∈ 𝒯 do
5        compute the degree of interest DOI(t)
6        assign this degree of interest to the respective object in G
7    od
8    foreach o ∈ G do
9        determine the drawing style depending on DOI(o)
10       determine drawing parameters depending on attributes of o
11       draw o
12   od
```

ALGORITHM 10.2 Creating an illustration for a given text segment S.

The degree of interest for an object (DOI(o)) can be determined in several ways. Based on the position in the text, there is an "a priori importance" for each object name. A name appearing in a chapter or section heading is then more important than the same name appearing in the text body or in an additional explanation in parentheses. This a priori importance is independent from the user's interaction. However, to compute the DOI value, user interaction has to be taken into account. Thus, different kinds of interactions change the importance value in different ways. A direct manipulation of the respective name should have a bigger influence than just the fact that while scrolling through the text a name becomes visible for a short time. Hence, computing the DOI depends on the a priori importance as well as on user interaction.

Figure 10.15 shows an example of such an illustration taken from a system called the TextIllustrator. Generally, it is possible to produce such or similar illustrations in real time. In this case, it is interesting to note that if we let S be the currently visible portion of text within a text editing or reading system, manipulating the scroll bar will lead to the illustration changing over time. This corresponds to an animation of the text.

10.4.2 Generating Labels

Textual labels are an important part of illustrations because they serve as explicit pointers from parts of the illustration to corresponding tokens and sentences within the text. Objects that are candidates for being labeled are those that are visible in an illustration and appear in the text that they accompany.

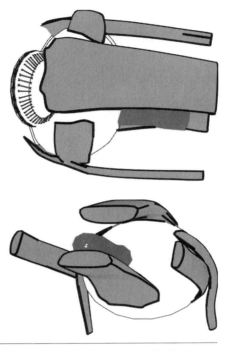

Extraocular Muscles

There are six extraocular muscles which act to rotate an eye about its vertical, horizontal, and antero-posterior axes: the *medial rectus (MR)*, the *external rectus (ER)*, the *superior rectus (SR)*, the *inferior rectus (IR)*, the *superior oblique (SO)*, and the *inferior oblique (IO)*.

muscle movements

A given extraocular muscle moves an eye in a specific manner, as follows:

- **medial rectus (MR)**—moves the eye toward the nose
- **external rectus (ER)**—moves the eye away from the nose
- **superior rectus (SR)**—primarily moves the eye upward and secondarily rotates the top of the eye toward the nose
- **inferior rectus (IR)**—primarily moves the eye downward and secondarily rotates the top of the eye away from the nose
- **superior oblique (SO)**—primarily rotates the top of the eye toward the nose and secondarily moves the eye downward
- **inferior oblique (IO)**—primarily rotates the top of the eye away from the nose and secondarily moves the eye upward

The primary muscle that moves an eye in a given direction is known as the "agonist." A muscle in the same eye that moves the eye in the same direction as the agonist is known as a "synergist," while the muscle in the same eye that moves the eye in the opposite direction of the agonist is the "antagonist." According to "Sherrington's Law," increased innervation to any agonist muscle is accompanied by a corresponding decrease in innervation to its antagonist muscle(s).

anatomical arrangement

All of the extraocular muscles, with the exception of the inferior oblique, form a "cone" within the bony orbit. The apex of this cone is located in the posterior aspect of the orbit, while the base of the cone is the attachment of the muscles around the midline of the eye. This conic structure is referred to as the "annulus of Zinn," and within the cone runs the *optic nerve* (cranial nerve II), and within the optic nerve are contained the ophthalmic artery and the ophthalmic vein.

The superior oblique muscle, although part of the cone-shaped annulus of Zinn, differs from the recti muscles in that before it attaches to the eye it passes through a ring-like tendon, the "trochlea" (which acts as a pulley), in the nasal portion of the orbit. The inferior oblique, which is not a member of the annulus of Zinn, arises from the lacrimal fossa in the nasal portion of the bony orbit and attaches to the inferior portion of the eye.

FIGURE 10.15 Example of a medical text and illustrations generated automatically by the TextIllustrator.

For the sake of clarity, many illustrations in medical books have their labels neatly aligned on the side of the image. This model has been adapted in the system called the ZoomIllustrator; Figure 10.16 shows an example. Note that the labels are dynamic in the sense that the user can manipulate them with well-defined operations. In particular, each label can be expanded so as to display more text. The ZoomIllustrator assumes that this text is available; it can either be fixed or itself generated with a text generation system.

The object-space zoom algorithm of Chapter 9 is applied to the region in which the labels are placed. This means that if a label is expanded, less space is available for the other labels, eventually meaning that labels have to

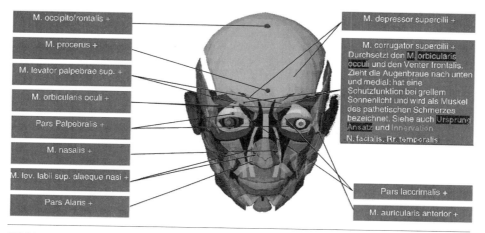

M. occipitofrontalis +

M. procerus +

M. levator palpebrae sup. +

M. orbicularis oculi +

Pars Palpebralis +

M. nasalis +

M. lev. labii sup. alaeque nasi +

Pars Alaris +

M. depressor supercilii +

M. corrugator supercilii +
Durchsetzt den M. orbicularis
occuli und den Venter frontalis.
Zieht die Augenbraue nach unten
und medial; hat eine
Schutzfunktion bei grellem
Sonnenlicht und wird als Muskel
des pathetischen Schmerzes
bezeichnet. Siehe auch Ursprung
Ansatz und Innervation
N. facialis. Rr. temporalis

Pars laccrimalis +

M. auricularis anterior +

FIGURE 10.16 Example of label placement and handling by the zoom algorithm in the ZoomIllustrator. The second label in the right-hand column is enlarged to show more information.

disappear. Care must then be taken to make sure that the user can retrieve the missing label (for example, by keeping a reference to the object no longer being labeled).

A particularly appealing part of the ZoomIllustrator is that the zoom algorithm now can be applied directly to the relevant parts of the three-dimensional model. This means that if the user has enlarged a label to get more information, the corresponding object can also be enlarged so as to show its relationship to the other objects. Experience has shown that the movement in the illustration as a result of a zoom operation is very helpful for enabling a user to assess the overall structure of an object.

Care must be taken in such a system to maintain consistency in the overall illustration. For example, if a user manipulates the illustration (for example, by turning it by 180° in the image plane), lines from a label to the object that did not cross beforehand will cross afterward. If the rotation is carried out in one of the other two planes, objects that were previously visible and labeled may no longer be visible; what is the system to do with the labels? These and other related questions are beyond the scope of this book.

10.4.3 Generating Figure Captions

Illustrations in medical textbooks always are accompanied by figure captions. Two kinds of captions dominate.

1. *descriptive captions*   These captions describe for the user what is visible. In principle, these captions describe the use of the NPR resources. For example, if an object is slightly enlarged, this is generally mentioned in the caption; objects that are emphasized are also mentioned. Such information is available as a by-product of the input to the algorithms for generating the illustrations in the first place (or possible user interaction) and can thus be generated automatically.

2. *instructive captions*   These captions give the user information about what the illustration is asking the viewer to do. For example, an illustration might show how the hand of a surgeon folds back a piece of skin; the caption may verbalize this operation. Such captions are very difficult to generate automatically, but would rely heavily on hardwired information associated with specific geometric models.

Figure 10.17 shows an example of a figure caption generated for a medial illustraion in the ZoomIllustrator system. Note that figure captions for automatically generated illustrations now have appealing interaction possibilities not available in printed books. For example, a user can manipulate the caption to obtain an alternative image. Hence the figure caption becomes a possibility to interrogate the system with the illustration being the output medium. Care must be taken by the system designer, however, to enable only such manipulations of the caption as can actually be covered by the illustrator. A solution here is to restrict editing of the caption to working with menus that provide the alternative objects actually available in the system.

The face of a man **from the** ventral side. **The main interest is on the** eye muscles, jaw muscles **and** nose muscles, the skin **and** bones **are** translucent. **All** 20 **objects of interest are labeled. The** Pars laccrimalis **explained above is** slightly enlarged.

FIGURE 10.17   Automatically generated figure caption produced for the image in Figure 10.16 by the ZoomIllustrator.

10.5 Tactile Rendering for Blind People

As a final application of NPR, we will study tactile graphics for blind people. In particular, we will take a closer look at tactile maps.

10.5.1 Hardware

Over the years, a variety of graphical output devices have been developed for blind people. Most notable are Braille output devices where users are given an array of, for example, 40 characters with 6 or 8 pins each. Text can be displayed in Braille without any problem. If the pins are close enough together, they can be used to display simple graphics.

Force feedback devices have also been used to display information for blind people. Such devices lend themselves particularly well to displaying three-dimensional graphical information. However, experience has shown that without visual feedback, blind people quickly get lost in the three-dimensional space. One approach that has been used successfully has been to map the three-dimensional information onto several two-dimensional layers that can be explored separately.

Perhaps the most popular method of producing tactile images uses so-called swell paper. This is paper with a thin layer of chemical material that expands when heated. A printer is used to deposit ink on the paper in selected places. The paper is subsequently placed under a bright light (as used in some photocopy machines); those parts of the paper that were printed on absorb more heat and swell up. This is what a blind person can feel when moving his or her fingers over the page.

10.5.2 Haptic Perception

Blind people can perceive graphical information by touching surfaces with their fingers. Three factors are of particular relevance:

1. *Speed of perception*   It is evident that blind people who touch tactile presentations are much slower at obtaining information than their sighted counterparts viewing visualizations. Indeed, it has been estimated that blind people perceive such information at 10% the speed of sighted people. This means that the information presented in a tactile form must be reduced to a minimum so as not to overload the user with unnecessary information.

2. *Area of perception*   When blind people run their fingers over a tactile presentation, at any given time they can perceive only what is directly under the tip of each finger. This means that they cannot perceive a surface as such, but must integrate mentally the impressions gained over time when moving

their fingers about. Care must thus be taken that local graphic attributes do not confuse the user with respect to the overall structure of a presentation. For example, in visualizations, it is not uncommon to annotate an object by drawing a line from the object in question to a text. When presented in a tactile form, points at which the lines cross may be mistaken for part of the object. Breaking up the annotation line may also influence the semantics that the blind user associates with the presentation.

3. *Discernibility of a presentation*   Studies have shown that when a blind person touches a tactile presentation, objects that are less than about 1.6 mm apart are perceived as though they were one object. When the user's hands are allowed to move about in a tactile presentation, matters are even worse: two objects less than about 3 mm apart are perceived as one object.

    This has far-reaching consequences for the design of computer graphics for blind people. In principle, the images must have a very low level of detail, and all objects must be at least 2–3 mm apart so as to be discernible from one another. Parallel lines must even be 4–6 mm apart so as not to be perceived as a single object. Individual symbols (like icons) should have edges that are at least 5 mm in length so that their shape can be ascertained. Objects of similar or like shape must differ in size by at least 30% if the difference is to be noticeable.

10.5.3   Converting Visualizations into Tactile Presentations

The material presented in the last section implies that if visualizations are to be converted into a tactile form for blind people, certain operations either on the image or on the underlying model must be carried out:

1. *Reduction of detail*   Much of computer graphics emphasizes details of images just right. In the case of tactile images for blind people, such detail can only confuse the user. Indeed, the problem is in some sense related to rendering images for a computer screen without color and of very low resolution.

    Some of the methods discussed in this book can be used here. For example:

    ◆ *Abstraction of detail or indication*   This method described in Section 5.2 varies the level of detail in an image based on interactively placed "detail segments." The user may specify which areas are presented with a high level of detail; the level of detail decreases with increasing distance to the detail segments.

♦ *Dithering with low resolution*   This "smudges" the image to remove local detail. In a post-processing step, coarse dither blocks representing lines must be reunited to form curves. The drawback is that the algorithm cannot differentiate between important and unimportant details.

♦ *Specialized prioritized stroke textures*   Special stroke textures can be designed for ease of touch.

2. *Image distortion*   As indicated a tactile representation must satisfy certain criteria with respect to the distribution of symbols or lines. Hence a distortion is necessary so as to separate objects by enough space so that they can be discerned even though they are physically close together. The methods discussed in Chapter 9 can be adapted to achieve an appropriate distortion.

10.5.4 Tactile Maps

Tactile maps are great because they help blind people find their way around unknown environments. Indeed, surveys and studies have shown that a large percentage of blind people say that they do not go out because of the fear of getting lost.

One of the problems encountered when designing maps for blind people is that routes (for example, streets, footpaths) must be enlarged. This application comes up when a blind person has chosen a destination and expects an interactive system to produce a map that details the way to be taken from a familiar place to the destination.

The method described in Chapter 9 can be applied to the routes on maps. Figure 10.18(a) shows an example of a map that was already prepared for blind people: in keeping with the recommendations given earlier, streets appear quite wide (over 3 mm in width in the tactile map), while the blocks between the streets have been made correspondingly smaller. Once a user has defined the path to be taken, a so-called focus line is applied automatically to it. With respect to the construction of Figure 9.1, the route in question is enlarged, while a drop-off function defines how the areas around the route are squeezed together to make room. Figure 10.18(b) shows an example of the new map emphasizing the specified route.

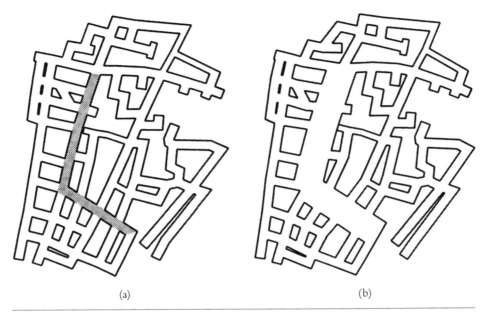

(a)   (b)

FIGURE 10.18 Creating a route map for blind people. The shaded route in (a) is enlarged while squeezing together all other parts of the route to produce (b).

Exercises

10.1   Extend the algorithm for computing speedlines in various different ways. For example, compute speedlines for the case when

     a. the movement is not straight but follows a curve. First try it when there are no inflection points on the curve, then try it when there are one or more inflection points;

     b. the speed of the object is also to be visualized;

     c. design and implement an algorithm to compute an aesthetically pleasing length for speedlines.

10.2   Devise and study algorithms for computing some of the other visualizations for object movement in still images (recall Figure 10.3).

10.3   Derive and explain Equation (10.1).

10.4   Experiment with different G-buffers as a source of data to compute parameters of the illustrations of trees, such as the line quality (line thickness, line waviness, and other parameters), the disc size, and the depth threshold. For example, use a shadow buffer to derive the line thickness and discuss the effect.

10.5 Derive a formula for the disc size as a function of the depth of a tree to achieve the effect of Figure 10.13(b).

10.6 Suggest a method to integrate shadows into the algorithms presented for rendering trees.

10.7 Study the effect of different dropoff functions for the distortion of tactile route maps. In particular, study their effect on rectilinear grids of streets on a map. Which dropoff function is best? Why?

Bibliographic Notes

An exciting study on how to communicate through comics has recently been published by McCloud (1993, 2000). These books contain a wealth of ideas on how to express information, usually through line drawings. Masuch (1999, see also 2001) first proposed the algorithm for computing speedlines automatically.

Non-photorealistic animation was born by the idea to use image processing filters on the single frames of an animation to achieve a "painted" look. This was explored in detail by Litwinowicz (1997) as well as by Hertzmann and Perlin (2000). Animations produced this way are rather noisy since there is no frame-coherent behavior of the strokes. The first "animated painting" has been presented by Meier in her paper on *painterly rendering* (1996). Since then, frame coherency has been a major concern for many authors, among them Kowalski (1999), Markosian et al. (2000), Masuch et al. (1997, 1998), and Curtis (1998).

Schumann et al. (1996) carried out an empirical study on the use of NPR in architectural drawings in CAD systems. They draw on a classification of effects of images proposed by Peeck (1987) and make use of the concept of projection discussed by Gombrich (1977) and normalization in Weidenmann (1994).

Deussen and Strothotte (2000) presented the algorithms for rendering pen-and-ink illustrations of trees as discussed in this chapter. Very early papers on this topic are by Guo and Kunii (1991) and Sasada (1987). The article by Lintermann and Deussen (1999) is a good reference for modeling trees as can be rendered with the algorithms discussed.

The abstraction and distortion of graphics for blind people have been studied in the education community. An exhaustive overview is given by Edman (1992).

However, the methods described there are geared toward practitioners who make tactile graphics by hand. The same questions have been studied algorithmically in the literature only to a small extent. An overview can be found in Strothotte and Strothotte (1997). Somewhat more recent material can be found in Strothotte et al. (1998). It is interesting to note that when blind people themselves draw images, certain features look very different than when sighted people are drawing for sighted people. This phenomenon has been studied from an algorithmic point of view by Kurze (1999).

Schlechtweg (1999) has carried out research into automatically generating illustrations from medical and technical texts. Labels in illustrations and a coherent zoom in labels and three-dimensional graphics were studied by Preim, Raab, and Strothotte (1997). Algorithms for generating figure captions in the ZoomIllustrator can be found in Hartmann et al. (1999). More details on the ZoomIllustrator and TextIllustrator can be found in Strothotte (1998) and Schlechtweg and Strothotte (1999).

The empirical study on architects discussed in this chapter stems from Schumann et al. (1996). The concept of projection stems from Gombrich (1977), and the concept of normalization demand stems from Weidenmann (1994). Recent empirical work has been carried out by Girshik et al. (2000). Empirical work on distortion has been carried out by Carpendale (1999).

11 A CONCEPTUAL FRAMEWORK FOR NPR

Kees van Overveld
Eindhoven University of Technology, The Netherlands

The previous chapters gave an overview of a variety of techniques that have been developed in NPR over the last few years. The field has developed thanks to the joint efforts of many researchers, and progress has been obtained in many different directions. It is not always clear to see the relations between one result and another, and the identification of promising open areas is therefore not trivial. Still, it may be expected that a further exploration of the field will add numerous new algorithms and paradigms. In this concluding chapter, we propose a line of thinking that may be helpful in this endeavor. We aim to give an onset for a conceptual background that could facilitate seeing the forest despite the trees.

11.1 Methodological Disclaimer

Many statements in this book are not true, not comprehensible, or not relevant. However, we assure you that the majority of the statements will be at least one of the three. Apparently, truthfulness, comprehensibility, and relevance are very different qualifiers of statements in scientific or technological texts. In the traditional methodology of science, most emphasis is on the *truthfulness* of statements.

For instance, in traditional mathematics texts, you ideally start from axioms that are true by definition; next, you construct true statements (theorems or lemmas) by applying accepted logic methods, such as deduction, complete induction, or the law of the excluded third. Since mathematics is a system that exists purely in itself (that is, it does not logically depend on assumptions or observations that are taken from the world outside mathematics), the goal of producing texts that are 100% true is, to a large extent, achievable. Notice that, for a pure mathematician, relevance and comprehensibility (in the sense of interpretability) are not issues.

In physics, the goal of producing a 100% true statement is already much more problematic. This is caused by the subtle interplay between empirical observations and models. Indeed, empirical observations are problematic due to such issues as reproducibility, intersubjectivity, accuracy, and the question if observations can be made without prior model assumptions. Models are problematic because every model is known to be an approximation, and every model is based on assumptions that never can be completely and formally verified. Further, all models are formulated in terms of concepts (such as "electric charge") that only follow indirectly from empiric observation. The outcomes of the models also can be verified at best indirectly with empiric observation. Finally, an experimental outcome that is consistent with a model prediction is nice, but it cannot prove the model to be *true*; conversely, an experimental outcome that is *inconsistent* with model prediction proves the model to be *false* (although it is not straightforward to prove that something is truly inconsistent, either!). Nevertheless, physical research is considered to be a highly valid endeavor, partially due to its *relevance* and its *comprehensibility*. The relevance of physical results relates to the practical applications of physics. Even though no one knows if Ohm's law is, in some sense, "true," it has paved the way to introducing electricity as an essential factor in everyday life. The comprehensibility of physics relates to our feeling that physics helps to (begin to) understand the world around us. Of course, it is unlikely that Mother Nature meticulously computes the value of the electric current I that flows through a resistor R every time when it is exposed to a voltage difference V by means of the formula $I = V/R$. Nevertheless, it helps in our comprehension to think that she still does so. We can effortlessly comprehend things that are not true. In fact, we do so all the time.

When we shift our attention from mathematics via physics into the direction of chemistry, biology, and psychology, the mix between truth, relevance, and comprehensibility gets more and more complicated (see, for instance, Sattler, 1986). Writers are often not explicit in labeling statements regarding their truthfulness, their relevance, or their comprehensibility. In some cases, the distinction follows from the context. For instance, a question is not a proposition, and therefore cannot be labeled true or false. Further, examples that clarify a certain concept are, strictly speaking, redundant. They carry no new meaning, so they could have been omitted. So they are irrelevant, but they can add to the comprehensibility of a text. Finally, consider the case where a first statement inspires[1] to a second statement. If this second statement is true, relevant, and comprehensible, the truthfulness of the first statement does not seem to matter. Instead, its relevance could lay entirely in the fact that it has inspired to a true statement.

In particular in the context of (technological) design, this last case quite often occurs. During a design project, many different utterances[2] are being made by the designer(s). Only a very small fraction of these will comprise the *final design document*. Here, the final design document is intended to be the set of all utterances about the designed artifact that are necessary to manufacture the artifact. All utterances that were made prior to writing the final design document could have been untrue without affecting the final artifact. The quality of these early utterances is in their relevance (did they inspire to true utterances?) and their comprehensibility (did they facilitate the communication among the designers?). Of course, we do not say that designers usually generate wrong utterances prior to writing the final design document. But if they would like, they are perfectly allowed to. Indeed, the merit and the validity of the majority of their utterances is *only* in their purpose of *inspiring* to the (true) utterances that make up the final design document. No more. And certainly no less.

This book is about design. In particular, this book is about the design of computer programs that play a role in visual communication, using other than photorealistic means. Given the previous observation, all but the sections that contain final design documents could contain plenty of wrong (untrue) statements without jeopardizing the final aim of presenting and explaining methods and techniques for non-photorealistic rendering. (In the case of software design, the final design documents are *algorithms*.)

Now we could have limited this book to a collection of algorithms that are in some sense useful in non-photorealistic rendering. Then we could have left out all the other material, and the book would contain only true statements. But we think that the main merit of this book is in the inspiration to possible new techniques, rather than *only* giving an exhaustive survey of known results.

---

1. If A inspires to B, it does not have to mean that B follows from A in some logic sense. It only means that we got the idea B as a result of contemplating A.

2. An utterance can be a statement, a question, a hypothesis, a formula, a diagram, a drawing, and so on.

In order to be a source of inspiration, we have imposed the structure that was outlined in the introduction (see Chapter 1). Nevertheless, writing a book involves ample reflection, looking at much of the material in a more global sense. Gradually, during the process of writing and reviewing, the outlines of another structure became apparent. This last chapter will address this alternative structure, a conceptual framework to argue about NPR. We present it because it may facilitate classifying future algorithms and techniques; it may inspire to work in the direction of validation of NPR methods; and in general, it may provide a language to communicate between workers in the field, computer scientists, and other professionals.

Our conceptual framework is inspired by various earlier concepts. We mention a few:

- The OSI model for data communication (Tanenbaum, 1998). This model distinguishes information in various semantic layers, and the interfaces between these layers.

- The human perceptual system, with its variety of built-in mechanisms that are assumed to have arisen from evolution in order to provide better ways to communicate with an environment and with other creatures. Now it is generally assumed that perception cannot be seen independent from cognition, so we deal with perception and cognition as two aspects of the same phenomenon. In doing so, we gratefully borrow from the work of Igor Aleksander (1994, 1996), although we use in some places a slightly different terminology.

- Some notions from classification theory. Indeed, perception may be seen as having been developed in order to perform classification tasks with increasing perfection, and therefore it is essential to be able to argue about classification, representation, and abstraction.

In the remainder of this chapter, we introduce concepts, such as *look-ahead sets, variants* and *invariants, semantic levels, equivalence relations* and *equivalence classes,* and *quotients.* All these schemes, models, and concepts help to search for relations between existing techniques, and may point to as yet missing techniques. Our classification schemes and reference models are based on what may *seem* to be physically, biologically, or psychologically correct, or at least plausible, arguments. To the best of our knowledge, however, the entire biological and psychological foundation of our approach could be dubious or even wrong. Almost everything that we write about the biologic evolution of visual perception systems is at best highly speculative. Much of it is founded neither in sound experiments nor in well-accepted models. Similarly, for many of our concepts we borrow shamelessly from mathematics (abstract algebra, linear algebra, function theory) without verifying the mathematical preliminaries. All this would make this chapter into obscure pseudoscience if our purpose was to state true claims on (the evolution of) visual perception, or mathematical models thereof. But as we mentioned, our only purpose is to inspire software engineers to come up with new ideas for visual communication and to facilitate arguing about such systems. Therefore, we think that our frivolous and speculative attitude toward mathematics, biology, perception theory, and cognitive psychology is, from the point of view of design methodology, at least partially acceptable.

Of course, we could have considered taking an alternative route, and put effort in founding our classification schemes and reference models only on well-established facts of mathematics, biology, perception, and cognitive psychology. Then this chapter should have been co-authored with representatives from these disciplines, which would have significantly complicated the process of writing it. But more important, we have the serious fear that the well-accepted understanding of (the evolution of) visual perception has not yet developed to a sufficiently mature level so as to cater to our needs. Further, many mathematical constructs are applicable only in very strict circumstances, and in perception (as a part of the phenomenology of the physical world) these circumstances are not always fulfilled. In particular, when we speculate about the higher levels in our semantic hierarchy, it seems that much understanding of the neurological principles is still missing—although our speculations are at least not inconsistent with some works in neural science and perception. We look forward to writing the next edition of this chapter in cooperation with specialists in the field if only to increase the level of semantics in our speculations.

11.2 Mathematical Preliminaries: Equivalence Relations, Equivalence Classes, and Quotients

Mathematical concepts are usually introduced in order to derive (or prove) *true* statements. We have a different purpose in mind: we use non-mathematical concepts that are chosen to be *similar* to mathematical concepts in order to facilitate the communication via *relevant* or *comprehensible* statements. Since we do not want to prove anything, we can afford some sloppiness in doing so, as long as we indicate precisely *when* we deviate from standard mathematical practice. The notions that we use are discussed in turn in the following sections.

11.2.1 Sets and Elements

Sets and elements are the fundamental concepts of modern mathematics. However, they are not defined (they are assumed to be *elementary notions*), so we do not have to attempt to define them either. We will consider such sets as the set of all shapes, a set of colors, a set of images, but also more esoteric things, such as the set of all features of an object or the set of interpretations of an image. We assume such notions as subset, intersection, and difference of two sets to be known. When necessary, we use the conventional notations for these notions.

11.2.2 Cartesian Products and Relations

A relation between two objects is an often used notion in everyday language: if John and Mary are married, they have a relation; if two objects have the same color, they have a relation; and so on. In mathematics, this same idea is introduced via a slightly less obvious intermediate concept, that of the *Cartesian product*. For two sets, U and V, the Cartesian product of U and V, written as $U \times V$, is the set of all pairs (u, v), where u is taken from U and v is taken from V. So if U is the set of all men and V is the set of all women, the pair (John, Mary) is one of the pairs in $U \times V$. But, for example, (Peter, Melany) are also in $U \times V$. We see that the fact that John and Mary are married (that is, have a marriage relation) corresponds to the fact that (John, Mary) is one of the pairs in $U \times V$. Every married couple corresponds to one of these pairs, and a way to define the relation "is married to" is to say that this relation corresponds directly to a *subset* of $U \times V$. A subset, indeed, since not all pairs in $U \times V$ correspond to married couples (Peter is not married to Melany, but the pair (Peter, Melany) is in $U \times V$). So we define a relation between u and v, where u in U and v in V is a subset of $U \times V$. We can also consider the Cartesian product of a set with itself: $U \times U$. Then we can see how the relation "has the same color as" is also a part of a Cartesian product. If $U = \{$tomato, banana, lemon$\}$, then "has the same color as"$=$ $\{$(tomato, tomato), (banana, lemon), (lemon, banana), (lemon, lemon)$\}$. Examples from NPR include $U =$ the set of technical drawings with a relation "depicts the same machine as" or $U =$ a set of geometric objects and $V =$ a set of NPR styles; then a relation between u in U and v in V is "object u is drawn in style v." A relation R between u and v is sometimes written as $R(u, v)$ or uRv. But if we know what relation we are talking about, we simply write $u \sim v$. In the following, we will reserve the word *relation* for a subset of the Cartesian product $U \times U$. A subset of a Cartesian product $U \times V$ will be called a *mapping*. An example of a mapping is the set $U \times V = \{(\text{banana, yellow}), (\text{tomato, red}), (\text{carrot, orange})\}$ where $U = \{\text{banana, tomato, carrot}\}$ and $V = \{\text{yellow, red, green, orange}\}$. We write mappings as prefix operators, so $M\text{banana} = \text{yellow}$, $M\text{tomato} = \text{red}$, $M\text{carrot} = \text{orange}$. In NPR, for instance, we can map NPR styles to geometric objects.

A relation between two things is called a *binary* relation. Relations, however, do not have to be binary. Red, yellow, and black have as a *ternary* relation that they occur in a flag (namely, the Belgian flag and the German flag), and the same relation holds for red, white, and blue (Dutch, British, French, U.S., and so on) and numerous other groups of three colors.

One particular type of a ternary relation that will be very important is the *product operation*. It takes three elements to define a *3-tuple* or *triple,* which is an element of $(U \times V) \times W$. We will often encounter the special case where product operations are subsets of $(U \times U) \times U$. Some well-known examples are the ordinary multiplication, with elements such as $(2, 3, 6)$ and $(3, 4, 12)$, to denote the more familiar expressions $2 \times 3 = 6$ and $3 \times 4 = 12$, respectively. Other important examples are *ordering relations*, also defined on numbers (but not only on numbers, as we will see later). For instance, $(3, 5, 5)$ or $(4, 0, 0)$ can be interpreted as "the maximum of 3 and 5 is 5," and "the minimum of 4 and 0 is 0," respectively. A nice property of product operations is that they can be denoted in tables, so-called *product tables*, such as the tables of multiplication. Indeed, if a set is *closed* under a product operation (as in $(U \times U) \times U$, where the result of taking the product of a first element of U with a second element of U is again an element of U), a product table completely characterizes everything that is to be known of the product operation without having to resort to an interpretation.

Consider Table 11.1, where U is some set with three elements $\{e_1, e_2, e_3\}$. This product table defines (e_1, e_2, e_2) to be part of the product operation, or $e_1 \cdot e_2 = e_2$, without bothering us with an interpretation of the operator. If we

$\cdot$	e_1	e_2	e_3
e_1	e_1	e_2	e_3
e_2	e_2	e_2	e_3
e_3	e_3	e_3	e_3

TABLE 11.1 Product table for the operation $\cdot$ on the set $\{e_1, e_2, e_3\}$.

like, we can assign the interpretation "e_2 is the maximum of e_1 and e_2," and then we see that this product table applies to such sets as $U = \{1, 2, 3\}$, $U' = \{1, 4, 7\}$, and $U'' = \{0, 100, 1000\}$. In NPR, an example of a product operator of the form $e_1 \cdot e_2$ could express, for a set of rendering styles e_1, e_2, e_3, . . . , which one, in pairwise comparison, would be favorable for a given context. The product table reveals a structure of the set, ignoring irrelevant details. Indeed, with this product table, U, U', and U'' have become in some sense equivalent or isomorphic (we give a more precise definition of isomorphic later).

11.2.3 Equivalence Relations and Variants

Relations come in various sorts. In particular, a binary relation on a set U (a subset of $U \times U$) can be reflexive, symmetric, or transitive. A relation $R \subset U \times U$ is *reflexive* if for all u in U, we have that $u \sim u$ holds. "Has the same age" is an example of a reflexive relation, but "is cheaper than" is not reflexive. A relation is *symmetric* if for all u and v, both from U, we have that either $u \sim v$ and $v \sim u$ or neither of the two. "Is married to" is an example of a symmetric relation, but "is the father of" is not symmetric. A relation is *transitive* if, for all u, v, and w from U, we have that from $u \sim v$ and $v \sim w$, it follows that $u \sim w$. We have a special notation for the repeated application of relation $\sim$, namely, $\sim^*$. So $a \sim^* b$ means either $a \sim b$ or there is a c so that $a \sim^* c$ and $c \sim b$. For transitive relations, we see that $\sim$ and $\sim^*$ are the same. This allows us to talk about the so-called transitive closure of a relation $\sim$. The *transitive closure* of a is the set of all b such that $a \sim^* b$. Loosely speaking, it is the set of all elements that can be reached from a, repeatedly using relation $\sim$. "Is younger than" is a transitive relation, as well as "has the same mother as." The transitive closure of "is younger than," applied to me, is the set of all people younger than I.

But, and this is a very important case, "is not too far from" is not transitive. Indeed, if I walk one meter, I have not moved very far. But if I repeatedly walk one meter, I can cross arbitrary large distances. The transitive closure of "is not too far from," starting at the place where I am, is the set of all possibly reachable places! So the distinction between "equal" and "almost equal" is very crucial. "Is equal to," in all its disguises (such as "has the same shape," "has the same color," "has the same meaning") is a transitive relation, and "is almost equal to," in all its disguises (such as "has almost the same shape," "has a similar color," "has about the same meaning") is *not* transitive. As we will see later, this means that relations with the word *almost* cannot form so-called equivalence classes, and they cannot form so-called quotients (see Section 11.2.5). In our approach to form a model for

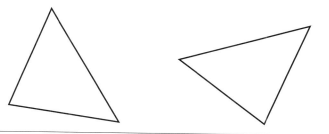

FIGURE 11.1 Two 2D images.

FIGURE 11.2 Two 2D images of three-dimensional objects.

visual perception, this is a serious blow, and we will put some effort in mitigating its effects. Strong mathematical results hold for equivalence classes and quotients, but much less can be proved in the weaker case where transitivity does not hold.

Relations that fulfill all three, the criteria symmetry, reflexivity, and transitivity, are called *equivalence relations*. In the context of perception, equivalence relations correspond to our notion of *variants*. We introduce this concept with some examples. Consider the images in Figure 11.1. There are various equivalence relations that hold between these two images, such as "has the same number of vertices as," "has the same area as," and "has the same perimeter as." At the same time, we recognize them as two rotated versions, or *variations*, of the same geometric object.

Next consider the example in Figure 11.2. In this case, the equivalence relations between the *images* (for now, consider them only as 2D images!) are quite limited since both the colors and virtually all (2D) geometric features are different. But if we interpret the images as projections (photographs) of 3D objects, we see that various equivalence relations between these 3D objects hold ("has the same 3D shape," "is illuminated from the same direction," "casts a shadow onto the same plane"). Again, we are able to identify the two images as *variations* from the same 3D object, thereby ignoring all the differences that result from the projection to 2D from two different viewpoints.

So it seems as if the mathematical notion of *equivalence relation* could be used to model the intuitive notion of *variants*. Since genuine transitivity in the case of the physical world is quite rare, there are a few cases where this association applies. Therefore, we will introduce a weaker concept *p-equivalence relation* (*p* for "pseudo") if the transitivity *almost* holds; for now, we do not attempt to give a precise definition of what "almost" means. Instead, at the end of Section 11.2.4, we give a construction that takes a p-equivalence relation and, under some special assumptions, turns it into a true equivalence relation.

11.2.4 Equivalence Classes and Invariants

Consider a set U and an equivalence relation $\sim$ on U. For example, let U be the natural numbers $0, 1, 2, 3, \ldots$, and let $\sim$ be defined as "has the same remainder when divided by 3." Then 6 and 9 are equivalent (both remainder 0). Also 7, 13, 16, and 22 are equivalent (all remainder 1), and 2, 11, and 32 are equivalent (all remainder 2). So we see that the introduction of this equivalence relation introduces three sets of numbers,

$$C_0 = \{0, 3, 6, 9, 12, \ldots\}$$
$$C_1 = \{1, 4, 7, 10, 13, \ldots\}$$
$$C_2 = \{2, 5, 8, 11, 14, \ldots\}$$

All numbers in each of these sets are equivalent among themselves. We see that C_0 is the transitive closure under $\sim$ starting in 0, C_1 is the transitive closure under $\sim$ starting in 1, and C_2 is the transitive closure of $\sim$ starting in 2. Further, these sets are disjoint, and finally, together they form all natural numbers. C_0, C_1, C_2 are said to *partition* the natural numbers. This is in fact a very general result: it can be proved that *every* equivalence relation on a set U introduces one or more disjoint so-called equivalence classes $C_0, C_1, C_2, \ldots$ that together partition U, such that all elements in one equivalence class are equivalent among themselves. For example, let U be the set of all polygons. Then the equivalence relation "has the same number of vertices" gives rise to the equivalence classes triangles, quadrilaterals, pentagons, hexagons, heptagons, and so on. The equivalence relation "has the same color" on the set of all objects gives rise to the equivalence classes red objects, yellow objects, green objects, and so on. The equivalence relation "has the same diet as" for animals gives rise to the classes of herbivores, carnivores, omnivores, and so on. In NPR, the equivalence relation "has the same average density as" gives rise to classes of hatching patterns (distinguished on the basis of darkness). But so does the equivalence relation "has the same average line direction as" (distinguished on the basis of orientation), and "uses the same line thickness as" (distinguished on the basis of a property that is more difficult to define visually), whereas all these classes of hatching patterns may be very different with respect to other attributes. In fact, these examples show that equivalence relations are extremely fundamental to our attitude of classifying objects (images, perceptual impressions, concepts, and so on) in the world. With some effort, it is often possible to associate an equivalence relation to a class of things.

In the context of perception, equivalence classes are associated with the notion of *invariants*. Indeed, despite that in Figure 11.1 the two images are different, there are equivalence relations between them. The equivalence relation "has the same number of vertices" introduces the equivalence classes triangles, quadrilaterals, and so on as before. Within each of these classes, the number of vertices is constant, and this number of vertices is an *invariant* of all the figures in that equivalence class. In perception, an invariant allows us to classify objects as being (for a certain purpose) identical, and all differences between these objects are regarded (for that same purpose) as *irrelevant*. You could say that an object, for instance, a dog, classifies as a dog in virtue of a number of invariants that should be different from those that classify an object as being a cat.

We can already anticipate that this notion is essential in NPR. There is a huge variety of images in all sorts of styles that are all being identified by a viewer as "an apple," and another (hopefully disjoint) set of images that are identified as "a pear." Apparently, there are some invariants among all these images, and NPR is concerned with conveying these invariants. If only a (sufficient) number of these invariants are sufficiently conveyed, the viewer will classify the seen object as "apple." A set of different invariants causes classification as "pear," but obviously, the two sets of invariants are not disjoint. (Both classes of images depict things that are in the same range of hues, that have a more or less bulky part (the fruit) and a skinny part (the stem), both have a little crown-like thing opposite the stem, and so on). A designer of NPR algorithms has to be aware both of the invariants and the variants of the images he or she wants to produce in order to make sure that the images will arouse (for an intended purpose) the correct classification.

Notice that it is indeed crucial that the equivalence relation is truly transitive. Even the slightest failure of transitivity destroys the entire notion of equivalence classes. A p-equivalence relation does not, unfortunately, introduce equivalence classes. If we consider the relation "has almost the same color as" (which is symmetric and reflexive, and *almost* transitive; in our terminology, it is a p-equivalence relation), and the objects in the set under consideration come in *all* existing colors, we can get smoothly from one object to another, each time taking together two objects that have *almost* the same color. In doing so, we can collect a series of objects with colors as diverse as in a candy shop, the extremes of this series having arbitrarily different colors. The transitive closure under "almost the same color as" starting in *any* color will produce *all* colors. So, in our continuum of colors there are no equivalence classes where one class consists of all red objects and another class of all green objects, and so on.

Now something curious happens. Suppose that the set of objects is finite, and that actually a quite limited variety of colors occurs. We see that then our procedure for getting from one color to an arbitrary other color does not work, and despite that our p-equivalence relation cannot, in strict mathematical sense, give rise to equivalence classes, it still does a fair job in separating the objects in similarly colored classes. We illustrate this with numbers. Consider the set $U = \{0.9, 1.1, 2.9, 3.0, 3.1, 9.9, 10.0, 10.2\}$. Let $\sim$ be the relation "differs no more than 0.3." This is not a transitive relation, so it cannot split U in equivalence classes. But it can split U in the classes $\{0.9, 1.1\}$, $\{2.9, 3.0, 3.1\}$, and $\{9.9, 10.0, 10.2\}$. We could call these classes U_i, where $i = 1, 2, 3$. Then we see that the p-equivalence relation "differs no more than 0.3," in virtue of the presence of a universe (the set U), which is finite and contains some "characteristic" elements, introduces a true equivalence relation after all, namely, "is in the same U_i." Notice that this relation does not contain the words *almost* or *differs no more than*. Indeed, the latter is a true equivalence relation, and its equivalence classes are U_1, U_2, U_3. This construction of a true equivalence relation out of a p-equivalence relation, under the conditions of a finite universe and some "characteristic" elements can be performed in general, and we give it in some length at the end of this section.

For NPR, an example would be the following. Consider simple cartoon faces, and the equivalence relation "shows the same emotion as." Then, in Figure 11.3, we can effortlessly distinguish two equivalence classes, one consisting of the left two images and the other consisting of the right two images. But the same would result for the p-equivalence relation "shows *almost* the same emotion as."

For now, all the aforementioned inspires us to use the less strict notion of p-equivalence classes, being the classes that are introduced by p-equivalence relations assuming that the set U permits this. In other words, the set U should possess "lumps" of similar objects, where one lump is sufficiently different from the next lump. A p-equivalence class is just such a lump. Every lump is associated

FIGURE 11.3 Simple cartoon faces to be classified with respect to the shown emotions.

(identified) with one of the "characteristic elements." In the preceding example, U_1 could, for instance, be identified with 1.1, U_2 with 3.0, and U_3 with 10.2, making 1.1, 3.0, and 10.2 the characteristic elements in this case, and U_1, U_2, and U_3 the lumps. In real life, this would be somewhat similar to associating the class of trees by a prototypical tree, the class of dogs by a prototypical dog, and so on. In fact, the way children learn new concepts is very similar to this: it is called *ostensive definition*. You might conjecture that a mental class (a class as it is used by the brain to classify a visual impression) consists of a prototypical characteristic element plus the allowed variants, where these variants are brought forward by (p-)equivalence relations. The prototypical characteristic element is also called the *default* element. For instance, the class "block" might have a red, axis parallel cube with 3-inch long sides as default. Suppose that relevant equivalence relations are "is identical up to a change of color," "is identical up to rotation," "is identical up to non-uniform scaling," and "is identical up to translation," then the set of allowed variants include those being generated by scaling, rotating, translating, and arbitrary coloring.

If we assume that classification in real life is adequately modeled by equivalence relations, equivalent classes, and variants and invariants, we see that this is only because the objects in real life come in sufficiently "lumpy" sets. There are, for instance, saxophones (tenor, alto, baritone, and so on) and crocodiles (tall, short, fat, skinny, mean, living in the Mississippi Delta, and so on) but not a continuum of classes that interpolate these two classes. Therefore, we can unambiguously distinguish saxophones and crocodiles. There are simply no hybrids like saxodiles and crocophones, so we should not be worried that we are not able to classify these hybrids unambiguously. But the p-equivalence relation "has about the same ethical value," which should give rise to p-equivalence classes of good things and bad things, is much more problematic—with all known ethical consequences.

We will use the notions of variants and invariants extensively when we discuss (visual) perception. Our own classification of objects in the real world amounts to distinguishing variants and invariants (large, small, brown, and black horses are all variants from the generic horse). "Horseness" is an invariant associated to the equivalence class "horse." Other invariants associated to the same class are, for example, "four-leggedness," "mammalness," and the like. This equivalence class is introduced by the equivalence relation "belongs to the same species." "Donkeyness" is the invariant that belongs to another equivalence class, namely, the equivalence class "donkey." But "belongs to the same species" is, upon closer inspection, a p-equivalence relation: we can interbreed horse with donkey, giving mule. So the equivalence classes are really p-equivalence classes. This is in practice not a serious problem since there is not a continuum of species: you cannot, for instance, interbreed donkey with dog and dog with cat. Still, the fact that we have to deal with p-equivalence classes instead of true equivalence classes is one of the reasons that a more rigorous mathematical foundation of our models and classifications is cumbersome. Therefore, we proceed with an algorithm that constructs true equivalence classes out of p-equivalence relations. Informally, the algorithm amounts to systematically constructing the transitive closure of the p-equivalence relation, starting in each of the defaults, and identifying the hybrids and removing these from the universe; the remaining elements can be uniquely partitioned in (true) equivalence classes, and if there were sufficiently few hybrids ("crocophones and saxodiles"), the resulting set of equivalence classes will do a reasonable job in classifying the original universe. The conditions to perform this construction are as follows:

♦ We are only considering a finite universe of elements (things we would like to classify).

♦ Among all these things there are a few characteristic elements (defaults, say, a particular saxophone and a particular crocodile).

The p-equivalence relation to start from does not hold between any two defaults (so whatever p-equivalence relation we are using, a saxophone and a crocodile are not p-equivalent). Let U be a finite set, and $S \subset U$ the set of defaults. Assume that for no two defaults, s_1 and s_2 in S, we have $s_1 \sim s_2$. We start by building sets P_s, one for each element $s \in S$, where elements v in P_s have $v \sim s$ or $v \sim^* s$. The sets P_s will form the formal representatives of our pseudoequivalence classes. We have a function $A(v)$ that tells how many p-equivalence classes v have been assigned already. Elements v for which $A(v) > 1$ apparently belong to two or more p-equivalence classes. These elements are hybrid. If $A(v) = 0$, v has not been assigned yet to any p-equivalence class. We initialize the entire process by making $A(v) = 0$ for all $v \in U$. Next, we iteratively extend the sets P_s one by one by including those $v \in U$ for $A(v) = 0$, for which $v \sim s$ for any $s \in P_s$. This is repeated until every $v \in U$ belongs to at least one P_s. Then for $U' = U \setminus \{v : A(v) > 1\}$, we can form a true equivalence relation, namely, "belongs to the same P_s as." The equivalence classes are $P_s \setminus \{v : A(v) > 1\}$, and provided that the number of elements $v \in U$ with $A(v) > 1$ is sufficiently small compared to the number of elements in U, we have a reasonable classification. For completeness, we write Algorithm 11.1 in pseudocode as shown below.

Figure 11.4 illustrates this algorithm for the case where U is a set of points in the plane, and the p-equivalence relation is "is closer by than . . . (some given distance)."

In NPR applications, the set U may contain, for instance, images or visual impressions. Provided that these sets are finite (for instance, in an experimental setup to assess the comprehensibility of NPR images), the algorithm can construct equivalence classes, and hence, quotient structures (see Section 11.2.5). In such cases, the equivalence relations are typically left implicit, to be applied by test subjects, and a meaningful experiment would consist of checking if in a population

---

1   **foreach** $v \in U$ **do** $A(v) := 0$ **od**
2   **foreach** $s \in S$ **do** $P_S = s; A(s) := 1$ **od**
3   **while** $(U \setminus \bigcup_s P_s) \neq \emptyset$ **do**
4   **foreach** $t \in S$ **do**
5         $Q_t := \emptyset$
6   **foreach** $q \in P_t$ **do**
7   **if** $A(q) == 1$ **then**
8   **foreach** $v \in (U \setminus \bigcup_s P_s)$ **do**
9   **if** $v \sim q$ **then** $Q_t := v \cup Q_t; A(v) := A(v) + 1$ **fi**
10   **od**
11   **fi**
12   **od**
13   **foreach** $t \in S$ **do** $P_t := P_t \cup Q_t$ **od**

ALGORITHM 11.1 Construction of true equivalence classes from p-equivalence relations. For simplicity, we assume that eventually every element belongs to one of the P_s.

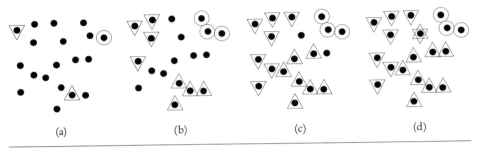

(a)   (b)   (c)   (d)

FIGURE 11.4 Construction of p-equivalence classes: S contains three defaults, indicated by an upward triangle ($s = u$), a downward triangle ($s = d$), and a circle ($s = c$) (a). After one iteration of the while loop, all three p-equivalence classes have been extended; P_u with three elements, P_d with three elements, and P_c with two elements (b). In the second iteration of the while loop, P_u claimed another three elements, and P_d also three elements. P_c did not acquire any further elements (c). In the third iteration, the single remaining element, say, v, was claimed both by P_d and P_u (it was added both to Q_u and Q_d, and therefore has $A(v) = 2$ (d)). It is a hybrid element. There are no further elements w with $A(w) = 0$, so the algorithm terminates. The entire set U, except for the single element with $A(v) = 2$, allows a partitioning in equivalence classes.

of test subjects everybody finds the same quotient structure (the same classification scheme) over a set of test images—and, for instance, if the found quotient structure depends on the chosen NPR rendering style. Conversely, the algorithm may be used to clarify what equivalence relations test subjects (implicitly) use. For our purposes, the major relevance of the algorithm is to show that equivalence classes in principle can be constructed out of p-equivalence classes that form a reasonable model of a classification in real-life situations provided that there are sufficiently few hybrid cases. The construction in the algorithm clearly shows that the number of hybrid elements dramatically increases with the tolerance (the "sloppiness") implied in the used p-equivalence relation.

11.2.5 Quotients, (Iso)morphism, and Abstraction

We have seen that equivalence relations give rise to equivalence classes. Equivalence classes impose a structure onto a set, such as the structure of biological species onto the set of all animals, or the structure of emotions on the set of all images of human faces. Once we have divided the set of all animals into species, or the set of all images of human faces into emotions, we do not have to take individual differences between one horse and another horse into account if, for example, we want to study the difference between horse and cow.

A set that is subdivided in equivalence classes is called a *quotient*. For instance, let $U = \{0, 1, 2, 3, 4, 5\}$, and let $\sim$ be given as "has the same remainder when divided by 2," then the two equivalence classes $C_0 = \{0, 2, 4\}$ and $C_1 = \{1, 3, 5\}$ result. The set that has C_0 and C_1 as elements, which can be written as $\{\{0, 2, 4\}, \{1, 3, 5\}\}$, is the quotient that results from partitioning U over $\sim$. We write $U/\sim$. The difference between U and $U/\sim$ is that the latter not only tells us what the contents of U is, but it also reflects how the contents is lumped together as a result of the equivalence relation $\sim$. If $\sim$ would have the meaning "has the same remainder when divided by 3," we would find $U/\sim = \{\{0, 3\}, \{1, 4\}, \{2, 5\}\}$. Although U has the same elements in both cases, the elements of $U/\sim$ differ in dependence of the meaning of $\sim$. The quotient, or the grouping of equivalence classes of U, really reflects the structure that is induced by $\sim$. Let $U = \{\text{carrot, lemon, tomato, banana, mandarin}\}$, and let $\sim$ have the meaning "has the same color," then $U/\sim = \{\{\text{lemon, banana}\}, \{\text{tomato}\}, \{\text{carrot, mandarin}\}\}$. If $\sim$ means "has the same shape" (distinguishing round and oblong), we get $U/\sim = \{\{\text{lemon, tomato, mandarin}\}, \{\text{banana, carrot}\}\}$.

Now let us introduce two sets, the set of shapes $V = \{\text{round, oblong}\}$ and the set of colors $W = \{\text{yellow, orange, red}\}$. Then we can see that we can make a mapping between the elements of $U/\sim$ ($\sim$ in the meaning of "has the same shape") and V: $M = \{m_1, m_2\} = \{(\{\text{lemon, tomato, mandarin}\}, \text{round}), (\{\text{banana, carrot}\}, \text{oblong})\}$.

For clarity, we summarize: the mapping M is a set; its elements are pairs, say, $m_1 = (\{\text{lemon, tomato, mandarin}\}, \text{round})$ and $m_2 = (\{\text{banana, carrot}\}, \text{oblong})$; each pair associates (maps) one element from $U/\sim$ to one element from V, and the elements of $U/\sim$ are the equivalence classes induced by $\sim$ on the elements of U. All this is encoded in the various parentheses and braces in the definition of M. The mapping M is an example of a mapping between a quotient on a concrete set and a set of abstractions. Shape is an abstraction, for instance, "round" is the shared property of all round objects. These mappings happen all the time in perception: we observe things; we classify them on the basis of equivalence (variants) into the equivalence classes (invariants) in a quotient, and we conclude properties on the basis of a mapping of this quotient to another, abstract set. It is often more convenient to argue in the latter abstract set, in particular if there are suitable relations defined in this abstract set.

We clarify this with an example taken from NPR. Consider the set U consisting of a set of images of human faces (either photographs, photorealistic or non-photorealistic images), and the set V of different basic emotions. In psychology texts, six basic emotions are normally distinguished, so V has six elements. An equivalence relation $\sim$ on U is "according to a particular group of test subjects, shows the same emotion as," and in V we use the familiar equivalence relation denoted by $=$. Indeed, equality is an equivalence relation. Notice that V is equal to {happy, sad, angry, startled, . . .}, whereas $V/=$ is equal to {{happy}, {sad}, {angry}, {startled}, . . .}. This last distinction is not very useful, so we work with V rather than with $V/=$. The quotient $U/\sim$ is the set of equivalence classes, each equivalence class consisting of faces that show the same emotion according to our test subjects. Notice that $U/\sim$ does not necessarily have to have six elements. It could be, for instance, that none of the faces in U is looking happy, or that our test subjects decide that there are two varieties of happy faces. A relation G that can be defined on $U/\sim$ is the relation "looks more sympathetic than," which is again to be decided by our group of test subjects. So both $U/\sim$ and the relation G have to be established, in this case, by means of sociopsychological experiments. Notice that G is a transitive relation, in particular a so-called partial ordering.[3] Of course, this is no equivalence relation since it is not reflexive.

Now we introduce the mapping M, which attributes to every equivalence class face images showing their same *basic* emotion (which is an element of V). Of course, M has not to be 1 to 1: it could be that some elements of V map to multiple elements of $U/\sim$, and others map to no element of $U/\sim$. Conversely, every element of $U/\sim$ maps to precisely one element of V (because all elements of V are basic emotions, no two of them could be considered the same). Next, assume that the relation G maps to a relation onto the set of emotions, say, a relation called $\rightarrow$. The relation $\rightarrow$ should also be a binary operator, and it should also be transitive (hence, a partial ordering). The existence of a mapping between G and $\rightarrow$ is not guaranteed. Suppose that there are two equivalence classes in $U/\sim$ that both map to "sad," say, sad1 and sad2, and one equivalence class in $U/\sim$ that maps to "startled," say, startled. Next, assuming that sad1 is considered to look more sympathetic than startled, and startled is considered to look more sympathetic than sad2, we have the problem that the relation G ("looks more sympathetic than") cannot be mapped to the relation $\rightarrow$. On the one hand, we should have "sad"$\rightarrow$"startled," and at the same time we should have "startled"$\rightarrow$"sad." But let us assume that this problem does not occur, and indeed a consistency between

---

3. A partial ordering of a set is an ordering relation that does not have to apply to any pair of elements in the set.

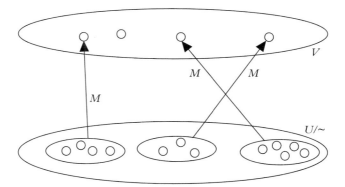

FIGURE 11.5 Mapping M between a quotient and an abstract set. Small circles in V denote basic emotions; small circles in $U/\sim$ denote elements of U (images of human faces). Ellipses in $U/\sim$ are the equivalence classes induced by "has the same emotion"; they form the elements of $U/\sim$.

G and $\rightarrow$ is found. If we have two sets (in this example, $U/\sim$ and V), each with a product operator relation defined on them (here G and $\rightarrow$), such that pairs according to the product operator in one set (here G) are mapped to a pair according to the associated product operator in the other set (here $\rightarrow$), we call this a *morphism*. If the mapping M is bi-jective (that is, for every element in V there is at most one element in $U/\sim$ that maps to it, and every element in $U/\sim$ maps to one element in V), it is called an *isomorphism*. In Figure 11.5, since M is probably not bi-jective, we do not have an isomorphism.

Let u_1 and u_2 be two elements of $U/\sim$, and v_1 and v_2 two elements of V. Then we see that morphism amounts to the scheme in Figure 11.6.

As we can see from the example, (iso)morphisms that result from mappings between quotients and abstract sets will turn out to be a very helpful tool to discuss images, meaning in images, and relations between the various images that, in some sense, hold the same meaning.

For instance, consider the example where we would like to draw a world map that is distorted in such a way that countries are drawn schematically as shapes (polygons) with an area that is proportional to their population—for instance, to study certain demographic properties. We could describe this problem in terms of sets, equivalence relations, and morphisms as follows:

- V is the set of all the countries we would like to consider.
- U is the set of all polygons.

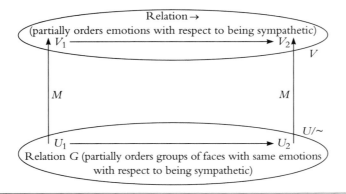

FIGURE 11.6 A morphism between $U/\sim$ and V that allows us to transpose relations from one domain to another, more abstract domain.

- An equivalence relation $\sim$ between two polygons could be "represents the borderline of the same country."

- An equivalence class (that would represent a country) would consist of all possible polygons that would be identified as a schematic representation of the shape of that country.

- The quotient $U/\sim$ is the set of all polygons, partitioned in collections of polygons that each represent one country (note that in this case, there definitely would be one very big equivalence class containing all polygons that represent no country at all).

- The relation G on elements of $U/\sim$ expresses "has larger area than."

- The relation $>$ on elements of V expresses "has larger population than."

- The (iso)morphism between V and $U/\sim$ is the implied semantics of the map.

Since our main topic is non-photorealistic rendering, where meaning has to be conveyed via images, we will constantly have to deal with equivalence, equivalence classes, and (iso)morphisms.

In the following, when we deal with the semantics of images, we will encounter expressions such as "from (image) A we conclude that B." This usually is indicative of the fact that A and B refer to sets, and there is some morphism between these sets. Consider the following example:

$$U = \left\{ \quad \right\}$$

$$V = \{3, 4, 5\}$$

Here we see a series of images (elements of U), and when inspecting U we will after a short while conclude that we see only 3-sided and 4-sided prisms, but no 5-sided prisms. This classification process can be modeled by assuming that we first apply an equivalence relation $\sim$ onto U, meaning "the same when viewed from a probably different 3D direction and ignoring different sizes." Under this equivalence relation, we find two equivalence classes, and the quotient $U/\sim$ contains two elements, namely, the set of 3-sided prisms and the set of 4-sided prisms. Next, we map each of these sets to the number of sides of the prisms in each set. This mapping is well defined, since all prisms in each of the sets in $U/\sim$ have the same number of sides by virtue of the equivalence relation $\sim$. We construct the morphism between $U/\sim$ and V, and we conclude that nothing maps to the element 5.

11.2.6 Summary of Mathematical Preliminaries

We have seen various devices to reveal the structure in sets. The structure within a set U is expressed by the *quotient* with respect to a (binary) equivalence relation, which itself is a subset of $U \times U$ that is symmetric, reflexive, and transitive. This equivalence relation gives rise to equivalence classes, and the collection of all equivalence classes forms the quotient, $U/\sim$. If a binary relation is symmetric, reflexive, and *almost* transitive, we call it a p-equivalence relation, and the associated concepts are p-equivalence classes and p-quotients. Under the assumption of a finite universe and some "characteristic" elements in the universe, we can construct a true equivalence relation out of the p-equivalence relation. If the universe is sufficiently "lumpy" (that is, there are saxophones and crocodiles but nothing in between), this equivalence relation introduces a quotient that is in many respects an adequate model of a classification. Equivalence relations serve to model the notion of *variants* in perception; equivalence classes serve to model *invariants* in perception. A second way to reveal the structure within U is by writing down the product table associated to a suitable product operator. This product table reveals the structure of the set with respect to that particular product operator.

The structure that is shared between two sets is expressed with (iso)-morphisms. For two sets U and V, each equipped with its own *product operation* (say, p and q, respectively subsets of $(U \times U) \times U$ and $(V \times V) \times V$), their individual structures can be reflected in the product tables of these operators. If a (bi-jective) mapping M can be found between the two sets such that $M(u_1pu_2) = (v_1qv_2)$, we say that there is an (iso)morphism between U and V. In many cases, one of the two sets will be a set of equivalence classes (say, cow, deer, tiger, and wolf) and the other set will be a set of abstract notions (say, herbivores and carnivores). Morphisms help us in arguing about deductions from the set of equivalence classes to the set of abstract notions (say, the rule that in common territories, herbivores should watch out for carnivores can be deduced from the fact that cow and deer are frequently being eaten by tiger and wolf, whereas this relation is not symmetric).

11.3 Physical Preliminaries: Communication via Light Rays

Visual perception forms a means of communication between human beings and their environment. If (part of) the environment is replaced by one or more images, information can still be regarded as being conveyed from the image to the viewer, and you can speculate that basically the same perception principles are at play. This still holds if the image is not generated by a photographic camera, but by a human being (an artist) or a software program running on a computer connected to a video screen. Therefore, in order to propose a reference model for visual communication, such that we can classify non-photorealistic rendering techniques and propose new ones, it is advisable to start looking at the key elements in the visual communication process: light rays, visual properties of the physical environment, and the eye–brain system.

Although our reasoning will be purely speculative, we will try to make it as reasonable as possible. We will state our assumptions explicitly. Very fundamental assumptions are as follows:

◆ Biological systems have evolved, from simple to complex, coarsely along the lines of natural evolution.

◆ The physical environment of this natural evolution has behaved largely the same as it does today.

◆ Natural evolution of neural systems is an optimization process where, with respect to data processing, the basic resources are time, memory, and connectivity (that is, the number of nervous cells to which information can be passed directly).

11.3.1 Physical Context

The evolution of higher animals has taken place over the last 10^8–10^9 years. During this period, it is assumed that Maxwell's laws did not change. Maxwell's laws model the propagation of electromagnetic fields through space and time. This propagation is governed by so-called partial differential equations of the form

$$\left(\frac{\partial^2}{\partial^2 x} + \frac{\partial^2}{\partial^2 y} + \frac{\partial^2}{\partial^2 z}\right) E(x, y, z, t) = c^{-2}\frac{\partial^2}{\partial^2 t} E(x, y, z, t) \tag{11.1}$$

Here $E(x, y, z, t)$ is a physical quantity (electric or magnetic field) that can vary as a function of time and space. Variations of these quantities are the information that is propagated by the equation. The general solution of this equation is a summation of all possible terms $E = E_0 \sin(k_x x + k_y y + k_z z - wt)$, where the vector $k = (k_x, k_y, k_z)$ is the so-called wave vector (the wavelength in a given direction) and w is a quantity called *frequency* (the number of oscillations per second). By substituting back into Equation(11.1), we find that $c^2|k|^2 = w^2$, where c is the speed of light. From the form of the solution follows that if a particular term E takes a certain value at a certain time t and a certain place (x, y, z), it takes the same value at all other time points t' and places (x', y', z') with $k_x x + k_y y + k_z z - wt = k_x x' + k_y y' + k_z z' - wt'$. This is the equation of a set of parallel planes, moving in the direction of k with speed c. The vector k and the frequency w depend on the initial conditions. In particular, it follows from symmetry considerations that with a unit pulse of E at $t = 0$, $(x, y, z) = (0, 0, 0)$, we get a superposition of these plane waves such that outgoing spherical waves result (Huygens's principle). The center, say, $(0, 0, 0)$, of these outgoing spherical waves will be called a *point light source*.

The information contained in a point light source is its color, which is light energy as it is distributed over the various w's. This distribution is called the *spectrum*. In all points p that are *visible* from a point light source S on a sphere with radius $r = |p - S| = ct$ we find the same values[4] E for the different frequencies w, and hence, the same spectra. Here, visible means that there is no opaque surface blocking the light between S and p. This spectrum is the information that is propagated. Hence the color is constant during the propagation—at least if no absorption occurs. Because of atmospheric conditions, however, there is some absorption of light energy. Low-frequency components are absorbed slightly more, and light that travels through the atmosphere over large distances turns to bluish-gray. The energy per square inch surface area also decreases since the same amount of light energy has to be emitted in all directions. If we call C_1 and C_2 the colors (spectra) at two different distances from S, both in the same direction, we see that there is a p-equivalence relation "almost the same color" between C_1 and C_2. This p-equivalence will be called "light ray attenuation equivalence," or LRA.

11.3.2 Detecting Light: Basic Principles of Viewing

The interaction between light and surfaces can be modeled such that every point of a surface that is either a light source or visible from another (point) light source acts as a point light source. Hence, the world around us is filled with a continuum of point light sources. As a result, in a given point p in 3D space, we get a superposition of the light information that has originated from a continuum of directions, each direction pointing to one point light source, distributed spherically around p. The color we receive in p is therefore the result of summing up all spectra of all point light sources that are visible from p. So we receive a mixture of all the colors that are present in the visible environment of p. In order to be able to distinguish one direction from another, and therefore to distinguish light from different regions, we have to be able to select on the basis of incoming light direction. Notice that this is not possible with just an array of light detectors adjacent to each other. In this case, every light detector will receive more or less the same information.

To study this problem a little better, we refer to Figure 11.7. Here, we have two different light sources, one with red light and one with green light. One detector seeing both of them would receive a mixture of both colors. Even if

---

4. We ignore the fact that E is a vector and hence has a direction. We are interested only in the information that is propagated by light rays. We do not study the precise way in which this information is encoded in the electromagnetic quantities.

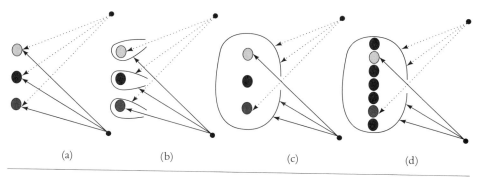

FIGURE 11.7 Different light detector strategies: every light detector sees incoming light of all directions, and multiple detectors all get the same information (a); if the detector is equipped with a collimator that restricts the directions of incoming light rays, multiple detectors can receive light from different directions, and hence can distinguish between different light sources (or different regions in the environment) (b); instead of one collimator per cell, we can also have one collimator for multiple cells (pupil) (c); if every cell does not have to have its own collimator, it can get closer together, hence give a better angular resolution (d).

we have multiple detectors, every detector will detect a mixture of both colors. But a simple device can overcome this problem. If every detector is equipped with a collimator that shields incoming light in all but a restricted part of spherical directions, the different detectors are capable of distinguishing the light information as it originates from different points in the environment. This is the way in which faceted eyes of insects work. Notice that all collimators have to be directed very accurately in a slightly different direction from their neighbors. Fortunately, the mechanically stable arrangement where the orientation of each collimator tube is the average of the orientations of its neighbors is also optimal from an optical point of view. So evolution did not have to cope with awkward compromises when developing the faceted eye.

Although a faceted eye can see spatial distributions of light, the resolution (the capability to distinguish colors from light that comes in from nearby directions) is limited. Indeed, for mechanical reasons, an insect's eye cannot be arbitrarily large. Because of the collimator that surrounds it, each light cell (detector) requires quite a large space—they cannot get too close together, and therefore, there is only room for a limited number. However, the same effect can be obtained if not every cell has its own collimator, but multiple cells share one collimator (the pupil in the eye of higher animals, or the pinhole in a camera obscura).

There is a strange side effect. Incoming light from below is detected by the topmost detector, and conversely. The image that is projected onto the retina that is, the collection of optical cells, is inverted! If the animal would have no other means for interrogating its environment than via optical means, this would not matter. But there are also senses (touch, sound, smell) that receive information that could (and should) correlate with the optical information. But tactile, sound, and smell information is not geometrically inverted. So it must have required a significant evolutionary effort to develop the required neural circuitry to cope with this inconsistency. Even stronger, if we assume that the single-pupil eye was preceded by the faceted eye, there is no way that— without the neural system to invert the image—the single-pupil eye had any advantage over the faceted eye. There is no way to gradually develop inverting systems: either an image is inverted or it is not. There is no smooth transition between non-inverting and inverting. If we assume that evolution works along paths of continuity, we can argue as follows. As long as the inverter is not operational, the single-pupil eye is worthless, and as long as the single-pupil eye is worthless (blind), evolution is not going to put effort in developing neural circuitry for correcting it. So we can provisionally conclude that it is likely that the single-pupil eye had developed separately from the faceted eye. But once a rudimentary single-pupil eye is functioning, it is clear that an increase of the resolution, simply by adding the number of optic cells in the retina, is immediately advantageous.

In the rest of our argumentation, we will consider only single-pupil eyes. We already have seen one p-equivalence relation that holds for 3D distributions of point light sources and their images on the retina. The emitted color of a point light source S and the color that is detected in the optic cell(s) p onto which S projects are almost the same, the (small) differences are caused by atmospherical absorption and the (significant) distance-related attenuation. Indeed, if someone lights a match in a 500-meter distance, we might be able to see the person because his or her body corresponds to a vast number of point light sources. But the visible area of the flame of his or her match is, at this distance, negligible. We can consider the flame a point light source. Therefore, the attenuation is proportional to $|p - S|^{-2}$, which is a direct result from Huygens's principle and energy conservation: the same amount of energy propagates to all subsequent spheres with increasing radii $r = ct$. Since the energy is distributed uniformly over each sphere, the energy density, that is, the energy per spherical angle, decreases inversely proportionally to the area of the sphere, or to r^{-2}.

There are quite a few further p-equivalence relations. Some have to do with geometry. The relation between a position of a point light source S and the position p on the retina onto which it projects is a mapping M. This mapping models the mechanism of the pupil. M depends on the position of the pupil, say, e, and the distance between the pupil and the retina, say, f. We assume that the retina is a plane with a normal vector k. Further, we complete k to an orthonormal basis (k, h, v) by introducing two normal vectors in the plane of the retina, h (defining the horizontal direction) and v (defining the vertical direction). Then, the mapping M can be derived from intersecting a line through S and e with the retina plane. We find

$$p_h = M_h S = f \frac{(S - e, h)}{(S - e, k)} \quad p_v = M_v S = f \frac{(S - e, v)}{(S - e, k)}$$

Here, (a, b) means the dot product of vectors a and b. The mapping produces the horizontal and vertical coordinates of the position on the retina that receive the projection of S. But it is not guaranteed that any cell will really be exactly at this position. Further, there is likely more than one cell activated at once, due to imperfections of the optical system and cross talk between adjacent optic cells. So the signal is actually sampled in some positions q, where $q_h = p_h + r_h$ and $q_v = p_v + r_v$. The vector r is a small random vector that causes an uncertainty in the interpretation of a detected color signal in q. This uncertainty means that there is a relation between various points p, p', p'', meaning "causes a color detection to take place in the same optic cell q." This relation is a p-equivalence relation, to be called "retina sample jitter" equivalence or RSJ. We will come back to it in the following.

A further equivalence relation is directly caused by the fact that a detector can be placed anywhere on a light ray. Apart from the LRA p-equivalence, all positions on the light ray carry the same information (provided that no occlusion occurs). Hence, for a given point p on the retina, there is a 1D set of possible points S that could have been the source of the detected color signal. All these points S have a relation, and this is an equivalence relation, to be called "light ray projection," or LRP equivalence. As a consequence of this projection, some additional equivalence relations and invariants have been extensively studied in projective geometry. We do not go into projective geometry here in a quantitative way; we merely give some qualitative results. First, there is an equivalence relation that we will call relative view position equivalence, or RVP. We have illustrated it in Figure 11.2. Depending on the position of the viewer, an illuminated cylinder can appear as in the left or the right image. Two 2D point sets are RVP equivalent if there is one 3D point set that can project on both of them by assuming different view positions. All parameters e, h, k, and v can be changed between these two view positions (here we assume the internal parameter f to be constant). So there is actually a 6-degrees-of-freedom family of possible projections (all orientations form a 3D set and all positions in 3D space form a 3D set; a view configuration consists of a position of the pupil and an orientation of the h, k, v-base). Projective geometry has studied the invariants under this equivalence relation. The most important invariants are incidence and double ratio. Incidence means that if two lines l and m intersect in a point p, then the images under varying projective views, l' and m', will intersect in a point p', which is the image under the same projective view of p. Similarly, for a line l that passes through two points p and q the image l' will under all projective views pass through the images p' and q' of p and q, respectively. Double ratio means to consider a line with four points, a, b, c, and d. Then we write $c = \lambda_0 a + \mu_0 b$; $d = \lambda_1 a + \mu_1 b$. This uniquely defines $\lambda_0 \dots \mu_1$. Now the double ratio $DR(a, b, c, d)$ is defined as $(\mu_0/\lambda_0)/(\mu_1/\lambda_1)$, and it can be proved that $DR(a, b, c, d)$ is a projective invariant. It stays the same from whatever direction we look at the line.

A next p-equivalence has to do with the interaction between the light of an incoming light ray and the light of a surface onto which this light ray reflects. A red piece of paper looks red in white light, but it looks almost black in green light. Still, it is the same piece of paper in both cases, and the apparent color differences form a p-equivalence relation. Under normal circumstances, the colors of incident light vary not so dramatically, and we deal with this relation again as a p-equivalence relation: to be called "proper surface color" p-equivalence, or PSC. So, two shades of green, observed from a field of grass at dawn (when the sunlight is bluish) and at sunset (where it may be reddish) are p-equivalent in PSC sense. For mirrorlike surfaces, this relation is not even a pseudoequivalence. The reflected light from a mirror takes hardly any information of the proper color of the mirroring surface. But even humans can sometimes be fooled by mirrors. Mirrors may lead to wrong conclusions about variants and invariants, and many magicians take advantages of this.

Also in the realm of color-related pseudoequivalences, we introduce the "shadow surface color" p-equivalence, abbreviated SSC, and the "incoming light direction" p-equivalence, ILD. Strictly speaking, they are both special cases of PSC, but they appear quite often in arguments about lighting circumstances as distinct phenomena. SSC is illustrated in Figure 11.8.

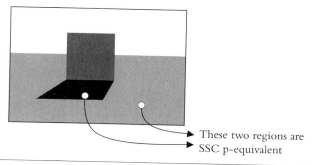

These two regions are
SSC p-equivalent

FIGURE 11.8 If a color C_1 transforms into a second color C_2 as a result of a shadow being cast, then the colors (and hence, the regions in which these colors are seen) are p-equivalent in SSC sense.

FIGURE 11.9 Five images that are p-equivalent in ILD sense.

The working of the ILD p-equivalence is illustrated in Figure 11.9. Further, the positions of highlights, which depend on the incoming light direction, are part of the ILD p-equivalence.

It goes without saying that in all but very specific cases, variants under the ILD, SSC, and PSC p-equivalences take place all together. Moreover, with a change of the viewpoint (a p-equivalence in RVP sense), the positions of highlights change, which gives rise to a variant in PSC sense.

The last p-equivalence class that is a direct result of the physics of light propagation is the "occlusion" p-equivalence, abbreviated OCC. We illustrate it in Figure 11.10. It often appears concurrent with p-equivalence in RVP sense, as is illustrated in Figure 11.11. The p-equivalence associated with the fact that the retina has a finite area, which means that the projections of objects can be clipped against the retina border (as illustrated in Figure 11.12), will be considered as a special case of OCC.

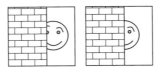

FIGURE 11.10 There is a p-equivalence relation in OCC sense between the smileys in the left and right image.

FIGURE 11.11 This form of OCC p-equivalence is related to parallax. We move to the left, and as a result of RVP p-equivalence, objects seem to move to the right. Their amount of movement depends on their distance, and different occlusion relations result.

FIGURE 11.12 Because of the finite size of the retina, a special case of OCC p-equivalence occurs for objects that are in the periphery of our field of view.

11.3.3 Summary of Viewing-Related (p-)Equivalence Relations

In the previous section, we have seen eight (pseudo-)equivalence relations that were directly caused by the physical properties of light. As we will see in the next section, for living beings to take advantage of visual communication, there have to be devices to form the (pseudo-)equivalence classes that are caused by these (p-)equivalences in order to distinguish variants and invariants. Before we discuss this, we summarize the (p-)equivalence relations, their causes, and their effects in Table 11.2.

There are, in fact, many more (p-)equivalence relations, for instance, the mechanism in human perception that recognizes faces. Someone can make a virtually infinite range of facial expressions. A nice example can be found on the back cover of a Paul McCartney and Wings album where each of the artists being photographed goes over some 20 rather extreme facial expressions. The equivalence relations here are not simply to be expressed in geometric terms.

Name	Abbre-viation	Equivalence (e) or p-equivalence (p)	Affects	Study together with
Light ray attenuation	LRA	p	Color and intensity	
Retina sample jitter	RSJ	p	Geometry (details)	
Light ray projection	LRP	e	Cannot distinguish an object shrinking or getting further away	RVP, OCC
Relative viewpoint	RVP	Special case: in the absence of occlusion, it is possible with two views to invert the projection, so to reconstruct the 3D relative positions. In that case, it is an equivalence relation. With one view, it is not possible, and RVP is at best a p-equivalence.	Shape (quantitative): angles and lengths are not constant; however, double ratio and incidences are invariant. Also qualitative: due to occlusions, some features may be invisible due to blocking (OCC).	LRP, OCC
Proper surface color	PSC	p (or not even p with very shiny surfaces)	Absolute color	SSC, ILD
Surface shadow color	SSC	p	Color differences in the shape of shadow patches	PSC, ILD
Incoming light direction	ILD	p	Relative intensity. With light shining from the left, the left part may seem brighter than the right part, and vice versa.	PSC, SSC
Occlusion	OCC	p	Arbitrary features may be missing.	LRP, RVP

TABLE 11.2 Summary of viewing-related (p-)equivalence relations.

The facial muscles apply complicated non-linear warps to the geometry of the skin. Nevertheless, this group of transformations has a distinct invariant: Paul McCartney stays Paul McCartney and Linda McCartney stays Linda McCartney. A skilled cartoon artist is capable of exploiting this invariant while taking the (p-)equivalence class to the limits.

More sophisticated equivalence relations result from more advanced physical, biological, or social mechanisms in our surrounding world. Human beings have developed into a physical, ecological, social, technical, and cognitive environment that behaves according to many invariants. The branch of philosophy called evolutionary epistemology assumes that the way our cognitive system works has been adapted, over the millions of years of evolution, to all these invariants. For instance, if I leave home in the morning, I may kiss my wife goodbye while she is still in her nightgown. When I get back in the evening, I expect to see her dressed in her regular daytime outfit, so despite the visual difference between these two outfits, they are equivalent in the sense that they generate perfectly normal variants within the class "the appearances of my wife during the day." (Even stronger, if I found her still in a nightgown when I get back home, I might assume that she has taken ill.) The same holds for the seasons' changes of trees and plants, the fact that sometimes my house is covered with snow and sometimes has all doors and windows open, though I still classify it as inhabiting the same category, namely, my house. Similarly, the very different appearances of a baby, a young child, a teenager, an adult, and an elderly person while all the time he is John Smith indicate the existence of very complex, but at the same time very natural, (p-)equivalence classes, and our cognitive system has become so much acquainted to these changes that we would be surprised if they would not occur.

As a conceptual simplification, we may model the neural processes underlying perception and cognition as being essentially similar, and in what follows we will use the same terminology to refer to both. An example where a conflict between a mainly perception-related p-equivalence relation and a p-equivalence relation of a much more sophisticated level occurs is exemplified in Figure 11.13.

At first, this image can be explained as being one extraordinary long dog behind a house, using the working of the OCC p-equivalence relation. Next, there is (probably) a p-equivalence relation associated to the class "dog" that causes an object to be classified as a "dog" if it can be transformed by means of a scaling transformation with a scale factor between (say) 0.5 and 2 from the default "dog." Let us call this p-equivalence relation DOG. According to this (p-)equivalence relation (together with the prototypical default), the observed object cannot be a dog. We can assume (using our model of perception and cognition that we propose in Section 11.5) that both p-equivalence relations associate to mental processes, in this case one in a relatively early stage (mainly perception related, namely, the OCC), and one in a later stage (mainly cognition related, namely, the DOG). Often a conflict between two interpretations at two different stages

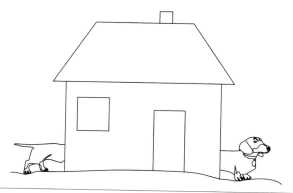

FIGURE 11.13   Illustration of the conflict between p-equivalence relations on different levels.

of mental processing gives rise to surprise, alienation, or laughter. As we will see later, many forms of non-naturalistic art as well as many cases of optical illusions can be directly related to p-equivalence relations, and you may speculate that this is not only true for the visual arts but also applies to non-strictly visual forms of mental processing.

However, as far as the topic of this book is concerned, we will focus on variants and invariants that relate to perception more than to cognition, and therefore we do not attempt to extend Table 11.2 with (p-)equivalence relations related to, for instance, the change of seasons, the growth of biological creatures,[5] or the social habit of wearing different clothes during the night and during the day. Most NPR practitioners do not take these variants into account either.

We have now already several times alluded to layered structures, both in mental processes (perception and cognition) and in our formal framework (connecting the semantic contents of layers by means of (iso-)morphisms). Let us try to carry this a bit further in Section 11.5, where we use the OSI model for data communication as a template for visual communication. However, for the mechanisms described

---

5. There is one well-known example where the anticipated variant due to biological growth directly affects our perception. Baby animals of most higher species have a relatively large forehead (due to the fact that in newborns, the brains are relatively far developed compared to the other body parts). At the same time, newborns are volatile and harmless and should receive protection by the adult individuals in the group more than grown-up individuals. Therefore, there is an almost irresistible affection to faces with a larger forehead compared to faces with a smaller forehead. Cartoon characters almost invariably make use of this phenomenon.

in this model to be at least a bit plausible, we have to go into some aspects of perception and cognition in neurological systems.

11.4 Neurobiological Context: Look-Ahead Sets and Look-Around Sets

A vast amount of literature exists on issues related to visual perception and perception-related cognition. It is certainly not our intention to summarize this material here. We also think that it may not be necessary for our purpose. Instead, we want to introduce a simple paradigm that should give sufficient support for our lines of reasoning. This is the notion of *look-ahead sets*.

The term *look-ahead set,* to be abbreviated as LAS (plural, LASses), is taken from the construction of compilers for computer languages; it is also not uncommon in linguistic studies. In a compiler or translator, the term *LAS* means the collection of given tokens (letters, symbols, words, and so on) that could occur as the next token in a given state. For example, suppose a computer language contains the construct (grammar rule)

IF (< condition >) THEN < statement1 > [ELSE < statement2 >];

where the terms in capitals refer to literally occurring strings of characters, and the terms in sharp brackets follow from further grammar rules. The term in rectangular brackets is optional. Then, after having recognized the word *IF*, the only meaningful character to follow can be a (. We say that in the state where the word IF has been recognized, the LAS equals a singleton (a set with only one element), namely, (. After having recognized the construct <statement1>, the LAS equals ELSE, ;, and so forth. We observe the following properties of LASses:

- In the case of a correct piece of text (that is, a piece of text that obeys the grammar rules of the compiler), in any state the next token is in the current LAS.

- The LAS is, in any state, typically much smaller than the set of all tokens that are recognized by the compiler. So restricting the search for matching to the LAS, apart from anything else, has significant efficiency advantages over exhaustive matching with all tokens.

- The collection of LASses in every state of the compiler, in some sense, reflects "everything that could occur" in a piece of text that is to be recognized by the compiler. All regularities of the language in which the pieces of text are written are reflected in the set of LASses.

- A LAS could easily be extended with a probability distribution, expressing the chance for each token to follow. For instance, in natural English, the LAS in the state where the most recently read tokens are "compi," the immediate LAS is "l", and if we look one step further, it is "la," "le," "li," respectively, for the words "compilation," "compilations," "compile," "compiled," "compiler," "compiles," and "compiling." If we have no further knowledge about the context (higher level semantics), the probabilities of "la," "le," and "li" therefore would be 2/7, 4/7, and 1/7, respectively. However, if we do have knowledge about the current state at a higher semantic level (for instance, because the grammar dictates that, if we are attempting to recognize a correct English sentence, we have to be in the process of recognizing a verb), the LAS reduces to "le" with 100% certainty. So LASses can co-exist at various semantic levels, and LASses at a higher semantic level could help reduce the size of LASses at lower semantic levels.

- Conversely, an "intelligent" compiler, that is, a compiler that should try to figure out what the LASses are of the language it should recognize, could attempt to acquire information about LASses using statistics. Indeed, this is the method that is used in various code-breaking techniques. In our context, we will call this process "learning." A compiler is fed with vast amounts of text fragments in a given (fixed) language, and it constructs the LAS statistics under way. For now, we do not make any allusions about the automatic occurrence of LASses at higher semantic levels, but it can be easily shown by experiments that a statistics-based set of LASses for a compiler to recognize words in any given natural language can be constructed in this way.

To summarize, LASses allow for more efficient recognition (that is, classification) of input patterns than exhaustive searching of the entire set of all possible input patterns. LASses tie in with the statistics of input patterns, and provided these statistics are sufficiently stable over time, LASses can be learned in an unsupervised manner. One way to put it is that to a compiler (or "classifying agent" or "recognizer"), the set of LASses represents the pool of patterns that it should recognize or classify.

Once a set of LASses is constructed that has shown to be adequate in a given environment (here the word *environment* refers to the set of input patterns that the classifying agent has to classify; the word *adequate* refers to the fact that the next token to be classified is with sufficient certainty in the current LAS), the

```
1   while (true) do
2     fetch new token t
3     q := undefined
4     bestmatchqualitythusfar := −∞
5     foreach possible input p
6       if (matchquality(t, p) > bestmatchqualitythusfar) then
7         q := p;
8         bestmatchqualitythusfar := matchquality(t, p);
9       fi
10    od
11    report found and recognized q
12  od
```

ALGORITHM 11.2   Strategy 1: exhaustive matching.

```
1   while (true) do
2     fetch new token t
3     q := undefined
4     bestmatchqualitythusfar := −∞
5     foreach possible input p in current LAS
6       if (matchquality(t, p) > bestmatchqualitythusfar) then
7         q := p;
8         bestmatchqualitythusfar := matchquality(t, p);
9       fi
10    od
11    update LAS on the basis of recognized q
12    report found and recognized q
13  od
```

ALGORITHM 11.3   Strategy 2: LAS-based matching.

process of classification can be further simplified. Indeed, we can distinguish three classification strategies:

1. exhaustive matching (see Algorithm 11.2),

2. LAS-based matching (see Algorithm 11.3), and

3. higher semantics LAS-based matching (see Algorithm 11.4).

We shall study these in turn.

```
 1   while (true) do
 2      fetch new token t
 3      q := undefined
 4      bestmatchqualitythusfar := 0
 5      foreach token p* in current highersemanticLAS do
 6         generate default input p out of p*
 7         if (matchquality(t, p) > bestmatchqualitythusfar) then
 8            q* := p*
 9            bestmatchqualitythusfar := matchquality(t, p)
10         fi
11      od
12      update highersemanticLAS on the basis of recognized q*;
13      report found and recognized q*
14   od
```

ALGORITHM 11.4   Strategy 3: higher semantics LAS-based matching.

In order to assess the match quality between t and p, the function matchquality (t, p) should take into account all the variants ((p-)equivalence relations) that belong to the semantic level of the input tokens. On the other hand, it should focus only on the invariants that belong to that level. If, for instance, we take the p-equivalence relation LRA (see Section 11.3.3) into account, we know that we do not have to attempt to assess the precise color since it may have turned a bit bluish gray because of atmospheric attenuation. But at this semantic level, the shape would be an invariant. In the example of compilers, the distinction between variants and invariants could amount to ignoring the difference between capitals or lowercase characters, tabs or redundant spaces. In the more interesting case of visual recognition, the equivalence relations depend on the semantic layer we are currently studying (in Section 11.5 we propose a reference model for such semantic layers in visual communication). For now we give as an example that an equivalence relation might be that straight lines of different thickness are to be considered equivalent, and therefore to check if t is a straight line (as opposed to, for instance, a circle). The function matchquality(t, p) should be resistant against the difference in thickness between p and t.

In the next strategy, we replace the set of all possible input tokens by a current LAS. The LAS is thought to have the structure of a quotient, either obtained from true equivalence relations, or by upgrading from p-equivalence relations under the assumption of a finite set of input patterns and sufficient defaults. The function matchquality(t, p) has to take the allowed equivalence relations of the current LAS into account. This strategy is clearly more efficient than the first strategy, provided that

- LASses are not too large,
- taking the equivalence relations into account is not too expensive,
- LASses are adequate with respect to our environment, and
- updating a LAS is not too complicated.

The efficiency of this second strategy is largely determined by the efficiency of dealing with the equivalence relations associated to the current LAS and the number of elements in that LAS. As we have seen in our example with natural language recognition, the migration to a higher semantic level might bring a significant reduction, both of the size of the LASses involved and their associated (p-)equivalence relations. For instance, the number of words in an average natural language is $O(10^5)$–$O(10^6)$, but the number of word categories (verbs, nouns, and so on) is only $O(10^1)$–$O(10^2)$. First assessing which word category we may expect (based on the quotient structure of a higher-level semantic LAS) significantly reduces the size of the LAS on the lower semantic level. In visual context, the number of distinct polygons (triangle, quadrilateral, pentagon, hexagon, and so on) is by far less than the number of different ways a triangle (quadrilateral, pentagon, and so on) could be drawn into a raster image. The following strategy makes use of this fact by performing the actual matching not at the semantic level of the current token t, but at a higher semantic level.

In the third strategy, we still have the disadvantage of a complicated matching function (because of the large and complicated set of equivalence relations in the lower semantic level LAS), but we have the advantage of only using elements p^* of a higher semantic LAS to perform the match with. An obvious variation of strategy 3 would therefore be to also do the matching between elements of the semantically higher quotient. This, however, requires "lifting" t to the higher semantic level—and that would confront us with a chicken-egg problem since the entire purpose of matching is to classify things. We conclude the overview of matching strategies with the following remarks:

- Strategy 3 does not necessarily need to be restricted to one higher semantic level: we can also conceive strategies where we bring in multiple higher semantic LASses at the same time. We even propose that the classifications as reported by the various (simultaneous) versions of strategy 3 should occur at the same time. We see that a drawing represents a triangle (and not a quadrilateral) and that its lines are curved (and not straight) and of unequal width (instead of equal width), and so on.

- When using either strategy 2 or 3, we might find that the reported q (or q^*) does not give a satisfyingly high value for the best match quality. That might be a trigger for extending the LASses of the various involved levels with a new characteristic element ("default"), and applying the already existing (p-)equivalents to generate an associated equivalence class to it. This could be called learning.

- We notice that strategies 2 and 3 as they are given here (so without the option for extending LASses) will produce meaningful (seemingly recognized) outputs even if the token t did not occur in any of the involved LASses. We can even imagine a scenario where a sequence of input tokens t is offered to the algorithm that are purely random. The internal sequence of states of the recognizer, as they are characterized by the subsequent LASses, generated by the internal "update LAS" steps in the algorithms, still would make sense. Indeed, they would correspond to a "synthesized" series of environments that would resemble a sequence of environments that at least locally would be consistent. You could call this "dreaming." The recognizer does not receive its input tokens from a true, physically existing dynamic environment, but it still goes through a sequence of state transitions (a sequence of LASses at various semantic levels) that seems to have some local consistency (due to the update from one LAS to the next, where every individual update would make sense in a truly occurring sequence of environments). Global consistency, of course, does not have to occur. In a non-dreaming situation, the experienced global consistency comes from the (assumed) consistency of the offered input tokens.

- The matching process is described here as a sequential linear search. It is neither necessary that the search is linear nor that it is sequential. Dropping the first assumption would give rise to alternative scenarios where statistics comes in. Check plausible elements p or p^* first, and stop as soon as a sufficient high best match quality has been obtained. This scenario could model a type of mistakes that, for instance, occur in young children that have not fully mastered reading. They conclude having read a particular word upon recognition of the first few characters of that word, which may be wrong. Dropping the assumption of sequential search gives rise to a slightly broader definition of LAS that is particularly useful in visual communication: instead of a look-ahead set, we can just as well consider a "look-around set," consisting of elements (equivalence classes) that can be expected in nearby regions of the visual field, instead of nearby temporal instants. When we come to discuss the (p-)equivalence relations such as introduced in Table 11.2, we will see that most of these follow quite naturally from the LAS model when interpreted as look-around sets.

Of course, we do not claim that perception and cognition in biological systems take place in the form of (variants of) strategies 1, 2, or 3. Neither do we claim that somewhere in the brain or the nervous system such things as LASses really occur. Even stronger, until a couple of years ago (we started thinking of this model around 1996) we would not even dare publicly speak or write about it, afraid of being ridiculed by the neurological community. There are a number of reasons that we dare to do it now.

◆ Our model only has to serve in arguing about (algorithms for) NPR. It does not have to be true (see our observations in Section 11.1), as long as it is relevant or comprehensible. It should only inspire to novel NPR techniques or NPR–related experiments. It seems that an approach in terms of variants and invariants, enhanced with the model of semantic layers of visual communication as we will introduce it in Section 11.5, is convenient because it simplifies the terminology.

◆ Our model seems not inconsistent with the ideas of Igor Aleksander (1996), in particular as far as the occurrence of dreaming is considered, but also learning, classification, and various types of mistakes follow both from his model and ours. In Alexander's work, however, a much more reductionistic view is developed as he departs from neural network models.

◆ As we will see, we no longer need to make a distinction between perception and cognition. There is just one stack of semantic layers where representation transformations occur that preserve invariants and exploit variants in order to achieve classification. Each layer has its own (p-)equivalence classes and defaults, and as a result, each layer can be described in principle as a quotient structure (more about this stack in Section 11.5).

- If we assume that biological evolution aims to optimize efficiency, we can see why a progression from strategy 1 to strategy 2 (the introduction of LASses), and next a step from 2 to 3 (introducing LASses from different semantic levels) would be a possible way to go.

- Our thinking is consistent with various forms of optic illusions and non-naturalistic painting (we will say more about optic illusions and non-naturalistic painting in Section 11.5 since these topics are closely related to NPR). For now, we refer to well-known phenomena from perception psychology: seeing faces in clouds and (under poor illumination conditions) in abstract patterns (for example, wallpaper in children's bedrooms is known to develop faces of witches and monsters). These phenomena, known as "gestalt," can be related to our scenarios 2 and 3 if the token t is really not in any of the LASses and just one of the defaults, q or q^*, is reported to have been recognized. Notice that the gestalt phenomenon in these forms seems to occur predominantly in states of reduced concentration: maybe concentration helps to enforce (guard?) global consistency of the sequence of LAS updates.

- The way to argue, in our model, about the connection between the LASses of various semantic levels is in terms of (iso)morphisms. This is convenient since this is also the language to use in formally specifying computer programs and designing experimental setups for validating, for example, the comprehensibility or equivalence of various NPR styles.

11.4.1 Perceptual Context

In terms of the LAS model that we presented in the previous section, we now give a brief discussion of some of the (p-)equivalence relations from Section 11.3.3. In the last years, much experimental research has been done on the mechanisms of early vision processing in the retina, the optic nerve, and the first couple of visual synapses in the pathways between the eye and the visual cortex. Without going into many technical details, we summarize some salient features of this system.

We start by observing that we assess relative brightness rather than absolute brightness. Indeed, consider the image in Figure 11.14.

Despite that the small rectangles have all the same absolute luminance, they appear increasingly bright due to increasingly darker backgrounds when going from left to right. To understand this, way may conjecture that our sense for absolute brightness is deduced from relative brightness that is obtained earlier in

FIGURE 11.14 Absolute versus relative brightness.

the vision system. A simple model for obtaining relative brightness from readout values in retina cells is to assume a second layer of neurons, immediately behind the retina cells, that compute the differences in small groups of adjacent retina cells. Such neurons will be called *operators*, mathematically speaking they behave as differential operators or (in a discrete view) finite difference operators of various kinds: directional derivatives in various orientations as well as (more or less) isotropic operators. Microscopic studies of the retina have revealed that these connections indeed exist in terms of appropriate interconnections of second-layer neurons and retina cells. A directional derivative in direction v is the operator $(v \cdot \nabla)$, and an example of an isotropic operator is $D = (\nabla \cdot \nabla)$. Here, ∇ is the operator $(\partial/\partial x, \partial/\partial y)$ and $(\cdot)$ is the dot product of two vectors. A minor variation to ∇, say, ∇^*, defined as the so-called logarithmic derivative $\nabla^* I = \nabla \log(I) = \nabla I/I$ (where I is the luminance, $I = I(x, y)$), explains the invariance for global changes in the luminance. If the luminance is globally multiplied by a constant factor, $I' = fI$, with f constant, we get $\nabla^* I' = \nabla^* I$. This not only implements parts of the p-equivalence relations LRA, PSC, and SSC, it also makes better use of the limited dynamic range of nerve cells. Indeed, the absolute difference between maximal brightness (say, direct sunlight) and nearly absolute darkness would require a signal range of many orders of magnitude. Using the logarithms brings this down to a much more modest variation. With a given dynamic range of the firing values of neurons, this allows a much more fine-grained distinction of (relative) luminance values. Further, we observe that difference operators implement the LAS that corresponds to the semantically lowest level (here, LAS is intended to mean look-around set). Indeed, in those regions where the output of the difference operators vanishes, we can conclude that the value in one retina cell exactly predicts those of its neighbors. A further type of connection that has been experimentally verified in the retina is that of

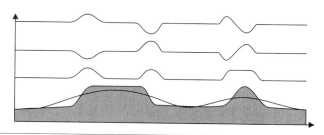

FIGURE 11.15 Schematic representation of a 1D luminance distribution and the result of some operators.

the (directional) averaging operator. It can be regarded as the opposite of the (directional) derivative operator. It does not fire in response to the difference of retina cells, but in response to the equality of retina cells. In our jargon, this implements part of the RSJ p-equivalence relation. In the schematic image in Figure 11.15, we give a one-dimensional luminance distribution, and we depict the output of the directional derivative in the x direction, the directional derivative in the $-x$ direction, the isotropic derivative (second derivative), and the averaging operator. If we assume the retina cells to be uniformly distributed, the working of the three operators can be described as a convolution with footprints, respectively, $(1, 0, -1)$, $(-1, 0, 1)$, $(-1, 2, -1)$, and $(0.25, 0.5, 0.25)$ (in Figure 11.15, these are the curves from top to bottom).

Since isotropic operators are (in good approximation) invariant for rotations, they implement part of the RVP equivalence relation. However, although their output value may be invariant under rotations and other 2D geometric transformations associated to LRP and RVP, the region of the retina where they report geometric singularities still varies. No local operators are able to achieve these invariants, so in order to explain how the geometric part of the LRP and RVP equivalences can be obtained, we have to look a bit more in detail. The key observation seems to be that repeated application of averaging is capable of producing a so-called scale space version of the retina's luminance distribution. A scale space is a series of images of a given input image at increasingly reduced scale. In Figure 11.16, we give an example of a scale space of a character K.

This example was obtained by repeatedly applying two anisotropic versions of the averaging operator. It can be shown that by superimposing various scaled copies of an image, an approximation of its so-called Fourier transform can be

FIGURE 11.16 Scale space for the character K.

obtained. The Fourier transform $F(I)$ of an image I is a mathematical quantity that has the property that when applying translation or rotation or scaling to I, for example, $I' = T(I)$, the Fourier transform is replaced by the Fourier transform multiplied by a complex number: $F(T(I)) = cF(I)$. In a similar way as the logarithmic derivative was capable of dealing with the effect of a global (real) multiplication factor of the luminance distribution, variants of the logarithmic derivative can eliminate these complex multiplication factors, and again we obtain invariants. The combined working of the Fourier transform together with the post-processing to obtain rotationally invariant representations is called the Fourier-Mellin transform, and it is considered not unlikely that the neural processing in the early visual pathway is similar to this transform. The invariants obtained by the Fourier-Mellin transform are (in reasonable approximation) part of the invariants associated with LRP and PSC. It is likely that operators, associated with further details of the LRP and RVP equivalence relations, require more advanced processing of neural networks higher up in the visual pathways.

We continue our short introduction in the perception of shape and the associated invariants with an example of how the working of some of the mechanisms, related to eliminating (p-)equivalence relations, can directly cause perceivable, visual sensations. First, consider Figure 11.17. We observe two rectangles (Figure

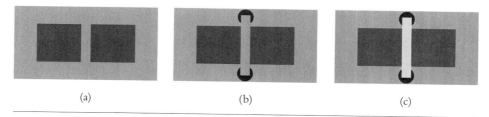

FIGURE 11.17 Subjective shapes: classification takes place without OCC involved (a), classification is simplified due to OCC causing a subjective rectangle to appear (b), and the subjective rectangle has been emphasized (c).

11.17(a)), and these are perceived as two isolated objects. Next, we add the two circular-shaped objects (Figure 11.17(b)), and suddenly the operator responsible for eliminating the OCC variants comes into play and generates the default (the characteristic prototype) of an object that is not at all present, but that can be explained by following strategy 3. Indeed, assuming the presence of the light-colored rectangle, as in Figure 11.17(c), makes classification of the four shapes in the second image easier, and apparently our visual system prefers the introduction of so-called *subjective shapes* (shapes that are perceived but do not really exist) if that can facilitate classification at other semantic levels.

The next example shows that the processes related to the LRP and RVP equivalence relations may force us to interpretations that are inconsistent with OCC. Consider the seemingly normal perspective drawing of a house (Figure 11.18(a)). As soon as we add windows, in Figure 11.18(b), the process that accounts for the LRP and RVP equivalence relations forces us into an interpretation where the OCC equivalence is violated. It looks as if the front and right walls of the house are transparent with respect to the windows! This inconsistency is accepted rather than an interpretation that is fully consistent both with LRP and RVP, *and* with OCC, but that would lead to an interpretation where the windows are not aligned with the horizontal and vertical sides of the walls. Indeed, an architect could have decided to plan windows as indicated in the two subsequent images— but rather than accepting this, our visual system overrides the OCC equivalence process.

As a last example we show that simple interpretations sometimes can enforce violation of equivalence. Considering Figure 11.19, we would rather interpret the arrangement of the cubes as representing an impossible figure (similar to the so-called Penrose triangle, shown in Figure 11.19(b)), than accept an interpretation

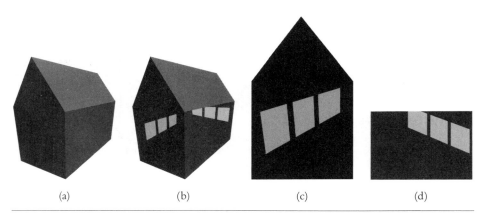

(a) (b) (c) (d)

FIGURE 11.18 Interpretation of occlusion: perspective image of a house (a), image that is interpreted as a house with missing walls (b), unconventional window layouts (c) and (d).

where the cubes are glued together in a manner such that incident faces only overlap for one quarter (which is in fact a construction to really *build* this object!). In this case, our visual system assumes that line segments that are on the same line in 2D also should be on the same line in 3D. This assumption can clearly be seen to be part of the OCC-related system: indeed, because of occlusion, lines can appear to be broken, but in reality they should be interpreted as being one line. This "trick" helps us out in many OCC-related cases, so it is considered so fundamental to our visual system that it is even applied where this would lead to inconsistent interpretations at higher semantic levels. The OCC-related mechanism escapes conscious control, indicating that it takes place in an early stage of the visual pathway.

Because of an "overenthusiastic" OCC-related process, Figure 11.19(a) is mistakenly interpreted as a "sort of" partially fragmented Penrose triangle (Figure 11.19(b)). The latter, however, is fundamentally inconsistent (cannot correspond to the projection of a solid 3D object), whereas the left figure is perfectly consistent with an arrangement of nine cubes, stuck face-to-face to each other.

After we have dealt with a layered model of the various semantic layers that can be thought of to be involved in visual processing, we give some more examples of optic illusions and non-naturalistic painting styles that can be related to the hidden working of neural processes, analogous to strategy 3, that aim at exploiting (p-)equivalence relations.

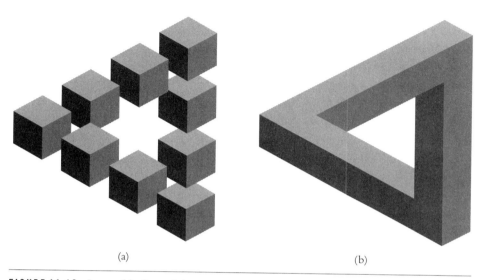

(a)   (b)

FIGURE 11.19 Impossible figures? An arrangement of cubes that can be realized in 3D but that would require all pairs of adjacent cubes to be nonaligned (a). This arrangement would result in the need for a non-consistent 3D interpretation by the viewer, and a non-existing 3D object (b).

11.5 A Model for Visual Communication

Long before the advent of computers, information was communicated via mechanical or electronic means. Alexander Graham Bell's invention is only one example in a vast range. With computer technology, there was a rapid increase in algorithms and protocols for *coding* and *decoding* information from one format into another. Coding and decoding refer to forms of transformation where certain characteristics of the processed information are kept, whereas others are changed. We could call the maintained aspects of information the *invariants* of the (de-)coding process, and the aspects that are changed the *variants*. The notions of equivalence classes, and of isomorphisms that we introduced earlier, again apply to the process of (de-)coding. For instance, consider Morse coding. In traditional Morse coding, no difference is made between capitals and lowercase letters, so the message SOS and sos are *equivalent*. In fact, the equivalence class with default sos is *SOS, SOs, SoS, Sos, sOS, sOs, soS, sos*. The coded version of this message

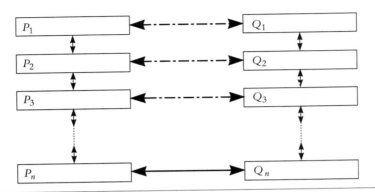

FIGURE 11.20 Simplified view of the OSI model for data communication.

is $\cdots -- - \cdots$, but again, there is an equivalence relation here because the absolute duration of a dot and a dash can vary; dots as well as dashes each are in a p-equivalence class defined by "has about the same length as," that can be made into a true equivalence class by introducing the default dot of (say) 0.2 second and the default dash of (say) 0.6 second, and next applying Algorithm 11.1 (Section 11.2.4). A hybrid here would be of duration 0.4 second, and every telegrapher is trained to avoid these hybrids. So we see two representations that carry the same semantic bearing, both in the form of a quotient structure, and an (iso-)morphism between them. Indeed, for a trained telegrapher, the message $\cdots -- - \cdots$ will cause the same flush of adrenaline as the message SOS for a layperson. This similarity with respect to the production of adrenaline is the iso-morphism, tying the representations together. When computer communication caused the increase of protocols for coding and decoding—in association with more and more complex sets of variants, invariants, and morphisms to connect them—the idea of a *layered structure* was born. This is the so-called OSI model, and it is extensively described elsewhere (see Tanenbaum, 1998). Schematically, it can be depicted as in Figure 11.20.

Since we do not go into the details of the OSI model here, we will not explain what the precise meaning of the boxes $P_1 \ldots Q_n$ is. We only mention the most salient features of the model.

There are two communicating agents, P and Q, that exchange messages with certain semantics, that is, the invariants of that message. Box P_1 contains the original message. In fact, box P_1 can be seen as a quotient structure on all the messages that can be represented, where the collection of various messages that carry the same meaning (semantics) is one element, namely, the equivalence class generated by the equivalence between all messages that have that same semantics. As an example, suppose that the communication structure is set up to convey subject–verb–object sentences, and the possible subjects could be "John," "Peter," or "Mary"; the possible verbs could be "paints," "bakes," or "buys"; and the objects could be "the floor," "a sausage," and "a new suit." Then the sentences "My friend John paints the floor of his room" would have the same semantics as "Mr. J. colors the ground part of his apartment." The equivalence class associated to "subject" is $P_1 = \{$John, my friend John, Mr. J., Johnnie, . . .$\}$. In box P_2 is another representation of the message that again can be represented by a quotient structure, and the relation between P_1 and P_2 is an isomorphism such that the semantics (the invariants) of the contents of P_1 are preserved. The arrow between P_1 and P_2 is a process that transforms you representation into the other. Finally, the message has been subsequentially transformed in a number of steps until the format is suitable for physical transfer. This can be in the form of any means that is understood by boxes P_n and Q_n. Finally, by means of a number of isomorphisms between the boxes Q_i, $i = 1 \ldots n$, the message is transformed (preserving the invariants and making efficient use of the freedom offered by the variants) until the format is understandable (or serves any other purpose) in Q. Notice that the actual communication takes place only between P_n and Q_n. Nevertheless, you could *pretend* that communication takes place between any P_j and Q_j, $j > n$.

In the original OSI model, communication is assumed to be bi-directional. For visual communication, this is not the case. Our eyes work as one-way communicators only, and so does the rest of our visual system. Similarly, a computer graphics rendering pipeline (be it photorealistic or not) is a one-way device. This significantly simplifies the communication model. This one-way version of the OSI model will serve as a blueprint for our model of *visual* communication in Section 11.5.1.

11.5.1 Layers and Semantic Transformations in Visual Communication

For our purpose, we propose a model with nine layers. In the diagram in Figure 11.21, which will serve as our reference model for the semantic layers in visual communication, the top-level information transfer is indicated by T_{18}.

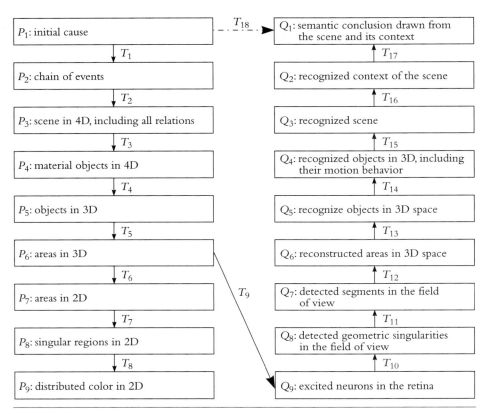

FIGURE 11.21 The layered model of data communication applied to visual communication.

However, it actually is the combined effect of transformations (morphisms) $T_1 \ldots T_5$ and $T_9 \ldots T_{17}$, where only T_9 is the optical communication via light rays. First, we explain the process steps $P_1 \ldots P_9$ in Table 11.3 and $Q_9 \ldots Q_1$ in Table 11.4 by means of an example; next, we describe the transformations.

Most transformations, in particular those in the lower regions of the Q-stack ($T_{10} \ldots T_{12}$) can be related to the equivalence classes introduced in Section 11.3. For example, at level T_{10} we can see the p-equivalence relation RSJ in action. In order not to be confused by the jitter due to the discrete distribution of retina cells, we assume that we have developed neural "correction hardware." In this case, cells near the LAS, associated with one optic cell receiving a color, may very well

	Interpretation	Some invariants	Some variants
P_1	A week ago, I bought an expensive Chinese vase and put it on top of a cabinet in my office so that everybody could have a good look at it.	"I," "expensive," "on top of"	"about a week ago," "cabinet"
P_2	Because of construction work going on near the office building, there is heavy traffic. Small vibrations in the ground propagate through the walls and the floors, and make the cabinet tremble slightly. The cumulated effect of all this, however, is that the vase has moved to the rim of the cabinet and now topples over.	"vibrations," "topples over"	"due to construction work," "through the walls and floors"
P_3	A falling Chinese vase that goes through a complicated trajectory due to the combined effects of gravity, the inertia of the solid object, air friction, and a first light collision with the side of the cabinet.	"gravity," "inertia," "collision"	"side of"
P_4	The relevant objects are the cabinet, the ground floor, and the Chinese vase. At this very instance, the cabinet and the floor are not moving, and the vase is taking part in a rotation around a given point P with a given axis A and a translation over a given vector T. Notice the parameters of this so-called rigid motion, i.e., P, A, and T themselves depend on time, and at the next time point they will be different. All this is described by suitable evolution equations.	P, A, T and all relevant objects	The time dependence of P, A, and T
P_5	If we only consider a static description of the situation, we have the cabinet and the floor in their usual positions and orientations, and the Chinese vase in a somewhat peculiar position and orientation.	All relevant objects, their positions and orientations	"peculiar"
P_6	The outside of the vase consists of, say, 12 piecewise smooth surfaces with given reflectivity (due to the glaze) and texture; moreover, there is a shadow of the cabinet on some of these surfaces. Each of these surfaces can be seen as a collection of light sources (as described in Section 3.1). All these light sources emit light rays in all directions in the hemisphere of directions above the surface. However, by far most light rays cannot contribute to the visual communication because they are not directed to the pupil of the observer.	All surfaces that are visible from the viewpoint of the viewer; shadows and textures	All surfaces that are not visible from the viewpoint of the viewer

TABLE 11.3 Example to clarify the proposed model *(continued)*.

Interpretation		Some invariants	Some variants
P_7, P_8, P_9	P_7, P_8, and P_9 normally don't refer to physical processes. However, they can be brought into correspondence with the layers Q_7, Q_8, and Q_9 in the stack of representation transformations on the side of the receiving agent (the viewer), therefore we include them in the stack of representation transformations of the sender (the object that the viewer is watching). Moreover, in a computer graphics model (either photorealistic or non-photorealistic), they are typically included, and the associated transformations $T_6 \ldots T_8$ correspond with meaningful classes of computer graphics algorithms.		

TABLE 11.3   *(continued)*

receive the same color. Having these LASses available in the early vision process means that one LAS represents the part of continuous color distribution, to be projected on the retina, which is consistent with the various patterns of adjacent optic cells that report the detection of a certain color. So, the p-equivalence class associated with a small collection of adjacent firing optic cells is in fact the collection of all continuous color distributions that could have given rise to the observed firing pattern. All further conclusions (distinctions between variants and invariants) are based on this equivalence class, not on the individual cell readings anymore.

This mechanism allows us to replace a continuous color shade by a stochastic stippling. At the lowest level of firing patterns of optic cells, these will be different in response; the produced equivalence class, however, will be the same, and we are willing to believe that the pattern should be interpreted as a continuous color distribution. If we force ourselves, we can "see" through the stack of subsequently lower and lower semantic contents (as we mentioned in Section 11.4, we can think of executing strategy 3 with various semantic layers in parallel, including low levels). We cannot help getting our interpretations immediately from the higher levels, and drawing a conclusion, "aha, this is a smoothly curved surface that is part of the back plate of a grass hopper" before we see "oh by the way, it was rendered using stippling, and oh by the way, it is actually a 2D projection, and oh by the way, the colors are really those of black toner on white paper,

	Interpretation	Some invariants	Some variants
Q_9	Every color-sensitive retina cell receives a color spectrum and samples it in three quantities.	Relative luminance, rough color distribution	Spectral energy distribution, precise location
Q_8	Cells along the visual pathway report local extremes in luminance, saddle points, contour lines, and dominant directions of texture.	Parallelism, periodicity, incidences	Orientation, distance and absolute position, number
Q_7	Segments that correspond to projected visual portions of surfaces of the Chinese vase, shadow regions are "automatically" attributed to the segment they belong to.	Proper color distribution due to the texture	Shadow borders
Q_6	A representation of the spatial shape of the surfaces that project onto the segments in Q_7. Occlusions are resolved, perspective distortions are adequately interpreted (so despite the fact that, due to the apparent non-rigid movement of the shape of the 2D segments, we conclude that the shape of the 3D surfaces is only subject to translation and rotation).	The current 3D shape of the perceived surface	Silhouette borders (indeed, the perception of a silhouette border depends on the position of the viewer)
Q_5	The Chinese vase in its current position and orientation.	The Chinese vase, the fact that it is not in a stable upright position	Its reflection into the shiny cabinet window
Q_4	The Chinese vase in its current state of motion.	Its global speed	The lack of perceived sharpness due to motion
Q_3	A falling Chinese vase that soon will collide with the ground.	Its collision course	The internal centrifugal forces due to the rotation of the vase
Q_2	A falling Chinese vase that soon will shatter due to a collision to the ground.	The prospective damage that will occur	The number of fragments that it will break into
Q_1	I was stupid putting the expensive vase in a high position.	My feeling bad about the accident	Insurance may be paying for the damage

TABLE 11.4 Example to clarify the proposed model.

and . . . ." For the stippling artist (or algorithm), it has to be such that the correct equivalence class is generated as a result of the stipples.

In Table 11.5, we present three versions of all the layers in our model: one from a physical point of view, one from a point of view of "photorealistic rendering (PR)," and one from a point of view of "non-photorealistic rendering (NPR)." Now we should treat the notion "(non-)photorealistic rendering" in a liberal way. Of course, the levels P_1 up to and including P_5 do not have anything to do with rendering. There we interpret the abbreviation (N)PR as "(non-)physical realization."

In general, to each of the transformation steps $T_1 \ldots T_8$, an algorithm or a procedure could be attributed (either physical, physically based modeled, or non-physically based modeled); to each of the semantic levels, P_1 up to and including P_9, a data representation can be attributed. For the layers Q_9 up to Q_1, we could do similarly, but then we embark onto the field of image processing and image understanding, where the distinction between PR and NPR loses its meaning.

After the transition from the external, objective representation layers of reality to the internal, perceived representation layers, the distinction between photorealistic and non-photorealistic representations vanishes. In the layers in Table 11.6, we only give the physical processes as they may occur in the human perceptive system, and the analogous computer algorithms.

In the image in Figure 11.22, we classify the various types of singularities in a static configuration. Of these singularities, we indicate their cause and their dimension. For simplicity, we leave out color information here. The depicted configuration consists of a rectangular block B with a rectangular patch P of different color on the top face, and two cylinders. The left cylinder L is attached to the top face of B, and the right cylinder is at some distance above B. The entire configuration is illuminated with a point light source. The numbers in the image refer to 1D singularities (lines or curves) of various kinds. Notice that various lines classify in more than one category. Some (but not all) 0D singularities (points) are indicated by lowercase letters. For the 1D singularities, we get the categories in Table 11.7.

In Table 11.7, C^0 refers to discontinuities ("jumps"), and C^1 refers to discontinuous derivatives (creases or folds). The latter can be convex or concave. C^∞ means that the discontinuity does not result from any shape singularity, the surface can be infinitely smooth, that is, all derivatives exist, but the line results from a discrete jump in optic qualities. In computer graphics, this is often modeled with texture mapping. Some of the 0D singularities are indicated. Most often

	Reality	Photorealistic (PR)	Non-photorealistic (NPR)
P_1	The Big Bang?	Some historical state that denotes the starting point of a simulation, a film, a story, or a documentary account by any other medium, from whereon the course of events is assumed to follow by causal relations. This may be on a large historical scale, such as "the fall of the Roman empire," but also of a much smaller scale (like setting up a collection of domino stones and toppling over the first one—all of this being simulated in a computer program). **Representation** A synopsis that has a connection to history and is internally consistent. Currently, this abstract level of semantics is only represented informally.	Most philosophical and religion systems start with creation myths. These could be considered to be initial causes. In the realm of fiction, it is the "Once upon a time" phrase that sets the stage for anything to follow. **Representation** A synopsis that does not necessarily have to have a connection to history and only has to be locally consistent. (For instance, Donald Duck is supposed to live in a house. But in some scenes, the kitchen in this house may be west of the living room, whereas in other scenes it may be east of the living room. "Local consistency" now means that within one scene, the relative position of the kitchen and the living room don't change, so presumably nobody will notice, but for aesthetic reasons (or from oversight) globally inconsistent discontinuities are allowed.) As with PR, this abstract level of semantics is only represented informally.
T_1	Transition between P_1 and P_2.	The transformations consist of all physical laws we want to take into account.	For a given didactic, artistic, or propagandistic purpose, we may want to allow non-physical cause–and–effect relations. A significant example is non-Newtonian physics where force is assumed to be proportional to speed instead of acceleration. Strictly speaking, all approximations that are necessary even in intended "exact" physics belong in this layer.

TABLE 11.5 Topmost levels of the reference model for semantic layers in visual communication. Column one: identification of levels $(P_1, P_2, \ldots)$ and identification of transitions $(T_1, T_2, \ldots)$. Second column: issues as found in reality. Third column: representation of these issues in PR applications. Last column: representation of these issues in NPR applications (*continued*).

	Reality	Photorealistic (PR)	Non-photorealistic (NPR)
P_2	The flow of mechanical causality by means of all known physical laws and processes plus the actions in biological systems that are initiated by intentions. P_2 represents the interconnectedness of the whole universe.	Since computers are finite, it is fundamentally impossible that in PR a simulation of the total universe can be achieved (for one reason since the universe would include the computer on which the simulation is running, and no finite system can contain itself completely). So the distinction between P_2 and P_3, which is basically a whole–part relation, does not make sense.	Same as PR
T_2	Transition between P_2 and P_3.	The translation of the synopsis into either a storyboard or a simulation script is typically performed by hand.	Same as PR
P_3	A physical system that can be considered on its own, because interactions with other systems outside P_3 either do not occur or can be assumed to be adequately represented by given boundary conditions and initial conditions.	A simulation script. **Representation** Representations for the part of reality that gives rise to visual phenomena can be globally classified into 4 types. 1) Descriptions of the occurring objects, including their geometric and dynamic properties (inertia, stiffness, internal degrees of freedom, resistance against breaking, . . .). 2) Descriptions of the (mostly mechanical) interactions between them (forces, force fields, handling of collision conditions, . . .). 3) Active controllers (to impose intentionality, e.g., simulated humans or animals) including their high-level behavior (AI scripts, neural networks, . . .) or tools for human interaction (motion capturing, . . .). 4) Models for participating media (water, air (damping, friction, . . .)). All this resulting in a set of coupled (partial) algebraic differential equations.	In NPR, we can either work with simulation scripts (see PR), where the equations or other components may be altered for artistic, didactical, or propagandistic reasons, or with *keyframe animation* (KFA). **Representation for KFA** In KFA, the storyboard is translated to a number of characteristic states (either stills or stills with instantaneous motion states), and interpolation is performed in between them. There are two variations that link KFA to simulation: (a) simulation could be used to generate keyframes, and if the motion sequences are smooth enough, it might save simulation effort not to explicitly solve for the simulation equations for all time steps but do cheaper interpolations instead and (b) the interpolation between keyframes might involve some form of (pseudo) physics, for instance, to achieve smooth motion, ensure constraints are being met, effort (energy) is minimized, or a final goal is being achieved (e.g., a thrown ball that should land in a bucket).

TABLE 11.5 *(continued)*

	Reality	Photorealistic (PR)	Non-photorealistic (NPR)
T_3	Transition between P_3 and P_4.	To go from P_3 to P_4, we simply leave out all the terms in the simulation script that do not correspond to objects that can be visualized.	If we used KFA, the transition from P_3 to P_4 is void since P_3 and P_4 are identical.
P_4	The manifestation of physical interactions as far as they are observed visually (e.g., electromagnetic waves that are part of P_3 are removed by T_3, but the visible behavior of a radio-controlled model race car are part of P_4).	**Representation** In common practice, geometric object components are represented either as polygon (typically triangle) meshes (well-suited for rendering) or implicit surfaces (object borders are the null sets of well-chosen functions, $f(x, y, z) = 0$; well-suited for non-linear deformations and collision detection). For convenient motion representation, components are arranged in a hierarchical structure, where the nodes correspond to (time-dependent) affine transformations. An affine transformation is a linear transformation plus an optional translation. In order to account for motion blurring (see P_5), it is necessary to represent motion information explicitly.	**Representation** The motion state is not necessarily encoded as affine transforms. In particular, the interpolation between keyframes in KFA may give rise to motion patterns that are defined on the vertex level in polygon meshes.

TABLE 11.5 *(continued)*

	Reality	Photorealistic (PR)	Non-photorealistic (NPR)
T_4	Transition between P_4 and P_5.	Between P_4 and P_5, time dependency has to be removed. Removing time dependency amounts, physically speaking, to taking a snapshot. Any measurement (a snapshot is a form of measurement), however, requires a finite amount of time, since otherwise the information transmission rate from the measured object to the measuring device would be infinitely high. In general, the measured system will move during the measurement, and motion uncertainty results. In physical systems, this gives rise to convolution with an apparatus-specific temporal filter profile. In PR rendering, the effect of this temporal filtering is realized with motion blurring. If motion blurring is omitted, temporal aliasing occurs: a moving object may appear to pop in and out.	In NPR, the impression of motion in a single frame may be conveyed by all sorts of devices, including velocity lines, repeated copies, blurring in motion direction, simulated dust particles, and wavy lines.
P_5	Any frozen snapshot of a part of reality, projected on its attributes of shape, size, position, and orientation; photometric properties—optional emission of light (light sources) and interaction with light (reflection, absorption, transmission).	**Representation** One way in PR to achieve motion blurring is to supersample the animation (i.e., to compute a number of frames at time instances in between those time instances for which animation frames are required). The resulting images should be accumulated and weighted with suitable coefficients that represent the apparatus-specific temporal filtering profile. This so-called *explicit* approach amounts to repeated traditional rendering. Alternatively, an *implicit* approach that falls in the *raytracing* paradigm, consists of, per pixel P, estimating the convolution with the temporal profile over that part of the scene that was visible through pixel P during the time interval associated to the exposure time of the snapshot.	**Representation** The additional visual attributes that were obtained in T_4 (either as 3D graphical objects, such as 3D speedlines or simulated dust particles, or in 2D, such as 2D speedlines) are joined to the object representation and merged in the rendering phases.

TABLE 11.5 *(continued)*

	Reality	Photorealistic (PR)	Non-photorealistic (NPR)
T_5	Transition between P_5 and P_6.	The decomposition of objects into 3D surfaces is typically performed during the design of the objects.	Same as PR
P_6	T_5 doesn't have an intrinsic physical interpretation. The difference between P_5 and P_6 is that an "area" refers to a connected region of homogeneous geometric and photometric properties. Whether or not an "area" could be equipped with a distribution of photometric properties ("texture," including distributions of reflectivity, transparence, etc.), or if it should be considered as a collection of smaller areas, each with constant photometric properties ("constant color," etc.) is left undecided.	For the two types of rendering paradigms, 3D surfaces should satisfy different requirements. For explicit rendering, or *scan converting*, it should be possible to enumerate all pixels that fall within (a projection of) the surface onto the image plane, where for every pixel, the photometric properties should be known. Suitable **representations** are triangle (meshes) or parametric patches that in turn are subdivided into meshes. Subdivision should be compatible with *level of detail* (LOD) strategies, where more triangles are generated upon demand (if more, smaller details are visible, more triangles should be rendered for an accurate image). For implicit rendering, or *raytracing*, it should be possible to find the intersection between a 3D surface and a straight line. This means that apart from polygon meshes, **representations** can also include *algebraic primitives*, such as spheres, quadrics, implicit surfaces, and Boolean combinations thereof. The control flow in explicit rendering is characterized by a per-surface approach; implicit rendering is characterized by a per-pixel approach.	Regarding the control flow, NPR is not different from PR. Here, as well, we might loop over the surfaces and perform rendering per surface, or we might loop over the pixels and perform rendering per pixel (or screen region—where a screen region could be any NPR drawing primitive, such as a hatch line, a brush trace, a blotch of simulated paint). An interesting hybrid consists of first using a PR rendering algorithm (e.g., to obtain a 2D segmentation in screen space in accordance to screen regions and their coverage by projected 3D surface, and next apply NPR techniques in accordance to the optometric properties of the 3D surface that projects onto that region. In this case, occlusion handling and perspective projection are being taken care of by PR.

TABLE 11.5   *(continued)*

	Reality	Photorealistic (PR)	Non-photorealistic (NPR)
T_6	Transition between P_6 and P_7.	The transformation from 3D to 2D can take place in either of two forms. For explicit rendering, every surface element (typically a triangle) is projected onto a 2D screen region (a collection of pixels). In this projection, occlusion is to be taken into account—most often using a depth buffer. For implicit rendering, projection takes place by computing the closest intersection to the eye of a backwardly traced light ray. Taking the *closest* intersection automatically solves the occlusion problem; using a ray that passes through the optic center (pupil) automatically gives the correct perspective transformation.	NPR variations to traditional 3D→2D mapping should be distinguished to the achieved transformations that take place as a result of this mapping. Geometric (central projective) deformation can be replaced by non-standard, non-central perspective (fisheye, local zoom, warping). Occlusion handling can be replaced by non-standard occlusion handling, such as partial transparency, priority-based ordering, and exploded views.

TABLE 11.5 *(continued)*

	Reality	Photorealistic (PR)	Non-photorealistic (NPR)
P_7	Physically speaking, it does not make sense to argue about 2D surfaces with photometric properties: even toner grains on a piece of paper are 3D. However, in many circumstances, it is convenient to consider 2D images as physical entities because for any practical purpose their shape in the 3rd dimension can be ignored. Therefore, T_6 can be seen as the projection operator that simply "flattens" the 3rd dimension in 2D images.	The 2D regions that result in explicit rendering can be shaded with any of a variety of shading techniques. Some issues are smooth interpolation of photometric conditions (Gouraud shading, Phong shading, and more advanced techniques; this includes also rendering of scenes that have been processed with radiosity-type global illumination algorithms), (perspective correct) texture mapping, where a texture can represent any varying photometric parameter, and transparency, environment mapping, and reflection mapping. **Representation** In its most complete form, local photometric conditions are represented in the *bi-directional reflection function* (bdrf) that, per wavelength, represents the reflected energy intensity for an incoming light ray in any one direction and an outgoing light ray in any other direction. In most cases, the bdrf is simplified, for instance, to be isotropic (i.e., it depends only on the *angle* between incoming and outgoing light rays). A full account of the bdrf is only possible in implicit rendering.	NPR rendering of 2D areas in screen space includes all forms of hatching, stippling, mosaicing, simulated brushstrokes, pencil strokes, airbrushes, interactions between paper and medium, and so on. Often, the algorithms to achieve these effects take their input from a PR rendering for that same region. Also techniques that imply screen space transformations to the 2D region, such as enlarging, highlighting, annotating, and replacing simulated shading by text fall into this semantic layer.

TABLE 11.5 *(continued)*

	Reality	Photorealistic (PR)	Non-photorealistic (NPR)
T_7	Transition between P_7 and P_8.	In PR, 1D or 0D singularities in 2D images occur in the rendering process, either they directly follow from singularities in 3D (e.g., a local maximum of the surface curvature), or they follow from the mapping T_6, or they result from discontinuities (C^0 or C^1) in the illumination (shadow borders, but also highlights may fall in this category). Their purpose in explicit rendering is to impose boundary conditions for the scan conversion algorithm. In implicit rendering they normally don't play a role, unless for efficiency reasons (e.g., for contour anti-aliasing it may be useful to know which pixels *are* on contours. For a general classification of 1D and 0D singularities, see Figure 11.22.	In NPR, singularities may be very relevant clues to determine rendering styles. In particular, an outline drawing *is* nothing but a rendition based on singularities. 1D (lines, curves) and 0D (points) singularities can be achieved from the segments in P_7 relatively straightforwardly with standard flood fill algorithms that can build on distributions of photometric values as obtained by PR rendering in P_6.
P_8	Singularities border two adjacent areas of relative homogeneous photometric or geometric properties. In Figure 11.22, we classify the various singularities.	In explicit rendering methods, the singularities of a geometric nature (either intrinsic or resulting from the 3D→2D mapping as mentioned above) are **represented** as projected corner vertices of triangles. The singularities related to illumination are most often not explicitly represented, unless by techniques that treat shadows as explicitly represented objects (e.g., *shadow volumes*). In implicit rendering, they typically don't occur.	Similarly as in P_6, a variety of line style options can be thought of. In particular, it may be useful to explicitly maintain the classification as presented after this table. Labeling the various singularities with their type may be useful to adjust the render styles in accordance with the singularity type.

TABLE 11.5 *(continued)*

	Reality	Photorealistic (PR)	Non-photorealistic (NPR)
T_8	Transition between P_8 and P_9.	Scan conversion enumerates the pixels within the 2D regions (P_7), delimited by the singular regions (P_8). In order to assign a color to pixels, however, anti-aliasing has to be taken into account. Anti-aliasing basically comes in two varieties: (a) shape-related anti-aliasing should appropriately blur the geometry-related singularities from P_8 and (b) texture-related anti-aliasing should assure that single texture elements (often called *texels*) are adequately low-pass filtered. Many techniques have been developed for both types of anti-aliasing, where techniques in the context of implicit rendering are directly related to convolution (supersampling and filtering with well-chosen low-pass filters). Techniques in explicit rendering still can use filtering to treat with texture anti-aliasing, but for shape anti-aliasing other methods have to be followed. Indeed, the projected shape of a geometric object is not simply represented as a signal on a discrete domain that can be convolved. (A full treatment of anti-aliasing falls outside our scope.)	If, in NPR, a rendering style is chosen with certain picture elements (say, stipples), the region is determined onto which stippling should be applied, and the luminance distribution that should be approximated is known, decisions should be made for the location of each individual stipple. This could be a priori fixed (dithering), adjusted to give pleasing distributions (e.g., no regular patterns and no clusters), adjusted to the luminance distribution, and adjusted to give uniform or variable density and/or shape of stipples. All these dimensions for choices apply in principle to all types of picture elements.

TABLE 11.5 *(continued)*

	Reality	Photorealistic (PR)	Non-photorealistic (NPR)
P_9	Layer P_9 models the coupling between individual surface points with given photometric (optic) properties and the light rays that depart from these points in the direction of the pupil of the eye of a beholder.	In PR, this is the **representation** of the image in terms of colored pixels.	In NPR, this is the **representation** of the image in terms of whatever picture elements have been chosen.
T_9	Physical transition by means of light rays from external reality to perceived reality.	In transferring from computer-generated images to computer-understandable images, of course the physics of light ray plays no role.	Same as PR

TABLE 11.5 *(continued)*

	Human perceptive system	Computer algorithm
Q_9, T_{10}	The first few layers of neurons behind the retina contain operators that detect 0D and 1D geometric singularities. Many of these operators have the character of differential operators. The LRA, RSJ, and part of the PSC, SSC, and ILD equivalence relations can be thought of to be handled here. That is, the semantic representation to be handed over to Q_8 largely consists of invariants with respect to the mentioned (p-)equivalence relations.	Examples of algorithms that mimic the behavior of the first few layers of neurons in the optical pathway fall into two categories. First, the operators that deal with the LRA, PSC, and SSC equivalence relations are commonly called *image-enhancing* algorithms. They operate, for instance, by means of histogram equalization in order to ensure that an optimal usage is made from the available dynamic range of luminance values throughout the image. The second category is formed by various feature detectors, such as edge—or corner—detectors, and Laplacian–of–Gaussian operators. Often, these have filter profiles that actually resemble the neurobiological structures that have been found in the visual pathway. This is also true for multiscale operators and so on.
Q_8, T_{11}	Following layers are active in shape analysis. These operators cannot be purely local, and a commonly used model works on the basis of the multiscale and Fourier–Mellin transforms.	Identifying segments requires segmentation algorithms. Basically two types are commonly used: (1) those that start from borders as found in Q_8 and build the segments in an inward growing manner and (2) those that start from areas that are guaranteed inside a segment (very homogenous areas) and grow outward. During the segmentation process, size and shape of segments should be controlled, for instance, by appropriate merging and splitting of segments under construction.

TABLE 11.6 Lowermost levels of the reference model for semantic layers in visual communication. Column one: identification of levels (Q_9, Q_8, . . .) and identification of transitions (T_{10}, T_{11}, . . .). Second column: issues as found in reality. Third column: representation of these issues in computer software. *Note:* because these levels regard the interpretation and reconstruction of meaning out of images, we do not need the distinction between PR and NPR *(continued)*.

Human perceptive system	Computer algorithm
Q_7, T_{12}	Once sufficient confidence has been obtained that perceived shapes are equivalent (with the LRP, RVP, and OCC (p–)equivalence relations) to simple shapes, the backward mapping from perspectively distorted and maybe even partially occluded 2D areas in the retina to 3D areas can be performed. Notice the condition of simplicity here: as we have seen, the vision system sometimes prefers to "live" with inconsistencies at higher semantic levels if an interpretation in terms of simple shapes at lower levels can be obtained. Simplicity here refers to, among other things, few objects preferred over many objects (see Figure 11.13), and parallel and coincident lines in 2D are preferably assumed to be projections from parallel and incident lines in 3D as well (see Figure 11.19). 2D lines that move in the direction of a vanishing point are assumed to be projections of 3D lines that are parallel.*	The inverse mapping from 2D regions to 3D regions traditionally takes place via the inverse mapping of the features (singularities) that border the 2D regions. If features can be found in several images that were taken with different camera settings, the 3D position of such a feature can be obtained by (advanced forms of) triangulation, similar to the technique followed by surveyors that measure positions in a landscape. Direct reconstruction of 3D surfaces on the basis of matched 2D regions is not (yet) a common technique in the image recognition literature.

TABLE 11.6 *(continued)*

* From a point of view of evolutionary epistemology, this preoccupation with interpretations that involve straight lines in them is curious. In the natural environment, where humans are supposed to have evolved, very few straight lines occur, except from the horizontal lines in water surfaces and the horizon. It may seem that the human visual system has "invented" straight lines before technology has introduced them: this makes us curious about what other geometric objects we may not yet be familiar with, we have built-in detectors.

	Human perceptive system	Computer algorithm
Q_6, T_{13}	At this level, the borderline between "perception" and "cognition" is commonly assumed to be crossed. What is understood to be "an object" is closely related to language and linguistics. It would carry us too far from our topic to go over these issues here.	Automated recognition of objects out of images of these objects (where perspective viewing, various illumination conditions, and possibly partial occlusion come into play) almost invariably requires *world knowledge* in the form of descriptions of the objects that can be expected. Recognition is then accomplished by a matching process, similar to our strategy 3. Every element in this finite set of *defaults* gives rise to an equivalence class, and the classification process amounts to identifying in which equivalence class a given image belongs. This field of applications is called *model-based* image understanding, and it is the counterpart of *cognition-based* image understanding in humans (i.e., those parts of the viewing process that can be thought of to involve the higher semantic layers). The opposite collection of techniques, called *model-independent* image understanding, then correspond to those semantic layers that we called *perception-based* viewing.
Q_5, T_{14}	In attributing motions to objects, successful subsequent matches in the LRP and RVP-induced equivalence classes may play a role, as well as in the OCC-induced class. Also the interpretation of *lacking* interpretation (e.g., due to frequency bandwidth limitation of the neural–optical system, it is impossible to assess if a fast-spinning object rotates clockwise or counterclockwise) should be mentioned here.	These two areas of computer-based image understanding are still largely unexplored except in very specific, application-domain specific applications (e.g, tracking of vehicles in automated surveillance systems).

TABLE 11.6 *(continued)*

	Human perceptive system	Computer algorithm
Q_4, T_{16}, Q_3, T_{16}, Q_2, T_{17}, Q_1	These layers and the involved mappings between them rely on a substantial body of world knowledge, but also cognitive faculties such as memorizing and reasoning. Therefore they fall outside the scope of the current study. Still the concept of LASses may be useful here, for instance, to argue about stereotypic high-level classifications (e.g., associated to social background, political preference, confession, or developed taste).	See Q_5, T_{14}

TABLE 11.6 *(continued)*

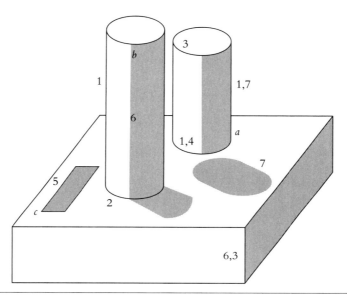

FIGURE 11.22 Possible singularities in a static image.

(a, b), these come from bifurcations where three or more 1D singularities meet. However, they can also result from a geometric singularity in just one 1D singularity (for example, c). A comprehensive scheme to classify a shape or an image in terms of its 0D, 1D, 2D and (in case of a shape, 3D) singular components or cells is by means of cellular structures. A cellular structure is a graph where the nodes are cells (either 0D, 1D, 2D, or 3D singularities). Edges between two cells indicate an incidence relation. For instance, a curve that terminates in two points corresponds to three nodes: one for a 1D cell and two for the two 0D cells, and two edges that connect the two 0D cells to the 1D cell.[6] We leave it as an exercise to verify for what sorts of incidents 1D singularities and 0D singularities can exist.

---

6. A full treatment of cellular structures falls beyond the scope of this text; we refer to textbooks on algebraic topology and the work of T. L. Kunii on the application of cellular structures in computer graphics, geometric modeling, and image processing (Kunii, 1999).

Number	Name (if any)	Type of discontinuity	View dependent, light dependent, or shape intrinsic	Related to shape or related to shadow
1	Silhouette	C^0	View dependent	Shape
2		C^1, concave	Shape intrinsic	Shape
3		C^1, convex	Shape intrinsic	Shape
4	Occlusion border	C^1, convex	Shape intrinsic	Shape
5	Texture or coplanar feature border	C^∞	Shape intrinsic	None
6	Separatrix (e.g.,the line that divides dark and light parts of the moon when it is in first or last quarter phase)	C^1	Light dependent	Shadow
7		C^0	Light dependent	Shadow

TABLE 11.7 Possible singularities in a static image (the numbers refer to Figure 11.22).

11.6 Summary and Practical Connection with NPR

We introduce a terminology that allows us to argue about "similar" and "dissimilar" images. Similarity is expressed in terms of (p-)equivalence classes, and we show that under the assumption of a finite set of stimuli, and a sufficient set of defaults, p-equivalence classes can be turned into true equivalence classes. With true equivalence classes, we can build a quotient structure, which is basically a partition of a collection of things into categories of things that are similar—according to particular definitions of the notion "similar." When studying the physics of the viewing process, we see that a number of (p-)equivalence relations are inevitable because a certain object can give rise to large varieties of visual impressions on the retina. We conjecture that, apart from the eight p-equivalence relations that we identify and that can be related immediately to the physics of optical communication, there are many more p-equivalence relations, and we adopt the notion of (p-)equivalence relations as a generic concept to argue about images and image classification. With respect to classification, we observe that an object should be identified under a variety of viewing conditions as the same object each time, and therefore the p-equivalences (due to the physical particularities) should be "filtered out." Therefore, it is convenient to depict images (represented in some semantic layer) as quotient structures.

Next, we see that between quotient structures relations can be defined, so-called (iso-)morphisms, and these relations help to express transforming a piece of information from one format into another format. Particular features of that piece of information are preserved (the so-called invariants), whereas other pieces of information may get lost (variants). The pieces that get lost impose again an equivalence relation upon the elements that we are considering.

We use this notion of mappings between various representations of images because there is strong evidence that the human visual process takes place as a sequence of transformations where at each step, the semantic contents of the representation increases. This notion of layers that each specialize on one semantic level is taken from a successful model for data communication, the OSI model.

To tie our thinking about mappings between various semantic levels into a conjectured mechanism of how this might work, we postulate the notion of look-ahead sets (or look-around sets, abbreviated as LAS and LASses). LASses are convenient to think about how the effect of (p-)equivalence relations may be dealt with, and we propose some strategies for how viewing and classification at various semantic levels indeed might take place.

After all this preparatory work, we propose our layered semantic structure since this gives a convenient classification of rendering algorithms (rendering is seen as a transformation from one semantic layer to a next lower layer, where these transformations are the matching transformations with those that could be conjectured in the vision system). Conventional rendering attempts, at every transformation, to be a close model of a physical (photorealistic) process, but confronting every step with the invariants that should be conveyed to the next lower level, automatically inspire to variants that may be used for *non-photorealistic* rendering. The main result of this section can therefore be seen as a classification structure for NPR algorithms, with ample open slots for future extensions.

For a practitioner of NPR, we dare to give the following recommendations:

1. Try to formulate the semantic levels between which your algorithm should transform.

2. For these levels, and for your application domain, try to formulate what the governing invariants are. In any case, the algorithm should map these invariants between the input and the output of your algorithm.

3. Once the invariants are clear, try to identify the variants. These variants span the design space (the space of your "fantasy") because any variant should give rise to equivalent semantic transfer.

4. Experiment with algorithms that exploit the variants as much as possible.

REFERENCES

Aleksander, I. (1994). Artificial Consciousness? In Thalmann, N. M., and Thalmann, D., editors, *Artificial Life and Virtual Reality*, pages 73–81. New York: John Wiley and Sons.

Aleksander, I. (1996). *Impossible Minds: My Neurons, My Consciousness*. London: Imperial College Press.

Appel, A., Rohlf, F. J., and Stein, A. J. (1979). The Haloed Line Effect for Hidden Line Elimination. In *Proceedings of SIGGRAPH'79* (Chicago, August 1979), Computer Graphics Proceedings, Annual Conference Series, pages 151–157. New York: ACM SIGGRAPH.

Arnheim, R. (1984). *Art and Visual Perception. A Psychology of the Creative Eye*. Berkeley: University of California Press.

Barr, A. H. (1984). Global and Local Deformations of Solid Primitives. In *Proceedings of SIGGRAPH'84* (Minneapolis, July 1984), Computer Graphics Proceedings, Annual Conference Series, pages 21–30. New York: ACM SIGGRAPH.

Bartels, R. H., Beatty, J. C., and Barsky, B. A. (1996). *An Introduction to Splines for Use in Computer Graphics and Geometric Modeling*. San Francisco: Morgan Kaufmann.

Bartram, L., Ho, A., Dill, J., and Henigman, F. (1995). The Continous Zoom: A Constrained Fisheye Technique for Viewing and Navigating Large Information Spaces. In *UIST '95: Proceedings of the ACM Symposium on User Interface Software and Technology*, pages 207–216. New York: ACM Press.

Bartram, L., Ho, A., Dill, J. C., and Henigman, F. (1995). The Continous Zoom: A Graphical Interface Technique for Viewing and Navigating Large Information Systems. Technical Report CCS-IS 95-01, Simon Fraser University.

Bleser, T. W., Sibert, J. L., and McGee, J. P. (1988). Charcoal Sketching: Returning Control to the Artist. *ACM Transactions on Graphics*, 7(1):76–81.

Blum, H. (1967). A Transformation for Extracting New Descriptors of Shape. In Wathen-Dunn, W., editor, *Models for the Perception of Speech and Visual Form*, pages 362–380. Cambridge: The MIT Press.

Buchanan, J. W. (1996). Special Effects with Half-Toning. *Computer Graphics Forum*, 15(3):97–108.

Buchanan, J. W., and Sousa, M. C. (2000). The Edge Buffer: A Data Structure for Easy Silhouette Rendering. In *Proceedings of NPAR 2000, Symposium on Non-Photorealistic Animation and Rendering* (Annecy, France, June 2000), pages 39–42. New York: ACM Press.

Buchanan, J. W., Streit, L. M., and Veryovka, O. (1998). Edge Enhancement Issues in Half-Toning. In Davis, W., Booth, K., and Fournier, A., editors, *Proceedings of Graphics Interface'98* (Vancouver, Canada, June 1998), pages 209–216. San Francisco: Morgan Kaufmann.

Buck, I., Finkelstein, A., Jacobs, C., Klein, A., Salesin, D. H., Seims, J., Szeliski, R., and Toyama, K. (2000). Performance-Driven Hand-Drawn Animation. In *Proceedings of NPAR 2000, Symposium on Non-Photorealistic Animation and Rendering* (Annecy, France, June 2000), pages 101–108. New York: ACM Press.

Canny, F. J. (1986). A Computational Approach to Edge Detection. *IEEE Transactions on Pattern Analysis and Machine Intelligence*, 8(6):679–698.

Carpendale, M. S. T. (1999). *A Framework for Elastic Presentation Space*. Ph.D. thesis, School of Computer Science, Simon Fraser University.

Carpendale, M. S. T., Cowperthwaite, D. J., and Fracchia, F. D. (1995). 3-Dimensional Pliable Surfaces: For the Effective Presentation of Visual Information. In *Proceedings of the ACM Symposium on User Interface Software and Technology, UIST'95* (Pittsburgh, November 1995), pages 217–226. New York: ACM Press.

Carpendale, M. S. T., Cowperthwaite, D. J., and Fracchia, F. D. (1997). Making Distortions Comprehensible. In *IEEE Symposium on Visual Languages'97* (Capri, Italy, September 1997), pages 36–45. Los Alamitos: IEEE Computer Society Press.

Cockshott, T., and England, D. (1991). Wet and Sticky: Supporting Interaction with Wet Paint. In Diaper, D., and Hammond, N. G., editors, *People and Computers IV, Proceedings of the HCI'91 Conference* (Edinburgh, August 1991), British Computer Society Conference Series, pages 199–208. Cambridge: Cambridge University Press.

Cockshott, T., Patterson, J., and England, D. (1992). Modelling the Texture of Paint. In Kilgour, A., and Kjelldahl, L., editors, *Proceedings of Eurographics'92* (Cambridge, UK, September 1992), pages 217–226. Oxford: NCC Blackwell Ltd.

Cohen, J. M., Hughes, J. F., and Zeleznik, R. C. (2000). Harold: A World Made of Drawings. In *Proceedings of NPAR 2000, Symposium on Non-Photorealistic Animation and Rendering* (Annecy, France, June 2000), pages 83–90. New York: ACM Press.

Curtis, C. (1998). Loose and Sketchy Animation. In *SIGGRAPH'98 Conference Abstracts and Applications*, page 317. New York: ACM SIGGRAPH.

Curtis, C. J., Anderson, S. E., Seims, J. E., Fleischer, K. W., and Salesin, D. H. (1997). Computer-Generated Watercolor. In Whitted, T., editor, *Proceedings of SIGGRAPH'97* (Los Angeles, August 1997), Computer Graphics Proceedings, Annual Conference Series, pages 421–430. New York: ACM SIGGRAPH.

Decaudin, P. (1996). Rendu de scènes 3D imitant le style "dessin animé." Technical Report 2919, INRIA, Rocquencourt, France.

Deussen, O. (1998). Pixel-Oriented Rendering of Line Drawings. In Strothotte (1998), Chapter 6, pages 105–119.

Deussen, O., Hamel, J., Raab, A., Schlechtweg, S., and Strothotte, T. (1999a). An Illustration Technique Using Intersections and Skeletons. In *Proceedings of Graphics Interface'99* (Kingston, Canada, June 1999), pages 175–182. San Francisco: Morgan Kaufmann.

Deussen, O., Hiller, S., van Overveld, C. W. A. M., and Strothotte, T. (1999b). Computer-Generated Stipple Drawings. In Girod, B., Niemann, H., and Seidel, H.-P., editors, *Proceedings of VMV'99, Workshop on Vision, Modelling and Visualization* (Erlangen, Germany, November 1999), Sankt Augustin, Germany: infix.

Deussen, O., Hiller, S., van Overveld, C. W. A. M., and Strothotte, T. (2000). Floating Points: A Method for Computing Stipple Drawings. In Gross, M., and Hopgood, F. R. A., editors, *Proceedings of Eurographics 2000* (Interlaken, Switzerland, August 2000), volume 19, pages 40–51. Oxford: NCC Blackwell Ltd.

Deussen, O., and Strothotte, T. (2000). Computer-Generated Pen-and-Ink Illustration of Trees. In Akeley, K., editor, *Proceedings of SIGGRAPH 2000* (New Orleans, July 2000), Computer Graphics Proceedings, Annual Conference Series, pages 13–18, New York: ACM SIGGRAPH.

Dill, J. C., Bartram, L., Ho, A., and Henigman, F. (1994). A Continuosly Variable Zoom for Navigating Large Hierarchical Networks. In *Proceedings of the IEEE Conference on Systems, Man and Cybernetics* (San Antonio, October 1994), pages 386–390. Los Alamitos: IEEE Computer Society Press.

Dooley, D. L., and Cohen, M. F. (1990a). Automatic Illustration of 3D Geometric Models: Lines. In Riesenfeld, R., and Sequin, C., editors, *Proceedings of 1990 Symposium on Interactive 3D Graphics* (Snowbird, UT, March 1990), pages 77–82. New York: ACM SIGGRAPH.

Dooley, D. L., and Cohen, M. F. (1990b). Automatic Illustration of 3D Geometric Models: Surfaces. In *Proceedings of Visualization'90* (San Francisco, October 1990), pages 307–314. Los Alamitos: IEEE Computer Society Press.

Duden (1977). *Duden. Bildwörterbuch*. Mannheim, Germany: Dudenverlag.

Edman, P. K. (1992). *Tactile Graphics*. American Foundation for the Blind, New York.

Elber, G. (1995). Line illustrations ∈ computer graphics. *The Visual Computer*, 11(6):290–296.

Elber, G. (1998). Line Art Illustrations of Parametric and Implicit Forms. *IEEE Transactions on Visualization and Computer Graphics*, 4(1):71–81.

Elber, G. (1999). Interactive Line Art Rendering of Freeform Surfaces. In Brunet, P., and Scopigno, R., editors, *Proceedings of Eurographics'99* (Milano, Italy, September 1999), pages 1–12. Oxford: NCC Blackwell Ltd.

Elber, G. (2001). Rendering with Parallel Stripes. *IEEE Computer Graphics and Applications*, 21(3):44–52.

Elber, G., and Cohen, E. (1990). Hidden Curve Removal for Free Form Surfaces. In Baskett, F., editor, *Proceedings of SIGGRAPH'90* (Dallas, August 1990), Computer Graphics Proceedings, Annual Conference Series, pages 95–104. New York: ACM SIGGRAPH.

ELSA AG (1999). *ELSA Microlink TM56k PCI Manual*. ELSA AG.

Emhardt, J., and Strothotte, T. (1992). Hyper-Rendering. In *Proceedings of Graphics Interface'92* (Vancouver, Canada, May 1992), pages 37–43. Toronto: Canadian Computer-Human Communications Society.

Farin, G. E. (1996). *Curves and Surfaces for Computer-Aided Geometric Design: A Practical Guide*. Boston: Academic Press.

Fekete, J., Bizouarn, É., Cournarie, É., Galas, T., and Taillefer, F. (1995). TicTacToon: A Paperless System for Professional 2-D Animation. In Cook, R., editor, *Proceedings of SIGGRAPH'95* (Los Angeles, August 1995), Computer Graphics Proceedings, Annual Conference Series, pages 79–90. New York: ACM SIGGRAPH.

Finkelstein, A., and Range, M. (1998). Image Mosaics. Technical Report TR-574-98, Computer Science Department, Princeton University.

Finkelstein, A., and Salesin, D. H. (1994). Multiresolution Curves. In Glassner, A., editor, *Proceedings of SIGGRAPH'94* (Orlando, July 1994), Computer Graphics Proceedings, Annual Conference Series, pages 261–268. New York: ACM SIGGRAPH.

Floyd, R. W., and Steinberg, L. (1976). An Adaptive Algorithm for Spatial Gray Scale. In *Society for Information Display Digest*, volume 17, pages 75–77.

Foley, J. D., van Dam, A., Feiner, S. K., and Hughes, J. F. (1990). *Computer Graphics. Principle and Practice*, second edition. Reading, MA: Addison-Wesley.

Freeman, W. T., Tenenbaum, J. B., and Pasztor, E. (1999). An Example-Based Approach to Style Translation for Line Drawings. Technical Report TR-99-11, Mitsubishi Electric Research Laboratory.

Furnas, G. W. (1986). Generalized Fisheye Views. In *Proceedings of CHI'86 Conference on Human Factors in Computing Systems* (Boston, April 1986), pages 16–23. New York: ACM SIGCHI.

Gardner, M. (1983). The Game of Life, Parts I–III. In *Wheels, Life, and Other Mathematical Amusements*, Chapters 20–22. New York: W. H. Freeman.

Girshick, A., and Interrante, V. (1999). Real-Time Principal Direction Line Drawings of Arbitraty 3D Surfaces. In *SIGGRAPH'99 Conference Abstracts and Applications*, page 271. New York: ACM SIGGRAPH.

Girshick, A., Interrante, V., Haker, S., and Lemoine, T. (2000). Line Direction Matters: An Argument for the Use of Principal Directions in 3D Line Drawings. In *Proceedings of NPAR 2000, Symposium on Non-Photorealistic Animation and Rendering* (Annecy, France, June 2000), pages 43–52. New York: ACM Press.

Godenschweger, F., Strothotte, T., and Wagener, H. (1996). Presentation of Freeform Surfaces as Line Drawings. In Girod, B., Niemann, H., and Seidel, H.-P., editors, *3D Image Analysis and Synthesis'96* (Erlangen, Germany, November 1996), pages 87–93. Sankt Augustin, Germany: infix.

Godenschweger, F., and Wagener, H. (1998). Rendering Line Drawings of Curved Surfaces. In Strothotte (1998), Chapter 5, pages 91–103.

Gombrich, E. H. (1977). *Art and Illusion. A Study in the Psychology of Pictorial Representations*, fifth edition. London: Phaidron Press.

Gooch, A. A. (1998). Interactive Non-Photorealistic Technical Illustration. Master's thesis, Department of Computer Science, University of Utah.

Gooch, A. A., and Gooch, B. (1999a). Using Non-Photorealistic Rendering to Communicate Shape. In Green, S., editor, *SIGGRAPH'99 Course Notes. Course on Non-Photorelistic Rendering*, Chapter 8. New York: ACM SIGGRAPH.

Gooch, A. A., Gooch, B., Shirley, P., and Cohen, E. (1998). A Non-Photorealistic Lighting Model for Automatic Technical Illustration. In Cohen, M., editor, *Proceedings of SIGGRAPH'98* (Orlando, July 1998), Computer Graphics Proceedings, Annual Conference Series, pages 447–452. New York: ACM SIGGRAPH.

Gooch, B., and Gooch, A. A. (1999b). Interactive Non-Photorealistic Rendering. In Green, S., editor, *SIGGRAPH'99 Course Notes. Course on Non-Photorelistic Rendering*, Chapter 10. New York: ACM SIGGRAPH.

Gooch, B., and Gooch, A. (2001). *Non-Photorealistic Rendering*. Natick: AK Peters, Ltd.

Gooch, B., Sloan, P.-P. J., Gooch, A. A., Shirley, P., and Riesenfeld, R. (1999). Interactive Technical Illustration. In Spencer, S. N., editor, *Proceedings of the Conference on the 1999 Symposium on Interactive 3D Graphics*, pages 31–38. New York: ACM Press.

Goss, J. (1991). *City Maps of Europe*. London: Studio Editions, Ltd.

Grafton, C. B., editor (1990). *Trades and Occupations. A Pictorial Archive from Early Sources*. New York: Dover Publications.

Guo, Q., and Kunii, T. L. (1991). Modeling the Diffuse Paintings of Sumie. In Kunii, T. L., editor, *Modeling in Computer Graphics. Proceedings of the IFIP WG 5.10 Working Conference* (Tokyo, April 1991), IFIP Series on Computer Graphics, pages 329–338. Tokyo: Springer-Verlag.

Haeberli, P. (1990). Paint by Numbers: Abstract Image Representations. In Baskett, F., editor, *Proceedings of SIGGRAPH'90* (Dallas, August 1990), Computer Graphics Proceedings, Annual Conference Series, pages 207–214. New York: ACM SIGGRAPH.

Hall, P. (1995a). Comic-Strip Rendering. Technical Report CS-TR-95/2, Department of Computer Science, Victoria University of Wellington, New Zealand.

Hall, P. (1995b). Non-Photorealistic Shape Cues for Visualization. In Skala, V., editor, *Proceedings of WSCG'95* (Pilzeň, February 1995), pages 113–122.

Hall, P. (1999). Nonphotorealistic Rendering by Q-Mapping. *Computer Graphics Forum*, 18(1):27–39.

Hamel, J. (2000). *A New Lighting Model for Computer Generated Line Drawings*. Ph.D. thesis, School of Computer Science, Otto-von-Guericke University of Magdeburg.

Hamel, J., Schlechtweg, S., and Strothotte, T. (1998). An Approach to Visualizing Transparancy in Computer-Generated Line Drawings. In *Proceedings of Information Visualization '98* (London, July 1998), pages 151–156. Los Alamitos: IEEE Computer Society.

Hamel, J., and Strothotte, T. (1999). Capturing and Re-using Rendition Styles for Non-Photorealistic Rendering. In *Proceedings of Eurographics'99* (Milano, Italy, September 1999), pages 173–182. Oxford: NCC Blackwell Ltd.

Hartmann, K., Preim, B., and Strothotte, T. (1998). Describing Abstraction in Rendered Images through Figure Captions. In Rist, T., editor, *Workshop on Combining AI and Graphics for Intelligent User Interfaces of the Future*. European Conference on Artificial Intelligence (ECAI'98), pages 235–246. Brighton, UK.

Hartmann, K., Preim, B., and Strothotte, T. (1999). Describing Abstraction in Rendered Images Through Figure Captions. In *Linköping Electronic Articles in Computer and Information Science*, www.ep.liu.se/ea/cis/1999/015/, volume 15. Linköping University Electronic Press.

Hawkes, J. (1993). *The Atlas of Early Man*. New York: St. Martin's Press.

Hertzmann, A. (1998). Painterly Rendering with Curved Brush Strokes of Multiple Sizes. In Cohen, M., editor, *Proceedings of SIGGRAPH'98* (Orlando, July 1998), Computer Graphics Proceedings, Annual Conference Series, pages 453–460. New York: ACM SIGGRAPH.

Hertzmann, A. (1999). Introduction to 3D Non-Photorealistic Rendering: Silhouettes and Outlines. In Green, S., editor, *SIGGRAPH'99 Course Notes. Course on Non-Photorelistic Rendering*, Chapter 7. New York: ACM SIGGRAPH.

Hertzmann, A. (2000). Paint by Relaxation. Technical Report 2000-801, Media Research Laboratory, Department of Computer Science, New York University.

Hertzmann, A. and Perlin, K. (2000). Painterly Rendering for Video and Interaction. In *Proceedings of NPAR 2000, Symposium on Non-Photorealistic Animation and Rendering* (Annecy, France, June 2000), pages 7–12. New York: ACM Press.

Hertzmann, A., and Zorin, D. (2000). Illustrating Smooth Surfaces. In Akeley, K., editor, *Proceedings of SIGGRAPH 2000* (New Orleans, July 2000), Computer Graphics Proceedings, Annual Conference Series, pages 517–526. New York: ACM SIGGRAPH.

Hiller, S. (1999). Generierung relaxierter Punktmengen. Master's thesis, Department of Simulation and Graphics, Otto-von-Guericke University Magdeburg.

Hiller, S., and Deussen, O. (2001). Voronoi-Relaxierung allgemeiner Objekte. In Schulze, T., Schlechtweg, S., and Hinz, V., editors, *Simulation und Visualisierung 2001* (Magdeburg, Germany, March 2001), pages 223–234. Erlangen, Germany: SCS Europe.

Hodges, E. R. S. (1989). *The Guild Handbook of Scientific Illustration*. New York: van Nostrand Reinhold.

Hoppe, H. (1996). Progressive Meshes. In Rushmeier, H., editor, *Proceedings of SIG-GRAPH'96* (New Orleans, August 1996), Computer Graphics Proceedings, Annual Conference Series, pages 99–108. New York: ACM SIGGRAPH.

Hoppe, H., DeRose, T., Duchamp, T., McDonald, J., and Stuetzle, W. (1993). Mesh Optimization. In Kajiya, J. T., editor, *Proceedings of SIGGRAPH'93* (Anaheim, August 1993), Computer Graphics Proceedings, Annual Conference Series, pages 19–26. New York: ACM SIGGRAPH.

Houghton, H. A., and Willows, D. M., editors (1987). *The Psychology of Illustration. Instructional Issues*, volume 2. New York: Springer-Verlag.

Hsu, S. C., and Lee, I. H. H. (1994). Drawing and Animation Using Skeletal Strokes. In Glassner, A., editor, *Proceedings of SIGGRAPH'94* (Orlando, July 1994), Computer Graphics Proceedings, Annual Conference Series, pages 109–118. New York: ACM SIGGRAPH.

Hsu, S. C., Lee, I. H. H., and Wiseman, N. E. (1993). Skeletal Strokes. In *UIST'93 Proceedings of the ACM SIGGRAPH and SIGCHI Symposium on User Interface Software and Technology* (Atlanta, November 1993), pages 197–206. New York: ACM Press.

Isenberg, T., Masuch, M., and Strothotte, T. (2000). 3D Illustrative Effects for Animating Line Drawings. In *Proceedings of the IEEE Conference on Information Visualization*, (London, July 2000), pages 413–418. Los Alamitos: IEEE Computer Society.

Jähne, B. (1997). *Digital Image Processing*. Berlin: Springer-Verlag.

Kaplan, M., Gooch, B., and Cohen, E. (2000). Interactive Artistic Rendering. In *Proceedings of NPAR 2000, Symposium on Non-Photorealistic Animation and Rendering* (Annecy, France, June 2000), pages 67–74. New York: ACM Press.

Kaplan, C. S., and Salesin, D. H. (2000). Escherization. In *Proceedings of SIGGRAPH 2000* (New Orleans, July 2000), Computer Graphics Proceedings, Annual Conference Series, pages 499–510. New York: ACM SIGGRAPH.

Keahey, T. A., and Robertson, E. L. (1996). Techniques for Nonlinear Magnification Transformations. In *Proceedings of the IEEE Symposium on Information Visualization* (San Francisco, October 1996), pages 38–45. Los Alamitos: IEEE Computer Society Press.

Klein, A. W., Li, W. W., Kazhdan, M. M., Correa, W. T., Finkelstein, A., and Funkhouser, T. A. (2000). Non-Photorealistic Virtual Environments. In Akeley, K., editor, *Proceedings of SIGGRAPH 2000* (New Orleans, July 2000), Computer Graphics Proceedings, Annual Conference Series, pages 527–534. New York: ACM SIGGRAPH.

Knuth, D. E. (1987). Digital Halftones by Dot Diffusion. *ACM Transactions on Graphics*, 6(4):245–273.

Kowalski, M. A., Markosian, L., Northrup, J. D., Bourdev, L., Barzel, R., Holden, L. S., and Hughes, J. F. (1999). Art-Based Rendering of Fur, Grass, and Trees. In *Proceedings of SIGGRAPH'99* (Los Angeles, August 1999), Computer Graphics Proceedings, Annual Conference Series, pages 433–438. New York: ACM SIGGRAPH.

Kunii, T. L. (1999). Homotopy Modeling as World Modeling. In *Proceedings of Computer Graphics International '99* (CGI 99) (Canmore, Canada, June 1999), pages 130–141. Los Alamitos: IEEE Computer Society Press.

Kurlander, D., Skelly, T., and Salesin, D. H. (1996). Comic Chat. In Rushmeier, H., editor, *Proceedings of SIGGRAPH'96* (New Orleans, August 1996), Computer Graphics Proceedings, Annual Conference Series, pages 225–236. New York: ACM SIGGRAPH.

Kurze, M. (1999). *Methoden zur computergenerierten Darstellung räumlicher Gegenstände für Blinde auf taktilen Medien*. Ph.D. thesis, Department of Mathematics and Computer Science, Free University of Berlin.

Lake, A., Marshall, C., Harris, M., and Blackstein, M. (2000). Stylized Rendering Techniques for Scalable Real-Time 3D Animation. In *Proceedings of NPAR 2000, Symposium on Non-Photorealistic Animation and Rendering* (Annecy, France, June 2000), pages 13–20. New York: ACM Press.

Lam, L., Lee, S.-W., and Suen, C. Y. (1992). Thinning Methodologies—A Comprehensive Survey. *IEEE Transactions on Pattern Analysis and Machine Intelligence*, 14(9):869–884.

Lansdown, J., and Schofield, S. (1995). Expressive Rendering: A Review of Nonphotorealistic Techniques. *IEEE Computer Graphics and Applications*, 15(3):29–37.

Leister, W. (1994). Computer Generated Copper Plates. *Computer Graphics Forum*, 13(1):69–77.

Lintermann, B., and Deussen, O. (1999). Interactive Modeling of Plants. *IEEE Computer Graphics and Applications*, 19(1).

Litwinowicz, P. (1997). Processing Images and Video for an Impressionist Effect. In Whitted, T., editor, *Proceedings of SIGGRAPH'97* (Los Angeles, August 1997), Computer Graphics Proceedings, Annual Conference Series, pages 407–414. New York: ACM SIGGRAPH.

Luebke, D. P. (1998). *View-Dependent Simplification of Arbitrary Polygonal Environments*. Ph.D. thesis, Department of Computer Science, University of North Carolina at Chapel Hill.

Luebke, D. P. (2001). A Developer's Survey of Polygonal Simplification Algorithms. *IEEE Computer Graphics and Applications*, 21(3):24–35.

Mäntylä, M. (1988). *An Introduction to Solid Modelling*. Rockville: Computer Science Press.

Markosian, L., Kowalski, M. A., Trychin, S. J., Bourdev, L. D., Goldstein, D., and Hughes, J. F. (1997). Real-Time Nonphotorealistic Rendering. In Whitted, T., editor, *Proceedings of SIGGRAPH'97* (Los Angeles, August 1997), Computer Graphics Proceedings, Annual Conference Series, pages 415–420. New York: ACM SIGGRAPH.

Markosian, L., Meier, B. J., Kowalski, M. A., Holden, L. S., Northrup, J. D., and Hughes, J. F. (2000). Art-Based Rendering with Continuous Levels of Detail. In *Proceedings of NPAR 2000, Symposium on Non-Photorealistic Animation and Rendering* (Annecy, France, June 2000), pages 59–64. New York: ACM Press.

Marshall, T. (1995). Lively Pictures (Power Mac Image Editing). *Byte Magazine*, 20(1):171–172.

Martín, D., García, S., and Torres, J. C. (2000). Observer Dependent Deformations in Illustrations. In *Proceedings of NPAR 2000, Symposium on Non-Photorealistic Animation and Rendering* (Annecy, France, June 2000), pages 75–82. New York: ACM Press.

Martin, J. (1989). *Technical Illustration*. London: MacDonald Orbis.

Masuch, M. (2001). *Nicht-photorealistische Visualisierungen: Von Bildern zu Animationen*. Ph.D. thesis, School of Computer Science, Otto-von-Guericke University of Magdeburg.

Masuch, M., Schlechtweg, S., and Schönwälder, B. (1997). dali!—Drawing Animated Lines! In Deussen, O., and Lorenz, P., editors, *Simulation und Animation '97* (Magdeburg, Germany, March 1997), pages 87–96. Erlangen, Germany: SCS Europe.

Masuch, M., Schlechtweg, S., and Schulz, R. (1999). Speedlines: Depicting Motion in Motionless Pictures. In *SIGGRAPH'99 Conference Abstracts and Applications*, page 277. New York: ACM SIGGRAPH.

Masuch, M., Schumann, L., and Schlechtweg, S. (1998). Animating Frame-to-Frame Consistent Line Drawings for Illustrative Purposes. In Lorenz, P., and Preim, B., editors, *Simulation und Visualisierung'98* (Magdeburg, Germany, March 1998), pages 101–112. Erlangen, Germany: SCS Europe.

McCloud, S. (1993). *Understanding Comics*. New York: HarperCollins.

McCloud, S. (2000). *Reinventing Comics*. New York: HarperCollins.

McKenna, T., and Arce, G. R. (2000). New Image Mosaic Structures. Technical Report, Department of Electrical and Computer Engineering, University of Delaware.

Meier, B. J. (1996). Painterly Rendering for Animation. In Rushmeier, H., editor, *Proceedings of SIGGRAPH'96* (New Orleans, August 1996), Computer Graphics Proceedings, Annual Conference Series, pages 477–484. New York: ACM SIGGRAPH.

Meisel, L. K. (1989). *Photorealism*. New York: Harry N. Abrams.

Milne, A. A. (1992). *Winnie-the-Pooh*. New York: Puffin Books.

Mizuno, S., Okada, M., and Toriwaki, J. (1998). Virtual Sculpting and Virtual Woodcut Printing. *The Visual Computer*, 14(2):39–51.

Mohr, A., and Gleicher, M. (2001). Non-Invasive, Interactive, Stylized Rendering. In *Proceedings of the 2001 ACM Symposium on Interactive 3D Graphics* (Research Triangle Park, March 2001), pages 175–178. New York: ACM Press.

Northrup, J. D., and Markosian, L. (2000). Artistic Silhouettes: A Hybrid Approach. In *Proceedings of NPAR 2000, Symposium on Non-Photorealistic Animation and Rendering* (Annecy, France, June 2000), pages 31–37. New York: ACM Press.

Ostromoukhov, V. (1998). Mathematical Tools for Computer-Generated Ornamental Patterns. In Hersch, R. D., André, J., and Brown, H., editors, *Electronic Publishing, Artistic Imaging and Digital Typography*, pages 193–223. Berlin: Springer-Verlag.

Ostromoukhov, V. (1999). Digital Facial Engraving. In *Proceedings of SIGGRAPH'99* (Los Angeles, August 1999), Computer Graphics Proceedings, Annual Conference Series, pages 417–424. New York: ACM SIGGRAPH.

Ostromoukhov, V. (2000). Artistic Halftoning—Between Technology and Art. *SPIE*, 3963:489–509.

Ostromoukhov, V. (2001). A Simple and Efficient Error-Diffusion Algorithm. In Fiume, E., editor, *Proceedings of SIGGRAPH 2001* (Los Angeles, August 2001), Computer Graphics Proceedings, Annual Conference Series, pages 567–572. New York: ACM SIGGRAPH.

Ostromoukhov, V., and Hersch, R. D. (1995). Artistic Screening. In Cook, R., editor, *Proceedings of SIGGRAPH'95* (Los Angeles, August 1995), Computer Graphics Proceedings, Annual Conference Series, pages 219–228. New York: ACM SIGGRAPH.

Ostromoukhov, V., and Hersch, R. D. (1999). Multi-Color and Artistic Dithering. In Rockwood, A., editor, *Proceedings of SIGGRAPH'99* (Los Angeles, August 1999), Computer Graphics Proceedings, Annual Conference Series, pages 425–432. New York: ACM SIGGRAPH.

Ostromoukhov, V., Hersch, R. D., and Amidror, I. (1994). Rotated Dispersion Dither: A New Technique for Digital Halftoning. In Glassner, A., editor, *Proceedings of SIGGRAPH'94* (Orlando, July 1994), Computer Graphics Proceedings, Annual Conference Series, pages 123–130. New York: ACM SIGGRAPH.

Ostromoukhov, V., Rudaz, N., Amidror, I., Emmel, P., and Hersch, R. D. (1996). Anti-Counterfeiting Feature of Artistic Screening. *SPIE, Proceedings on Holographic and Diffractive Techniques*, 2951:126–133.

Parker, J. R. (1988). Extracting Vectors from Raster Images. *Computers and Graphics*, 12(1):75–79.

Pavlidis, T. (1980). Thinning Algorithm for Discrete Binary Images. *Computer Graphics and Image Processing*, 13(2):142–157.

Peeck, J. (1987). The Role of Illustration in Processing and Remembering Illustrated Text. In Willows and Houghton (1987), Chapter 4, pages 115–151.

Perlin, K., and Velho, L. (1995). Live Paint: Painting with Procedural Multiscale Textures. In Cook, R., editor, *Proceedings of SIGGRAPH'95* (Los Angeles, August 1995), Computer Graphics Proceedings, Annual Conference Series, pages 153–160. New York: ACM SIGGRAPH.

Pham, B. (1991). Expressive Brush Strokes. *Computer Vision, Graphics, and Image Processing: Graphical Models and Image Processing*, 53(1):1–6.

Phong, B.-T. (1975). Illumination for Computer Generated Pictures. *Communications of the ACM*, 18(6):311–317.

Plaisant, C., Carr, D., and Shneiderman, B. (1995). Image-Browser Taxonomy and Guidelines for Designers. *IEEE Software*, 12(2):21–32.

Pnueli, Y., and Bruckstein, A. M. (1996). Gridless Halftoning: A Reincarnation of the Old Method. *Graphical Models and Image Processing: GMIP*, 58(1):38–64.

Preim, B., and Hoppe, A. (1998). Enrichment and Reuse of Geometric Models. In Strothotte (1998), Chapter 3, pages 45–62.

Preim, B., Raab, A., and Strothotte, T. (1997). Coherent Zooming of Illustrations with 3D-Graphics and Text. In *Proceedings of Graphics Interface'97* (Kelowna, Canada, May 1997), pages 105–113. Toronto: Canadian Computer-Human Communications Society.

Preim, B., and Strothotte, T. (1995). Tuning Rendered Line-Drawings. In Skala, V., editor, *Proceedings of WSCG'95* (Pilzeň, February 1995), pages 228–238.

Preparata, F. P., and Shamos, M. I. (1985). *Computational Geometry—An Introduction*, second edition. New York: Springer-Verlag.

Press, W. H., Teukolsky, S. A., Vetterling, W. T., and Flannery, B. P. (1993). *Numerical Recipes in C: The Art of Scientific Computing*, second edition. Cambridge: Cambridge University Press.

Putz, R., and Pabst, R., editors (1993). *Sobotta. Atlas der Anatomie des Menschen*, 20th edition. München, Germany: Urban & Schwarzenberg.

Raab, A. (1998). *Techniken zur Interaktion mit und Visualisierung von geometrischen Modellen*. Ph.D. thesis, School of Computer Science, Otto-von-Guericke University of Magdeburg.

Raab, A., and Rüger, M. (1996). 3D-ZOOM Interactive Visualisation of Structures and Relations in Complex Graphics. In Girod, B., Niemann, H., and Seidel, H.-P., editors, *3D Image Analysis and Synthesis '96* (Erlangen, Germany, November 1996), pages 87–93. Sankt Augustin, Germany: infix.

Rademacher, C. (2000). Die Spur der Heiligen Zeichen. *GEO Epoche*, (3):86–98.

Rademacher, P. (1999). View-Dependent Geometry. In Rockwood, A., editor, *Proceedings of SIGGRAPH'99* (Los Angeles, August 1999), Computer Graphics Proceedings, Annual Conference Series, pages 439–446. New York: ACM SIGGRAPH.

Richens, P., and Schofield, S. (1995). Interactive Computer Rendering. *Architectural Research Quarterly*, 1(1).

Rogers, D. F. (1998). *Procedural Elements for Computer Graphics*, second edition. Boston: McGraw-Hill.

Rössl, C., and Kobbelt, L. (2000). Line Art Rendering of 3D-Models. In Barsky, B. A., Shinagawa, Y., and Wang, W., editors, *Proceedings of Pacific Graphics 2000* (Hong Kong, October 2000), pages 87–96. Los Alamitos: IEEE Computer Society Press.

Rössl, C., Kobbelt, L., and Seidel, H.-P. (2000). Line Art Rendering of Triangulated Surfaces Using Discrete Lines of Curvature. In Skala, V., editor, *Proceedings of WSCG 2000* (Pilzeň, February 2000), pages 168–175.

Rudaz, N., Hersch, R. D., and Ostromoukhov, V. (1998). An Interface for the Interactive Design of Artistic Screens. In Hersch, R. D., André, J., and Brown, H., editors, *Electronic Publishing, Artistic Imaging and Digital Typography*, pages 1–10. Berlin: Springer-Verlag.

Ruttkay, Z., and Noot, H. (2000). Animated CharToon Faces. In *Proceedings of NPAR 2000, Symposium on Non-Photorealistic Animation and Rendering* (Annecy, France, June 2000), pages 91–100. New York: ACM Press.

Saito, T., and Takahashi, T. (1990). Comprehensible Rendering of 3-D Shapes. In Baskett, F., editor, *Proceedings of SIGGRAPH'90* (Dallas, August 1990), Computer Graphics Proceedings, Annual Conference Series, pages 197–206. New York: ACM SIGGRAPH.

Salisbury, M. P. (1997). *Image-Based Pen-and-Ink Illustration.* Ph.D. thesis, Department of Computer Science and Engineering, University of Washington, Seattle.

Salisbury, M. P., Anderson, C., Lischinski, D., and Salesin, D. H. (1996). Scale-Dependent Reproduction of Pen-and-Ink Illustration. In Rushmeier, H., editor, *Proceedings of SIGGRAPH'96* (New Orleans, August 1996), Computer Graphics Proceedings, Annual Conference Series, pages 461–468. New York: ACM SIGGRAPH.

Salisbury, M. P., Anderson, S. E., Barzel, R., and Salesin, D. H. (1994). Interactive Pen-and-Ink Illustration. In Glassner, A., editor, *Proceedings of SIGGRAPH'94* (Orlando, July 1994), Computer Graphics Proceedings, Annual Conference Series, pages 101–108. New York: ACM SIGGRAPH.

Salisbury, M. P., Wong, M. T., Hughes, J. F., and Salesin, D. H. (1997). Orientable Textures for Image-Based Pen-and-Ink Illustration. In Whitted, T., editor, *Proceedings of SIGGRAPH'97* (Los Angeles, August 1997), Computer Graphics Proceedings, Annual Conference Series, pages 401–406. New York: ACM SIGGRAPH.

Sarkar, M., and Brown, M. H. (1992). Graphical Fisheye Views of Graphs. In Bauersfeld, P., Bennett, J., and Lynch, G., editors, *Proceedings of CHI'92 Conference on Human Factors in Computing Systems* (Monterey, May 1992), pages 83–91. New York: ACM SIGCHI.

Sasada, T. T. (1987). Drawing Natural Scenery by Computer Graphics. *Computer-Aided Design*, 19(4):212–218.

Sattler, R. (1986). *Bio-Philosophy: Analytic and Holistic Perspectives.* Berlin: Springer-Verlag.

Schaffer, D., Zuo, Z., Bartram, L., Dill, J., Dubs, S., Greenberg, S., and Roseman, M. (1993). Comparing Fisheye and Full-Zoom Techniques for Navigation of Hierarchically Clustered Networks. *Proceedings of Graphics Interface'93* (Toronto, Canada, May 1993), pages 87–96.

Schaffer, D., Zuo, Z., Greenberg, S., Bartram, L., Dill, J., Dubs, S., and Roseman, M. (1996). Navigating Hierarchically Clustered Networks Through Fisheye and Full-Zoom Methods. *ACM Transactions on Computer-Human Interaction*, 3(2):162–188.

Schlechtweg, S., and Raab, A. (1998). Rendering Line Drawings for Illustrative Purposes. In Strothotte (1998), Chapter 4, pages 65–89.

Schlechtweg, S., Schönwälder, B., Schumann, L., and Strothotte, T. (1998). Surfaces to Lines: Rendering Rich Line Drawings. In Skala, V., editor, *Proceedings of WSCG'98, The 6th International Conference in Central Europe on Computer Graphics and Visualization* (Pilzeň, February 1998), pages 354–361.

Schlechtweg, S., and Strothotte, T. (1999). Illustrative Browsing: A New Method of Browsing in Long On-Line Texts. In Sasse, M. A., and Johnson, C., editors, *Computert Human Interaction. Proceedings of INTERACT'99* (Edinburgh, UK, September 1999), pages 466–473. Amsterdam: IOS Press.

Schleich, R., and Dürst, M. J. (1994). Beyond WYSIWYG: Display of Hidden Information in Graphics Editors. In *Proceedings of Eurographics'94* (Oslo, Norway, September 1994), pages 185–194. Oxford: NCC Blackwell Ltd.

Schofield, S. (1994). *Non-photorealistic Rendering: A Critical Examination and Proposed System.* Ph.D. thesis, School of Art and Design, Middlesex University.

Schönwälder, B. (1997). Generierung charakteristischer Linienzüge aus 3D-Modellen. Master's thesis, Department of Simulation and Graphics, Otto-von-Guericke University of Magdeburg.

Schumann, J., Strothotte, T., Raab, A., and Laser, S. (1996). Assessing the Effect of Non-photorealistic Rendered Images in CAD. In *Proceedings of CHI'96 Conference on Human Factors in Computing Systems* (Vancouver, Canda, April 1996), pages 35–42. New York: ACM SIGCHI.

Sederberg, T. W., and Greenwood, E. (1992). A Physically Based Approach to 2D Shape Blending. In Catmull, E. E., editor, *Proceedings of SIGGRAPH'92* (Chicago, July 1992), Computer Graphics Proceedings, Annual Conference Series, pages 25–34. New York: ACM SIGGRAPH.

Shiraishi, M., and Yamaguchi, Y. (2000). An Algorithm for Automatic Painterly Rendering Based on Local Source Image Approximation. In *Proceedings of NPAR 2000, Symposium on Non-Photorealistic Animation and Rendering* (Annecy, France, June 2000), pages 53–58. New York: ACM Press.

Sklansky, J., and Gonzalez, V. (1979). Fast Polygonal Approximation of Digitized Curves. *Journal of the ACM*, 18(2):255–264.

Small, D. (1991). Simulating Watercolor by Modeling Diffusion, Pigment, and Paper Fibers. In Bender, W. R., and Plouffe, W., editors, *Image Handling and Reproduction Systems Integration*, volume 1460 of *Proceedings of SPIE*.

Sourin, A. (2001). Functionally Based Virtual Computer Art. In *Proceedings of the ACM Symposium on Interactive 3D Graphics, I3D 2001*, pages 77–84. New York: ACM Press.

Sousa, M. C. (1999). *Computer-Generated Graphite Pencil Materials and Rendering*. Ph.D. thesis, Department of Computing Science, University of Alberta, Edmonton, Canada.

Sousa, M. C., and Buchanan, J. W. (1999a). Computer-Generated Graphite Pencil Rendering of 3D Polygonal Models. In Brunet, P., and Scopigno, R., editors, *Proceedings of Eurographics'99* (Milano, Italy, September 1999), pages 195–207. Oxford: NCC Blackwell Ltd.

Sousa, M. C., and Buchanan, J. W. (1999b). Observational Model of Blenders and Erasers in Computer-Generated Pencil Rendering. In *Proceedings of Graphics Interface'99* (Kingston, Canada, June 1999), pages 157–166. Toronto: Canadian Computer-Human Communications Society.

Sousa, M. C., and Buchanan, J. W. (2000). Observational Model of Graphite Pencil Materials. *Computer Graphics Forum*, 19(1):27–49.

Stollnitz, E. J., DeRose, T. D., and Salesin, D. H. (1996). *Wavelets for Computer Graphics: Theory and Applications*. San Francisco: Morgan Kaufmann.

Strassmann, S. (1986a). Hairy Brushes. In Evans, D. C., and Athay, R. J., editors, *Proceedings of SIGGRAPH'86* (Dallas, August 1986), Computer Graphics Proceedings, Annual Conference Series, pages 225–232. New York: ACM SIGGRAPH.

Strassmann, S. (1986b). Hairy Brushes in Computer-Generated Images. Master's thesis, Department of Architecture, Massachusetts Institute of Technology.

Streit, L. (1998). Importance Driven Halftoning. Master's thesis, Department of Computing Science, University of Alberta, Edmonton, Canada.

Streit, L., and Buchanan, J. W. (1998). Importance Driven Halftoning. In *Proceedings of Eurographics'98* (Lisbon, Portugal, August 1998), pages 207–217. Oxford: NCC Blackwell Ltd.

Strothotte, C., and Strothotte, T. (1997). *Seeing Between the Pixels. Pictures in Interactive Computer Systems*. Berlin: Springer-Verlag.

Strothotte, T., (1998). *Computational Visualization: Graphics, Abstraction, and Interactivity*. Berlin: Springer-Verlag.

Strothotte, T., Masuch, M., and Isenberg, T. (1999). Visualizing Knowledge about Virtual Reconstructions of Ancient Architecture. In *Proceedings of CGI'99* (Canmore, Canada, June 1999), pages 36–43. Los Alamitos: IEEE Computer Society Press.

Strothotte, T., Preim, B., Raab, A., Schumann, J., and Forsey, D. R. (1994). How to Render Frames and Influence People. In *Proceedings of Eurographics'94* (Oslo, Norway, September 1994), pages 455–466. Oxford: NCC Blackwell Ltd.

Tanenbaum, A. S. (1998). *Computer Networks*. Englewood Cliffs: Prentice-Hall.

Tortora, G. J. (1996). *Introduction to the Human Body: The Essentials of Anatomy and Physiology*, fourth edition. Menlo Park: Addison-Wesley Longman.

Treavett, S. M. F. (1998). Art in the Pipeline. In *Proceedings of the 16th Eurographics UK Conference* (Leeds, UK, March 1998).

Treavett, S. M. F., and Chen, M. (1997). Statistical Techniques for the Automatic Generation of Non-Photorealistic Images. In *Proceedings of the 15th Eurographics UK Conference*.

Ulichney, R. (1987). *Digital Halftoning*. Cambridge: The MIT Press.

Ulichney, R. (1999). Halftoning. In *Wiley Encyclopedia of Electrical and Electronics Engineering*, volume 8, pages 588–600. New York: John Wiley and Sons.

Ulichney, R. (2000). A Review of Halftoning Techniques. In *Color Imaging: Device-Independent Color, Color Hardcopy, and Graphic Arts V*, volume 3963 of *Proceedings of SPIE*.

van Bakergem, W. D., and Obata, G. (1991). Free Hand Plotting. Is It Live or Is It Digital? In Schmitt, G. N., editor, *CAAD Futures '91. International Conference for Computer Aided Architectural Design*, pages 567–582. Braunschweig, Germany.

Velho, L., and de Miranda Gomes, J. (1991). Digital Halftoning with Space Filling Curves. In Sederberg, T. W., editor, *Proceedings of SIGGRAPH'91* (Las Vegas, July 1991), Computer Graphics Proceedings, Annual Conference Series, pages 81–90. New York: ACM SIGGRAPH.

Vermeulen, A. H., and Tanner, P. P. (1989). PencilSketch—A Pencil-Based Paint System. In *Proceedings of Graphics Interface'89* (London, Canada, June 1998), pages 138–143. San Francisco: Morgan Kaufmann.

Veryovka, O. (1999). *Texture Control in Digital Halftoning*. Ph.D. thesis, Department of Computing Science, University of Alberta, Canada.

Veryovka, O., and Buchanan, J. W. (1999a). Comprehensive Halftoning of 3D Scenes. In Brunet, P., and Scopigno, R., editors, *Proceedings of Eurographics'99* (Milano, Italy, September 1999), pages 13–22. Oxford: NCC Blackwell Ltd.

Veryovka, O., and Buchanan, J. W. (1999b). Halftoning with Image-Based Dither Screens. In *Proceedings of Graphics Interface'99* (Toronto, Canada, June 1999), pages 167–174. San Francisco: Morgan Kaufmann.

Veryovka, O., and Buchanan, J. W. (2000). Texture-Based Dither Matrices. *Computer Graphics Forum*, 19(1):51–64.

Viewpoint Digital (2000). Viewpoint Premier Catalog 2000 Edition.

Walther, I. F. (1992). *Pablo Picasso. Das Genie des Jahrhunderts*. Köln, Germany: Benedikt Taschen Verlag.

Watt, A. (2000). *3D Computer Graphics*, third edition. Reading: Addison-Wesley.

Watt, A., and Policarpo, F. (1998). *The Computer Image*. Reading: Addison-Wesley.

Weidenmann, B., editor (1994). *Wissenserwerb mit Bildern*. Bern: Verlag Hans Huber.

Willows, D. M., and Houghton, H. A., editors (1987). *The Psychology of Illustration—Basic Research*, volume 1. New York: Springer-Verlag.

Winkenbach, G., and Salesin, D. H. (1994). Computer-Generated Pen-and-Ink Illustration. In Glassner, A., editor, *Proceedings of SIGGRAPH'94* (Orlando, July 1994), Computer Graphics Proceedings, Annual Conference Series, pages 91–100. New York: ACM SIGGRAPH.

Winkenbach, G., and Salesin, D. H. (1996). Rendering Parametric Surfaces in Pen and Ink. In Rushmeier, H., editor, *Proceedings of SIGGRAPH'96* (New Orleans, August 1996), Computer Graphics Proceedings, Annual Conference Series, pages 469–476. New York: ACM SIGGRAPH.

Yun-Jie, P., and Hui-Xiang, Z. (1991). Drawing Chinese Traditional Painting by Computer. In Kunii, T. L., editor, *Modeling in Computer Graphics. Proceedings of the IFIP WG 5.10 Working Conference* (Tokyo, April 1991), IFIP Series on Computer Graphics, pages 321–328. Tokyo: Springer-Verlag.

Zhang, Q., Sato, Y., Takahashi, J., Muraoka, K., and Chiba, N. (1999). Simple Cellular Automaton-Based Simulation of Ink Behaviour and Its Application to Suibokuga-like 3D Rendering of Trees. *The Journal of Visualization and Computer Animation*, 10(1):27–37.

AUTHOR INDEX

SUBJECT INDEX

algorithms *(continued)*
  exhaustive matching, 372
  Floyd-Steinberg algorithm modified for
    hatching lines, 39–40
  Floyd-Steinberg error diffusion, 35–36
  fluid simulation approach to watercolor,
    125–127
  haloed line effect, 223
  higher semantics LAS-based matching, 373
  histogram computation, 44, 45
  illustration generation from given text,
    326–327
  image mosaics, 72, 76
  image-space distortion, 271–273
  intersection computation, 225
  intersection method for stippling, 62–63
  LAS-based matching, 372
  non-adaptive uniform histogram
    equalization, 45–46
  non-deterministic elements in, 306
  object-space distortion, 285, 286–288
  ordered dithering, 34
  painter's algorithm, 311
  paper fiber structures, 118, 119
  path and style approach to watercolor,
    102–103, 104
  point coverage of a surface, 239
  procedural screening, 50, 52
  raytracing approach for engraving, 139–140
  screening with texts, 53–54, 55
  skeleton computation for polygon meshes,
    231
  speedlines computation, 308–309
  stroke orientation, 167
  for stroke placement, 160–162
  for strokes reflecting light intensity, 159
  view-dependent model, 299, 300
aliasing artifacts
  contour-based screening and, 59
  in photorealistic rendering, 12–13
ambient light in Phong model, 253, 256
analysis filter for multiresolution curves,
    107

animation, 305–311
  computerized drawing techniques for, 93
  distorted transformations, 296–297
  distortions in, 269–270, 295–302
  key deformations, 299
  key viewpoints, 299, 300
  Latin root of term, 305–306
  morphing the model, 297–302
  motion representation in still images,
    307–309
  non-deterministic elements and, 306
  non-linear transformations, 296–297
  particle systems-based, 310–311, 312
  reference drawings, 298–299
  shower-door effect, 306
  speedlines, 307, 308–309
  text illustrations and, 327
  view-dependent model algorithms, 299, 300
  viewer-dependent distortions, 295–296
  visualizations of movement, 207
  wiggly lines for, 306
annotations as presentation variable, 205
applications for NPR, 305–336
  animation, 305–311
  architectural illustrations, 311–320
  medical and technical illustrations, 324–330
  rendering plants, 321–324
  tactile rendering for blind people, 331–334
  See also specific applications
approximation errors in polygonal models,
    213–214
arbitrariness, 21, 22
archeological illustrations
  combining photographs with NPR
    visualizations, 319, 320
  hand-drawn illustrations preferred for, 317
  as NPR role model, 27, 28
  photorealistic vs. NPR interpretations,
    319–320
  for reconstructions of ancient architecture,
    317, 318–320
architectural illustrations, 311–320
  empirical study of, 312–316

look-ahead sets (LASses), 370–378
  classification strategies and, 371–377
  in compilers or translators, 370–371
  defined, 370
  exhaustive matching strategy, 372, 373, 376, 377
  higher semantics LAS-based matching strategy, 373, 374–376, 377
  LAS-based matching strategy, 372, 373–374, 375, 376, 377
  properties of, 370–371
  RSJ p-equivalence and, 386, 388
  semantic levels of, 371
LRA (light ray attenuation) p-equivalence relation, 362, 367, 373
LRP (light ray projection) equivalence relation, 363, 367, 379, 381

Magazines and books, halftoning in, 33
Magdeburg building constructed by Otto the Great, 318–320
magnification
  regions of, 273–275
  zoom algorithm, 271–273, 329
Manhattan distance, 277
Manster, Sebastian, 5
mapping
  defined, 343
  function in procedural screening, 49–50
  as p-equivalence relation, 363
  semantic levels and, 407
maps, tactile, 333–334
marks
  along contours, 157, 158
  line-drawing techniques and, 84
  as very short lines, 84
"Martian Bananas," 145
material-buffers for interactive painting, 192
mathematical preliminaries, 341–358
  Cartesian products and relations, 342–344
  equivalence classes and invariants, 346–352
  equivalence relations and variants, 344–346

  quotients, (iso)morphism, and abstraction, 352–357
  sets and elements, 342
  summary of, 357–358
maximal compression in dropoff functions, 274, 276
Maxwell's laws, 359–360
McCartney, Paul and Linda, 366–367
mean curvature, 267
meaning. *See* communicating information; human cognition and perception
medical illustrations, 324–330
  algorithm, 326–327
  conventions, 25
  degree of interest for an object (DOI), 327
  for e-books (digital books), 9–10, 324
  edge detection for enhancing, 18, 19
  generating figure captions, 330
  generating from texts, 326–327
  generating labels, 327–329
  graphical abstraction in, 15
  line style applications, 99, 100
  relationship to text, 324–325
  role model for NPR, 25, 26
  TextIllustrator system, 327, 328
  ZoomIllustrator system, 328–329, 330
merging rules for engraving layers, 146–149
Mickey Mouse, 16, 17
microletters
  for counterfeit protection, 53
  for dither screens, 53, 55
  original output denoted by, 55
Mobile example, 144
model artifacts
  graphical abstraction and, 15–16
  necessity for, 16–17
  photorealistic rendering vs. NPR and, 14–15, 17
  See also geometric models
model for visual communication, 383–406
  coding and decoding process, 383–384
  discontinuities, 390, 405–406

FIGURE CREDITS

Figure 1.1 Ralph Goings' *Hot Fudge Sundae Interior,* 1972, oil on canvas. ©
Luis K. Meisel Gallery, New York. Used by permission.

Figures 1.2, 1.17, and 7.11–7.14 courtesy of Oliver Deussen.

Figure 1.3 from "Die Spur der heilige Zeichen" by Cay Rademacher, *GEO
Epoche,* April 2000. Used by permission.

Figure 1.4 from *City Maps of Europe* by John Gross. Studio Editions, Ltd.,
London, 1991. Used by permission.

Figure 1.5 Pablo Picasso's *Portrait de Dora Maar,* 1937, oil on canvas. *Das Genie
des Jahrhunderts* by Ingo F. Walther. Benedikt Taschen Verlag, Köln, 1992. Used
by permission.

Figure 1.6 courtesy of the City of Plzeň, Czech Republic.

Figures 1.7 and 1.22 from *The Atlas of Early Man* by Jacquetta Hawkes. St.
Martin's Press, New York, 1993. Used by permission.

Figure 1.9 from *Atlas der Anatomie des Menschen,* 20th edition, vol. 1, edited
by R. Putz and R. Pabst. Urban & Schwarzenberg, Munich, 1993. Used by
permission.

Figure 1.10 from *Duden Bildwörterbuch.* BI Mannheim, Vienna and Zurich,
1977. Used by permission.

Figure 1.11 from *Micky Maus, Das is mein Leben.* Silva-Verlag, Zurich, Switzerland, p. 20. © The Walt Disney Company. Used by permission.

Figure 1.12 courtesy of Regina Pohle.

Figures 1.13, 6.5, and 6.7 from "Comprehensible Rendering of 3-D Shapes" by Takafumi Saito and Tokiichiro Takahashi, *Proceedings of SIGGRAPH '90*. © 1990 Association for Computing Machinery, reprinted with permission.

Figure 1.14 courtesy of Bert Freudenberg.

Figure 1.16 courtesy of Stefan Hiller.

Figure 1.18 courtesy of Frank Goldenschweger.

Figure 1.20 from *Introduction to the Human Body: The Essentials of Anatomy and Physiology* by Gerard T. Tortora. Addison-Wesley, Reading 1996. Used by permission.

Figure 1.21 based on an illustration from the ELSA Microlink TM56k PCI Technical Manual.

Figure 1.23 from *Winnie-the-Pooh* by A. A. Milne. Puffin Books, New York, 1992. Used by permission.

Figures 2.15, 2.16, and 6.11–6.14 from "Halftoning with Image-Based Dither Screens" by Oleg Veryovka and John Buchanan. *Proceedings of Graphics Interface '99,* Morgan Kaufmann, San Francisco, 1999.

Figure 2.20 from "Gridless Halftoning: A Reincarnation of the Old Method" by Yachin Pruell and Alfred Bruckstein, *Graphical Models and Image Processing,* January 1996.

Figures 2.21–2.23 and 2.30 from "Artistic Screening" by Victor Ostromoukhov and Roger D. Hersch, *Proceedings of SIGGRAPH '95*. © 1995 Association for Computing Machinery, reprinted with permission.

Figures 2.24 and 2.29 courtesy of Peilian Yuan.

Figures 2.31–2.35 courtesy of Adrian Secord.

Figures 2.36 and 2.37 courtesy of Stefan Hiller.

Figure 2.38 courtesy of Marcel Götze.

Figure 2.41 from *Image Mosaics* by Adam Finkelstein and Marisa Range. Technical Report TR-574–98, Princeton University, Computer Science Department, March 1998.

Figure 3.1 from "Free Hand Plotting: Is it Live or Is It Digital?" by W. Davis van Bakergem and Gen Obata. *CAAD Futures '91,* Vieweg Verlag, Braunschweig, 1991.

Figures 3.10–3.12 courtesy of Lars Schumann.

Figure 3.15 courtesy of Steve Strassmann.

Figures 3.17 and 3.18 from "Multiresolution Curves" by Adam Finkelstein and David H. Salesin, *Proceedings of SIGGRAPH '94.* © 1994 Association for Computing Machinery, reprinted with permission.

Figure 4.5 based on an illustration from "Computer Generated Watercolor" by Cassidy J. Curtis, Sean E. Anderson, Joshua E. Seims, Kurt W. Fleischer, and David H. Salesin, *Proceedings of SIGGRAPH '97.* © 1997 Association for Computing Machinery.

Figure 4.6 from "Computer Generated Watercolor" by Cassidy J. Curtis, Sean E. Anderson, Joshua E. Seims, Kurt W. Fleischer, and David H. Salesin, *Proceedings of SIGGRAPH '97.* © 1997 Association for Computing Machinery, reprinted with permission.

Figures 4.7 and 4.11 based on an illustration from *Computer-Generated Graphite Pencil Materials and Rendering* by Mario Costa Sousa. Ph.D. Thesis, Department of Computing Science, University of Alberta, 1999.

Figures 4.8–4.10, 4.12 and 4.13 from *Computer-Generated Graphite Pencil Materials and Rendering* by Mario Costa Sousa. Ph.D. Thesis, Department of Computing Science, University of Alberta, 1999.

Figures 4.15 and 4.16 from "Computer Generated Copper Plates" by Wolfgang Leister. *Computer Graphics Forum,* March 1994. Used by permission.

Figures 4.17–4.22 from "Digital Facial Engraving" by Victor Ostromoukhov, *Proceedings of SIGGRAPH '99.* © 1999 Association for Computing Machinery, reprinted with permission.

Figures 5.1, 5.11–5.12, and 5.18 from "Scale Dependant Reproduction of Pen-and-Ink Illustration" by Mike Salisbury, Corin Anderson, Dani Lischinski, and David H. Salesin, *Proceedings of SIGGRAPH '96.* © 1996 Association for Computing Machinery, reprinted with permission.

Figure 5.2(a) from "Art-Based Rendering of Fur, Grass, and Trees" by Kowalski et al., *Proceedings of SIGGRAPH '99.* © 1999 Association for Computing Machinery, reprinted with permission.

Figures 5.2(b) and 10.6 from "Painterly Rendering for Animation" by Barbara J. Meier, *Proceedings of SIGGRAPH '96.* © 1996 Association for Computing Machinery, reprinted with permission.

Figures 5.3, 5.5–5.7, and 5.9 from "Computer-Generated Pen-and-Ink Illustration" by George Winkenbach and David H. Salesin. *Proceedings of SIGGRAPH '94.* © 1994 Association for Computing Machinery, reprinted with permission.

Figure 5.4 from "Interactive Pen-and-Ink Illustration" by Mike P. Salisbury, Sean E. Anderson, Ronen Barzel, and David H. Salesin, *Proceedings of SIGGRAPH '94.* © 1994 Association for Computing Machinery, reprinted with permission.

Figure 5.8 from "Paint by Numbers: Abstract Image Representations" by Paul Haeberti, *Proceedings of SIGGRAPH '90.* © 1990 Association for Computing Machinery, reprinted with permission.

Figure 5.10 from "Art Based Rendering with Continuous Levels of Detail" by Lee Markosian, Barbara J. Meier, Michael Kowalski, Loring S. Holden, J.D. Northrup, and John F. Hughes, *Proceedings of the First International Symposium of Non-Photorealistic Animation and Rendering.* © 2000 Association for Computing Machinery, reprinted with permission.

Figures 5.16 based on an illustration from "Scale Dependant Reproduction of Pen-and-Ink Illustration" by Mike Salisbury, Corin Anderson, Dani Lischinski, and David H. Salesin, *Proceedings of SIGGRAPH '96*. © 1996 Association for Computing Machinery.

Figures 6.2 and 6.3 courtesy of Axel Hoppe.

Figure 6.8 from the University of Cambridge, Department of Architecture Web site *www.arct.cam.ac.uk.research/cadlab/irender/gallery/*. Used by permission.

Figure 6.9 from Informatix Software International Web site *www.informatix .co.uk/pir_gallery_styles.htm*. Used by permission.

Figures 6.10 and 6.15 from *Texture Control in Digital Halftoning* by Oleg Veryovka. Ph.D. Thesis, Department of Computing Science, University of Alberta, 1999.

Figures 7.2–7.4, 7.18, 7.19, and 9.14–9.16 courtesy of Andreas Raab.

Figures 7.5 and 7.7 based on an illustration from "The Edge Buffer: A Data Structure for Easy Silhouette Rendering," *Proceedings of the First International Symposium on Non-Photorealistic Animation and Rendering*. © 2000 Association for Computing Machinery.

Figures 7.8 and 7.9 courtesy of Bert Freudenberg.

Figure 7.10 from *Procedural Elements for Computer Graphics,* 2nd Edition by David F. Rogers. McGraw Hill, Boston, 1998. Used by permission.

Figure 7.15 based on an illustration from the Viewpoint Digital Catalog, Summer 2000 edition. Used by permission.

Figures 7.20, 8.1, and 8.16 courtesy of Jörg Hamel.

Figure 7.21 from "Hidden Curve Removal for Free Form Surfaces," by Gershon Elber and Elaine Cohen. *Proceedings of SIGGRAPH '90*. © 1990 Association for Computing Machinery, reprinted with permission.

Figure 7.22 from "Line Art Illustrations of Parametric and Implicit Forms," by Gershon Elber. *IEEE Transactions on Visualization and Computer Graphics,* January 1998. Used by permission.

Figures 7.23–7.25 courtesy of Frank Godenschweger.

Figure 8.2 from *Art and Visual Perception: A Psychology of the Creative Eye* by Rudolph Arnheim, University of California Press, Berkeley, 1994. Used by permission.

Figure 8.3 from *Trades and Occupations: A Pictorial Archive from Early Sources* edited by Carol Grafton, Dover Publications, 1990. Used by permission.

Figures 8.4 and 8.15 from *The Guild Handbook of Scientific Illustration* by Elaine R.S. Hodges, van Nostrand Reinhold, New York, 1989. Used by permission.

Figures 8.7–8.10 from "A Non-Photorealistic Lighting Model for Automatic Technical Illustration" by Amy Gooch, Bruce Gooch, Peter Shirley, and Elaine Cohen, *Proceedings of SIGGRAPH '98.* © 1998 Association for Computing Machinery, reprinted with permission.

Figures 9.3–9.9 from *A Framework for Elastic Presentation Space* by Sheelagh Carpendale. Ph.D. thesis, School of Computer Science, Simon Fraser University, 1999. Used by permission.

Figure 9.10 courtesy of Sheelagh Carpendale.

Figure 9.17 from "Observer Dependent Deformations on Illustrations" by D. Martin, S. Garcia, and J.C. Torres, *Proceedings of the First International Symposium on Non-Photorealistic Animation and Rendering.* © 2000 Association for Computing Machinery, reprinted with permission.

Figures 9.18–9.20 from "View-Dependent Geometry" by Paul Rademacher, *Proceedimgs of SIGGRAPH '99.* © 1999 Association for Computing Machinery, reprinted with permission.

Figures 10.1–10.3 and 10.5 courtesy of Maic Masuch.

Figure 10.7 "Assessing the Effect of Non-Photorealistic Rendered Images in CAD" by Jutta Schumann, Thomas Strothotte, Andreas Raab, and Stefan Laser, *Proceedings of CHI '96 Conference on Human Factors in Computing Systems.* © 1996 Association for Computing Machinery, reprinted with permission.

Figures 10.8–10.10 from "Visualizing Knowledge about Virtual Reconstructions of Ancient Architecture" by T. Strothotte, Maic Masuch, and Tobias Isenberg, *Proceedings of CGI '99.* IEEE Computer Society Press, 1999. Used by permission.

Figures 10.11–10.15 from "Computer-Generated Pen-and-Ink Illustration of Trees" by Oliver Deussen and Thomas Strothotte, *Proceedings of SIGGRAPH '2000.* © 2000 Association for Computing Machinery, reprinted with permission.

Figures 10.16 and 10.17 courtesy of Bernhard Preim.

Figure 10.18 courtesy Rainer Michel.

ABOUT THE AUTHORS

Thomas Strothotte has a fundamental interest in scientific methods for studying language and graphics for communication between computers and users. His long-range goal is to equip computers with the expertise to communicate even subtle nuances to users through images. This goal has led him to carry out research combining the areas of language systems, human–computer interaction, and computer graphics in unison with one another. He considers non-photorealistic modeling, rendering, and animation, the topic of the current book, to be one of the important building blocks in future systems for communication of ideas between computers and users.

Strothotte is a Canadian citizen who was born in 1959 in Regina (Saskatchewan) and grew up in Vancouver, British Columbia. There he attended Simon Fraser University to earn a B.Sc. in 1980, majoring in physics with a minor in computing science. He continued for one more year to earn an M.Sc. in 1981 in computing science with a thesis on a parallel algorithm for specialized geometric transformations in graphics systems (see "Raster Display of a Rotating Object Using Parallel Processing" (1983) (with Brian Funt), *Computer Graphics Forum*, 2(4):209–217).

In his doctoral studies, he concentrated on studying differences between natural languages and computer languages. In particular, he found out that the *subjunctive* case in natural languages is intimately related to the notion of backtracking as expressed in computer algorithms. This led to the definition of a subjunctive construct for algorithmic programming languages that enables easy expression of backtracking and can be implemented efficiently (see "Structured Program Lookahead" (1987) (with Gordon V. Cormack), *Computer Languages*, 12(2):95–108). For various reasons, he moved twice during the three years of his doctoral studies, carrying out his research on scholarships for a year each at the University of Stuttgart (Germany), at McGill University (Montréal, Québec), and at the University of Waterloo (Ontario). He received his Ph.D. from McGill in 1984.

Concurrently with his thesis work, Strothotte developed his interest in the area of design and analysis of algorithms. He worked extensively with J. Sack at

Carleton University (Ottawa) and others (see, for example, "MinMax Heaps and Generalized Priority Queues" (1986), *Communications of the ACM*, 29(10):996–1000) and spent a year as postdoctoral fellow at the Institut National de Recherche en Informatique et Automatique in Rocquencourt, France, in the research group ALGO of Phillippe Flajolet.

In December 1985, Strothotte went to Germany to specialize in human-computer interaction. He concentrated on knowledge-based systems for integrated language and picture communication in dialog systems in the group of Rul Gunzenhäuser at the Universität Stuttgart where he completed a German postdoctoral degree ("Habilitation") in 1989. After that he worked for one year as a researcher in the software ergonomics department of the IBM Scientific Center in Heidelberg. From 1987 to 1991, he was a frequent visiting lecturer at the Institution für Teknisk Databehandling at the Universitetet i Uppsala, Sweden.

Strothotte took a faculty position in computer science at the Freie Universität Berlin in 1990, and after a sabbatical at the University of British Columbia (Vancouver) in 1993, he moved to the Institut für Simulation und Graphik of the Otto-von-Guericke-Universität Magdeburg in Germany as a full professor of computer science. There he heads the Computer Graphics and Interactive Systems Laboratory, which has about 20 graduate students and 5 postdoctoral fellows at any given time. In the last five years, he has graduated 14 Ph.D. and 18 M.Sc. students, and was the driving force behind the establishment of undergraduate and graduate degree programs in *computational visualistics,* as well as development of their curricula.

In Magdeburg, he has also contributed extensively as an administrator. He was the dean of his faculty from 1994 to 1996, the Vice President for Academic Planning and Budget of his university from 1996 to 1998, and the President pro tem of the university during 1998. Since March 2001, he has been the director of the Office of Information Technology of the State of Saxony-Anhalt, where he reports directly to the state's prime minister.

The results of Strothotte's research and those of the members of his laboratory have appeared in all major conferences in his areas of expertise, including ACM SIGGRAPH, ACM CHI, and Eurographics, as well as various scientific journals. He is the senior author of *Seeing Between the Pixels: Pictures in Interactive Systems* (Springer-Verlag, Heidelberg, 1997) and *Abstraction in Computational Visualization* (Springer-Verlag, Heidelberg, 1998). He has worked on and headed EU-funded research projects and served as a scientific advisor to the European Union in Brussels. He has also contributed to various international conferences by engaging in their program committees (for example, Eurographics, Computer Graphics International, Pacific Graphics, and currently the International Symposium on Non-Photorealistic Animation and Rendering, NPAR 2002). While living in Germany for over 15 years now, he proudly keeps up contact to his native Canada through frequent visits home, as well as by regularly serving on the program committee of the Canadian *Graphics Interface* conferences, and teaching as an adjunct professor at Simon Fraser University.

Stefan Schlechtweg has been interested in non-photorealistic computer graphics since he started his master's thesis in 1994. He mainly focused on the area of computer-generated line drawings but also on the overall structure and development of NPR. Together with Thomas Strothotte, he developed a graduate course on this topic, which has become a regular teaching subject at the University of Magdeburg, Germany, and which was also held at Simon Fraser University in Canada. This course had a major influence on the development of this book.

Schlechtweg was born in 1971 in Bad Salzungen, in the state of Thuringia in Germany. He went to the University of Magdeburg to study Computer Science in 1990. During his studies, his main focus was on artificial intelligence and information systems before he became acquainted with the idea of non-photorealism in computer graphics. Fascinated with this area, he decided to focus on this in his master's thesis. Schlechtweg finished his studies in 1995 with a thesis on the topic "Limitation of Drawing Resources in Computer Generated Line Drawings" and received the Best Annual Graduate Award from the School of Computer Science of his university.

Schlechtweg then moved to Ann Arbor, Michigan, for five months where he worked in the virtual reality laboratory at the University of Michigan. There he was involved in projects on VR design studies and human computer interaction in virtual environments, which were supported by the automotive industry. He then went back to the Otto-von-Guericke-Universität Magdeburg to work as a research assistant under the supervision of Thomas Strothotte. Starting with a publicly funded project on "Adaptive Graphical Zoom," Schlechtweg began to focus on the connection of NPR techniques and user interaction that set the stage for his thesis topic. He received his Ph.D. in 1999 for his work on "Interactive Scientific Illustration of Texts."

Currently, Schlechtweg is an assistant professor at the Institut für Simulation und Graphik of the Otto-von-Guericke-Universität Magdeburg working on his German postdoctoral degree. The results of Schlechtweg's work have been published in several papers on smaller and major conferences, including INTER-ACT and SIGGRAPH. He also contributes to the community as a reviewer for conferences and journals. His current research focus lies on the use of NPR techniques in visualization and on visualizations for small screens. He is co-chairing the International Symposium on Non Photorealistic Animation and Rendering, NPAR 2002, and is serving in the organizing committee of the International Symposium on Smart Graphics 2002.

Kees van Overveld, born in 1957, obtained both an M.Sc. (1981) and a Ph.D. in physics (1985) at Eindhoven University of Technology (EUT). Also in 1985, he joined the computing science department of the faculty of mathematics and computer science of EUT as a university lecturer; since 1990, he has been an associate professor. From 1989 to 1998, he was head of the computer graphics group. In 1992–1993, he worked at the University of Calgary and at the University of Pennsylvania in Philadelphia. As of December 1995, he became research consultant for Philips Research. In June 1998, he founded Van Overveld Coaching, a consultancy company in the field of creativity, innovation, and the methodology of technological design. In May 2000, he joined the Stan Ackermans Institute (SAI, the EUT institute for post-graduate programs in technological design) as associate professor. He is now head of the SAI research group in design methodology. He joined IEEE as an adjunct member (1995–1997), and he was a member of ACM (1996–1997).